First World War
and Army of Occupation
War Diary
France, Belgium and Germany

3 DIVISION
76 Infantry Brigade
Gordon Highlanders
1st Battalion
1 March 1915 - 10 April 1919

WO95/1435

The Naval & Military Press Ltd
www.nmarchive.com
Published in association with The National Archives

Published by

The Naval & Military Press Ltd

Unit 10 Ridgewood Industrial Park,

Uckfield, East Sussex,

TN22 5QE England

Tel: +44 (0) 1825 749494

www.naval-military-press.com

www.nmarchive.com

This diary has been reprinted in facsimile from the original. Any imperfections are inevitably reproduced and the quality may fall short of modern type and cartographic standards.

Contents

Document type	Place/Title	Date From	Date To
Heading	76 Infantry Brigade 1 Battalion Gordon Highlanders 1915 Nov To 1919 Apr		
Heading	76 Infantry Brigade 1 Battalion Gordon Highlanders 1915 Nov To 1919 Apr.		
Heading	3rd Division 76th Inf Bde 1st Battalion Gordon Highlanders Jan-Dec 1916		
Heading	3rd Division 1st Battn. Gordon Highlanders November & December 1915		
Heading	76th Inf. Bde. 3rd Div. Battn. Transferred From 8th Inf. Bde. 3rd Div. 19.10.15 War Diary 1st Battn. The Gordon Highlanders November 1915		
War Diary	Billets At Eecke	01/11/1915	20/11/1915
War Diary	Reninghelst B.Camp	21/11/1918	21/11/1918
War Diary	I 34 b & c	22/11/1915	27/11/1915
War Diary	Reninghelst	28/11/1918	30/11/1918
Miscellaneous	Roll Of Officers Serving With 1st Battalion Gordon Highlanders On 31st November 1915		
Heading	76th Inf. Bde. 3rd Div. War Diary 1st Battn. The Gordon Highlanders December 1915		
War Diary	Reninghelst	01/12/1915	03/12/1915
War Diary	I 34 b & c	04/12/1915	09/12/1915
War Diary	Reninghelst	10/12/1915	15/12/1915
War Diary	I 34 b & c	16/12/1915	22/12/1915
War Diary	Reninghelst	23/12/1915	29/12/1915
War Diary	I34 B&c	30/12/1915	31/12/1915
Miscellaneous	1st Battalion Gordon Highlanders		
Heading	76th 3rd Division War Diary 1st Battalion Gordon Highlanders March 1916		
War Diary	Reninghelst	01/03/1915	01/03/1915
War Diary	I34b	02/03/1915	03/03/1915
War Diary	Scottish Lines	04/03/1915	10/03/1915
War Diary	Gordon Terrace Reserve	11/03/1915	12/03/1915
War Diary	Gordon Terrace	13/03/1915	13/03/1915
War Diary	I34b	14/03/1915	17/03/1915
War Diary	Reninghelst	18/03/1915	24/03/1915
War Diary	Scottish Wood	25/03/1915	25/03/1915
War Diary	J Camp Reninghelst	26/03/1915	27/03/1915
War Diary	Reninghelst	28/03/1915	28/03/1915
War Diary	Dickebusch	29/03/1915	31/03/1915
Miscellaneous	1st Battalion The Gordon Highlanders	07/03/1915	07/03/1915
Miscellaneous	1st Battalion The Gordon Highlanders	04/03/1915	04/03/1915
Miscellaneous	1st Bn. Gordon Highlanders	31/03/1916	31/03/1916
Heading	76th Brigade 3rd Division War Diary 1st Battalion Gordon Highlanders January 1916		
Miscellaneous	1/Gordon Highrs. Jan 1916 Vol XVI		
War Diary	Reninghelst	29/12/1915	29/12/1915
War Diary	I34 B&C	30/12/1915	05/01/1916
War Diary	Reninghelst	06/01/1916	12/01/1916
War Diary	I34 B&C	13/01/1916	17/01/1916
War Diary	Reninghelst	20/01/1916	26/01/1916

War Diary	I34 B&C	27/01/1916	31/01/1916
Miscellaneous	Roll of Officer Serving With 1st Bn. Gordon Highlrs On 31st January 1916		
Heading	76th Brigade 3rd Division War Diary 1st Battalion Gordon Highlanders February 1916		
War Diary	I34 B&C	01/02/1916	02/02/1916
War Diary	Reninghelst	03/02/1916	06/02/1916
War Diary	Serques	07/02/1916	15/02/1916
War Diary	Poperinghe	16/02/1916	16/02/1916
War Diary	H14c	17/02/1916	17/02/1916
War Diary	I34c	18/02/1916	18/02/1916
War Diary	I34 B&C	19/02/1916	22/02/1916
War Diary	Reninghelst	23/02/1916	29/02/1916
Miscellaneous	1st Bn. Gordon Highlanders	29/02/1916	29/02/1916
Heading	76th Brigade 3rd Division War Diary 1st Battalion Gordon Highlanders1916		
Heading	1 Gordon Hrs Vol 19		
War Diary	St Eloi	01/04/1916	03/04/1916
War Diary	Reninghelst	04/04/1916	04/04/1916
War Diary	Thieushoek	05/04/1916	19/04/1916
War Diary	La Clytte	20/04/1916	21/04/1916
War Diary	Thieushouk	21/04/1916	26/04/1916
War Diary	Locre	27/04/1916	28/04/1916
War Diary	Kemmel	29/04/1916	30/04/1916
Miscellaneous	1st Battn. Gordon Highlanders	09/05/1916	09/05/1916
Heading	76th Brigade 3rd Division War Diary 1st Battalion Gordon Highlanders May 1916		
War Diary	Trenches Nr. Kemmel	01/05/1916	06/05/1916
War Diary	Locre	07/05/1916	13/05/1916
War Diary	Kemmel	14/05/1916	17/05/1916
War Diary	Trenches Kemmel	18/05/1916	20/05/1916
War Diary	Kemmel Shelters	21/05/1916	26/05/1916
War Diary	Thieusheuk	27/05/1916	31/05/1916
Miscellaneous	1st. Battn. The Gordon Highlanders	02/06/1916	02/06/1916
Heading	76th Brigade 3rd Division War Diary 1st Battalion Gordon Highlanders June 1916		
War Diary	Thieshouk	01/06/1916	05/06/1916
War Diary	Bailleuil S6d 08 Sheet 78 S.W.	06/06/1916	10/06/1916
War Diary	Bailleuil	11/06/1916	11/06/1916
War Diary	Zermezeele	12/06/1916	12/06/1916
War Diary	Wulverdinghe	13/06/1916	13/06/1916
War Diary	Houlle	14/06/1916	30/06/1916
Miscellaneous	1st Bn. The Gordon Highlanders	30/06/1916	30/06/1916
Heading	1st Bn Gordon Highlanders July 1916		
Heading	War Diary Of 1st Bn. Gordon Highlanders 1st-31st July 1916		
War Diary	Houlle	01/07/1916	01/07/1916
War Diary	Gezaincourt	02/07/1916	03/07/1916
War Diary	Naours	04/07/1916	04/07/1916
War Diary	Rainville	05/07/1916	05/07/1916
War Diary	Franvillers	06/07/1916	06/07/1916
War Diary	Bois Les Celestin	07/07/1916	08/07/1916
War Diary	Bronfay Farm	09/07/1916	13/07/1916
War Diary	Moutauban Alley	14/07/1916	14/07/1916
War Diary	Caterpillar Valley	15/07/1916	18/07/1916
War Diary	W. Longueval Trenches	19/07/1916	19/07/1916

War Diary	Breslau Redoubt	20/07/1916	21/07/1916
War Diary	Delville Wood	22/07/1916	26/07/1916
War Diary	Bois Des Tailles	27/07/1916	28/07/1916
War Diary	Mariecourt L'Abbe	29/07/1916	31/07/1916
Miscellaneous	1st Battalion The Gordon Highlanders	29/07/1916	29/07/1916
Miscellaneous	1st Battalion The Gordon Highlanders	31/07/1916	31/07/1916
Heading	76th Brigade 3rd Division War Diary 1st Battalion Gordon Highlanders August 1916		
War Diary	Mericourt L'Abbe	01/08/1916	11/08/1916
War Diary	Sandpits	12/08/1916	14/08/1916
War Diary	Great Bear	15/08/1916	16/08/1916
War Diary	Talus Bois	17/08/1916	17/08/1916
War Diary	Chimpanzee Trench	18/08/1916	18/08/1916
War Diary	Maltz Horn	19/08/1916	19/08/1916
War Diary	Happy Valley	20/08/1916	21/08/1916
War Diary	Morlancourt	22/08/1916	23/08/1916
War Diary	Maillard	24/08/1916	25/08/1916
War Diary	Boubers	26/08/1916	26/08/1916
War Diary	Oeuf	27/08/1916	27/08/1916
War Diary	Heuchin	28/08/1916	28/08/1916
War Diary	Bours	29/08/1916	29/08/1916
War Diary	Bruay	30/08/1916	31/08/1916
Miscellaneous	1st Battalion The Gordon Highlanders	24/08/1916	24/08/1916
Miscellaneous	1st Battalion The Gordon Highlanders	03/09/1916	03/09/1916
Heading	76th Brigade 3rd Division War Diary 1st Battalion Gordon Highlanders September 1916		
War Diary	Noeux Les Mines	01/09/1916	25/09/1916
War Diary	Estree Blanche	26/09/1916	30/09/1916
Miscellaneous	1st Battalion The Gordon Highlanders	30/09/1916	30/09/1916
Operation(al) Order(s)	76th Infantry Brigade Operation Order No.49	21/09/1916	21/09/1916
Operation(al) Order(s)	76th Infantry Brigade Operation Order No.48	20/09/1916	20/09/1916
Operation(al) Order(s)	76th Infantry Brigade Operation Order No.50	22/09/1916	22/09/1916
Heading	76th Brigade 3rd Division War Diary 1st Battalion Gordon Highlanders October 1916		
War Diary	Estree Blanche	01/10/1916	05/10/1916
War Diary	Heuchin	05/10/1916	08/10/1916
War Diary	Acheux	09/10/1916	16/10/1916
War Diary	Vauchelles	17/10/1916	18/10/1916
War Diary	Courcelles	19/10/1916	26/10/1916
War Diary	Trenches	27/10/1916	28/10/1916
War Diary	Bus	29/10/1916	31/10/1916
Miscellaneous	1st Battalion The Gordon Highlanders	31/10/1916	31/10/1916
Operation(al) Order(s)	76th Infantry Brigade Operation Order No.54	17/10/1916	17/10/1916
Operation(al) Order(s)	76th Infantry Brigade Operation Order No.61	28/10/1916	28/10/1916
Heading	76th Brigade 3rd Division War Diary 1st Battalion Gordon Highlanders November 1916		
War Diary	Bus	01/11/1916	12/11/1916
War Diary	Trenches	13/11/1916	17/11/1916
War Diary	Courcelles	18/11/1916	18/11/1916
War Diary	Vauchelles	19/11/1916	26/11/1916
War Diary	Trenches	27/11/1916	30/11/1916
Miscellaneous	1st Battalion The Gordon Highlanders	30/11/1916	30/11/1916
Miscellaneous	Amendment No.4 to 76th Infantry Brigade Operation Order No.57	08/11/1918	08/11/1918
Miscellaneous	Amendment No.3 to 76th Infantry Brigade Operation Order No.57	02/11/1916	02/11/1916

Operation(al) Order(s)	76th Infantry Brigade Operation Order No.68	17/11/1916	17/11/1916
Operation(al) Order(s)	76th Infantry Brigade Operation Order No.71	30/11/1916	30/11/1916
Heading	76th Brigade 3rd Division War Diary 1st Battalion Gordon Highlanders December 1916		
War Diary	Trenches	01/12/1916	01/12/1916
War Diary	Courcelles	02/12/1916	05/12/1916
War Diary	Loovencourt	06/12/1916	13/12/1916
War Diary	In Trenches	14/12/1916	17/12/1916
War Diary	Courcelles	18/12/1916	22/12/1916
War Diary	Couin	23/12/1916	29/12/1916
War Diary	Trenches	30/12/1916	01/01/1917
Operation(al) Order(s)	76th Infantry Brigade Operation Order No.75	20/12/1916	20/12/1916
Operation(al) Order(s)	76th Infantry Brigade Operation Order No.77	31/12/1916	31/12/1916
Operation(al) Order(s)	76th Infantry Brigade Operation Order No.72	05/12/1916	05/12/1916
Heading	3rd Division 76th Inf. Bde 1st Battalion Gordon Highlanders 1917		
War Diary	In The Trenches Serre Area	01/01/1917	01/01/1917
War Diary	Courcelles	02/01/1917	03/01/1917
War Diary	In Trenches	04/01/1917	05/01/1917
War Diary	Courcelles	06/01/1917	06/01/1917
War Diary	Rubempre	07/01/1917	08/01/1917
War Diary	Pernois	09/01/1917	31/01/1917
Miscellaneous	1st Battalion The Gordon Highlanders	31/01/1917	31/01/1917
Operation(al) Order(s)	76th Infantry Brigade Operation Order No.1	02/01/1917	02/01/1917
Operation(al) Order(s)	76th Infantry Brigade Operation Order No.2	04/01/1917	04/01/1917
Operation(al) Order(s)	76th Infantry Brigade Operation Order No.3	05/01/1917	05/01/1917
Miscellaneous	Embussing Table Issued With 76th Infty. Brigade Operation Order No.3	05/01/1917	05/01/1917
Miscellaneous	Time Table Of Reliefs Issued With 76th Infty Brigade Operation Order No.3	05/01/1917	05/01/1917
Miscellaneous	Amendment to March Table In 76th Bde. O.O.70		
Operation(al) Order(s)	76th Infantry Brigade Operation Order No.6	28/01/1917	28/01/1917
War Diary	Penin	01/02/1917	08/02/1917
War Diary	Wanquetin	09/02/1917	11/02/1917
War Diary	In The Line	12/02/1917	15/02/1917
War Diary	Arras	16/02/1917	19/02/1917
War Diary	In The Line	20/02/1917	23/02/1917
War Diary	Arras	24/02/1917	27/02/1917
War Diary	Wanquetin	28/02/1917	28/02/1917
War Diary	Houvin-Houvigneul	01/03/1917	01/03/1917
Miscellaneous	76th Infantry Brigade Operation Order (Special)	01/02/1917	01/02/1917
Operation(al) Order(s)	76th Infantry Brigade Operation Order No.13	22/02/1917	22/02/1917
Miscellaneous	1st Bn The Gordon Highlanders Operation Orders by Lt Col G L G Burnett D.S.O.	22/02/1917	22/02/1917
Miscellaneous	Amendment Reference 76th Infantry Brigade O.O. No.14	26/02/1917	26/02/1917
Operation(al) Order(s)	76th Infantry Brigade Operation Order No.14	25/02/1917	25/02/1917
Miscellaneous	March And Relief Table To Accompany 76th Infy. Brigade Operation Order No.14	25/02/1917	25/02/1917
Operation(al) Order(s)	76th Infantry Brigade Operation Order No.10	09/02/1917	09/02/1917
Miscellaneous	Relief Table To Accompany 76th Infantry Brigade Operation Order O.10		
Operation(al) Order(s)	76th Infantry Brigade Operation Order No.11	14/02/1917	14/02/1917
Operation(al) Order(s)	Operation Order No.21 By Capt. X. Commanding 'B' Company		
Miscellaneous	Trench To Trench Attack Narrative		

War Diary	Houvin-Houvigneuil	01/03/1917	08/03/1917
War Diary	Magnicourt	09/03/1917	17/03/1917
War Diary	Liencourt	18/03/1917	31/03/1917
Miscellaneous	1st Battn. The Gordon Highlanders	31/03/1917	31/03/1917
War Diary	Liencourt	01/04/1917	04/04/1917
War Diary	Wanquetin	05/04/1917	07/04/1917
War Diary	Arras	08/04/1917	08/04/1917
War Diary	Arras (Trenches)	09/04/1917	13/04/1917
War Diary	Arras	14/04/1917	23/04/1917
War Diary	Monchy Lepreux	24/04/1917	30/04/1917
Miscellaneous	1st Battalion The Gordon Highlanders	30/04/1917	30/04/1917
Miscellaneous	Report On Operations At Arms 9th To 11th April 1917		
Miscellaneous	Operations Orders By Lieut-Col, J.G. Burnett, D.S.O. Commanding 1st. Battalion The Gordon Highlanders	06/04/1917	06/04/1917
War Diary	Tilloy	01/05/1917	09/05/1917
War Diary	Monchy-le-Preux	10/05/1917	14/05/1917
War Diary	Duisans	15/05/1917	16/05/1917
War Diary	Noyellette	17/05/1917	17/05/1917
War Diary	Ambrines	18/05/1917	31/05/1917
Miscellaneous	1st Battalion The Gordon Highlanders	31/05/1917	31/05/1917
War Diary	Ambrines	01/06/1917	01/06/1917
War Diary	Arras	02/06/1917	12/06/1917
War Diary	In The Field	13/06/1917	14/06/1917
War Diary	Arras	20/06/1917	20/06/1917
War Diary	Grenas	21/06/1917	30/06/1917
Miscellaneous	Nominal Roll Of Officers Serving With Battalion	30/06/1917	30/06/1917
Miscellaneous	Account Of Operations Against Infantry Hill-East Of Monchy	24/06/1917	24/06/1917
War Diary	Grenas	01/07/1917	01/07/1917
War Diary	Bihucourt	02/07/1917	03/07/1917
War Diary	Beugny	04/07/1917	10/07/1917
War Diary	In The Field	11/07/1917	19/07/1917
War Diary	Beugny	20/07/1917	25/07/1917
War Diary	In The Field	26/07/1917	31/07/1917
Miscellaneous	1st. Battn. The Gordon Highlanders	31/07/1917	31/07/1917
War Diary	In The Field	01/08/1917	02/08/1917
War Diary	Beugny	03/08/1917	11/08/1917
War Diary	In The Field	12/08/1917	18/08/1917
War Diary	Beugny	19/08/1917	26/08/1917
War Diary	In The Field	27/08/1917	31/08/1917
Miscellaneous	1st Battalion The Gordon Highlanders		
War Diary	In The Field	01/09/1917	03/09/1917
War Diary	Beugny	04/09/1917	05/09/1917
War Diary	Barastre	06/09/1917	17/09/1917
War Diary	Move	18/09/1917	18/09/1917
War Diary	Watou	19/09/1917	24/09/1917
War Diary	Ypres	25/09/1917	26/09/1917
War Diary	Vlamertinghe	30/09/1917	30/09/1917
Miscellaneous	1st Battalion The Gordon Highlanders	30/09/1917	30/09/1917
Miscellaneous	Report On The Recent Operations At Zonnebeke	04/10/1917	04/10/1917
Miscellaneous	1st Battalion The Gordon Highlanders	25/09/1917	25/09/1917
War Diary	Winnezeele	01/10/1917	11/10/1917
War Diary	In The Field	12/10/1917	18/10/1917
War Diary	Moray	19/10/1917	26/10/1917
War Diary	Bullecourt	27/10/1917	31/10/1917

Miscellaneous	Nominal Roll Of Officers Serving With Battalion On 31/10/17	31/10/1917	31/10/1917
War Diary	Bullecourt	01/11/1917	03/11/1917
War Diary	Mory	04/11/1917	10/11/1917
War Diary	Bullecourt	11/11/1917	15/11/1917
War Diary	Mory	16/11/1917	25/11/1917
War Diary	Bullecourt	26/11/1917	29/11/1917
War Diary	Mory	30/11/1917	30/11/1917
Miscellaneous	Roll Of Officers On Strength Of Battalion on 30th November 1917	30/11/1917	30/11/1917
War Diary	Abbaye Mory	01/12/1917	03/12/1917
War Diary	Bullecourt	04/12/1917	10/12/1917
War Diary	Railway Embankment Ecoust	11/12/1917	11/12/1917
War Diary	Railway Embankment	11/12/1917	14/12/1917
War Diary	Embankment	15/12/1917	15/12/1917
War Diary	Bullecourt	16/12/1917	21/12/1917
War Diary	Bullecourt Abbaye Mory	22/12/1917	28/12/1917
War Diary	Mory Abbaye	29/12/1917	29/12/1917
War Diary	Hendecourt	29/12/1917	31/12/1917
Miscellaneous	1st. Battalion The Gordon Highlanders	31/12/1917	31/12/1917
Heading	3rd Division War Diaries 1st Gordon Highlanders January To 1st 31st December 1918		
Heading	76th Brigade 3rd Division 1st Battalion Gordon Highlanders January 1918		
War Diary	In The Field	01/01/1918	31/01/1918
Miscellaneous	1st. Battalion The Gordon Highlanders	31/01/1918	31/01/1918
Heading	76th Brigade 3rd Division 1st Battalion Gordon Highlanders February 1918		
War Diary	Wancourt Guemappe	01/02/1918	28/02/1918
Miscellaneous	1st. Battalion The Gordon Highlanders	28/02/1918	28/02/1918
Miscellaneous	To Officer Commanding 1st. Bn. The Gordon Highlanders	03/02/1918	03/02/1918
Heading	76th Brigade 3rd Division 1st Battalion Gordon Highlanders March 1918		
War Diary	Wancourt Sector Right	01/03/1918	02/03/1918
War Diary	Support Dugout	03/03/1918	06/03/1918
War Diary	Left Sector Wancourt	07/03/1918	12/03/1918
War Diary	Wancourt Sector Support Dugout	13/03/1918	31/03/1918
Miscellaneous	The Boche Offensive (March 1918) In So Far As It Concerned Me		
Miscellaneous	1st Battalion, The Gordon Highlanders. Appendix		
Heading	76th Bde. 3rd Div War Diary 1st Battalion The Gordon April 1918		
War Diary	In Route In The Field	01/04/1918	01/04/1918
War Diary	Ourton	02/04/1918	03/04/1918
War Diary	Route	04/04/1918	04/04/1918
War Diary	Fosse 10	05/04/1918	11/04/1918
War Diary	Hinges Sector	12/04/1918	13/04/1918
War Diary	Oblinghem	14/04/1918	18/04/1918
War Diary	Le Chouquaox Sector	19/04/1918	22/04/1918
War Diary	In Support Vendin	23/04/1918	23/04/1918
War Diary	In Bethune	24/04/1918	30/04/1918
Heading	76th Brigade 3rd Division 1st Battalion Gordon Highlanders May 1918		
War Diary	Chocques	01/05/1918	07/05/1918
War Diary	Locon	08/05/1918	16/05/1918

War Diary	Chocques	17/05/1918	24/05/1918
War Diary	Hinges	25/05/1918	31/05/1918
Heading	76th Brigade 3rd Division 1st Battalion Gordon Highlanders June 1918		
War Diary	Hinges	01/06/1918	04/06/1918
War Diary	Chocques	05/06/1918	12/06/1918
War Diary	Hinges	13/06/1918	30/06/1918
Miscellaneous	Letter Written By. Lt. D.D.A. Lockhart,	29/06/1917	29/06/1917
Heading	76th Brigade 3rd Division 1st Battalion Gordon Highlanders July 1918		
War Diary	Chocques	01/07/1918	05/07/1918
War Diary	Hinges	05/07/1918	17/07/1918
War Diary	Chocques	18/07/1918	23/07/1918
War Diary	Hinges	24/07/1918	31/07/1918
Heading	76th Brigade 3rd Division 91st Battalion Gordon Highlanders August 1918		
War Diary	Hinges	01/08/1918	06/08/1918
War Diary	Lieres	07/08/1918	14/08/1918
War Diary	Sus-St-Leger	14/08/1918	19/08/1918
War Diary	Berles Au Bois	20/08/1918	20/08/1918
War Diary	Ayette	20/08/1918	24/08/1918
War Diary	Douchy	25/08/1918	30/08/1918
War Diary	Mory & Ecoust	30/08/1918	31/08/1918
Miscellaneous	In The Field	05/09/1918	05/09/1918
Miscellaneous	1st Battn. The Gordon Highlrs	31/08/1918	31/08/1918
Heading	76th Brigade 3rd Division 1st Battalion Gordon Highlanders September 1918		
War Diary	Vrauxourt	01/09/1918	03/09/1918
War Diary	Ayette	04/09/1918	06/09/1918
War Diary	Gaudiempre	07/09/1918	11/09/1918
War Diary	Adinfer Wood	11/09/1918	11/09/1918
War Diary	Sapignies	12/09/1918	15/09/1918
War Diary	Fremicourt	15/09/1918	16/09/1918
War Diary	Beumetz-Les-Cambrai	17/09/1918	30/09/1918
Miscellaneous	Report On Operations Carried Out 1st Bn The Gordon Highlanders	27/09/1918	27/09/1918
Miscellaneous	Remarks On The Operations	03/10/1918	03/10/1918
Miscellaneous	1st Battalion The Gordon Highlanders	30/09/1918	30/09/1918
Heading	76th Brigade 3rd Division 1st Battalion Gordon Highlanders October 1918		
War Diary	Rumilly	01/10/1918	02/10/1918
War Diary	Masnieres	03/10/1918	10/10/1918
War Diary	Havrincourt	11/10/1918	13/10/1918
War Diary	Marcoine	14/10/1918	19/10/1918
War Diary	Cattenieres	19/10/1918	20/10/1918
War Diary	Quievy	20/10/1918	22/10/1918
War Diary	Romeries	23/10/1918	26/10/1918
War Diary	Escarmain	26/10/1918	27/10/1918
War Diary	Ruesnes	28/10/1918	29/10/1918
War Diary	St. Python	30/10/1918	31/10/1918
Miscellaneous	Report On The Capture Of Rumilly By 1st Bn. The Gordon Highlanders Assisted By The 2nd Bn The Suffolk Regt	02/10/1918	02/10/1918
Miscellaneous	Report On Operations By 1st Bn. The Gordon Highlanders	02/10/1918	02/10/1918

Miscellaneous	Report On Operations Of 1st Bn The Gordon Highlanders	08/10/1918	08/10/1918
Miscellaneous	Report On Operations By 1st Bn. The Gordon Highlanders	24/10/1918	24/10/1918
Miscellaneous	1st Battalion The Gordon Highlanders	31/10/1918	31/10/1918
Heading	76th Brigade 3rd Division 1st Battalion Gordon Highlanders November 1918		
War Diary	Carnieres	01/11/1918	03/11/1918
War Diary	Quievy	03/11/1918	04/11/1918
War Diary	Romeries	05/11/1918	08/11/1918
War Diary	Gommegnies	09/11/1918	09/11/1918
War Diary	Le Grand Sart	10/11/1918	10/11/1918
War Diary	Longueville	11/11/1918	13/11/1918
Miscellaneous			
War Diary	Longueville	13/11/1918	16/11/1918
War Diary	Monplaisir	17/11/1918	18/11/1918
War Diary	Louvroil	19/11/1918	20/11/1918
War Diary	Bousignies	21/11/1918	24/11/1918
War Diary	Lobbes	25/11/1918	25/11/1918
War Diary	Thy Le Chateau	26/11/1918	26/11/1918
War Diary	Mettet	27/11/1918	28/11/1918
War Diary	Anhee	29/11/1918	29/11/1918
War Diary	Braibant	30/11/1918	30/11/1918
Miscellaneous	Reinforcement Officers	15/11/1918	15/11/1918
Miscellaneous	Roll Of Officers Serving With Battalion	15/11/1918	15/11/1918
Heading	76th Brigade 3rd Division 1st Battalion Gordon Highlanders December 1918		
War Diary	Ciney	01/12/1918	04/12/1918
War Diary	Sinsin	05/12/1918	06/12/1918
War Diary	La Fosse & Oster	07/12/1918	07/12/1918
War Diary	Ottre	08/12/1918	08/12/1918
War Diary	Courtil	09/12/1918	09/12/1918
War Diary	Beho	10/12/1918	11/12/1918
War Diary	Neidingen Breitfeld	12/12/1918	12/12/1918
War Diary	Manderfeld Krewinkle	13/12/1918	13/12/1918
War Diary	Hallschlag	14/12/1918	14/12/1918
War Diary	Dahlem	15/12/1918	15/12/1918
War Diary	Tondore	16/12/1918	16/12/1918
War Diary	Munstereifel	17/12/1918	17/12/1918
War Diary	Euskirchen	18/12/1918	18/12/1918
War Diary	Erp Kierdoff Bruggen	19/12/1918	19/12/1918
War Diary	Bruggen & Kierdoff	20/12/1918	31/12/1918
Miscellaneous	1st Battalion The Gordon Highlanders	31/12/1918	31/12/1918
Heading	3rd Division War Diaries 1st Gordon Highlanders August To 31 December 1915 And 1919 Jan-1919 April		
War Diary	Kierdoff & Bruggen	01/01/1919	31/01/1919
Miscellaneous	1st Battalion The Gordon Highlanders	31/01/1919	31/01/1919
War Diary	Bruggen & Kierdorf	01/02/1919	28/02/1919
Miscellaneous	1st Bn The Gordon Highlanders		
War Diary	Kierdorf	01/03/1919	04/03/1919
War Diary	Cologne	05/03/1919	31/03/1919
Miscellaneous	1st Battalion The Gordon Highlanders	31/03/1919	31/03/1919
War Diary	Cologne	01/04/1919	10/04/1919

76 INFANTRY BRIGADE.

1 BATTALION GORDON HIGHLANDERS.

1915 NOV TO 1919 APR.

1435

76 INFANTRY BRIGADE.

1 BATTALION GORDON HIGHLANDERS.

1915 NOV TO 1919 APR.

1435

3RD DIVISION
76TH INF BDE

1ST BATTALION

GORDON HIGHLANDERS.

JAN - DEC 1916.

3rd Division

1st Battn. Gordon Highlanders

November + December

1915

From 8 BDE SAME DIV

76th Inf.Bde.
3rd Div.

Battn. transferred from 8th Inf.Bde. 3rd Div. 19.10.15.

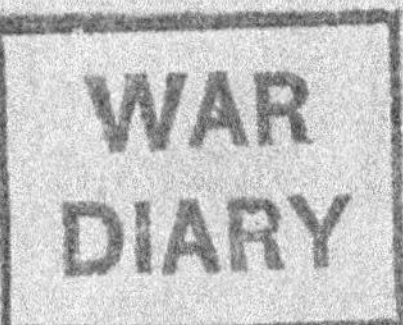

1st BATTN. THE GORDON HIGHLANDERS.

N O V E M B E R

1 9 1 5

Attached:

Roll of Officers.

1st Gordon Highlanders.

WAR DIARY
or
INTELLIGENCE SUMMARY

(Erase heading not required.)

Army Form C. 2118

Instructions regarding War Diaries and Intelligence Summaries are contained in F. S. Regs., Part II. and the Staff Manual respectively. Title Pages will be prepared in manuscript.

November 1915

Place	Date	Hour	Summary of Events and Information	Remarks and references to Appendices
BILLETS AT EECKE.	1st November – 5th Nov.		Wet Weather which hampered Training. Many Classes of Instruction. On 3rd Capt. A de L. Long arrived on transfer from 3rd Batt: A + S. Hrs. He took over command of C Coy from 2nd Lieut. Colquhoun.	
do.	3rd Nov.		The Rev. I. Logan left the Battalion on transfer to 8th Brigade.	
do.	6th November		Fine Day. General holiday in 3rd Division on account of final of Divisional Football Competition. The Battalion provided the Guard of Honour of 3 Officers and 200 O.R. under the command of Capt. A. de L. Long to take part in the ceremony of Presentation of French Decorations to certain officers and men of the 2nd Army. A French Guard of Honour was also present. General Hely D'Oissel commanding 36th French Corps made the presentation. The Ceremony took place in the Market Place of STEINVOORDE.	
do.	7th November		Fine Day. Church Parade. Capt. I. L. Stewart, R.A.M.C. reported for duty with the Battalion. Lieut. E. M. Hackett transferred to 8th Field Ambulance.	
do.	8th November		Fine Day. Companies at work visited by G.O.C. 3rd Division.	
do.	9th November		Stormy. Battalion at work visited by General Sir H. Plumer, commanding 2nd Army, who congratulated the Battalion on the very smart and soldier-like appearance of the Guard of Honour provided on the 6th inst.	
do.	10th November		Fine Day. Lt. Col. P. W. Brown having proceeded on leave, Capt. A. de L. Long took over temporary Command of the Battalion.	

1875 Wt. W593/826 1,000,000 4/15 J.B.C. & A. A.D.S.S./Forms/C. 2118.

1st Gordon Highlanders

2

WAR DIARY
or
INTELLIGENCE SUMMARY
(Erase heading not required.)

November 1915

Army Form C. 2118

Instructions regarding War Diaries and Intelligence Summaries are contained in F. S. Regs., Part II. and the Staff Manual respectively. Title Pages will be prepared in manuscript.

Place	Date	Hour	Summary of Events and Information	Remarks and references to Appendices
BILLETS AT EECKE	11th November		Fine Day. Training by Companies.	
	12th Nov.		Very Wet Day. Brig-General Pratt, 46th Brigade, inspected trenches dug by Companies. Lecture on "Trench Duties" by Capt. W. Fraser.	
do.	13th Nov.		Stormy. Wet morning – Route March cancelled. Outpost Scheme in afternoon.	
	14th Nov.		Fine. Capt. the Rev. J. Thomson took the service.	
do.	15th November		Fine. The G.O.C. 46th Brigade visited some of the Companies during the morning. Lecture on "Musketry" by Capt. A. deL. Long. Arrangements were made by the Brigade for 80 men of C Coy. to go to the Divisional Cinema Theatre. Motor buses were provided. Unfortunately somebody blundered and it fell through. The Pipers, together with part of the Fife band of the 11th Gordon Highlanders played "Retreat" in EECKE village. In the evening, our Pipers played at the Brigade Mess. The final of the Brigade Boxing Tournament for a cup presented by Brig-General A. R. Hoskins D.S.O. was contested. Our representative Sgt. Hogg, was beaten by the representative of the 2nd Royal Scots in the Light Weights.	
do.	16th November		Fine morning. Company training. Lecture on "Discipline and Personal Conduct" by Capt. A. deL. Long.	
do.	17th November		Showery. The G.O.C. 46th Infantry Brigade inspected the Regimental Transport and the kits of A Company. He expressed satisfaction at what he had seen.	

1875 Wt. W593/826 1,000,000 4/15 J.B.C. & A. A.D.S.S./Forms/C. 2118.

1st Gordon Highlanders

WAR DIARY
or
INTELLIGENCE SUMMARY
(Erase heading not required.)

November 1915

Army Form C. 2118

Instructions regarding War Diaries and Intelligence Summaries are contained in F. S. Regs., Part II. and the Staff Manual respectively. Title Pages will be prepared in manuscript.

Place	Date	Hour	Summary of Events and Information	Remarks and references to Appendices
BILLETS AT EECKE	18th November		Fine morning. Route March. In afternoon, Lantern Exhibition of Aeroplane Photos at RENINGHELST attended by Commanding Officer, Adjutant, Company Commanders and Intelligence Officer. Received orders to prepare to move to RENINGHELST on 20th inst.	
do.	19th November		Fine. No Parades. Filling in Trenches. Cleaning Billets.	
do.	20th November		Fine but cold. Battalion marched to RENINGHELST via BOESCHEPE. Company Commanders visited trenches. Specialists arrived in evening having been conveyed by Motor-bus.	
RENINGHELST B Camp.	21st November		Fine - Frosty. Specialists consisting of Grenadiers, Snipers, Machine Gunners, + Signallers left for trenches at 2.30 am. They had 3 casualties on the way up. The Battalion marched at 2.30 pm to trenches near VERBRANDENMOLEN I 34 b+c. Nos. 32 - 35 inclusive taking over from 1st Royal Fusiliers 24th Division and Trench 32 from 8th Buffs. The relief was carried through without casualties. The trenches run across a wooded Ravine. The ground slopes gently back from the front line which is level with the German trenches which vary from 125 to 35 yards from our front line. The Companies were arranged in the following order A on the right B C + D	
I 34 b+c.	22nd November		Fine and Frosty. Day spent cleaning up trenches detailing work and sending parties of N.C.O's and men round the trenches as these are very complicated. Quiet day - one casualty	
do.	23rd November		Fine - Work - draining, putting wire in front of D Coy. 2 casualties	

1875 Wt. W593/826 1,000,000 4/15 J.B.C. & A. A.D.S.S./Forms/C. 2118.

1st Gordon Highlanders.

Instructions regarding War Diaries and Intelligence Summaries are contained in F. S. Regs., Part II. and the Staff Manual respectively. Title Pages will be prepared in manuscript.

WAR DIARY
or
INTELLIGENCE SUMMARY
(Erase heading not required.)

November 1915

Army Form C. 2118

Place	Date	Hour	Summary of Events and Information	Remarks and references to Appendices
I 34 b d c	24th November		Thick fog. Officers of King's Own Royal Lancaster Regt. came up to look over trenches. During afternoon, our trenches & Head Qrs were shelled. Some trench mortar bombs fell in D Company trench. No casualties.	
do.	25th November		Cold and clear. 9.2 in. Howitzer fired on German Trenches. Casualties - two.	
do.	26th November		Fine after 11am. - Both sides active with Rifle Grenades and [illegible] with Trench Mortars. 2nd Lieut A. G. Keith, commanding D Company was killed and two men very severely wounded by a rifle grenade. Total casualties - [illegible]. The Belgian Batteries retaliated but things only became quiet after 4.5 in. guns had been turned on.	
do.	27th November		Fine - Specialists were relieved at 9am by 2nd K.O.R.L. Regt. - Quiet day. At 4.30pm the remainder of the Battalion was relieved by the same unit and returned to rest billets at RENINGHELST. Lovely moonlight night and hard frost. No casualties.	
RENINGHELST	28th November		Fine but Cold - Rev. [illegible] Chaplain to Liverpool Scottish took Service. Drainage scheme for Camp decided on.	
do.	29th November		Wet - Thaw - Digging main drains - Kit Inspection	
do	30th November		Damp - Inspection of camp by Commanding Officer. Work on drainage continued. Roll of Officers and Strength of Battalion at this date given on attached	

[illegible] Captain
Commanding 1st Gordon Highlanders

1875 Wt. W593/826 1,000,000 4/15 J.B.C. & A. A.D.S.S./Forms/C. 2118.

Roll of Officers serving with 1st Battalion Gordon Highlanders
on 30th November 1915.

Commanding Officer	Captain A. de L. Long.
Adjutant	Captain W. Morrison
i/c Pioneers	Captain W. Morrison
i/c Machine Gun Section.	2/Lieut J. A. H. Brown.
i/c Grenade Section	2/Lieut W. B. Campbell
i/c Light Section	2/Lieut J. McA. Cunningham
i/c Transport	2/Lieut L. S. Sinclair
"A" Company	Captain M. Dinwiddie - Commanding
	2/Lieut D. G. Watt.
	" A. J. Cleghorn.
	" H. W. Wright
	" C. R. Booth.
"B" Company	2/Lieut M. S. Robertson Commanding.
	" A. S. Reece
	" A. R. McR. Law
	" C. E. Humphrey.
	" A. H. Duncan.
	" W. R. Watt.
"C" Company	2/Lieut P. Colquhoun - Commanding
	" D. R. G. Renfrew.
	" S. Mackintosh
	" C. A. J. Chambers Hunter.
"D" Company	Captain W. A. Dyke - Commanding
	2/Lieut E. G. Saunders.
	" G. Mutch.
	" J. D. Robertson.

Quartermaster Captain J. MacLennan.
Chaplain
Medical Officer Captain J. L. Stewart. R. A. M. C.

Strength of Battalion on 30-11-15 = { 26 Officers
866 Other Ranks.

76th Inf.Bde.
3rd Div.

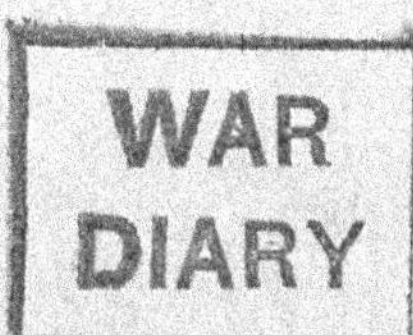

1st BATTN. THE GORDON HIGHLANDERS.

D E C E M B E R

1 9 1 5

Attached:

Roll of Officers.

1

1st Gordon Highlanders

WAR DIARY
or
~~INTELLIGENCE SUMMARY~~

(Erase heading not required.)

December 1915.

Army Form C. 2118

Instructions regarding War Diaries and Intelligence Summaries are contained in F. S. Regs., Part II. and the Staff Manual respectively. Title Pages will be prepared in manuscript.

Place	Date	Hour	Summary of Events and Information	Remarks and references to Appendices
RENINGHELST	1st DEC		Very wet Night. Company Inspection. The C.O. inspected M.G. Section. Pioneers at work laying trench boards and draining camp.	
do	2nd Dec.		Fine day. Physical drill and practice in Grenade Throwing. C.O. inspected the Draft	
do.	3rd Dec.		Wet day. Specialists left for trench area at 3 am. Morning spent in cleaning camp and laying trench boards. Battalion left camp at 2.30 pm and had a wet march to the trenches.	
I 34 b&c	4th Dec.		Mild - wind N.N.W. Situation quiet all day.	
do	5th Dec.		Strong wind - Stormy about 1 am. Trench 34 received some enemy trench mortar bombs. Trench mortars silenced by No. 4 Belgian Battery and 4.5 Howitzers. 1 Casualty. Machine Gun Relief under Brigade arrangements.	Belgium N.W. Sheet 28
do.	6th Dec.		Mild. wind S.W. Mortars again troublesome in evening.	
do.	7th Dec.		Mild and bright. wind S.W. In the afternoon Battalion Headquarters shelled by H.G. Howitzers. Little material damage. 1 Casualty. Work on Reserve line progressing favourably. 2 Lieut. S.M. Robertson joined the Battalion from home and was posted to D Coy.	
do	8th Dec.		Stormy in morning. wind S.W. Quiet day. 2nd Lieut. G.P. Ketchin joined the Battalion from home and was posted to D Coy.	

1875 Wt. W593/826 1,000,000 4/15 J.B.C. & A. A.D.S.S./Forms/C. 2118.

1st Gordon Highlanders

3

WAR DIARY
or
~~INTELLIGENCE SUMMARY~~
(Erase heading not required.)

December 1915

Army Form C. 2118

Instructions regarding War Diaries and Intelligence Summaries are contained in F. S. Regs., Part II. and the Staff Manual respectively. Title Pages will be prepared in manuscript.

Place	Date	Hour	Summary of Events and Information	Remarks and references to Appendices
I 34 b & c	9th Dec.		Mild. Divisional Commander visited the trenches, also three representatives of the Royal Navy. Belgian Batteries shelled the German front line, necessitating our line being cleared. In the afternoon, trench mortars very active against Trench 35 and were only stopped after a good deal of retaliation from 4.5 in. Howitzers. 1 Casualty. The Specialists were relieved about 8 am, the Battalion in the evening and marched back to B Camp. Reninghelst. Very ~~wet~~ wet night. Conditions between firing line and road very bad.	
Reninghelst	10th Dec.		Fine - Showery - Lieuts. R.I. Baird and G. Macdonald reported their arrival and posted to ~~D~~ & ~~D~~ C Coy. respectively. 2 Lieut. Coolquhoun transferred to A Company. Lt. Macdonald took over command of C Coy.	
do.	11th Dec.		Stormy. Battalion started on a route march but had to turn back owing to very heavy rain. Lt. Col. Cranford C.I.E., D.S.O., having rejoined the Battalion from Light Duty assumed command of the Battalion. Capt. A. de L. Long assumed the duties of Second in command	
do	12th Dec.		Bright with intermittent showers. Church parade in morning. C.O. inspected camp and transport lines	

1875 Wt. W593/826 1,000,000 4/15 J.B.C. & A. A.D.S.S./Forms/C. 2118.

1st Gordon Highlanders

Instructions regarding War Diaries and Intelligence Summaries are contained in F. S. Regs., Part II. and the Staff Manual respectively. Title Pages will be prepared in manuscript.

WAR DIARY
or
~~INTELLIGENCE SUMMARY~~
(Erase heading not required.)

December 1915.

Army Form C. 2118

Place	Date	Hour	Summary of Events and Information	Remarks and references to Appendices
Reninghelst	13th Dec.		Bright but cold. Battalion at Baths. Kit Inspection by Companies. Inspection of Camp and vicinity by C.O. Lecture to officers on Intelligence by Capt. Long. Lecture to N.C.O's on Duties in the Trenches by Capt. Morrison. Pioneers continued improvement of camp. Divisional Commander visited camp in afternoon.	
do.	14th Dec.		Fine but cold. Training by Companies in Smoke Helmet Drill and Throwing Dummy Grenades. Bayonet Fighting in afternoon.	
do.	15th Dec.		Fine. Specialists left for trenches at 2.30 am. Morning spent in cleaning up Huts. Battalion paraded at 2.15 pm. and relieved 8th K.O.R.L. in trenches about 6 pm. Bright moonlight night which facilitated relief. C.O. made a tour of inspection of the front line trenches during the night.	
Inverbac	16th Dec.		Damp and mild. G.O.C. Brigade and Brigade-Major made a lengthy tour of inspection of front line and support trenches at 11am. Some shelling about midday and again in the evening when the enemy also bombarded the left of our sector with trench mortars. 1 man killed and 2 wounded. The enemy blew up a small mine at 2 am. opposite 32. causing a small crater. No damage done. During the night Lts Watt and Booth reconnoitred crater and bombed enemy trenches. Surprise Stand to arms at midnight.	

1875 Wt. W593/826 1,000,000 4/15 J.B.C. & A. A.D.S.S./Forms/C. 2118.

1st Gordon Highlanders.

Instructions regarding War Diaries and Intelligence Summaries are contained in F. S. Regs., Part II. and the Staff Manual respectively. Title Pages will be prepared in manuscript.

WAR[4] DIARY
or
~~INTELLIGENCE SUMMARY~~
(Erase heading not required.)

December 1915

Army Form C. 2118

Place	Date	Hour	Summary of Events and Information	Remarks and references to Appendices
I 34 b&c	17th Dec		Mild and damp day. The C.O. made a tour of inspection of the Reserve line trenches. Some shelling of the Reserves during the day. Shelling and trench mortaring during the night. 4 casualties from shock. Germans bombed crater in 32 which was unoccupied. C.O. visited 8th Gordons on our left during the afternoon. Major F. L. M. Crichton-Maitland joined the Battalion and assumed the duties of second in command.	
do.	18th Dec		Misty morning. The C.O. inspected adjoining defences in VERBRANDENMOLEN. About noon enemy began to shell Reserve Sector working from Verbrandenmolen to centre of sector. No damage done. Heavy and effective retaliation by Belgians on enemy front line. Wiring was done on left sector at 4 am. Some shelling at night.	
do.	19th Dec.		Fine day brilliant sunshine. At 4 am. enemy musketry fire opened. At 5.30 am heavy rifle fire again broke out, accompanied by lachrymatory shells. Heavy shelling was also heard in a Northerly direction. This continued for some three hours. Desultory shelling however continued throughout the morning. An enemy aeroplane flew over our lines shortly after dawn. During the morning bombardment, about 7 am. 4 men of the R.E. Tunnelling Coy were killed and at 8 am. an officer and two Sergeants were wounded. At 3.30 pm. enemy commenced an intensive bombardment of the whole front of the Battalion. This lasted until 4.30 pm. 2nd Lieut. H.W. Wright and four men were killed and 15 wounded.	

1st Gordon Highlanders

5

WAR DIARY
or
~~INTELLIGENCE SUMMARY~~
(Erase heading not required.)

December 1915

Army Form C. 2118

Instructions regarding War Diaries and Intelligence Summaries are contained in F. S. Regs., Part II. and the Staff Manual respectively. Title Pages will be prepared in manuscript.

Place	Date	Hour	Summary of Events and Information	Remarks and references to Appendices
I 34 bac.	19th Dec ctd.		The parapet on A Company's front was badly knocked about. Parties of the 4th Gordons and East Yorks came up in the evening to repair damage. Shelling continued until midnight.	
do.	20th Dec.		Misty and damp. G.O.C. Brigade and Brigade Major visited front trenches with C.O. at 9 am. G.O.C. Division, Chief of Staff, and A.D.C. visited trenches at about 10.30 am. Slight shelling of Reserves during morning. Continuous desultory shelling during afternoon and well into night.	
do	21st Dec.		Misty and damp. Enemy quiet all day. Specialists relieved at dawn. Battalion not relieved as expected owing to 9th Brigade relief falling on the same night.	
do	22nd Dec.		Fine. At 4.15 am. our Artillery bombarded roads behind enemy's lines continuing at intervals until 7 am. Our Heavy Artillery bombarded sector on our right from 9 to 10 am. Enemy retaliated by bombarding our line from 10 to 11 am. G.O.C. Brigade accompanied by General Staff Officer, 5th Corps and Staff Captain inspected trenches. Quiet afternoon. Battalion relieved by 8th K.O.R.L. Regt. about 7 pm and marched back to billets undisturbed. One casualty.	

1875 Wt. W593/826 1,000,000 4/15 J.B.C. & A. A.D.S.S./Forms/C. 2118.

1st Gordon Highlanders

6

WAR DIARY
or
~~INTELLIGENCE SUMMARY~~
(Erase heading not required.)

December 1915

Army Form C. 2118

Instructions regarding War Diaries and Intelligence Summaries are contained in F. S. Regs., Part II. and the Staff Manual respectively. Title Pages will be prepared in manuscript.

Place	Date	Hour	Summary of Events and Information	Remarks and references to Appendices
Reninghelst	23rd Dec.		Mild. Companies at Baths morning and afternoon. Capt R.D. [illegible] reported his arrival and was posted to A Company.	
do.	24th Dec		Showery – Company inspections of kit & Smoke Helmets. Smoke Helmet drill. Lecture to Officers & N.C.O's by C.O. on 'Esprit de Corps'	
do	25th Dec		Showery. Day observed as a holiday. Short Service at 11 am. The C.O. & Staff visited 19th Canadian Regiment billeted at La Clytte with Christmas greetings, reminding them of South Africa associations. Battalion Officers Mess inaugurated.	
do	26th Dec.		Showery in morning, fine afternoon. Church Parade 11 am followed by Lecture on Gas by Major Maitland.	
do	27th Dec.		Dry. Platoon drill and Bayonet fighting etc during morning. Lecture by C.O. to Officers & N.C.O's on The History of the Regiment. The C.O. ~~[illegible]~~ accompanied by Major Maitland attended a Conference at Brigade Headquarters. Two Casualties in machine gun section.	
do.	28th Dec		Fine but cold. Companies carried out training during morning. Major Maitland was posted provisionally to command 10th Royal Welsh Fusiliers.	

1875 Wt. W593/826 1,000,000 4/15 J.B.C. & A. A.D.S.S./Forms/C. 2118.

1st Gordon Highlanders

Instructions regarding War Diaries and Intelligence Summaries are contained in F. S. Regs., Part II. and the Staff Manual respectively. Title Pages will be prepared in manuscript.

WAR DIARY
or
~~INTELLIGENCE SUMMARY~~
(Erase heading not required.)

December 1915.

Army Form C. 2118

Place	Date	Hour	Summary of Events and Information	Remarks and references to Appendices
Reninghelst	29th Dec.		Misty. Specialists left at 4.30 a.m. for trenches. The Divisional Commander visited camp during morning and stayed about an hour. The Battalion marched at 2.15 to trench area via La CLYTTE but on arrival there, found the village was being shelled and made a detour to avoid it, relieving 8th K.O.R.L.Regt. about 8 p.m. Night quiet.	
I34b&c.	30th Dec.		Mild Wind S.E. Special precautions taken for gas. Brigadier made a tour of the trenches with the C.O. Capt. Parker 3D.A.C. joined Battalion for the tour in the trenches.	
do.	31st Dec		Mild Wind S.E. Bombardment of enemy trenches opposite 34 & 35 from 9 to 11 a.m. Bombardment of same sector by machine guns, trench mortars & grenades at 2 p.m. Retaliation feeble at both times. Rain in afternoon. 2nd Lieut. A.J.E. Carey joined as grenade officer and posted to C Coy.	
			Roll of Officers and strength of Battalion at this date given on attached	
			S.G. Craufurd Lieut Col. Commanding 1st Gordon Highlanders	

1875 Wt. W593/826 1,000,000 4/15 J.B.C. & A. A.D.S.S./Forms/C. 2118.

1st Battalion Gordon Highlanders.

Roll of Officers serving with this Battalion, 31st, Dec. 1915.

Commanding.	Lieut, Col. S.G.Craufurd, C.I.E. D.S.O.
Adjutant.	Captain M. Dinwiddie.

Pioneer Section.	Captain W. Morrison.
Machine Gun Section.	Lieut. J.A.W. Brown.
" " "	2/Lieut. J.D. Robertson.
Grenade Section.	2/Lieut. W.B. Campbell.
" "	" D.G. Watt.
Light Section.	Lieut. J. Mc P.Cunningham.
Transport Officer.	2/Lieut. L.T. Sinclair.

"A" Company.

Captain. R.D. Oxley, Commanding.
2/Lieut. P. Colquhoun.
" A.J. Cleghorn.
" C.R. Booth.
" C.B. Humphrey.

"B" Company.

2/Lieut. M.S. Robertson. Commanding.
" H.S. Reece.
" H.R.McK. Law.
" A.H. Duncan.
" W.R. Watt.

"C" Company.

Captain A. de L. Long, Commanding.
Lieut. G. Macdonald.
2/ Lieut. D.R.G. Renfrew.
" T. Mackintosh.
" C.A.J. Chambers-Hunter.
2nd Lieut A.E.B. Carey CAREY

"D" Company.

Captain. W.A. Dyke, Commanding.
Lieut. R.I. Baird.
2/Lieut. G. Mutch.
" S.M. Robertson.
" R. Peterkin.

Quartermaster, Captain J. MacLennan.

Medical Officer, Captain J.L. Stewart. R.A.M.C.

Strength of Battalion on 31st Dec 1915.

32 Officers
900 Other Ranks.

76th Brigade.

3rd Division.

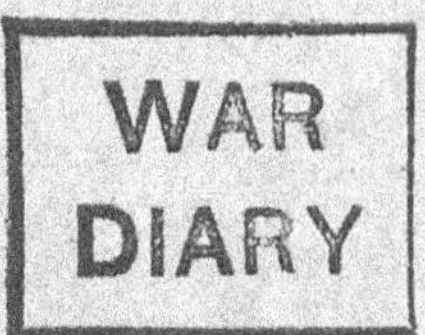

1st BATTALION

GORDON HIGHLANDERS

MARCH 1 9 1 6

Appendices attached:-

Report on the Action at the BLUFF
2/3rd March.

Nominal Roll of Officers.

1st Gordon Highlanders

Instructions regarding War Diaries and Intelligence Summaries are contained in F. S. Regs., Part II. and the Staff Manual respectively. Title Pages will be prepared in manuscript.

WAR DIARY
or
~~INTELLIGENCE SUMMARY~~
(Erase heading not required.)

March 1916

Army Form C. 2118

Place	1916 Date	Hour	Summary of Events and Information	Remarks and references to Appendices
RENINGHELST	1st March		Fine. Battalion spent forenoon in final preparations for attack. Voluntary Service at 2 pm. Battalion marched off at 3.30 to Camp 414 where a halt of an hour was made for tea. Battalion left 414 at 5.45 pm, ~~and [illegible]~~ relieving 2 Companies, 9th Northumberland Fusiliers and occupying Assembly trenches in rear of 32 & 33 S.	
I 34 b	2nd March		Fine. Assault made at 4.30 am without previous artillery bombardment. The assault was immediately successful on the right but left not secured until attack had been launched ~~[illegible]~~ for the third time. In the first assault on the left, 3 Platoons of A Coy taking part were practically annihilated by Machine Gun fire. (A detailed account of the action is attached). Casualties. Officers killed 3 wounded 5 slightly at duty 2. Other Ranks killed 68 Missing 12. Died of Wounds 3 Wounded 145. Officers killed Temp Capt M. S. Robertson 2Lt. D G Watt 2Lt. W. T. Sinclair. Wounded 2Lt P. Colquhoun 2Lt. T. J. Robertson 2Lt C R Booth 2Lt A. T. C. Carey 2Lt. G. P. Peterkin. Slightly at duty Lt G. McDonald, 2Lt G. Sanderson. Reserves and Support lines very heavily shelled by enemy during day. All counterattacks repulsed. Shelling continued throughout night mainly as a Barrage.	
I 34 b	3rd March		Cold. Position consolidated as much as possible. Shelling continuous and it was difficult even to remove the wounded. Shelling slackened towards evening. By 4 pm. a heavy Snow Storm was raging which continued throughout night	

1875 Wt. W593/826 1,000,000 4/15 J.B.C. & A. A.D.S.S./Forms/C. 2118.

1st Gordon Highlanders

WAR DIARY
or
~~INTELLIGENCE SUMMARY~~
(Erase heading not required.)

March 1916.

Army Form C. 2118

Instructions regarding War Diaries and Intelligence Summaries are contained in F. S. Regs., Part II. and the Staff Manual respectively. Title Pages will be prepared in manuscript.

Place	Date	Hour	Summary of Events and Information	Remarks and references to Appendices
SCOTTISH LINES ~~[illegible]~~	4th March		Battalion relieved by 8th East Yorks at 3.30 am. Relief not complete until 4.30 am. Conveyed by buses from Belgian Battery Corner to SCOTTISH LINES. Main portion of Battalion reached camp at 8 am. Men continued however to straggle in throughout the day. Desultory shelling continued throughout the whole relief but casualties were few.	
do.	5th March		Snowstorm continued throughout day. Proportion of Battalion went to Baths. Snow falling ~~throughout~~ night. Congratulatory telegram received (attached).	
do.	6th March		Snow still falling. Ground covered to depth of 4 inches. Army Commander inspected Battalion and expressed the thanks of himself and Commander-in-Chief for the good work done by the Battalion. Reinforcement of 88 joined in evening.	
do.	7th March		Fine but cold. Battalion bath parties, refitting and completing deficiencies.	
do.	8th March		Fine. Reorganisation continued. Draft inspected by C.O.	
do.	9th March		Fine. Work of refitting etc. continued. Visit from G.O.C. Brigade ~~who inspected~~ Battalion on parade. G.O.C. Corps later came round but did not wish the men turned out.	
do.	10th March		Dull. Battalion marched at 3.30 pm and relieved 12th West Yorks in Reserve Dugouts at GORDON TERRACE & KINGSWAY. Night spent in working parties.	
GORDON TERRACE RESERVE	11th March		Dry. Small working parties by day and Battalion at work during night. Slight shelling of KINGSWAY.	
do.	12th March		Fine. 5 men accidentally wounded examining noise cap. Working parties continued. 1 casualty.	

1875 Wt. W593/826 1,000,000 4/15 J.B.C. & A. A.D.S.S./Forms/C. 2118.

1st Gordon Highlanders — 3 — March 1916

Army Form C. 2118

WAR DIARY
or
~~INTELLIGENCE SUMMARY~~
(Erase heading not required.)

Instructions regarding War Diaries and Intelligence Summaries are contained in F. S. Regs., Part II. and the Staff Manual respectively. Title Pages will be prepared in manuscript.

Place	Date 1916	Hour	Summary of Events and Information	Remarks and references to Appendices
GORDON TERRACE	13th March		Fine. Specialists moved to trenches at dawn relieving 8th King's Own R.L. Regt. Battalion moved up at dusk, taking over trenches 32, 33 and 34. One casualty.	
I 34 b	14th March		Clear day. Many enemy aeroplanes otherwise quiet. Battalion hard at work clearing trenches, rebuilding whole sector, draining and clearing C.T.s and burying dead. One casualty.	
I 34 b	15th March		Brilliant sunshine. Work principally done at night. Enemy sniping very active. This was gradually reduced by our snipers.	
I 34 b	16th March		Bright and warm. Repair of trenches continued at high pressure. 2Lt. Smith and Brown joined the Battalion and were posted to A and D Coys respectively. 2Lt. Clephan returned from Hospital. Casualties 3 killed 2 wounded.	
do	17th March		Fine. Capt. Russell joined Battalion and posted to B Coy. Some shelling in afternoon. One casualty - wounded.	
RENINGHELST	18th March		Fine and warm. Specialists relieved at dawn by 8 K.O.R.L. Day quiet. Battalion relieved by K.O.R.L. in evening and marched to B Camp. During this spell in the trenches Battalion rebuilt and repaired 850 yards of parapet. 20,500 sandbags were filled and used in this work. In addition 6 dugouts were built and 10 more constructed except for roofing. This was in addition to general repairs and drainage of trenches and C.T.s, burial parties and salvage.	
do.	19th March		Warm and fine. Following immediate awards announced. 2Lt Sanderson D.S.O. Lieut McDonald and 2Lt. Reece M.C. Sgt Walker, Ptes. Allardyce and Smith, D.C.M. Voluntary service in evening.	

1875 Wt. W593/826 1,000,000 4/15 J.B.C. & A. A.D.S.S./Forms/C. 2118.

1st Gordon Highlanders

Army Form C. 2118

WAR DIARY
or
INTELLIGENCE SUMMARY
(Erase heading not required.)

March 1916

Instructions regarding War Diaries and Intelligence Summaries are contained in F. S. Regs., Part II. and the Staff Manual respectively. Title Pages will be prepared in manuscript.

Place	Date	Hour	Summary of Events and Information	Remarks and references to Appendices
RENINGHELST	20th March		Fine. Col. Craufurd left for Gordon Terrace to take over command of Brigade vice Gen Pratt invalided from shell shock. Kit inspection & Refitting	
do	21st March		Showery. Company training in forenoon. In evening, Battalion supplied a working party of 250 men for filling sandbags in ST. ELOI Sector.	
do.	22nd March		Wet. Battalion again supplied working parties for ST. ELOI sector.	
do.	23rd March		Fine. Battalion visited by Commander in Chief who inspected Companies at their training. Battalion again supplied working parties at night. ~~Sick~~ Casualties 1 Killed 3 wounded	
do.	24th March		Snow. Battalion left for Reserve in VOORMEZEELE and SCOTTISH WOOD Employed on Carrying fatigue all night.	
SCOTTISH WOOD	25th March		Fine. B & C Coy at VOORMEZEELE heavily shelled. Battalion relieved in evening after working parties had returned. Casualties Capt Russell wounded. 1 man wounded.	
J Camp RENINGHELST	26th March		Fine but cold. Battalion, on relief by East Yorks, marched back to J Camp. Divisional Commander visited Battalion at 3 pm and presented ribbons for immediate awards granted for operations 2.3rd March. He complimented the Battalion both on their good work in operations at BLUFF and also on the good work done in the trenches during the last tour of duty. 2Lt. R. K. Gordon joined & posted to A Coy. 1 casualty (self-inflicted)	
do.	27th March		Dry but cold; rain in evening. Day spent in cleaning up. 2Lt. O. Horsley and 2Lt. D. Miller and draft of 70 men arrived.	

1875 Wt. W593/826 1,000,000 4/15 J.B.C. & A. A.D.S.S./Forms/C. 2118.

Instructions regarding War Diaries and Intelligence Summaries are contained in F. S. Regs., Part II. and the Staff Manual respectively. Title Pages will be prepared in manuscript.

1st Gordon Highlanders

5 WAR DIARY or ~~INTELLIGENCE SUMMARY~~

(Erase heading not required.)

March 1916

Army Form C. 2118

Place	Date	Hour	Summary of Events and Information	Remarks and references to Appendices
RENINGHELST	28th March		Windy. Company training during forenoon. Battalion marched to DICKEBUSCH in evening, obtaining billets with some difficulty. Dickebusch was slightly shelled. A & B Companies on working parties all night.	
DICKEBUSCH	29th March		Fine & bright. Whole Battalion on fatigue in evening. G.O.C. Division visited Battalion during day along with G.O.C. Brigade.	
do.	30th March		Fine but cold. Battalion again on working parties at night. Two Companies were recalled and A Company was sent up to support of 10th Royal Welsh Fusiliers.	
do.	31st March		Stormy. At 3 am A Company marched to trenches and occupied support line to 10th Royal Welsh Fusiliers in captured trenches at St. ELOI. Great delay in getting into position. No gumboots were available. Trenches on an average 3 feet in water. A Company badly shelled by 5.9 during morning; 22 casualties 10 killed 12 wounded. Remainder of Battalion marched up in afternoon to P trenches in relief of 10th Royal Welsh Fusiliers in captured trenches. A Company relieved with Welsh and returned B Camp. Stormy night.	

1875 Wt. W593/826 1,000,000 4/15 J.B.C. & A. A.D.S.S./Forms/C. 2118.

1st Battalion The GORDON HIGHLANDERS.

Account of the Action about the BLUFF March 2/3rd.1916.

The Battalion left Billets at Camp I at 3.30pm.on the evening of March,1st. A halt was made for one hour at Camp H for teas and Battal finally marched off at 5.45 reaching CAFE BELGE at 7pm. After leaving Camp H no lights or sinking of any description was allowed. The Battalion moved from the R.E.dump to the trenches by Companies 200 yards interval. The relief was completed by 10.45 The disposition of the Battalion was then as follows:- On the right in 32 S "B"Coy. under Captain M.S.Robertson.

Captain Robertson had received instructions to charge silently with his whole company at the hour of assault to be given later and capture the then German front line,his objective being our old front line 32 from the continuation of the DRIVE to the left edge of the BEAN in continuation of HEDGE ROW. A party of bombers and one Lewis Gun detachment had been detailed under his orders for the special consolidation of the left edge of the BEAN. On the left in 33 Support three platoons of A Coy.under 2/Lieutenant COLQUHOUN - objecti 33. These two Companies together with 52 Grenadiers (detailed to clear the C.T's) comprised the front line - strength 280.

A detached post consisting of a personeel of 28 Grenadiers and their support had been detailed to co-operate on the left of the RAVINE.

In support there were two platoons of D coy.,2 platoons of C Coy.,1 platoon of A Coy.,which,together with carriers to the Grenadi formed the second line - a total strength of 225 - and occupied the first line assembly trenches from HEDGE ROW to DEESIDE.

In reserve 2 platoons D Coy.,2 platoons C Coy.,which,together with Machine Gunners and Pioneers occupied the second line assembly trenches with a total strength of 175.

"D" Coy. was commanded by Captain LONG and "C" Coy.by Lieut. MACDONALD.

The assault was timed to take place at 4.30am.

Wiring parties were sent out at 11.30pm. That on the right was furnished by D Coy. under 2/Lieut.MUTCH and that on the left by C Coy. under 2/Lieut.CAREY. It had been found impossible to stop our trench morters whilst this work was going on.

Bayonets and wire breakers were fixed at 4.15am.and at 4.25am. parties detailed for the assault silently left the parapet. At 4.30am. the assault was carried out in silence. B Coy. on the right owing to the suddenness of the attack gained possession of the German lines without serious opposition and the left platoon commenced to bomb down the trenches to join up with A Coy.

A Coy. on the left likewise reached the German parapet in the first rush but were met with a sharp bomb attack from the bombing posts to their front and left and by a murderous rifle and machine gun fire from their left flank. Our Grenadiers failed to subdue the

P.T.O.

to subdue the German bombers and the Company was forced to retire suffering heavy casualties. Only 20 men under 2/Lieut SANDERSON succeeded in entering the German trench. This party being reduced to six men and being unsupported were forced to retire.

2/Lieut.SINCLAIR was killed in the first rush and 2/Lieuts.BOOTH and COLQUHOUN wounded.

On the assault taking place the two supporting lines in the Assembly trenches moved forward, the line in the front assembly trench occupying the S line. The remaining platoon of A Coy.and one platoon of C Coy.were immediately sent up in support as soon as it was evident that the attack on the left had not fully succeeded. They were, however, forced to retire along with the remnants of A Coy. It was now just on dawn and Lieut.MACDONALD made a fresh attack with two other platoons of C Coy. under 2/Lieuts.CHAMBERS-HUNTER and CAREY .This attack however, missed its direction though they succeeded in gaining the German trench failed to secure our left flank and join up with the bombing post on the WEST of the RAVINE.

The situation on the left flank now seemed critical and I called up the company of the 7th LINCOLNS from the "R" line to the "S" line. I also asked for a company of the STAFFORDS to be placed at my disposal in the reserve. It was now daylight and Lieut. MACDONALD collected one intact platoon together with the disorganised parties of "A" and "C" Companies who had been driven back from the front line. Reinforced by the bombers of the 7th LINCOLNS he then made a determined charge for the German trenches which he then carried.

In this he was greatly aided by 2/Lieut. SANDERSON and Private ALLERDYCE who pushed on ahead down the left C.T. and bombed out of action two German bombing posts and a German machine gun, thereby securing Lieut. MACDONALD'S left flank.

Communication was then established with "B" Company and with the WEST RIDINGS to the left of the RAVINE.

Meanwhile on the right reinforcements had been asked for and one platoon of "D" Company together with Grenadiers were sent up. Some of these were later seen in the German second line and recalled.

A working party was also sent up to connect 82 with the BEAN . These men were, however, all killed.

At 6.45 it was reported that a C.T. had been cut through between 82 and the BEAN but this proved not to be the case, nor was it found possible to cut this C.T. throughout the remainder of the action.

Further reinforcements having been urgently called for on the left I directed Captain LONG to send up a further two platoons in support at 6.25 a.m. to secure the ground won. Shortly after this the Germans began to surrender in large numbers and these two platoons were again withdrawn.

Captain M.S.ROBERTSON Commanding "B" Company had been killed early in the assault while trying to establish communication with the KING'S OWN on his right.

Three Lewis Guns had been sent up to reinforce the firing line as soon as it had been made good and 2/Lieut. J.D.ROBERTSON was wounded shortly afterwards about 7.a.m.

The following further casualties occurred during the assault:-

"A" Company	2/Lieut. BOOTH	(wounded)
"C" Company	2/Lieut. CAREY	"
"D" Company	2/Lieut. PETERKIN	"
"Headquarters Coy.	2/Lieut. GORDON WATT	(Killed)

LIEUT. MACDONALD and 2/LIEUT. SANDERSON were also slightly wounded.

At 8.a.m. I learnt that men of both the Gordon Highlanders and Kings Own had penetrated to beyond the German second line and as senior officer of that sector I sent to recall both regiments back to the line of our original objective.

It would appear as if at this time the German front had been evacuated to beyond their third lines and unconfirmed reports were received that forward field guns had been abandoned.

By 8.30. a.m. the Germans began shelling our front line fairly heavily.

At 10. a.m. they sent up two Green Star Shells opposite HEDGE ROW and an intensive bombardment of our whole position commenced. This continued till noon when a feeble attempt at a counter attack was made.

Shelling was maintained more or less continuously till about 6.30. a.m.on March 3rd. From 6.30.a.m. till 9. a.m. there was a lull after which shelling continued with varying intensity till dark. After dark shelling was maintained by two batteries on the C.T's. throughout the night.

Throughout the whole of March 2nd and 3rd there was very great congestion in all the trenches. The "R" line and much of the support line of the KINGS OWN on our right had become untenable.

Movement It had therefore been found necessary to move up the Company of the STAFFORD Regiment and many of the KINGS OWN supports into ours S line and assembly trenches. Trenches were also blocked with killed and wounded, most of whom it was impossible to evacuate till the afternoon of the 3rd.

On the night of the3rd/4tha heavy snowstorm fell which together with the bombardment rendered all C.T's except LOVERS LANE and DRIVE impracticable.

The N.C.Os sent as guides to the relieving Regiments lost their way on the return journey in the dark and snowstorm and the relief was not complete till 4.a.m. The congestion by this time was much intensifi Nine regiments were occupying the frontage normally held by three.

As already stated only two avenues of communication existed in our sector. Shelling was continuous if desultory and it was impossible that at any moment a barrage might be formed. I therefore directed all units under my command to file away in small parties as quickly as circumstances should permit and reform at CAFE BELGE. I left myself with Headquarters Staff as soon as it was reported to me that all unitshad left the trench area.

(Sd) S. G. Craufurd Lieut. Colonel,
Commandang 1st Battalion Gordon Highrs.

7th March, 1916.

1st. Battalion The Gordon Highlanders.

Copy of Message received on March, 4th. 1916.

BM 212 4-3-16.

Following messages were received during the operations aaa From 3rd. Division begins aaa My congratulations to yourself and all ranks of the Brigade please convey to all ranks my appreciation of the gallant manner in which the attack was carried out Message ends. From 51st. Infantry Brigade begins Hearty congratulations on your complete success Message ends aaa From 17th. Division Very hearty congratulations to all ranks on success gained Message ends aaa From Army Commander begins I am very pleased to have received reports of the success of your operations last night. Please convey my appreciationto all ranks of the troops engaged ends aaa From C. in C begins I have heard with very great pleasure the good news of the capture of the Bluff and trenches just north of the Canal aaa I have been kept informed from day to day of the careful thought and methodical preparations which have been devoted to this enterprise aaa Please convey to all ranks concerned in the operations my heartiest congratulations and thanks.

1st Bn. Gordon Highlanders.

Roll of Officers serving with the Battalion on 31/3/16

Major F. L. M. C. Maitland	Commanding Officer
Lieut. J. McA. Cunningham	A/Adjutant
Capt. W. A. Dyke	i/c Pioneer Section
2/Lieut. W. C. Watt	i/c Light Section
" W. B. Campbell	i/c Grenade Section
" D. C. G. Henfrew	i/c Transport Section
Lieut. H. S. Gammell	i/c Lewis Detachment

"A" Coy.

2/Lieut. J. B. Smith	Commanding.
" R. J. Cleghorn	
" A. Bothwell	
" C. K. Gordon	
" O. Horsley	

"B" Coy.

2/Lieut. H. S. Hunt	Commanding
" C. C. Humphrey	
" A. H. Duncan	
" D. A. Millar	

"C" Coy.

Lieut. G. MacDonald	Commanding
2/Lieut. T. Mackintosh	

"D" Coy.

Capt. A. de L. Long	Commanding
Lieut. C. G. Baird	
2/Lieut. G. P. Peterkin	
" H. H. Bruce	
" D. C. D. Munro	

Quartermaster	Major J. Mackennan
Medical Officer	Capt. J. L. Stewart
Chaplain	Capt. P. D. Thomson

Strength of Battalion – Officers 26
Other Ranks 715.

76th Brigade.

3rd Division.

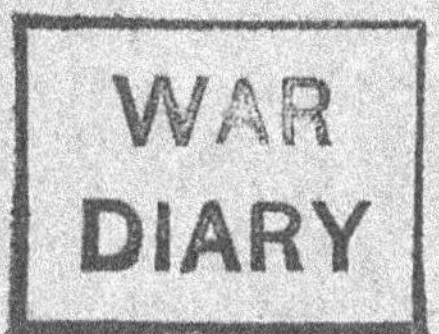

1st BATTALION

GORDON HIGHLANDERS

JANUARY 1 9 1 6

Nominal Roll of Offizers is attached.

Army Form C. 2118

WAR DIARY
or
INTELLIGENCE SUMMARY
(Erase heading not required.)

Instructions regarding War Diaries and Intelligence Summaries are contained in F. S. Regs., Part II. and the Staff Manual respectively. Title Pages will be prepared in manuscript.

Place	Date	Hour	Summary of Events and Information	Remarks and references to Appendices
	1915			
RENINGHELST	29th Dec		Misty. Specialists left at 4.30 am and relieved 8th K.O.L.R. at dawn. Battalion marched at 2.15 pm via LA CLYTTE but on arrival there, found that the village was being shelled and so made a detour to avoid it relieving the 8th KOLR about 8 pm. Night quiet.	
I 34 B+C	30th Dec		Mild wind S.E. Bombardment of enemy trenches opposite 34+35 from 9 am – 11 am. Bombardment of same sector by trench mortars, machine guns + grenades at 12 noon. Retaliation feeble at both times. Rain in afternoon.	
" "	30th Dec		Mild wind SE. Quiet. Special precautions taken for gas. [illegible] made a tour of trenches with C.O.	
	1916			
"	1st Jan		Fine but showery. Both Division Commander and Brigadier visited trenches in morning [illegible] for the year [illegible] with Gen Sir Ian Hamilton [illegible] [illegible]. Enemy very quiet all day.	
"	2nd Jan		Wet and stormy. Brigadier made tour of trenches. Work carried on as usual. Enemy quiet. [illegible] went out in evening but found all quiet.	
"	3rd Jan		Fine. Quiet morning. Our trench mortars bombarded enemy [illegible] opposite [illegible]. Enemy retaliated with mortars and field guns [illegible] 4 casualties.	
	4th Jan		Cloudy mild. Brigadier and Brigadier General [illegible] visited trenches during morning [illegible] Col Williams (Warwickshire Regt) attached to Battalion for a [illegible]. Little shelling during afternoon.	
	5th Jan		Fine Quiet day. Some shelling of Batteries. Many aeroplanes over trenches [illegible]. Battalion relieved in the evening and marched to billets at RENINGHELST [illegible]	

1875 Wt. W593/826 1,000,000 4/15 J.B.C. & A. A.D.S.S./Forms/C. 2118.

WAR DIARY
or
INTELLIGENCE SUMMARY
(*Erase heading not required.*)

Instructions regarding War Diaries and Intelligence Summaries are contained in F. S. Regs., Part II. and the Staff Manual respectively. Title Pages will be prepared in manuscript.

Place	Date 1916	Hour	Summary of Events and Information	Remarks and references to Appendices
RENINGHELST	6th Jan		Fine day spent in cleaning up. Paying out Companies in afternoon.	
"	7th Jan		Showery. Companies at Baths. Kit inspection, Commanding Officer inspected Transport	
"	8th Jan		Fine but cold. Company Training	
"	9th Jan		Fine. Church Parade in morning. Sentences on 4 men for offences on sentry duty by Courts Martial promulgated	
"	10th Jan		Route march. 150 men on Divisional fatigue laying cable. Regimental Concert in Reading Room in evening. Lecture by Capt Oxley on Map Reading. Capt + Adjutant Dinwiddie to Brigade as acting Staff Officer	
"	11th Jan		Showery + Cold. Grenade and helmet drill. 200 men on fatigue laying cable	
"	12th Jan		Fine but cold. Two Bombs near transport from aeroplane. No casualties. Morning spent cleaning Camp. Battalion marched via OUDERDAM + CAFE BELGE to trenches. Quiet night. Relief completed 7.30 pm (record time).	
I.34 b+c	13th Jan		Showery + cold. Very quiet day.	
" "	14th Jan		Mild. Brigadier visited trenches in morning. Morning quiet. In the afternoon 3 trench mortar shells thrown into enemy's lines. Enemy retaliated with some 40 rounds of Shrapnel + H.E. Casualties 2 Killed 2 severely wounded and 2 slightly wounded. In the evening one man was killed by a sniper. C.O. visited Brigade Headquarters with 38 men for interview.	
" "	15th Jan		Dull day. Very quiet day	
" "	16th Jan		Fine bright day. Considerable aerial activity. Enemy quiet.	
" "	19th Jan		Fine + clear. 8 inch howitzers bombarded enemy's trenches opposite 31 + 32 trenches. Shoot interfered with owing to enemy aeroplanes being over our guns. Specialists relieved in morning. Battalion relieved at 7 pm by 8th KOLR. Splendid night for relief	
" "	18th Jan		Dull. Quiet day	
" "	17th Jan		Fine. Brigadier visited trenches in afternoon. Belgian Battery gave farewell bombardment at Enemy opposite 32 + 33 trench. Enemy retaliated on Trench 35 reserve. Casualties 1 Killed + 4 wounded	

1875 Wt. W593/826 1,000,000 4/15 J.B.C. & A. A.D.S.S./Forms/C. 2118.

Instructions regarding War Diaries and Intelligence Summaries are contained in F. S. Regs., Part II. and the Staff Manual respectively. Title Pages will be prepared in manuscript.

WAR DIARY
or
INTELLIGENCE SUMMARY

(Erase heading not required.)

Army Form C. 2118

Place	Date 1916	Hour	Summary of Events and Information	Remarks and references to Appendices
RENINGHELST	20th Jan		Fine. Battalion held kit inspection in the afternoon.	
" "	21st Jan		Fine. Baths at RENINGHELST	
" "	22nd Jan		Fine. Battalion training carried out in morning. [illegible] in afternoon to officers and N.C.Os on "Some Causes of the War"	
" "	23rd Jan		Fine. Church parade at 11 am	
" "	24th Jan		Dry but dull. Battalion route march [illegible] via RENINGHELST [illegible] LOCRE and then to billets. Fatigue party of [illegible] and [illegible] NCOs [illegible] at work from 3pm laying Divisional cable in vicinity of DICKEBUSCH. Lt Colonel [illegible] [illegible] of Brigade on Br Gen Pratt going on leave.	
" "	25th Jan		Fine and clear. Aerial activity [illegible] over camp at various intervals in day.	
" "	26th Jan		Dull in morning brighter in afternoon. In morning cleaning [illegible] afternoon battalion marched to trenches at 2.45pm + relieved 8th KOLR at [illegible] [illegible] + relief consequently slightly delayed. Enemy quiet.	
I.34 b + c	27th Jan		Dull. Our artillery bombarded enemy trenches opposite 31. 32. 33 [illegible] and Field batteries. T.M batteries + rifle grenades also being used. Enemy's retaliation very feeble, only about 25. 4.1 H.E Shrapnel + a few light Shrapnel [illegible] in our area. Lt Colonel Craufurd visited our trenches in afternoon. 3 Sailors from the Grand Fleet joined us at midnight and spent a day with us. Battalion gave up 33 trench to 10th RWF. and took over 36 + 37.	
" "	28th Jan		Fine but slightly dull. Enemy quiet. Lt Col Craufurd visited trenches in morning [illegible] with him Captain Ferguson RN. who spent a good part of the day with us looking at our trenches. Enemy sent over 4 H.E. Shrapnel Shells in retaliation to our T.M. Captain Ferguson + sailors left at 3.30 pm. New communication trench to 36 named GRAND FLEET WALK in recognition of the visit of the representatives of the Navy	

1875 Wt. W593/826 1,000,000 4/15 J.B.C. & A. A.D.S.S./Forms/C. 2118.

Instructions regarding War Diaries and Intelligence Summaries are contained in F. S. Regs., Part II. and the Staff Manual respectively. Title Pages will be prepared in manuscript.

WAR DIARY
or
INTELLIGENCE SUMMARY
(Erase heading not required.)

Place	Date 1916	Hour	Summary of Events and Information	Remarks and references to Appendices
I 34 b + c	29th Jan		Fine but dull. Very quiet day. Lt Colonel Crauford visited trenches in afternoon. Towards night wind changed round to the East. necessary precautions taken against gas	
" "	30th Jan		Foggy. Very quiet day. Wind still Easterly	
" "	31st Jan		Dull but dry. Our artillery bombarded enemy's front and support line with 9.2" 8" + field batteries. Trench Mortars and rifle grenades also assisted	

1875 Wt. W593/826 1,000,000 4/15 J.B.C. & A. A.D.S.S./Forms/C. 2118.

Roll of Officers serving with 1st Bn. Gordon Highrs on 31st January 1916.

Lieut. Col. J.C. [illegible]
Capt. B. [illegible]
" A. [illegible] King
" N. [illegible]
" R.D. Oxley
" W.A. Dick
Lieut. J. McA. Cunningham
" G. F. H. Brian
" R.J. Baird
" G. MacDonald
2/Lieut. W.B. Campbell
" L.J. Sinclair
" A.J.E. Carey
" P. Colquhoun
" D.G. Watt
" C.E. Boalth
" A.J. Cleghorn
" M.S. Robertson
" S.M. Robertson
" J.D. Robertson
" H.S. Reece
" H.C. McK. Law
" C.E. Humphrey
" A.H. Duncan
" W.R. Watt
" C.A.J. Chambers-Hunter
" D.R.G. Renfrew
" T. Mackintosh
" G. Mutch
" R.P. Peteskin

Capt. J.L. Stewart, M.O.
Major J. Maclennan, Q.M.

No 6461 R.S.M. Neilson W.
7297 2/R.S.M. Ross R.
5841 R.Q.M.S. Farrant G.

76th Brigade.

3rd Division.

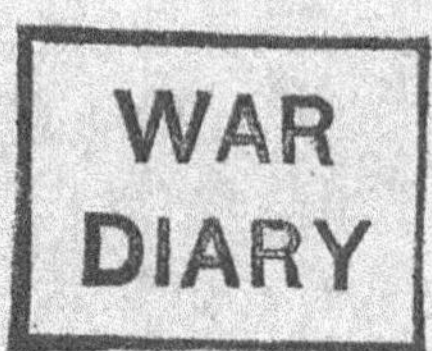

1st BATTALION

GORDON HIGHLANDERS

FEBRUARY 1 9 1 6

Appendix - Nominal Roll of Officers

1st Gordon Highlanders

Instructions regarding War Diaries and Intelligence Summaries are contained in F. S. Regs., Part II. and the Staff Manual respectively. Title Pages will be prepared in manuscript.

WAR DIARY
or
~~INTELLIGENCE SUMMARY~~
(Erase heading not required.)

~~March~~ February 1916

Army Form C.2118

Vol XVII

Place	Date 1916	Hour	Summary of Events and Information	Remarks and references to Appendices
I 34 b & c	1st Feb		Fine and clear Day quiet. Wind still Easterly. [illegible] visited trenches in afternoon	
" "	2nd Feb		Fine and clear Day again quiet throughout. Battalion relieved by 8th [illegible]. Captain Oxley sent to Field Ambulance suffering from Malaria.	
RENINGHELST.	3rd Feb		Fine. Kit inspection & battalion paying out in afternoon	
" "	4th Feb		Dull. Lt Colonel Campbell rejoined battalion from commanding 76th Brigade. Battalion at Baths	
	5th Feb		Fine. Major F. Crichton Maitland rejoined battalion from commanding 10th Royal Welch Fusiliers. Received orders to move to rest billets near St. Omer.	
"	6th Feb		Fine. Battalion marched to Godewaersvelde and entrained there for St. Omer, whence it marched to Serques and took over rest billets. Battalion arrived at dusk and the march from St Omer was made in a steady drizzle throughout.	
SERQUES	7th Feb		Fine but cold. Day occupied in settling down in billets	
do.	8th Feb		Showery and cold. Training commenced	

1875 Wt. W593/826 1,000,000 4/15 J.B.C. & A. A.D.S.S./Forms/C. 2118.

1st Gordon Highlanders

3

Instructions regarding War Diaries and Intelligence Summaries are contained in F. S. Regs., Part II. and the Staff Manual respectively. Title Pages will be prepared in manuscript.

WAR DIARY
or
~~INTELLIGENCE SUMMARY~~
(Erase heading not required.)

February 1916

Army Form C. 2118

Place	Date	Hour	Summary of Events and Information	Remarks and references to Appendices
SERQUES	9th Feb		Fine and frosty. Brigadier visited billets in morning. Training carried on.	
do.	10 Feb		Fine. Sir Douglas HAIG C-in-C. visited Battalion in afternoon. Officers and N.C.O's exercised in map Reading on ground by C.O.	
do.	11th Feb		Showery. No training in morning. Practice in location of sounds, light, [illegible] by night.	
do.	12th Feb		Morning wet, dry later. Battalion Route March. In the morning Col. Crawfurd assumed command of 76th Brigade on departure of Gen. Pratt to [illegible] manoeuvres.	
do.	13th Feb		Showery. Church Parade.	
do.	14th Feb		Fine. Company training carried out.	
do.	15th Feb		Showery. About 3 pm Battalion warned to be ready to move at short notice. At 4 pm orders received to entrain at WATTEN at 8.30 pm for POPERINGHE	
POPERINGHE	16th Feb		Fine. Battalion arrived at 7.30 am. Transport arriving by road at 11 am. Battalion billeted in town POPERINGHE. Col. Crawfurd rejoined Battalion. Visit by G.O.C. Brigade in afternoon. Battalion marched at 8 pm to huts at OUDERDOM (H14c) arriving there at 10 pm.	
H14c	17th Feb		Fine. Battalion marched to trenches at 4.30 pm and relieved 4th BORDER Regt. in trenches 32 S. 33 S. 34 & 35. Germans in occupation of front line of 32 and 33. Enfilade sniping in 34 and 35 bad in consequence	

1875 Wt. W593/826 1,000,000 4/15 J.B.C. & A. A.D.S.S./Forms/C. 2118.

1st Gordon Highlanders

3

WAR DIARY
or
~~INTELLIGENCE SUMMARY~~
(*Erase heading not required.*)

February 1916

Army Form C. 2118

Instructions regarding War Diaries and Intelligence Summaries are contained in F. S. Regs., Part II. and the Staff Manual respectively. Title Pages will be prepared in manuscript.

Place	Date	Hour	Summary of Events and Information	Remarks and references to Appendices
I 34 c	18 Feb		Fine. Enemy shelled foot of GORDON WOOD and top of trench railway, also Batt^n reserve about 2.30 pm. Our Artillery retaliated by bombardment of his trenches at 4 pm, on which enemy commenced intense barrage of wood behind our line, presumably under impression that we were about to attack. Artillery activity quiet at 6 pm. Desultory shelling of Battalion dump by 5.9" continued throughout night. Casualties 1 killed & 8 wounded.	
I 34 b & c	19 Feb		Fine. ~~Day quieter~~ Enemy sent over three aerial torpedoes in direction of Batt^n cookhouses which had to be evacuated. Casualties 1 killed by sniper, 1 shell shock.	
I 34 b & c	20th Feb		Very bright & fine. Great aerial activity on both sides. Day otherwise quiet. Several Zeppelins seen at night as well as many aeroplanes. 1 killed & 2 wounded by our own shells.	
do	21st Feb		Dull, frost in morning. Considerable aerial activity. Enemy shelled gun positions in our rear during afternoon [illegible] be killed by our guns. 1 wounded by sniper.	
do	22nd Feb		Day fine. Quiet. Battalion relieved at night by 12th Manchester Regt. and marched to I Camp, Reninghelst.	
RENINGHELST	23rd Feb		Cold with snow. Hard frost at night.	
do	24th Feb		Fine but frosty. Snow on ground. Battalion at Baths during morning. Officers and N.C.O.'s went over [illegible] position of trenches to be recaptured.	

1875 Wt. W593/826 1,000,000 4/15 J.B.C. & A. A.D.S.S./Forms/C. 2118.

4

1st Gordon Highlanders

Army Form C. 2118

WAR DIARY
or
~~INTELLIGENCE SUMMARY~~
(Erase heading not required.)

February 1916

Instructions regarding War Diaries and Intelligence Summaries are contained in F. S. Regs., Part II. and the Staff Manual respectively. Title Pages will be prepared in manuscript.

Place	Date 1916	Hour	Summary of Events and Information	Remarks and references to Appendices
RENINGHELST	25th Feb		Fine. Snow still on ground. Battalion practised attack in conjunction with 8th King Own R L Regt.	
do.	26th Feb		Wet, frost in evening. Battalion again rehearsed attack.	
do.	27th Feb		Dull. Thaw. Battalion practised attack	
do	28th Feb		Fine. Battalion made final practice of assault before attack.	
do.	29th Feb		Fine. Battalion made final arrangements before going into action.	

1875 Wt. W593/826 1,000,000 4/15 J.B.C. & A. A.D.S.S./Forms/C. 2118.

[illegible]

[illegible]

[illegible]

[illegible] D. G. [illegible]	[illegible]
[illegible] B [illegible]	[illegible]
[illegible]	[illegible]
Lieut. J. A. H. Brown	[illegible] Transport [illegible]
	[illegible] Detachment

"A" Coy.

[illegible]	[illegible]
" A. J. [illegible]	
" C. H. Booth	
L. J. Sinclair	

"B" Coy.

Capt. M. S. Robertson	Commanding
2/Lieut. W. H. [illegible]	
" A. H. McK. Jones	
" C. C. Humphrey	
" A. G. Duncan	
" H. L. Reece	

"C" Coy.

Lieut. G. MacDonald	Commanding
2/Lieut. E. A. J. Chambers-Hunter	
" T. Mackintosh	
" A. J. E. Carey	

"D" Coy.

Capt. A. de L. Long	Commanding
Lieut. A. J. Baird	
2/Lieut. G. C. Ritchie	
" G. Mutch	
" J. D. Robertson	
" C. Sanderson	

Quartermaster	Major J. MacLennan
Medical Officer	Capt. J. L. Stewart

Strength of the Battn. O. 30
Other Ranks 841

76th Brigade.

3rd Division.

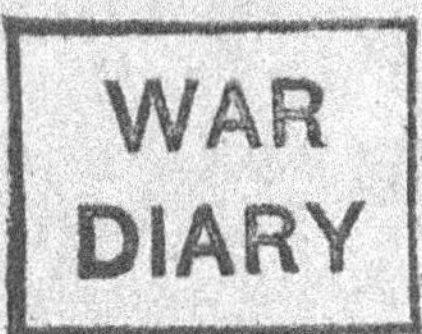

1st BATTALION

GORDON HIGHLANDERS

APRIL 1 9 1 6

Appendix:- Nominal Roll of Officers.

3

1 Gordon Hos

Vol 19

1st Gordon Highlanders

1

WAR DIARY
or
INTELLIGENCE SUMMARY
(Erase heading not required.)

April 1916

Army Form C. 2118

76/3

Instructions regarding War Diaries and Intelligence Summaries are contained in F. S. Regs., Part II. and the Staff Manual respectively. Title Pages will be prepared in manuscript.

Place	Date	Hour	Summary of Events and Information	Remarks and references to Appendices
ST ELOI trenches	1st April		Cold. Relief of 10th R.W.F. was just completed when enemy commenced bombing attacks on points 44 and 45. These were repulsed. During the day trench 44-45 was heavily shelled necessitating evacuation. This trench together with point 55 were reoccupied after bombardment ceased. Point 64 was, however held by the enemy. Condition of the trenches was very bad, being in some cases three foot deep in water and mud. C Company suffered heavily and was relieved by D Coy in the evening. 2 Lieuts Chambers-Hunter was killed, 2Lt Reece died of wounds. 2 Lts Macintosh Humphrey and Miller wounded.	
do.	2nd April		Fine. Three attempts were made in early morning to get back point 64 which the enemy was still holding. Canadian and Royal Scots bombing parties took part but attempts failed owing to the enemy occupation of a shallow trench in rear from which he could bomb 64 thereby preventing our occupation. There was some heavy shelling during the day. 2Lt. W. B. Campbell was wounded.	
do.	3rd April		Fine but cold. Assault on No 5 Crater was delivered by 8th Kings Own R.L. Regt at 2am. This resulted in occupation of front line from 64 to 77 and the capture of 4 officers and 40 other ranks of the enemy from Crater 5. The Battalion joined up with the Kings Own at 44. The enemy carried out an intense bombardment throughout the day. B Company suffered heavy casualties in the afternoon. Officers of 27 Canadian Regt visited trenches in afternoon. 2Lt. Bothwell wounded.	

1st Gordon Highlanders

WAR DIARY
or
~~INTELLIGENCE SUMMARY~~
(Erase heading not required.)

April 1916

Army Form C. 2118

Instructions regarding War Diaries and Intelligence Summaries are contained in F. S. Regs., Part II. and the Staff Manual respectively. Title Pages will be prepared in manuscript.

Place	Date	Hour	Summary of Events and Information	Remarks and references to Appendices
REMINGHELST	4th April		Cold. The Battalion was relieved by 27th Canadian Regt at 1.30 a.m. and returned to E Camp Reninghelst. Busses were provided. Men were very tired but cheerful. Machine Gun teams not relieved until late at night.	
THIEUSHOEK	5th April		Cold. Battalion moved at 9 a.m. to Q30c 19 near Thieushoek into rest billets, arriving at 1.30 p.m. They were there joined by A Company which had gone on ahead. Billets in good barns and farmhouses. Very little officers accommodation. Capt. Long left to take over temporary command of 10th Royal Welsh Fusiliers and Capt Dinwiddie assumed temporary command of the Battalion.	
do.	6th April		Fine. Day spent in refitting and kit inspection.	
do.	7th April		Cold. Refitting and clothing under Company arrangements.	
do.	8th April		Very fine but cold. Reinforcement of 125 men arrived from Base. Companies inspected by C.O. during morning.	
do.	9th April		Fine. Companies at Baths during morning. Church Parade followed by Celebration of Communion. Companies paid out.	
do.	10th April		Fine. Parades under Company arrangements. Col. Crauford returned to command Battn. on arrival of General Kentish as G.O.C. 76th Brigade.	
do.	11th April		Work in morning. Lectures by O.C. Companies on Discipline. Visit by G.O.C. Brigade. Inoculation started. Company Tie for Brigade Football Cup played off, B Coy defeating C by 1 goal to 0.	

1875 Wt. W593/826 1,000,000 4/15 J.B.C. & A. A.D.S.S./Forms/C. 2118.

1st Gordon Highlanders

WAR DIARY
or
~~INTELLIGENCE SUMMARY~~
(Erase heading not required.)

April 1916

Army Form C. 2118

Instructions regarding War Diaries and Intelligence Summaries are contained in F. S. Regs., Part II. and the Staff Manual respectively. Title Pages will be prepared in manuscript.

Place	Date	Hour	Summary of Events and Information	Remarks and references to Appendices
THIEUSHOEK	12 April		Stormy. Parades impossible. Lectures by Coy officers. 1 Casualty Cpl. Taylor, attached Div. Drainage Section (self-inflicted).	
do.	13 April		Fine. G.O.C. Brigade inspected Battalion and Transport in morning. He expressed his satisfaction at the turn-out of the Battalion and especially ~~[illegible]~~ commented on good turn out of the Transport. Football Tie D Coy being defeated by A 5-1.	
do.	14 April		Stormy. Lectures by O.C. Companies. Final of Inter Coy Football Contest played B Coy defeating A Coy 1-0.	
do.	15 April		Windy. Companies at training during morning. B Coy Football team played A Coy 10 Royal Welsh Fusiliers and defeated 6-2 in Brigade Cup Contest. Battalion Concert and Boxing at night. G.O.C. Brigade present.	
do.	16 April		~~[illegible]~~ Fine. Church Parade 11.30 am	
do.	17 April		Showery. Companies lectured on Bayonet fighting by Major Campbell, Gordon Highlanders and Gymnasium Instructor, G.H.Q. Remainder of morning spent in Bayonet practice.	
do.	18 April		Unsettled weather. Company training. At 2.30 pm Battalion inspected by D.M.S. 2nd Army accompanied by A.D.M.S. 3rd Divn and G.O.C. Brigade. Football match with Brigade M.G. Coy for Brigade Cup. B Coy won 1-0. Night operations postponed owing to wet. 2nd Lt. T.C. Scoones joined. 2nd Lt. Miller rejoined from hospital.	

1875 Wt. W593/826 1,000,000 4/15 J.B.C. & A. A.D.S.S./Forms/C. 2118.

Instructions regarding War Diaries and Intelligence Summaries are contained in F. S. Regs., Part II. and the Staff Manual respectively. Title Pages will be prepared in manuscript.

4

WAR DIARY
or
INTELLIGENCE SUMMARY
(Erase heading not required.)

Army Form C. 2118

Place	Date	Hour	Summary of Events and Information	Remarks and references to Appendices
THIEUSHOUK	19 April		Fine. Wet in afternoon. Companies at Baths during morning. Heats for Divisional Sports postponed owing to stormy weather. Battalion Concert at D Coy's billet in evening.	
LA CLYTTE	20 April		Fine. Battalion marched at 9.30 am to LA CLYTTE for Pioneer work, arriving at Camp on RENINGHELST – LA CLYTTE road at 1.45 pm. Work on Reserve Line, wiring and construction of strong points round VIERSTRAAT.	
do.	21 April		Wet. A.M.B. Returned to Camp about 3 am. Day spent resting. Work at night at [illegible]. Lieut Norman joined; took over command of 'D' Coy.	
THIEUSHOUK	22 April		Very wet. Battalion marched back to THIEUSHOUK at 9.30 am arriving about 1.30 pm. Continual rain during afternoon & evening. Major Maitland and Lieut. [illegible] rejoined from Hospital. Captain R.H. Gordon joined, took over command of 'B' Coy.	
do.	23 April		Fine. Church parade at 11 am. 2/Lt. D.S. Inglis joined. Posted to 'C' Coy. 2/Lt. T.D. Lammie joined. Posted to 'B' Coy.	
do.	24 April		Warm. Lecture to Officers & N.C.O's by G.O.C. Brigade on Discipline. Cross-country Race in afternoon. Battalion second. Brigade Concert and Boxing Tournament in evening. Battalion won [illegible] Contest.	
do.	25 April		Hot. Lecture and demonstration on Drill to all officers & N.C.O's of Brigade by G.O.C. Final of Brigade Football Tie in afternoon. Battalion beat 8th K.O.R.L. 8-2 and won G.O.C's cup. Lecture by C.R.A. Division to officers & N.C.O's in evening.	
do.	26 April		Hot. Training in morning. Coys at Baths in afternoon. Battalion Concert in evening.	

1875 Wt. W593/826 1,000,000 4/15 J.B.C. & A. A.D.S.S./Forms/C. 2118.

1st Gordon Highlanders

WAR DIARY
or
INTELLIGENCE SUMMARY
(Erase heading not required.)

April 1916.

Army Form C. 2118

Instructions regarding War Diaries and Intelligence Summaries are contained in F. S. Regs., Part II. and the Staff Manual respectively. Title Pages will be prepared in manuscript.

Place	Date	Hour	Summary of Events and Information	Remarks and references to Appendices
LOCRE.	27th April		Very Hot. Battalion marched at 9 am to billets in LOCRE arriving about 12.30 pm. March hot and trying. Battalion billeted in huts at LOCRE.	
do	28th April		Fine and warm. Specialists left for trenches at 1.30 am. Remainder of Battalion marched to trenches East of KEMMEL at 7 pm. Relief complete from 5th Durham Light Infantry at 10.10 pm. Night quiet. Trenches in good repair with exception of sector on right. No support line.	
KEMMEL	29th April		Fine quiet day. Two prisoners surrendered to Battalion on our right at dusk reporting gas attack imminent. Gas attack made at 12.30 am with bombardment lasting two hours. Gas was liberated opposite our right company (A) but owing to direction of wind did not drift over our line. Main attack took place to our immediate right. Shelling ceased at dawn. Casualties – Lieut. A. M. B. Norman, 2Lts. Saunders and Lawrie wounded 14 OR. killed 21 wounded. No gas casualties.	
do	30th April		Hot. Day quiet on our front. Enemy harassed Battalion on our left with Trench Mortars. Gas alarm at 11.30 pm. Lasted about an hour. Little gas felt. 2/Lt R.W. Preston & R.W.G. Lawson joined. Posted to 'D' and 'B' Coys respectively.	

E G Crawford Lt Col.
Comdg. 1st Gordon Highlanders

1875 Wt. W593/826 1,000,000 4/15 J.B.C. & A. A.D.S.S./Forms/C. 2118.

1st.BATTN.GORDON HIGHLANDERS.

Roll of Officers serving with Battalion on the 30/4/16.

Lieut.Col.S.G.Craufurd.
Major F.L.M.C.Maitland.
Capt.M.Dinwiddie.
" P.H.Gordon.
" W.A.Dyke.
" C.MacDonald.
Lieut.A.M.B.Norman.
" W.H.Smith-Grant.
" H.I.Baird.
" J.McA.Cunningham.
2/Lieut.J.D.Lammie.
" E.G.Saunders.
" J.F.Smith.
" T.C.Scoones.
" R.F.Gordon.
" D.S.Inglis.
" A.J.Cleghorn.
" H.H.Brown.
" D.R.G.Renfrew.
" A.R.Duncan.
" D.C.D.Munro.
" G.P.Peterkin.
" D.A.Miller.
" W.P.Watt.
" R.H.Preston.

Captain J.P.Hunter.	M.O.
" P.D.Thomson.	Chaplain.

DETAILS.

Major J.McLennan.	In Hospital in U.K.
Capt.A.de L.Long.	Temp.Comm.10th.R.W.F.
" W.Morrison.	a/Adjt.& QM.2nd.Army N.C.O's. School of Instruction.
Lieut.J.A.H.Brown.	Base Training Camp.
2/Lieut.S.M.Robertson.	Attached 8th.Bde.M.G.Coy.

9/5/16.

S G Craufurd Lieut.Colonel,
Comndg.1st.Battn.Gordon Highlanders

Strength of Battn. on 30/5/16.
Fighting Strength O 30, O.R. 878
Details O 5, O.R. 156.

76th Brigade.

3rd Division.

WAR DIARY

1st BATTALION

GORDON HIGHLANDERS.

M A Y 1 9 1 6

Appendix :- Nominal Roll of Officers.

1st Gordon Highlanders

May 1916

1 Gordon Hrs

Vol 20

Army Form C. 2118.

WAR DIARY
or
~~INTELLIGENCE~~ SUMMARY

(Erase heading not required.)

Instructions regarding War Diaries and Intelligence Summaries are contained in F. S. Regs., Part II. and the Staff Manual respectively. Title Pages will be prepared in manuscript.

Place	Date	Hour	Summary of Events and Information	Remarks and references to Appendices
Trenches nr. Kemmel.	1st May		Fine. Quiet day. Some trench mortaring on our left.	
do.	2nd May		Hot. Quiet day. At 8pm. gas alarms were sounded owing to gas attack to the South. No hostile artillery demonstration on our front.	
do	3rd May		Fine. All precautions taken for gas owing to wind [illegible]	
do.	4th May		Hot. Quiet day. Some shelling of [illegible] [illegible] reported for duty and posted to D Coy.	
do	5th May		Warm. Some fishtail bombs burst in left Company sector. Casualties [illegible] Sniping increased at night. Batt. Headquarters received attention of [illegible] shells.	
do.	6th May		Warm. Special [illegible] returned at 1.30 am [illegible] Quiet day. Battalion relieved by 8th K.O.R.L. complete at 11pm. Some shelling of areas in rear of trenches at [illegible] Battalion returned to billets in LOCRE.	
LOCRE	7th May		Fine. Church Parade 3pm.	
do	8th May		Stormy. Battalion training during morning. Football match with 10th Royal Welch Fusiliers in afternoon. Working party of 150 supplied at night.	
do.	9th May		Wet. Battalion at baths. Gas demonstration during [illegible] for half Battalion. Working party of 150 again supplied at night.	

2449 Wt. W14957/M90 750,000 1/16 J.B.C. & A. Forms/C.2118/12.

1st Gordon Highlanders — 2 — May 1916

Army Form C. 2118.

Instructions regarding War Diaries and Intelligence Summaries are contained in F. S. Regs., Part II. and the Staff Manual respectively. Title Pages will be prepared in manuscript.

WAR DIARY
or
~~INTELLIGENCE SUMMARY~~

(Erase heading not required.)

Place	Date	Hour	Summary of Events and Information	Remarks and references to Appendices
LOCRE	10th May		Fine. Route March. Lecture by G.O.C. Brigade at 5.30pm on Patrols and Scouts.	
do.	11th May		Wet in morning, fine in evening. Patrol competition at 9pm. 1 N.C.O. and 3 men from each Platoon. 1st Signallers, 2nd Bombers. Prize to the 1st two leading patrols – match box embossed with Regt'l Crest.	
do.	12th May		Showery. Battalion in training. Lecture to Officers and N.C.O.s on Gas. 2Lt G.W. Nelson joined Battalion and posted to B Coy.	
do.	13th May		Wet. Lecture to Officers and N.C.O.s on Field Telephones. Lecture by M.O. [illegible]. Specialists left for trenches at 12.15 am. Remainder of Battalion at 9pm in relief of 8th K.O.R.L. Regt. Quiet night.	
KEMMEL	14th May		Fine. Quiet day.	
do.	15th May		Fine. Wiring party under 2Lt. Smith Grant found some dead Germans in crater near Glory hole. Three land mines were found. Some 20 of the enemy were counted. Draft of 52 men, most of them from Argyll and Sutherland Highrs.	
do.	16th May		Fine, very warm. Lt Col. H.S. Turnbull, 3/7th Gordons attached for 3 days. Day very quiet.	
do.	17th May		Fine. Eight Cadets from Cadet School attached for 48 hrs. Day quiet. Lt Baird went sick to Field Ambulance.	

2449 Wt. W14957/M90 750,000 1/16 J.B.C. & A. Forms/C.2118/12.

1st Gordon Highlanders

WAR DIARY
or
~~INTELLIGENCE SUMMARY~~
(Erase heading not required.)

May 1916

Army Form C. 2118.

Instructions regarding War Diaries and Intelligence Summaries are contained in F. S. Regs., Part II. and the Staff Manual respectively. Title Pages will be prepared in manuscript.

Place	Date	Hour	Summary of Events and Information	Remarks and references to Appendices
[illegible] KEMMEL	18th May		Fine. Enemy shelled heavily during day with Trench Mortars and [illegible]. Casualties 3 wounded.	
do.	19th May		Fine. Enemy active with Trench Mortars. Casualties [illegible]	
do.	20th May		Fine. Specialists relieved at 2 am by 8th K.O.R.L. Regt. Battalion relieved at 10 pm and marched to KEMMEL SHELTERS. Enemy again active. Casualties [illegible]. 2Lt. E. G. Saunders joined for duty and posted to [illegible] Coy.	
KEMMEL SHELTERS	21st May		Fine. Very warm. Church Parade.	
do.	22nd May		Fine & warm. Battalion at training.	
do.	23rd May		Fine. Very hot. Training. Football Match against R.W.F. Gas alarm about 10 pm.	
do.	24th May		Fine & warm. Lecture by G.O.C. 76th Bde on OPEN WARFARE. Lt. J.A.H. Brown rejoined Battn from Base depot Rouen. 2Lt. W.T. Currie joined for duty and posted to D Coy. Lt. W. Blair, 2/3rd Scottish Horse joined as Transport Officer.	

2449 Wt. W14957/M90 750,000 1/16 J.B.C. & A. Forms/C.2118/12.

1st Gordon Highlanders

4

WAR DIARY
or
~~INTELLIGENCE SUMMARY~~
(Erase heading not required.)

May 1916

Army Form C. 2118.

Instructions regarding War Diaries and Intelligence Summaries are contained in F. S. Regs., Part II. and the Staff Manual respectively. Title Pages will be prepared in manuscript.

Place	Date	Hour	Summary of Events and Information	Remarks and references to Appendices
KEMMEL SHELTERS	25 May		Showery. Football match with R.W.F. in afternoon. Concert in evening.	
do	26 May		Fine. Battalion relieved in KEMMEL SHELTERS by 4th YORKS and marched to Divisional Rest Area near FLETRE via BAILLEUL and METEREN. Arrived in rest area at 6 pm.	
THIEUSHEUK ~~do~~	27 May		Fine. Kit Inspection by Companies. Officers Football match with Officers of 10th R.W.F.	
do.	28		Very warm. Church parade.	
do.	29		Fine. Companies at training. Saluting and Squad drill. Practice in Marching past. Officers played N.C.Os at Football.	
do.	30		Warm. Companies trained in Guard Duties. ~~[illegible]~~ Played R.W.F. at Football.	
do.	31		Very warm. Practice in Saluting and Guard Duties.	

2449 Wt. W14957/M90 750,000 1/16 J.B.C. & A. Forms/C.2118/12.

1st.BATTN. THE GORDON HIGHLANDERS.

Roll of Officers with Battalion on 31/5/16.

Lieut.Col.S.G.CRAUFURD.
Major F.L.M.C.MAITLAND.
Capt.M.DINWIDDIE.
" R.H.GORDON.
" G.MACDONALD.
Lieut.J.A.H.BROWN.
" H.S.GAMMELL.
" J.McA.CUNNINGHAM.
" R.I.BAIRD.
" W.BLAIR.
2/Lieut.E.G.SAUNDERS.
" W.H.S.GRANT.
" J.B.SMITH.
" R.K.GORDON.
" D.S.INGLIS.
" A.J.CLEGHORN.
" H.H.BROWN. On Leave.
" D.R.G.RENFREW. "
" A.H.DUNCAN.
" D.C.D.MUNRO.
" G.P.PETERKIN.
" D.A.MILLER.
" W.R.WATT.
" R.W.PRESTON.
" R.W.G.LAWSON.
" G.W.NELSON.
" T.C.SCOONES.
" W.T.CURRIE.

Capt.J.L.STEWART. M.O.
" P.D.THOMSON. Chaplain.

DETAILS.

Major A.de L.LONG. Temp.Comm. 10th. R.W.F.
" J.McLENNAN. On sick furlough.
Capt.W.MORRISON. A/Adjt.& QM.2nd ARMY NCO's School.
" W.A.DYKE. A/Bombing Officer,76th Inf.Bde.

STRENGTH OF BATTALION ON 31/5/16.

FIGHTING STRENGTH.	32O.	973O.R.
DETAILS.	8 O.	187 O.R.

2/6/16.

S G Craufurd Lieut.Colonel,
Commdg.,1st.Battn. The Gordon Highlanders.

76th Brigade.

3rd Division.

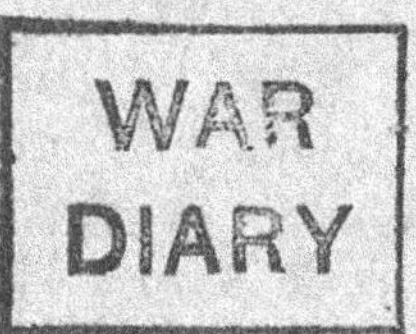

1st BATTALION

GORDON HIGHLANDERS

JUNE 1916

Appendix :- Nominal Roll of Officers.

1st Gordon Highlanders

Instructions regarding War Diaries and Intelligence Summaries are contained in F. S. Regs., Part II. and the Staff Manual respectively. Title Pages will be prepared in manuscript.

WAR DIARY
or
~~INTELLIGENCE SUMMARY~~
(Erase heading not required.)

June 1916

1 Gordon Hrs

Vol 21

Army Form C. 2118.

3

Place	Date	Hour	Summary of Events and Information	Remarks and references to Appendices
THIESHOUK	June 1st		Very warm. Route march to MONT DES CATS. Battalion Drill and practice in March past. 2Lt. R. Rish joined Battalion as Signalling Officer.	
do.	2nd		Warm. Practice in Brigade Ceremonial Drill and Marching Past.	
do.	3rd		Fine. Kings Birthday. Brigade Ceremonial Parade to celebrate Royal birthday. Royal Salute given and Brigade marched past G.O.C. Remainder of day observed as a holiday. Battalion Standing-by ready to move at 4 hrs. notice. 2Lt. W. Waring joined Battalion & posted to B Coy.	
do.	4th		Fine. Church Parade.	
do.	5th		Cloudy but fair. Battalion marched to Billets near BAILLEUIL and took over from 12th West Yorks. Some showers on march. Destination reached at 12.15 pm. Companies paid out during afternoon.	
BAILLEUIL S6d08 Sheet 28 S.W.	6th		Very wet. Lectures by Coy. inside billets. Working party of 100 supplied for BAILLEUIL STATION. 2Lt. Dove joined Battn. and posted to C Coy.	
do.	7th		Fine. Officers & N.C.O's went over battle of METEREN under guidance of G.O.C. Brigade. Companies at Bayonet Fighting. Working party provided for BAILLEUIL. 2Lts. S. P. T. Fine & B. C. Law joined Battn. & posted to [illegible] Coy respectively.	
do.	8th		Showery. Companies at Baths. Very wet in evening.	
do.	9th		Fine. Companies at training during morning in extended order. Heats for Battn. Sports run off in afternoon.	
do.	10th		Fine. Training during morning. Battalion Sports during afternoon. Very successful.	

2449 Wt. W14957/M90 750,000 1/16 J.B.C. & A. Forms/C.2118/12.

1st Gordon Highlanders

2

WAR DIARY
or
~~INTELLIGENCE SUMMARY~~

(Erase heading not required.)

June 1916.

Army Form C. 2118.

Instructions regarding War Diaries and Intelligence Summaries are contained in F. S. Regs., Part II. and the Staff Manual respectively. Title Pages will be prepared in manuscript.

Place	Date	Hour	Summary of Events and Information	Remarks and references to Appendices
BAILLEUIL	11th		Warm. Battalion commenced march to Training Area via METEREN, CAESTRE, CASSEL, to temporary billets near ZERMEZEELE. March commenced at 11 a.m. Halt for dinners at ST. SYLVESTER CAPPEL at 2 p.m. March of 14 miles arriving at 6 p.m. Day warm for marching. 76th Brigade marched as Brigade, Battalion marching in rear of Royal Welch Fusiliers.	
ZERMEZEELE	12th		Very wet. Brigade march continued from ZERMEZEELE at 11 a.m. to WULVERDINGHE (11 miles) arriving at 4.30 p.m. Halt of 1½ hrs for dinners. Battalion ~~in front~~ at head of Brigade Column.	
WULVERDINGHE	13th		Showery & cold. March completed from WULVERDINGHE to HOULLE in Brigade Training Area. Marched at 10.30 a.m. arriving at 1.30 p.m. Billets good for both officers & men. ~~[illegible]~~	
HOULLE	14th		Cold with showers. Kit inspections for men during morning. Officers & N.C.O's attended demonstration by G.O.C. Brigade on Companies in the Attack.	
do.	15th		Showery. Battalion marched to Training Area and witnessed demonstration by one Company of the different stages of the Attack in the open. One Company at Range for Musketry during afternoon.	
do.	16th		Fine. Companies practised attack formations in the open after demonstration. One Company at range for Musketry during afternoon. 2Lt. G. Ritchie joined Batt. & posted to B Coy.	
do.	17th		Fine. Battalion at training and demonstration in attack formations	

2449 Wt. W14957/M90 750,000 1/16 J.B.C. & A. Forms/C.2118/12.

1st Gordon Highlanders

WAR DIARY
or
~~INTELLIGENCE SUMMARY~~

(Erase heading not required.)

June 1916

Army Form C. 2118.

Instructions regarding War Diaries and Intelligence Summaries are contained in F. S. Regs., Part II. and the Staff Manual respectively. Title Pages will be prepared in manuscript.

Place	Date June	Hour	Summary of Events and Information	Remarks and references to Appendices
HOULLE	18th.		Fine. Church Parade. A number of officers and N.C.O's permitted to proceed to CALAIS for the day	
do.	19th.		Fine. Battalion at Training in open warfare and attack formations. Baths for 2 Companies during afternoon. A Court of Enquiry as to loss of kit held during afternoon.	
do.	20th.		Cloudy. Battalion at Training in Companies in attack formations. Baths for 2 Companies during afternoon. One Company at range for Musketry.	
do.	21st.		Fine. Further practice in attack formations. One Company at Musketry.	
do.	22nd.		Warm & Sultry. Companies at disposal of O.C. Coys during morning. Brigade Training in attack formation and liaison between Infantry & Aircraft demonstration and practised during afternoon & evening.	
do.	23rd.		Sultry. Companies at training during morning. Preliminary Brigade Sports in afternoon. R.S.M. R Ross accidentally killed by bomb.	
do.	24th		Very wet in morning and fine later in day. Brigade Gds Field Race & Sports cancelled owing to rain.	
do.	25th.		Fine. Church Parade. Funeral of R.S.M. Ross. 2 Lts. N.M. Paton & H.F. [illegible] joined Battn. [illegible]	
do.	26th.		Fine. Brigade Route March to NORDAUSQUES.	
do.	27th.		Showery. Training under Company arrangement in attack formations. Two Companies at range for musketry.	

2449 Wt. W14957/M90 750,000 1/16 J.B.C. & A. Forms/C.2118/12.

1st Gordon Highlanders.

Instructions regarding War Diaries and Intelligence Summaries are contained in F. S. Regs., Part II. and the Staff Manual respectively. Title Pages will be prepared in manuscript.

WAR DIARY
or
~~INTELLIGENCE SUMMARY~~
(Erase heading not required.)

June 1916

Army Form C. 2118.

Place	Date	Hour	Summary of Events and Information	Remarks and references to Appendices
HOULLE	June 28th		Very wet in morning but fine later. Battalion Route March to EPERLECQUES Forest, returning about 4 pm. 2Lt. D. K. Templeton joined Battn: & posted to A Coy.	
do.	29th		Fine. Companies at training in area. Two Companies at Range for Musketry. Distribution of Medal Ribbons by G.O.C. Division. Lt.Col. S. G. Crawford C.M.G. C.I.E. D.S.O. Capt. J. L. Stewart R.A.M.C. Ptes. Smith & Begg received ribbons.	
do.	30th		Cold & showery. Brigade Route March to MENCQUE & Forêt Nationale. Officers spent morning on training area with G.O.C. Brigade.	

2449 Wt. W14957/M90 750,000 1/16 J.B.C. & A. Forms/C.2118/12.

1st Bn. THE GORDON HIGHLANDERS.

Roll of Officers serving with Battalion on 30th June 1916.

Lieut.Col.S.G.CRAUFURD.
Major F.L.M.G.MAITLAND.
Capt.& Adjt.[illegible].DINWIDDIE.
Capt.J.BARTHOLOMEW.
" R.H.GORDON.
" R.F.BAIRD.
Lieut.J.A.H.BROWN.
" H.S.GAMMELL.
2/Lieut.J.D.SMITH.
" W.H.S.GRANT.
" A.J.CREIGHTON.
" R.K.GORDON.
" R.RISK.
" D.C.LOW.
" D.E.TEMPLETON.
" A.H.DUNCAN.
" W.R.WATT.
" L.G.SAUNDERS.
" R.W.G.LAWSON.
" G.W.NELSON.
" W.T.CURRIE.
" G.RITCHIE.
" D.R.G.RENFREW.
" D.A.MILLER.
" T.C.SCOONES.
" D.S.INGLIS.
" P.E.DOVE.
" N.M.PATON.
" G.P.PETERKIN.
" D.C.D.MUNRO.
" H.H.BROWN.
" R.W.PRESTON.
" P.T.PIRIE.
"" H.W.PUNTAN.

Capt.J.L.STEWART.	M.O.
Rev.P.D.THOMSON.	Chaplain.

DETAILS.

Lieut.Col.A.de L.LONG.	Temp.Comm. 10th R.W.F.
Major J.McLENNAN.	On sick furlough.
Capt.W.A.DYKE.	To England:training Reserve Bn
" J.McA.CUNNINGHAM.	Base Training Camp.
" W.WARING.	A/Adjutant, 8th K.O.R.L.

Strength of Battalion on [illegible]

76 Brigade
3 Division

1st Bn
Gordon Highlanders
July 1916

War Diary

of

1st Bn Gordon Highlanders.

1st – 31st July, 1916.

1st Gordon Highlanders

WAR DIARY

or

~~INTELLIGENCE SUMMARY~~

(Erase heading not required.)

July, 1916.

76

Vol 3 22

Army Form C. 2118.

Instructions regarding War Diaries and Intelligence Summaries are contained in F. S. Regs., Part II. and the Staff Manual respectively. Title Pages will be prepared in manuscript.

Place	Date July	Hour	Summary of Events and Information	Remarks and references to Appendices
HOULLE	1st		Hot day. Orders received at 5.10 am to march to new area. Bn marched at 8 am and entrained at Saint OMER at 11 am, arriving in DOULLENS at 7 pm. After tea in the station Bn marched to billets in GEZAINCOURT and BEGNAUX. From this date Bn became part of IV Army being attached to 2nd Corps.	
GEZAINCOURT ~~DOULLENS~~	2nd		Fine warm day. Church parade at 11 am. Working parties supplied to DOULLENS Station also guard and volunteer stretcher party of 200 men supplied to 29 C.C.S. at GEZAINCOURT.	
– do –	3rd		Hot day. Bn marched at 9 am via BEAUVAL to billets in NAOURS, where it arrived at 1 PM.	
NAOURS	4th		Sultry, with thunderstorms in afternoon. Morning spent at baths. Bn marched at head of Brigade at 8.45 PM via TALMAS, VILLERS-BOCAGE to billets in RAINEVILLE, arriving about 12.30 am. 2/Lt DIPPIE joined the Bn and was posted to B Coy.	
RAINVILLE	5th		Fine. Bn at rest. Brigade marched at 9 PM to billets at FRANVILLERS, arriving about 1 am. Billets very crowded. 2/Lt M'INTOSH joined and was posted to C Coy.	
FRANVILLERS	6th		Showery. CO. Adjt and Coy Comdrs left at 10 am to visit field of battle. Brigade marched at 9 PM to LES CELESTINS WOOD via TREUX passing the billets of the 2nd Bn at the latter place, and arriving about 1 am.	
BOIS LES CELESTIN	7th		Continual rain. Bn at rest.	
– do –	8th		Showery, fine in afternoon. Bn marched at 3.45 PH to BRONFAY FARM arriving in bivouac for the night at 7 pm. Bn practised deployment in attack formation at 10 P.M	

2449 Wt. W14957/M90 750,000 1/16 J.B.C. & A. Forms/C.2118/12.

1st Gordon Highlanders

Instructions regarding War Diaries and Intelligence Summaries are contained in F. S. Regs., Part II. and the Staff Manual respectively. Title Pages will be prepared in manuscript.

WAR DIARY

~~or~~

~~INTELLIGENCE~~ SUMMARY

(Erase heading not required.)

July 1916.

Army Form C. 2118.

Place	Date July	Hour	Summary of Events and Information	Remarks and references to Appendices
BRONFAY FARM	9th		Day fine. Brigade practised assault of position [illegible] and by night. Some shelling of next camp. [illegible] Voluntary church service in [illegible] [illegible]	
"	10th		Fine day - cold at night. Enemy shelled camp during afternoon [illegible] at MONTAUBAN. Bn practised assault.	
"	11th		Cloudy with some rain. [illegible] MONTAUBAN. 2Lt R. RISK and 2Lt [illegible] and [illegible]	
"	12th		Fine though cloudy. Bn moved camp at [illegible] [illegible] 90 [illegible] to MONTAUBAN.	
"	13th		Showery. Bn marched at [illegible] to MONTAUBAN ALLEY [illegible] position (German 2nd Line defences) 2Lt [illegible] F.W. Clarke joined.	
MONTAUBAN ALLEY	14th		Thick haze, followed later by some showers. Attack on German 2nd line [illegible] German 2nd line captured. [illegible] 10 am Bn moved [illegible] to CATERPILLAR VALLEY [illegible] heavily shelled by 6" gun in the afternoon. [illegible]	
CATERPILLAR VALLEY	15th		Day fine - cool in the evening. [illegible] LONGUEVAL. O.P. [illegible] and 3 men established [illegible]	
- do -	16th		Day fine. Very quiet.	
- do -	17th		Showery. Patrol went out at 2 am under 2Lt [illegible] [illegible] patrol wounded & missing. 2Lt [illegible] did not succeed [illegible] received to attack LONGUEVAL village next morning.	

2449 Wt. W14957/M90 750,000 1/16 J.B.C. & A. Forms/C.2118/12.

1st Gordon Highlanders

Instructions regarding War Diaries and Intelligence Summaries are contained in F. S. Regs., Part II. and the Staff Manual respectively. Title Pages will be prepared in manuscript.

WAR DIARY

~~or~~

~~INTELLIGENCE SUMMARY~~

(Erase heading not required.)

July 1916

Army Form C. 2118.

Place	Date July	Hour	Summary of Events and Information	Remarks and references to Appendices
CATERPILLAR VALLEY	18th		Day dull in forenoon but cleared later. Moved forward to position of assembly at 2 am. Assault took place at 3.45 am. Village was successfully carried, but ~~the~~ several strong pts N of DELVILLE WOOD remained in enemy's hands. About 12.30 pm the troops were forced to evacuate all but the southern end of village and wood owing to continued and intense bombardment lasting some seven hours followed by strong and determined counter attack. Casualties 4 Offrs killed 7 wd. 321 O Ranks Kd wd and missing. A detailed account of operations is attached.	
W. LONGUEVAL TRENCHES	19th		Day fine. Bn shelled throughout the day. At 8 PM, (Remnants of) Bn was relieved by 1 Coy DCLI. Bn moved to BRESLAU REDOUBT Trench N.W. of CARNOY.	
BRESLAU REDOUBT	20th		Day fine, spent in reorganisation. Reserve Division rejoined.	
"	21st		Day fine. Bn moved into Trenches at southern edge of LONGUEVAL and DELVILLE WOOD in relief of 8th NORFOLKS and 1 Coy ESSEX Regt, arriving about midnight after a check of 1 hour in CATERPILLAR VALLEY through heavy barrage.	
DELVILLE WOOD	22nd		Day fine. Trench system found to be very disorganised. Day spent organising defences. Draft of 240 joined transport in HAPPY VALLEY. Corpl HEARNS in patrol killed one German and wounded 3 others.	
"	23rd		Day fine. Line further consolidated. Attack by 9th Brigade on N end of village at 3-40 am unsuccessful. Heavy and persistent shelling of S end of village and Bn H.Q. by enemy. Six casualties. 2Lts Clarke and Russell and 129 O.R. joined transport in HAPPY VALLEY. Gas shell attack.	

2449 Wt. W14957/M90 750,000 1/16 J.B.C. & A. Forms/C.2118/12.

1st Gordon Highlanders

Instructions regarding War Diaries and Intelligence Summaries are contained in F. S. Regs., Part II. and the Staff Manual respectively. Title Pages will be prepared in manuscript.

WAR DIARY

~~or~~

~~INTELLIGENCE SUMMARY~~

(Erase heading not required.)

July 1916

Army Form C. 2118.

Place	Date July	Hour	Summary of Events and Information	Remarks and references to Appendices
DELVILLE WOOD	24th		Day fine though dull. Consolidation of trenches continued. [illegible] Heavy shelling on both sides from [illegible] [illegible] wounded. Casualties mostly confined to [illegible]	
"	25th		Day fine. 1st KRR arrived shortly before M.N. [illegible]	
"	26th		Day fine. Relief completed at [illegible] Bn marched to BOIS DES TAILLES. [illegible] stragglers. 2Lt. H.R.S. Clarke posted to [illegible] Coy 2Lt A [illegible]	
BOIS DES TAILLES	27th		Day fine. Day spent in reorganisation. [illegible] SOMME river.	
	28th		Day very hot. Bn marched to MARICOURT L'ABBÉ [illegible] fairly comfortable.	
MARICOURT L'ABBÉ	29th		Day very hot. Day spent in reorganisation. Bathing [illegible] evening.	
"	30th		Day very hot. Church parade in morning.	
"	31st		Day hot. Two Coys rifle inspection by [illegible]	

[illegible signature]
Comdg 1st Gordon Highlanders
1st August 1916

2449 Wt. W14957/M90 750,000 1/16 J.B.C. & A. Forms/C.2118/12.

1ST BATTALION. THE GORDON HIGHLANDERS.

Account of Operations North of MONTAUBAN from 14th July, 1916 to 26th July 1916, inclusive.

13th. At 9-15 P.M. on the night of the 13th. July 1916, the Battalion moved into Trenches in MONTAUBAN ALLEY in support of the 8th. and 9th. Brigades, who were to assault and carry the LONGUEVAL position at dawn on the 14th.

14th. The assault was carried out at 3-25 A.M. amongst thick mist, and it was not until about 6 A.M. that the light became sufficiently good to show that the main position had been successfully carried.

At 10 A.M. the Battalion moved down into CATERPILLAR VALLEY and dug in under the bank on arrival. There was some shelling during the forenoon, but no casualties took place. About 3 P.M. the Battalion came under enfilade fire from a 6" gun. The trench was twice caught and seven casualties were sustained.

15th. The Battalion remained in Reserve. Officers patrols went forward to reconnoitre the position in front of LONGUEVAL, and an Observation Post, consisting of a Lance-Corporal and three men was established in the front line trenches. Battalion again came under enfilade fire from a 6" gun, sustaining two casualties.

16th. The Battalion continued in Reserve in CATERPILLAR VALLEY.

Two Officers patrols were sent out to reconnoitre the enemy's position near HIGH WOOD. One of these patrols came into close contact with the enemy and Sgt. BEATTIE was wounded and captured. 2/Lt. PUNTAN did not succeed in recrossing the German patrol line to rejoin his unit till Mid-day on the 18th.

17th. Orders were received to attack LONGUEVAL village at dawn on the 18th., and all Officers moved forward to the front line trenches to reconnoitre the position previous to attack. Orders as to disposition, etc., were issued during the night, but final instructions were not received from the Brigade until after midnight.

18th. The Battalion moved forward at 2 A.M. to take up the position of assembly for attack. Dispositions were as follows:-

"A" Coy. under Captain J.B. SMITH was to move round the northern edge of LONGUEVAL, keeping clear of the village with the two suspected strong points 400 yards North of Village, as their main objective.

"B" Coy. under Captain R.H. GORDON was to clear the Orchards and enclosures abutting the village at the north end, and also to push on patrols through the N.W. corner of DELVILLE WOOD and so gain touch with the 9th. Division.

P.T.O.

18th. contd. Both these companies moved with three platoons in the Firing Line and one in Support.

"C" Coy. under Captain J. BARTHOLOMEW was to clear the houses in the village immediately south of the avenue which connects the LONGUEVAL village with the road to HIGH WOOD. This company moved with two platoons in Support. Battalion Bombers were equally distributed amongst the three attacking companies. Two Lewis Guns went with "A" Company where the flank was open.

"D" Coy. under Captain R.I. BAIRD was in Support and dug in along the LONGUEVAL- HIGH WOOD road, guarding the left flank and rear. Two Lewis Guns and Battalion Reserve Bombers were attached to this Company.

Battalion Headquarters were in advanced trenches near the Windmill.

There had been a steady bombardment of the position for one hour previous to the assault with one or two intense bursts lasting five minutes. There was also a five minutes intense bombardment previous to the assault, when the barrage lifted 200 yards and after a further five minutes bombardment lifted to the open country to the north of the Wood.

The assault took place at 3-45 A.M. and was completely successful with the exception of the two strong points north of the village. One of these - the easterly one - was actually entered by six men who were, however, driven out.

Great difficulty was experienced in gaining touch with the 9th Division. Consequently, "B" and "C" Coys wheeled to their left and took up a position on the northern edge of the Wood. From there, it was found that the Germans were entrenched some 200 yards to the north in the open. An attempt was made to carry this position by a charge, but the wire was uncut, and the assailants were all shot down by rifle and machine gun fire. No definite information was obtained about the situation till 7 A.M..

By this time very heavy casualties had been suffered, and two companies of the KINGS OWN ROYAL LANCASTERS Regt. were immediately pushed down through the village to assist in the consolidation. Lt. Col. SMITH, K.O.R.L. accompanied these two companies.

The orchards to the north of the village proved to be veritable quagmires from the recent rain and the line taken up was that running along the north west edge of DELVILLE WOOD through the north of the village and along the avenue to the west.

Meanwhile "D" Coy. found that the Germans were entrenched along the sunken road which joins the strong points north of the village to the LONGUEVAL-HIGH WOOD road. They dug in but could not advance.

At 9 A.M., the situation was as follows:-

All movement north and north west of the village was rendered almost impossible from machine gun fire. Machine guns had been located at the following points in order from east to west:-

(1) In the north east corner of the small oblong orchard on the LONGUEVAL-FLERS road.

(2 & 3) At the two strong points on the two tracks running north from LONGUEVAL.

(4) At end of the trees in the outer hedge running north west from the avenue.

(5) In the sunken road at its junction with the track running from the east of HIGH WOOD towards LONGUEVAL.

At 9 A.M., the Germans commenced shelling the wood and village. At midday this developed into an intense bombardment

P.T.O.

18th. centd. lasting 4½ hours, and at roughly 4-30 P.M. the Germans counter-attack was delivered.

Meanwhile the northern half of the village and wood as well as the avenue had become untenable. The troops gradually gave way under the pitiless shelling and on the assault taking place, the remnants of the troops withdrew to the trenches.

The German counter-stroke was delivered in four main waves; the troops apparently moving from the direction of HARTINPUICH as well as FLERS. The attack was unable to make headway to the west of the village owing to our machine gun and lewis gun fire, and on one occasion, one of the German lines was seen to be driven back in confusion. They however, reformed on the horizon and advanced further to the east. Unfortunately, the artillery barrage was directed too far to the west to break up the German attack north of the wood.

As soon as the intense bombardment ceased, a fresh attempt was made to re-occupy the avenue and hedges facing the village to the south. This proved however, to be impracticable.

At dusk, the situation on the right appeared to be serious . The troops of the 9th. Division appeared to be disorganised and as "D" Coy. was entirely " in the Air", it was withdrawn with a view to strengthening and holding the right flank.

About this time reinforcements from the 2nd. Suffolk Regiment began to arrive. One company was immediately detailed to watch and hold the right flank at all costs.

With evening, the situation cleared. It was found that the 9th Division were established in the southern end of the village and as the troops were sufficient to hold all ground, the request for further reinforcements from the Suffolks was cancelled.

Very heavy shelling continued till dawn on the 19th.

Casualties in the Regiment were 4 Officers killed, 7 Officers wounded and 321 other ranks killed, wounded and missing.

19th. Desultory shelling continued throughout the day. At 8 P.M. the Battalion was relieved by one company of the D.C.L.I. and moved back to the BRESLAU REDOUBT trench northwest of CARNOY.

20th. Day was spent in reorganisation and the reserve Officers were called up to replace casualties.

21st. The Battalion received orders to take over trenches along the southern edge of DELVILLE WOOD.

On meeting the guides in CATERPILLAR VALLEY the Battalion came under a heavy barrage from gas and other shells and was unable to move forward from 10 P.M. till 11 P.M. Two casualties occurred from gas and helmets had to be put on. The trenches were reached about midnight, but the relief was not complete till 4-30 A.M.

The Battalion was detailed to take over the trenches held by the 8th NORFOLK Regt and one company ESSEX Regt.

The trench system was found to be far from organised. Units were mixed up in some confusion and trenches were only held at certain points, euphemistically called " strong points ". Owing to the confusion, one company of the NORFOLKS occupying the eastern edge of SOUTH STREET did not get relieved till dark when the Battalion Bombers and Snipers were sent up to take their place.

P.T.O.

22nd. A heavy mist remained on the ground till 8 A.M. Advantage was taken of this to get a real grip of the situation and to disentangle the different posts from their former confusion. Arrangements were made to strengthen the existing trenches, and to connect up the various posts into an organised line of resistance.

The line of defence was carried along the southern end of the wood from the road junction northwest of WATERLOT FARM to the western post held by the ROYAL FUSILIERS, along the line of ROTTEN ROW. A bombing post, near the corner of ROTTEN ROW and facing the German strong point at eastern end of PRINCES STREET was also connected up with the main system of defences.

An old second line running to the east of KING STREET was also rendered tenable for defence.

Owing to shelling and sniping, work during the day time had to be done cautiously.

Digging and wiring were continued throughout the night.

During the morning mist, Corporal MEARNS on patrol shot six Germans and wounded three others.

23rd. By dawn, the system of defence was roughly connected throughout. An attack, made by the 9th Brigade at 3-40 A.M. in the northern end of the village brought on some heavy shelling which much delayed the work of consolidation. A bombardment by gas shells also took place, but did no damage.

Shelling continued throughout the day. Battalion suffered six casualties from this cause.

During the night the K.S.L.I. connected up CHEAPSIDE with SOUTH STREET.

24th. Work of consolidation was continued. Reports were received that the enemy was massing in trenches east of DELVILLE WOOD. From 8-40 P.M. till midnight the enemy bombarded the position heavily directing special attention to the southern end of the village. There was a further burst at 3 A.M. Casualties, which were almost entirely confined to Battalion Headquarters were One Officer (2/Lt. PUNTAN) and eighteen servants and orderlies wounded.

25th. At dawn the shelling died down. The Battalion was relieved during the night by the 1st K.R.R.C. and 2nd H L I.

Owing to a misunderstanding, the portion of the trench between ROTTEN ROW and SOUTH STREET was not relieved as falling outside the boundary of each brigade.

26th. Battalion Headquarters reported at Headquarters 99th. Brigade at 5 A.M. Relief complete with the exception of "D" Coy. "D" Coy was relieved at midday reaching MONTAUBAN at 1-30 P.M.

The conditions obtaining in the wood were very bad. Friend and foe, living and dead, lying practically, side by side in many cases. A rough attempt at burial was made where possible but only shell holes could be used for the purpose. In some cases, bodies were disenterred by shell fire after burial, and throughout the wood and along the trenches in places exposed to shell fire bodies still lay unburied from the fighting of ten days before.

The trenches from the road junction of SOUTH STREET and HIGH HOLBURN to PALL MALL at southern end of village were continually exposed to enfilade fire.

P.T.O.

It was found however, inadvisable to shift Battalion Headquarters however exposed, as it was the one spot known to all orderlies, and formed the forwarding centre for messages to the three battalions in the line.

A persistent barrage at the southern end of the village made all communication with Brigade Headquarters difficult.

In the Field.
29/7/16.

S. G. Craufurd

Lieut. Colonel.

Commanding, 1st Battn., The Gordon Highlanders.

1ST. BATTALION, THE GORDON HIGHLANDERS.

ROLL OF OFFICERS SERVING WITH BATTALION ON 31ST. JULY 1916.

Lieut. Colonel S. G. CRAUFURD.
Major F.L.M.C. MAITLAND.
2/Lieut. & Adjt. D.C.D. MUNRO.
Captain J. McA. CUNNINGHAM.
Lieut. O. HORSLEY.
" J.A.H. BROWN.
" H.S. GAMMELL.
" W. BLAIR.
2/Lieut. D.R.G. RENFREW.
" A.H. DUNCAN.
" N.M. PATON.
" E.G. SAUNDERS.
" A.J. CLEGHORN.
" R.K. GORDON.
" A. RIDDELL.
" W.T. CURRIE.
" G. RITCHIE.
" D.K. TEMPLETON.
" J. BROADHURST.
" T.C. SCOONES.
" D.S. INGLIS.
" J. McINTOSH.
" R.W. PRESTON.
" G.P. PETERKIN.
" P.T. PIRIE.
" H.R.S. CLARKE.

Lieut. & QM. F. CLARKE.
Captain J.L. STEWART. M.O.
Rev. P.D. THOMSON. C.F.

DETAILS.

Lieut. Col. A.de L. LONG.	Temp. Comm. 10th R.W.F.
Major J. McLENNAN.	Sick in U.K.
Capt. W.AM DYKE.	Att. Reserve Bn.
" W. WARING.	A/Adjt. 8th K.O.R.L.

DAILY STRENGTH RETURN.		31-7-16.
Fighting Strength.	31 O.	980 O.R.
Details.	4 O.	90 O.R.

F.C. Maitland Major for Lieut. Colonel.

31/7/16. Commanding 1st Battn., The Gordon Highlanders.

76th Brigade.

3rd Division.

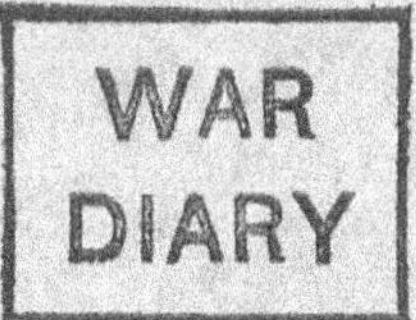

1st BATTALION

GORDON HIGHLANDERS

AUGUST 1 9 1 6

Appendices :- Report on the Operations in MALTZ HORN RAVINE 16th-20th Aug.

Nominal Roll of Offficers.

1st Gordon Highlanders

Instructions regarding War Diaries and Intelligence Summaries are contained in F. S. Regs., Part II. and the Staff Manual respectively. Title Pages will be prepared in manuscript.

7/6/3

WAR DIARY
or
~~INTELLIGENCE SUMMARY~~
(Erase heading not required.)

Army Form C. 2118.

August '16

Vol 23

Place	Date 1916	Hour	Summary of Events and Information	Remarks and references to Appendices
MÉRICOURT L'ABBÉ	1st		Day fine and very hot. Bn training. Squad drill – Arm drill and Bayonet Fighting.	
"	2nd		Very hot. Bn training. Inspection of Draft by G.O.C. Brigade.	
"	3rd		Very hot. Route march in the morning via Ribemont – BUIRE – [illegible] and TREUX.	
"	4th		Hot. Bn training.	
"	5th		Hot. Cards for Gallant Conduct 18th – 20th July given out [illegible]. At 5 P.M. a working party of 5 Officers and 2[illegible] NCOs & men proceeded to the CITADEL for work on trenches South and East of TRONES WOOD. Major Maitland took over duties of Camp Commandant of BOIS des TAILLES.	
"	6th		Day fine. Church parade at 10 am followed by Communion Service. Lecture by Brigadier on Recent Operations at 11.30 am.	
"	7th		Fine but cloudy. Fatigue party of 70 NCOs & men to Station. Bn training.	
"	8th		Fine. Bn training.	
"	9th		Hot. Route march via camps of 4th, 5th, 6th, 7th & 8th Battalions of the Regt.	

2449 Wt. W14957/M90 750,000 1/16 J.B.C. & A. Forms/C.2118/12.

1st Gordon Highlanders

Instructions regarding War Diaries and Intelligence Summaries are contained in F. S. Regs., Part II. and the Staff Manual respectively. Title Pages will be prepared in manuscript.

WAR DIARY
or
~~INTELLIGENCE SUMMARY~~
(Erase heading not required.)

August, 1916

Army Form C. 2118.

Place	Date 1916	Hour	Summary of Events and Information	Remarks and references to Appendices
MERICOURT L'ABBÉ	10th		Showery. Fatigue party of 40 men making ~~rifle~~ Range butts for Battalion at MARRETT WOOD.	
"	11th		Hot. Bn marched at 3.15 P.M. to bivouacs at SANDPITS where they were joined by the working party from the CITADEL. Bn arrived at 6.30 P.M.	
SANDPITS	12th		Very warm. Bn practised assault over flagged course at 4 P.M. Working party from CITADEL marched to baths at VILLE SUR AUBE in the morning.	
"	13th		Very warm during day cold in the evening. Bn practised assault at 4 P.M. Church parade at 10 a.m.	
"	14th		Cold and wet. Bn practised assault in the morning. Moved at 6 P.M. to bivouac near GREAT BEAR arriving about 7.30 P.M. Carrying party of 80 taking up ammunition for Machine Gun Company during the evening.	
GREAT BEAR	15th		Showery. Officers visited MALTZ HORN Trench System at 11 a.m. ~~Bn at rest~~ Party heavily shelled on return journey. Bn at rest.	
"	16th		Cool. Bn moved to TALUS BOIS at 2 P.M. arriving about 3 P.M. B & C Coys moved forward to DUBLIN TRENCH. Sgts MacLennan, Nearns and Rennie provisionally promoted 2nd Lieuts	

2449 Wt. W14957/M90 750,000 1/16 J.B.C. & A. Forms/C.2118/12.

1st Gordon Highlanders

WAR DIARY
or
~~INTELLIGENCE SUMMARY~~
(Erase heading not required.)

Army Form C. 2118.

August 1916.

Instructions regarding War Diaries and Intelligence Summaries are contained in F. S. Regs., Part II. and the Staff Manual respectively. Title Pages will be prepared in manuscript.

Place	Date 1916	Hour	Summary of Events and Information	Remarks and references to Appendices
TALUS BOIS	17th		Heavy Shower at 1 P.M. Carrying party of 4[illegible] to STANLEY DUMP at [illegible]. H.Q. Rs A & D Coys moved forward to CHIMPANZEE TRENCH at 6 P.M. Rear party came in for shelling from 5.9s and lost 6 killed & 3 very seriously wounded.	
CHIMPANZEE TRENCH	18th		Hazy with heavy mist in the morning. Some showers later. Bn moved at daylight to trenches in front of MALTZ HORN FARM for the assault. Bn objective Sunken road from ANGLE WOOD to GUILLEMONT, time to take place at 2.45 P.M. 1st objective gained and consolidated for some 400 yards linking up with the 4[illegible] French Infantry Regt on the right. Left Attack gained 2nd objective but as both flanks were "in the air" it was forced to retire to the 1st objective at dusk. Casualties:- 3 Offrs Killed 2 Offrs [illegible] wounded & 2 wounded. O.Ranks 350 killed wounded & missing.	
MALTZ HORN	19th		Fine with showers. Misty in the morning. New line taken over by two Coys Royal Scots Fus[illegible]. Desultory shelling throughout the day while the evacuation of the wounded was [illegible]. LONELY TRENCH occupied about 5 P.M. by K.S.L.I. B.C. & D Coys returned to [illegible] TRENCH about noon. A Coy remained burying dead and generally clearing the trenches till relieved by the 12th Manchester Regt (Bantams) at midnight. Bn then proceeded back to HAPPY VALLEY.	
HAPPY VALLEY	20th		Fine. Voluntary service at 6 P.M. (farewell to Rev. P.W. Thomson)	

2449 Wt. W14957/M90 750,000 1/16 J.B.C. & A. Forms/C.2118/12.

1st Gordon Highlanders

Instructions regarding War Diaries and Intelligence Summaries are contained in F. S. Regs., Part II. and the Staff Manual respectively. Title Pages will be prepared in manuscript.

WAR DIARY
or
~~INTELLIGENCE~~ SUMMARY

(Erase heading not required.)

August, 1916.

Army Form C. 2118.

Place	Date	Hour	Summary of Events and Information	Remarks and references to Appendices
HAPPY VALLEY	21st		Fine. Bn marched to MORLANCOURT, 6 miles arriving at 10 am. Draft of 220 OR. arrived at 4 P.M. chiefly men from 2/4 2/5 & 2/7 Battalions.	
MORLANCOURT	22nd		Fine. Transport left for new area at 10.45 am. Rev P.W. Thomson left at 7 am. Draft of 125 O.Ranks arrived, chiefly men of 2/5 & 2/7 Battalions. ~~[illegible]~~.	
"	23rd		Showery. Bn marched at 6.30 am. to MÉRICOURT STATION and entrained for CANDAS at 9.30 am. Arrived CANDAS at 2 P.M. and marched to MAILLARD arriving about 4 P.M. Billets poor and very dirty. 7 miles.	
MAILLARD	24th		Fine. Draft inspected by Comdg: Officer at 2.30 P.M. Rev W H LEATHEM arrived.	
"	25th		Hot. Marched at 9 am to BOUBERS. 8 miles. Billets good with one exception which collapsed at midnight. Following Officers arrived. 2nd Lts W.H. Lyle, G.M Berry, K.C Davidson; J Russell; C.C Thorburn; C Gimmill; H.B Cook W.G Forbes and T Merrilees.	
BOUBERS	26th		Showery. Bn marched at 8.50 am. to OEUF - 8 miles. arriving in billets at 12 noon. Billets good.	
OEUF	27th		Cool, some showers. Bn marched at 7.50 am to HEUCHIN - 11 miles - arriving 12.30 P.M. Billets exceptionally good. Inhabitants very friendly.	

2449 Wt. W14957/M90 750,000 1/16 J.B.C. & A. Forms/C.2118/12.

1st Gordon Highlanders

Instructions regarding War Diaries and Intelligence Summaries are contained in F. S. Regs., Part II. and the Staff Manual respectively. Title Pages will be prepared in manuscript.

WAR DIARY
or
~~INTELLIGENCE~~ SUMMARY
(Erase heading not required.)

August 1916.

Army Form C. 2118.

Place	Date	Hour	Summary of Events and Information	Remarks and references to Appendices
HEUCHIN	28th		Showery. Bn marched at 10.30 am to BOURS. 9 miles – arriving about 2PM. Billets good but scattered.	
BOURS	29th		Showery with very heavy rain in afternoon. Bn marched at 11.30 am to BRUAY 8 miles – arriving about 3 PM. Billets in houses of mining village, 10 to 12 men in each.	
BRUAY	30th		Showery. Baths for whole Bn in bathhouses of mine No III. Very good. ~~Lt.~~ 2/Lt G.W.A. Alexander joined.	
"	31st		Fine. Bn marched at 2.15 PM to NOEUX les MINES. – 7½ miles – arriving about 5 P.M. Bn in huts, offrs in town. 2/Lt Wm Hendrie joined with draft of 28 O.R. Lt Hendrie's kit damaged by shell fire in station. ~~Bn~~ An account of operations at MALTZ HORN RIDGE is attached.	

S. G. Craufurd Lt Col.
Comdg; 1st Gordon Highlanders

2449 Wt. W14957/M90 750,000 1/16 J.B.C. & A. Forms/C.2118/12.

1ST. BATTALION. THE GORDON HIGHLANDERS.

Report on Operations in MALTZ HORN RAVINE 16th to 20th August 1916.

On the afternoon of the 16th August, the Battalion moved from the Camp at GREAT BEAR to the Support position and was distributed as follows:-

"B" and "C" Coys = **DUBLIN TRENCH.**
"A" "D" & Hd Qr" Coys = TALUS BOIS.

On the evening of the 17th "A" "D" and Hd.Qr" Coys moved to CHIMPANZEE TRENCH in relief of the 10th R.W.F. who were proceeding to the attack.

Early on the morning of the 18th, orders were received for the Battalion to move into the front line for the attack in the afternoon.

The morning was misty and the Battalion filed out of CHIMPANZEE TRENCHES about 7 A.M. and reached their position in the front line trenches between 10 and 11 A.M.

DISPOSITIONS.

The disposition of the Coys. was as follows:-
COCHRANE ALLEY and part of SHUTE TRENCH "C" Coy under LIEUT. HORSLEY.
SHUTE TRENCH "B" Coy. under LIEUT BROWN.
ASSEMBLY TRENCH "D" Coy under 2/LT. SAUNDERS on the right.
"A" Coy. under CAPTAIN CUNNINGHAM on the left.

"A" Coy of K.S.L.I. was on the left of "A" Coy in ASSEMBLY TRENCH.

In the front line there was also one company 10th R.W.F. and one company K.S.L.I. on the left of "B" Coy 1st Gordon Highrs, in the trench facing the German LONELY TRENCH.

The assault was timed to commence at 2-45 P.M. and a further advance was to be made at 4-45 P.M.

"C" Coy. was detailed for the right of the advance in touch with the FRENCH and "B" Coy on the left.

1st objective, the first road running from the corner of MALTZ HORN RAVINE to GUILLEMONT. This road was battered out of recognition, but the position indicated was the crest of the ridge along which it presumably runs.

"B" and "C" Coys were under the command of Lieut. HORSLEY.

On the left of the Battalion a company of the 10th R.W.F. and a company of K.S.L.I. were to capture LONELY TRENCH and join up with the left of the Battalion.

A quarter of an hour previous to the assault "D" Coy was to start filing into SHUTE TRENCH as it was evacuated, from which it was to move in support by half companies and so strengthen the firing line.

Once SHUTE TRENCH was clear of the assaulting troops "A" Coy was to move in, ready to move forward when the advance on the 2nd. objective began at 4-45 P.M.

ASSAULT. At 2-30 P.M. ¼ of an hour before the assault an intense bombardment was opened on the enemy line and at 2-45 P.M. the Coys moved forward as directed. Owing to the configuration of the front line trenches which formed a deep re-entrant angle, the two inner platoons of the first two lines had to double to get into position while the two outer platoons proceeded in quick time.

The attack was made on two half Coy. frontages supported in each case by the remaining half company. Total frontage for the Battalion some 250 Yards.

During the preliminary bombardment it appears that the enemy left his trenches in the front line both on the Battalion frontage and in LONELY TRENCH and took up a position in shell holes in front.

Shell fire generally, previous to the attack, was not heavy.

The first two companies went over in perfect order as if on

parade, and this advance elicitated very favourable comments from the French.

As soon as the advance started heavy machine gun fire was opened on the assaulting line, chiefly from the FALFEMONT FARM position, and also from dugouts in the MALTZ HORN RAVINE which was in the FRENCH Sector. There was also a good deal of sniping from shell holes in front.

"C" Coy on the right flank suffered very heavy casualties losing eventually nearly 90 men out of a total of 110.

The right of the line reached its objective, but the two left platoons of "B" Coy under Sgts AITKEN and CRAIG got detach ed from the main line whilst in pursuit of the garrison of LONELY TRENCH which fled at our assault.

These two platoons reached 2nd sunken road 250 yards in front of the main position and started digging in. Meanwhile the 1st two platoons of "D" Coy advancing in rushes of from 30 to 40 yards had reinforced the left of the line. Shortly afterwards the other half company of "D" Coy under Cpl GERRARD advanced in perfect order in attack formation and reinforced the line on the right. To do this they had to make their way through heavy flanking machine gun fire from the RAVINE.

Within half an hour of Sgt AITKEN reaching the advanced position, LIEUT BROWN went down to give directions as to digging in and was killed shortly afterwards on returning to the main position for reinforcements.

During this time there was little shell fire on the position captured, such as there was, being chiefly confined to shrapnel.

At 2-45 P.M. the 418 FRENCH INFANTRY advanced in line with our right and later somewhere about 4-45 P.M. the CHASSEURS advanced forward on the right and gained touch with Sgt Aitkens party. Shortly afterwards they were however, driven back by a counter-attack.

It was now dusk and Sgt. Aitkenfinding himself isolated and running short of ammunition withdrew his men to the main posit- ion. The position then was as follows:-

On the right a trench was being constructed connecting up with the 418 French Infantry. A party of these latter had also dug a forward trench 50 yards in front which was also connected up. The company of the Suffolk Regt. carried on COCHRANE ALLEY to the new position, utilising the German defences in the Ravine. The left flank which was in the air was defended by machine gun and listening posts.

The work of consolidation was carried on throughout the night.

A company of K.S.L.I. who had been reported early in the afternoon to have advanced on our left did not in reality reach our new position till 2 A.M. when they assisted in the consolid- ation.

On the 1st Assault taking place the majority of the Germans opposed to our front as well as those on our immediate left cleared out in disorder back to the FALFEMONT position.

During the night there was very little shelling on our new position though a desultory rifle fire was maintained. German very lights would show that the enemy had retired to the FALFE- MONT FARM position. This contention is borne out by the fact that next day the only Germans seen was a company sent down to re-establish itself on the lower slopes of the FALFEMONT FARM ~~position~~ ridge. It was dispersed by our machine gun fire.

Support Line.

The first phases of the assault could be clearly followed from our old line and it was seen that the first objective had been gained and the work of consolidation commenced. Shortly after this the smoke from our barrage obscured all further view.

"A" Coy had originally been directed to occupy SHUTE TRENCH as soon as it was evacuated by "D" Coy. When however, an attempt was made to do this the trench was found to be full of men of various units, viz:- K.S.L.I., a few R.W.F. some of our own men who had filtered back and Suffolks driven from COCHRANE ALLEY by the shelling. All movement was impossible and the company had to be withdrawn to ASSEMBLY TRENCH. This was about 5 P.M.

Immediately after the assault took place the enemy opened a heavy barrage of 5.9's on COCHRANE TRENCH which was blown in in many places and became untenable. About 5-30 P.M. the enemy opened a heavy barrage previous to a counter attack on the French. This continued till 8 P.M. when it became intense. This barrage was chiefly directed on the French lines immediately to our right, Battalion Headquarters and Cochrane Alley which latter became quite untenable. There was also a heavy barrage on Edwards Trench which was empty.

About 10 P.M. in consequence of a report from Sgt. Craig who had come back from the front line which report was confirmed from the K.S.L.I. men of the R.W.F and by liason Officers from the 418 French Infantry and Chasseurs. I reported that our line had been forced to retire to our original position. These reports I afterwards found referred to the withdrawal of Sgts Aitken and Craig's party from the advanced position. I then sent down to verify and found out the truth about midnight.

All communication was by this time very difficult, the barrage continued nearly till dawn; and the trenches were blocked by KRR whom I could get neither to proceed nor withdraw, and by two companies R.S.F. who could not get down to the front line to reinforce till dawn, in spite of every effort they made. These two companies when they did manage to arrive did very good work in further consolidation under Captain Cranston.

Although the advance of the K.S.L.I. at the hour of assault did not mature, small parties of K.S.L.I. and R.W.F. accompanied Sgt. Aitken to the most advanced position on a sunken road.

The party of K.S.L.I. which reinforced at 2 A.M. were led up by 2/Lt. Gordon.

The morning of the 19th was occupied in removing the wounded. In the afternoon "A" Coy. was employed in removing the dead from Cochrane Alley. "B" "C" and "D" Companies who were now much reduced were withdrawn at midday as the two companies R.S.F. were strong enough to hold the trench. The remainder of the R.W.F. were previously withdrawn as well as the remaining company of the Suffolks.

In the afternoon the K.S.L.I. occupied LONELY TRENCH without opposition.

At dusk I withdrew "A" Coy from the work of cleaning the trenches and burying the dead with a view to their connecting up LONELY TRENCH with SHUTE TRENCH.

Before they filed out, however, the enemy opened a heavy barrage on our support trenches which was especially severe on the trenches of the troops on our left. Fearing a counter attack we stood to arms with fixed bayonets. By the time the barrage was over the Manchester Regt. (Bantams) had arrived in relief. As two more companies R.S.F. and two companies KRR had by this time arrived as digging parties and proved sufficient to connect up LONELY TRENCH both with the new line (GORDON TRENCH) and SHUTE TRENCH "A" Coy withdrew at Midnight.

The Battalion lost in casualties 4 Officers killed and 3 wounded and 257 other ranks, killed, wounded, and missing. -

S. G. Craufurd
Lieut. Colonel.
Commanding, 1st Battn., The Gordon Highlanders.

24/8/16.

1st BATTALION THE GORDON HIGHLANDERS.

Roll of Officers on strength of Battalion on 31st August 1916.

Lieut.Col.S.G.Craufurd.
Lieut.& Adjt.D.C.D.Munro.
Capt.J.McA.Cunningham.
" H.S.Gammell.
" G.W.A.Alexander.
Lieut.W.Blair.
2/Lieut.T.C.Scoones.
" D.R.G.Renfrew.
" N.M.Paton.
" W.H.Lyell.
" G.M.Berry.
" A.J.Cleghorn.
" R.K.Gordon.
" A.Riddell.
" K.C.Davidson.
" A.H.Duncan.
" W.T.Currie.
" G.Ritchie.
" J.Russell.
" C.C.Thorburn.
" J.McIntosh.
" H.B.Cook.
" J.Merrilees.
" W.W.Hendrie.
" G.P.Peterkin.
" P.T.Pirie.
" C.Gemmill.
" W.G.H.Forbes.
" R.W.Preston.

Lieut.F.W.Clarke.	Quartermaster.
Capt.J.L.Stewart.	M.O.
Rev.W.H.Leathem.	C.F.

DETAILS.

Major F.L.M.C.Maitland.	Camp Commandant. BOIS des TAILLES.
Capt.W.Waring.	A/Adjutant, 8th K.O.R.L.
2/Lieut.D.K.Templeton.	13th Corps. Heavy Ammunition Park.
" D.S.Inglis.	Admitted Field Ambulance.

STRENGTH OF BATTALION ON 31st AUGUST 1916.

Fighting Strength.	34 O.	1013 O.R.
Details.	4 O.	96 O.R.

DCD Munro Lt

Lieut.Colonel
Commdg.,1st BN. The Gordon Highlanders.

3/9/16.

76th Brigade.

3rd Division.

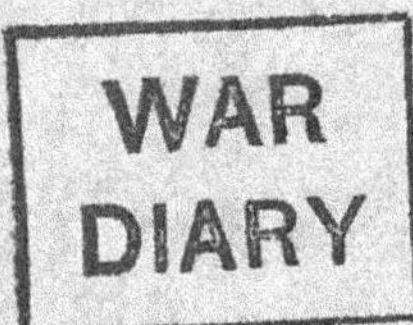

1st BATTALION

GORDON HIGHLANDERS

SEPTEMBER 1916

Appendix :- Nominal Roll of Officers.

1st Gordon Highlanders

Instructions regarding War Diaries and Intelligence Summaries are contained in F. S. Regs., Part II. and the Staff Manual respectively. Title Pages will be prepared in manuscript.

WAR DIARY
or
~~INTELLIGENCE SUMMARY~~
(Erase heading not required.)

1 Gordon Hrs. 76/3

September 1916

Vol 24 25

Army Form C. 2118

Place	Date	Hour	Summary of Events and Information	Remarks and references to Appendices
NOEUX LES MINES	1st		Day fine – The Battalion marched to MAZINGARBE by companies and billeted in the Northern Huts. Hutments good and accomadation ample for whole Battalion. The Battalion was in Brigade Reserve.	
	2nd		Fine day – Battalion training. Physical drill, bayonet fighting and Company drill	
	3rd		Fine – showery in the evening. Church parade at 10.30 a.m. The Commander [illegible] gave out cards for gallantry in action on Aug: 18th 1916. Carrying party of 10 officers and 280. O.Rs paraded at 6.30 p.m.	
	4th		Showery – fine during the evening. Battalion training. Carrying party of 2 officers and 248 O.Rs. paraded at 6.30 p.m. C.S.M. Brock joined	
	5th		Showery. Battalion training. Major R.A.N. TYLER joined and assumed 2nd in command. The Commanding Officer and Adjutant visited the trenches. An R.E. Class, in barbed wiring was started, of 1 off and 5 men from each Company.	
	6th		Fine day. Battalion training	
	7th		Fine. The Battalion was inspected by the G.O.C. Division at 11 a.m. Military Medal ribbons were presented to Sgt Bramah, Cpl Gellamont, Pte Ramsay and Greenless. 2nd Lieut A.J. Cloghorn died.	
	8th		Fine. Battalion took over the trenches in B.1.c 14 Sector from the 8th Kings Own. 3 Coys: occupied front line trenches and 1 Coy: in RESERVE trench. Parts of the front line required a great deal of work little or no wire existed in front of our own line while the enemy front was very strongly wired. Lieuts. D. Buchan, D. McFarlane, J. Cumming and R.J. Giles joined from 11th Battalion.	

1st Gordon Highlanders

Instructions regarding War Diaries and Intelligence Summaries are contained in F. S. Regs., Part II. and the Staff Manual respectively. Title Pages will be prepared in manuscript.

WAR DIARY
or
~~INTELLIGENCE SUMMARY~~
(Erase heading not required.)

September 1916

Army Form C. 2118.

Place	Date	Hour	Summary of Events and Information	Remarks and references to Appendices
	9th		Fine. Quiet day. Party of 100 men dug nests for gas cylinders in the left Coy: front. Coys: in the front line wired their respective fronts during the night.	
	10th		Fine. Quiet day. Digging party continued. Coys: wired at night. The trench mortar batteries bombarded the enemys wire in front of B is 14 at 5.0 p.m.	
	11th		Fine. several showers. Fairly quiet day. 2 O.Rs wounded. The trench mortars bombarded enemys wire at 5.40 p.m. at same objective. 2Lieuts Ritchie and McIntosh rejoined from 4th Army School.	
	12th		Fine. Quiet day. Coys: wired their front during the night. The trench mortars bombarded enemys wire at 12 noon at the same objective.	
	13th		Fine day. Quiet. Coys: wired their front.	
	14th		Fine. Quiet day. Trench mortars bombarded enemys wire at 6.30 a.m. Draft of 33 O.Rs reported and were posted to Coys:	
	15th		Fine. Quiet day. Trench mortars bombarded enemys wire at 10.30 a.m. 4 Officers and 80 O.Rs. carrying gas cylinders	
	16th		Day fine. The Battalion was relieved by 8th Kings Own Royal Lancasters and on relief went into support. B Coy: in GUN trench, A Coy in VILLAGE line and remainder with Battalion H.Qrs. in 10th AVENUE.	
	17th		Day fine. some rain after 8 p.m. Nearly the whole of the Battalion furnished various working and carrying parties, chiefly carrying trench mortar ammunition.	

1875 Wt. W593/826 1,000,000 4/15 J.B.C. & A. A.D.S.S./Forms/C. 2118.

1st Gordon Highlanders

Instructions regarding War Diaries and Intelligence Summaries are contained in F. S. Regs., Part II. and the Staff Manual respectively. Title Pages will be prepared in manuscript.

WAR DIARY
or
~~INTELLIGENCE SUMMARY~~
(Erase heading not required.)

September 1916

Army Form C. 2118

Place	Date	Hour	Summary of Events and Information	Remarks and references to Appendices
[illegible]	18th		Wet Day. The Battalion furnished parties the same as 17th. C Coy left at [illegible] for baths at MAZINGARBE.	
	19th		Wet day. The Battalion furnished similar parties as on 17th. A Coy proceeded to the baths.	
	20th		Wet day. The Battalion furnished parties as before. "B" Coy proceeded to the baths.	
	21st		Day fine, wet towards evening. All the battalion employed in [illegible] the support trench and a ~~[illegible]~~ wood party employed in wiring the support line.	
	22nd		Dull and changeable day. The Battalion employed in cleaning and [illegible] the trenches with a view to being relieved. Draft of 23 O.R. reported and were posted to Coys.	
	23rd		Fine day. The Battalion was relieved by the 13th EAST SURREY REGIMENT and billeted in MAZINGARBE	
	24th		Fine day. The Battalion moved at 9.30 a.m. en route for LOZINGHEM about 12 miles. Joined the Brigade West of NOEUX LES MINES and arrived at LOZINGHEM at about 2.30 p.m. where the regiment billeted for the night.	
	25th		Fine day. The Battalion moved at 9.0 a.m. for ESTREE BLANCHE about 12 miles via AUCHEL – FERFAY and RELY and arrived about 2.0 p.m.	
ESTREE BLANCHE	26th		Fine day. Company kit inspections and cleaning up generally	
"	27th		Fine day. Battalion marched to training area, practised artillery formations, finishing up with a march past. Musketry practise in 30 yds in the afternoon	

1875 Wt. W593/826 1,000,000 4/15 J.B.C. & A. A.D.S.S./Forms/C. 2118.

1st Gordon Highlanders

Instructions regarding War Diaries and Intelligence Summaries are contained in F. S. Regs., Part II. and the Staff Manual respectively. Title Pages will be prepared in manuscript.

WAR DIARY
or
INTELLIGENCE SUMMARY September 1916

(Erase heading not required.)

Army Form C. 2118

Place	Date	Hour	Summary of Events and Information	Remarks and references to Appendices
ESTREE BLANCHE	28th		Fine day. The Battalion marched to the training area in the morning and carried out the 1st phases of the attack. Musketry practise in the afternoon. 2Lieut W. T. Currie proceeded on leave.	
"	29th		Fine day. The Battalion marched to the training area in the morning and practised the attack normal and ceremonial.	
"	30th		Fine day. The Battalion marched to the training area and carried out the "attack". The Brigade marched past Brigadier General R. Kentish D.S.O. who afterwards presented medal ribbons to men of the Brigade including 2 V.Cs. to the 10th Royal Welsh Fusiliers. He also made a farewell speech on his leaving the Brigade for Staff Employment at Home.	

S G Crawford Lieut: Colonel
Commanding 1st Battn The Gordon Highlanders

1875 Wt. W593/826 1,000,000 4/15 J.B.C. & A. A.D.S.S./Forms/C. 2118.

1st Battalion The Gordon Highlanders.

List of Officers serving with the Battalion on 30/9/16.

[illegible] S. C. Crawford

Major [illegible] C. Maitland

Capt. [illegible] Dairy
[illegible] Alexander
Capt. [illegible] Campbell

[illegible]
Lieut. [illegible] McFarlane
Lieut. [illegible] Cumming
Lieut. [illegible] Buchanan
[illegible]
Lieut. [illegible] Munro

2/Lieut. [illegible] C. [illegible]
[illegible]
2/Lieut. [illegible] Palmer
2/ [illegible]
2/Lieut. J. [illegible]
2/Lieut. W. [illegible]
2/Lieut. [illegible] Ritchie
2/Lieut. [illegible]
2/Lieut. A. [illegible]
2/Lieut. J. McIntosh
2/Lieut. [illegible] Lyall
2/Lieut. [illegible] Cammell
2/Lieut. [illegible] C. Davidson
2/Lieut. J. Russell
2/Lieut. C. C. [illegible]
2/Lieut. H. B. Cook
2/Lieut. [illegible] M. Barry
2/Lieut. N. C. H. Forbes
2/Lieut. W. [illegible] Currie

Lieut. F. W. Oarke — Quarter Master
Capt. J. L. Stewart — M. O.
Rev. W. H. Lontrum — C. F.

Details

Major R. A. N. Tytler — Attached 2nd Bn Gordon Highrs
Capt. R. Waring — A/Adjt 8th K. O. R. L.
Capt. J. McCunningham — Attached 8th Brigade Headqrs
2/Lieut. D. R. Templeton — XIII Corps Ammunition Park
2/Lieut. R. A. Gordon — Base Etaples 24/9/16.

Strength of Battalion on 30th Sept 1916

Fighting Strength	37 O	1013 OR.
Details	7 O	110 OR.

[illegible signature]
Lieut Colonel
Commanding 1st Battn The Gordon Highlanders

S E C R E T.

Copy No. 3

76TH INFANTRY BRIGADE OPERATION ORDER NO.49. 21/9/16

1. Reliefs of Battalions will be carried out on the 22nd. instan as per 76th. Brigade Operation Order No.48 para 1. The UP route for incoming Battalions will be via LONDON Road; the DOWN route for outgoing troops will be NORTHERN UP.

2. Guides will be provided by outgoing Battalions at the rate of one per Platoon, one for Snipers, and one for Battalion Hd.Qrs.- and also in the case of the Support Battalion of one guide for Bombers and one per Lewis Gun. One Officer per Battalion will be detailed to be i/c of all guides.

3. (a) Left Battalion guides will be at junction of NORTH STREET and ENGLISH ALLEY at 10 a.m.
(b) Right Battalion guides at same place at 11 a.m.
(c) Support Battalion guides will be at 2 p.m. at a point in the VILLAGE LINE to be arranged between the Battalions concerned.

4. The incoming Battalions (less Reserve Battalion) will send advanced parties to be at 76th. Infantry Brigade Headquarters at 7 a.m. on 22nd instant as follows :-
(a) 1 Officer per Battalion and 1 N.C.O.per Company to take over Trench Stores.
(b) 1 Sniping Officer.
(c) 1 Officer to take over from Battalion Field Works Officers the scheme of work on trenches and the spoil arrangements for mine galleries and for dug-outs.
(d) These parties will be guided by Brigade Headquarters via NORTHERN UP as far as Advanced Brigade H.Q. at which point one guide per Battalion will meet them and conduct them to Bn. H.Q. where their opposite numbers will meet them.

5. On 22nd inst. after relief 8th. K.O.R.L. Regiment and 2nd. Suffolk Regiment will billet in MAZINGARBE and the 1st. Gordon Highlanders to NOEUX-les-MINES. The 10th. R.W.Fusiliers will mar to billets ~~MAZINGARBE~~ NOEUX-les-MINES so as to clear MAZINGARBE by 3 p.m. Billetting parties for MAZINGARBE will report to Town Major at 10 a.m. and those for NOEUX-les-MINES to Staff Captain at same hour at 76th. Brigade Headquarters.

6. The incoming Reserve Battalion are sending 1 Officer on a bicy and 1 Corporal and 13 men to be at 76th. Brigade Headquarters at 8 a.m. on 22nd. where they will be met by guides of 10th. R.W.Fus. for taking over keeps.

7. Completion of reliefs and of arrival in billets to be wired to Brigade Headquarters.

8. On 23rd. inst. the 76th. Brigade Group (less Artillery) marches to RAIMBERT-AUCHEL-LOZINGHEM-ALLOUAGNE-BURBURE and on the 24th. inst to the training area.

9. Acknowledge.

Issued at 3.30 p.m.

Major,
Brigade Major, 76th. Infantry Brigade.

SECRET. Copy No. 3

76th INFANTRY BRIGADE OPERATION ORDER No. 48.

20/9/16.

1. On the 22nd instant the 120th Infantry Brigade (who are at LE BREBIS) of 40th Division will relieve the 76th Infantry Brigade, but the relief of the Machine Gun Company, Trench Mortar Battery (Stokes) and Battalion specialists will take place 24 hours previously.

2. On the 22nd instant, the Right Battalion (2nd Suffolk Regt.) will be relieved by the 14th Bn. H. L. I.
The Left Battalion (8th Bn. K.O.R.L.Regt.) will be relieved by the 14th Bn. Argyll & Sutherland Highlanders.
The Support Battalion (1st Bn. Gordon Highlanders) will be relieved by the 13th Bn. E. Surrey Regiment.
The Reserve Battalion (10th Bn. Royal Welch Fusiliers) will be relieved by the 11th Bn. K. O. R. L. Regiment.
Further orders will be issued later.

3. On 21st instant
(a) The Commanding Officer and 4 Company Commanders and Bn. Intelligence and Signalling Officers of the two front and support battalions, and also the Bombing Officer of the two front battalions of the 120th Infantry Brigade will be reconnoitring the line, leaving 76th Brigade H.Q. at 9 a.m. They will be guided by Brigade H.Q. guides to Advanced Brigade H.Q., where the 76th Brigade Battalions concerned will have guides ready at 10 a.m. to take them to the respective Battalion H.Q's., where they are to be met by their opposite numbers.
(b) Battalion Signallers, Lewis Gunners, and Bombers of the two relieving front battalions, and the Signallers of the relieving Support Battalion will leave 76th Brigade H.Q. at 10 a.m. 21st instant to carry out relief. The 1st Gordon Highlanders will send six guides to be at Brigade H.Q. at 9-45 a.m. in order to guide the incoming Specialists as far as Advanced Brigade H.Q. Thence guides for specialists will be provided by Battalions concerned to be at Advanced Brigade H.Q. at 11 a.m. at the rate for each battalion of 1 guide for signallers, 1 guide for bombers, and 1 guide per Lewis Gun. Specialists of the 8th K. O. R. L. Regt. will ~~relieve~~ return to NORTHERN HUTS at MAZINGARBE, and those of the 2nd Bn. Suffolk Regt. and signallers of the 1st Gordon Highlanders to NOEUX-les-MINES. Orders for billets will be given by the Staff Captain to Battalion Quartermasters.

4. The 9th Infantry Brigade have been given permission to use NORTHERN UP on 21st for UP traffic for relief purposes from 11 a.m. to 1 p.m.

5. Lists of Trench Stores, etc., to be handed over, to reach Brigade H.Q. by 12 noon on 22nd instant.

6. Acknowledge.

J. R. Skipsmith

Major,
Brigade Major, 76th Infantry Brigade.

SECRET   Copy No....3.........

76th INFANTRY BRIGADE OPERATION ORDER No. 80.

Tranq Hill

Ref. Map 1/100,000 LENS 11.
and 1/100,000 HAZEBROUCK 5a.   22/9/16.

1. The 76th Infantry Brigade Group (less artillery) will march on 23/9/16 to the area RAIMBERT - AUCHEL - LOZINGHEM - ALLOUAGNE - BURBURE as follows :-

Starting Point cross roads at R in FOUR a CHAUX 9-45 a.m.
Route. Railway crossing at U in PLACE d BRUAY - MARLE - LES-MINES - LOZINGHEM.

ORDER OF MARCH

Units	Time.	Probable Billets.
Brigade H.Q.	9-45 a.m.	ALLOUAGNE
1/1st E.Riding Fld.Coy.R.E. }	9-45 a.m.	AUCHEL
76th T. M. Battery	9-45 a.m.	ALLOUAGNE
8th K. O. R. L. Regt.	9-55 a.m.	"
2nd Suffolk Regiment	10-2 a.m.	"
10th Royal Welch Fus.	10-9 a.m.	"
1st Gordon Highlanders	10-16 a.m.	"
76th Machine Gun Coy.	10-24 a.m.	AUCHEL
7th Field Ambulance	10-24 a.m.	ALLOUAGNE
~~No. 2 Company A. S. C.~~	10-24 a.m.	"
20th K. R. R. C.	10-31 a.m.	BURBURE
No. 5 a Sanitary Section	10-38 a.m.	"
NO 2 COY. A.S.C.	10-40 a.m.	ALLOUAGNE

2. BILLETTING PARTIES will meet the Staff Captain at ~~9~~ 8. a.m. 23/9/16 at starting point given above.

3. All Transport will follow in rear of the Brigade in same order of march as units, under O.C. No. 2 Company A.S.C.

4. Battalions marching from MAZINGARBE to NOEUX-LES-MINES will move by platoons at intervals of 100 yards until the level crossing of the LABOURSE - HERSIN Railway is passed, when they will close up into column of route. 76th M. G. Company will move similarly.

5. Battalions marching from MAZINGARBE in moving to starting point will leave by N. EXIT of the village as follows :-

10th Royal Welch Fusiliers 7.30
1st Gordon Highlanders 7.46
76th Machine Gun Company 8.6
20th K. R. R. C. 8.11 } - independently
5 a San. Section 8.25 }

Intervals of 1 minute will be left between platoons, i.e. Time allowed for battalions 25 minutes - for M. G. Coy. 10 minutes - from time of 1st platoon to time of 1st Platoon of successive unit. A halt of 10 minutes must be allowed for after rear of last unit has passed the railway crossing. The last unit is to clear NOEUX-LES-MINES by 10-15 a.m.

6. REAR PARTIES. The usual rear parties will be arranged for by units - and a return of stragglers to be sent Brigade H.Q. immediately on conclusion of the march.

7. Acknowledge.

Issued at 4.45pm

Ch. Cooper. Capt
for Major,
Brigade Major, 76th Infantry Brigade.

76th Brigade.

3rd Division.

WAR DIARY

1st BATTALION

GORDON HIGHLANDERS

OCTOBER 1 9 1 6

Appendix ;- Nominal Roll of Officers.

Instructions regarding War Diaries and Intelligence Summaries are contained in F. S. Regs., Part II. and the Staff Manual respectively. Title Pages will be prepared in manuscript.

WAR DIARY
or
INTELLIGENCE SUMMARY
(Erase heading not required.)

Army Form C. 2118.

1 Gordon Hrs
Vol 25

Place	Date	Hour	Summary of Events and Information	Remarks and references to Appendices
ESTRBE BLANCHE	Oct. 1	1916	Fine. Church parade 11 am. Afternoon funeral of Pte. TEMPLE accidentally killed by train at the Railway crossing. Regimental Mascot fox terrier "PYPER" died.	
	2.		Very Wet. March to trench practice ground. Brigade practice postponed owing to wet. 2/Lieut. E.L. MITCHELL reported on being posted to the Regiment.	
	3.		Wet morning. Fine afternoon. Practice attacks over trenches. Sports in the evening.	
	4.		Wet. Brigade & Divisional assault practice over trenches. Major F.L. Maitland left for Home Establishment. Major SWORDER reported for duty. In the evening big fire occurred in the village in the salvage of which the Battalion worked throughout the night, receiving next morning the thanks of the Brigadier for their work.	
	5.		Fine. Battalion marched to HEUCHIN at 2 p.m. arriving at billets at 5.45 pm, when they received the same cordial welcome from the inhabitants as previously.	
HEUCHIN	6		Showery. Battalion at rest.	
	7		Wet with heavy showers. Battalion marched at 5.40 am. to ST. POL arriving at 8 am. & entraining at 10 am. for RAINCHEVAL. After weary train journey detrained at BELLE EGLISE at midnight reaching billets at RAINCHEVAL at 1 am.	
	8		Very stormy morning. Marched at 1.20 pm. to ACHEUX arriving 5 pm. Billets in huts in ACHEUX WOOD.	
ACHEUX	9		Fine. Battalion resting. Fatigue party of 150 men found.	

2449 Wt. W14957/M90 750,000 1/16 J.B.C. & A. Forms/C.2118/12.

Army Form C. 2118.

WAR DIARY
or
INTELLIGENCE SUMMARY
(Erase heading not required.)

Instructions regarding War Diaries and Intelligence Summaries are contained in F. S. Regs., Part II. and the Staff Manual respectively. Title Pages will be prepared in manuscript.

Place	Date	Hour	Summary of Events and Information	Remarks and references to Appendices
ACHEUX	10		Fine. Practice assault of trenches to be captured over flagged course.	
	11		Wet morning. Fine afternoon. Practice assault of trenches in conjunction with K.O.R.L. In the afternoon combined sports K.O.R.L.R. & Gordon Highlanders.	
	12		Fine. Practice assault over flagged course.	
	13		Fine. Practice assault over flagged course.	
	14		Fine. Practically whole battalion on fatigue & trenches	
	15		Showery. Church parade in morning.	
	16		Fine. Battalion on fatigues. C.O. & Adjutant went round trenches in SERRE sector.	
VAUCHELLES	17		Fine. Battalion marched 2 p.m. to VAUCHELLES arriving 4 p.m. Billets in huts. Very muddy. Lieut. A.M.R. NORMAN reported on rejoining battalion	
	18		Wet & very cold. Battalion paraded 6.30 am & practised assault of trenches over flagged course in Brigade & Divisional training. Dinners on the ground at 5 p.m. Returned to billets 7.30 p.m.	
COURCELLES	19		Very Wet. Battalion marched at 9.45 am. to COURCELLES over very wet & muddy road arriving 12.30 p.m. Fatigue party to trenches of 300 men at 9 p.m.	
	20		Fine. Digging party of 200 men to trenches at 6 a.m.	

2449 Wt. W14957/M90 750,000 1/16 J.B.C. & A. Forms/C.2118/12.

Army Form C. 2118.

Instructions regarding War Diaries and Intelligence Summaries are contained in F. S. Regs., Part II. and the Staff Manual respectively. Title Pages will be prepared in manuscript.

WAR DIARY
or
INTELLIGENCE SUMMARY
(Erase heading not required.)

Place	Date	Hour	Summary of Events and Information	Remarks and references to Appendices
COURCELLES	21		Fine frosty & cold. Kit inspection. 300 men ~~to~~ trenches at night on fatigue.	
	22		Fine. Very cold chilly East wind. Divisional practice of trenches to be captured over flagged course. 200 fatigue party during night. Lieut. STEARNS, 2/Lt. CAMPBELL & 2/Lt. SCOTT joined for duty.	
	23		Fine. No parades during day. Battalion carrying trench mortar ammunition & cleaning Assembly trenches at night.	
	24		Wet. Fatigue party of 300 men at 4 p.m. carrying T. M. ammunition.	
	25		Wet. Battalion at rest.	
	26		Wet. Raiding party 2/Lt CURRIE, 2/Lt K.C. DAVIDSON & 47 other ranks ~~tried~~ to enter enemy trenches at 7.45 p.m. Day occupied in preparation. Raid unsuccessful owing to change of time of assault. Divisional artillery in consequence opened barrage ¼ hour ~~too~~ soon & raiding party could not leave our front trenches owing to enemy's counter barrage. 2/Lts. CURRIE & DAVIDSON wounded, Sgt. LESLIE killed.	

2449 Wt. W14957/M90 750,000 1/16 J.B.C. & A. Forms/C.2118/12.

Instructions regarding War Diaries and Intelligence Summaries are contained in F. S. Regs., Part II. and the Staff Manual respectively. Title Pages will be prepared in manuscript.

WAR DIARY
or
INTELLIGENCE SUMMARY
(Erase heading not required.)

Army Form C. 2118.

Place	Date	Hour	Summary of Events and Information	Remarks and references to Appendices
Trenches	27		Wet. Battalion less B Coy marched 7.30 am. & took over trenches in SERRE Sector from 8/K.O.R.L.R. Some shelling en route. ROB ROY (front line) badly damaged by T.M. fire. Trenches very muddy throughout. Support line knee deep in mud & in places hard to follow. Enemy activity quiescent during latter part of day.	
	28		~~Wet~~ Showery. Enemy shelled OBSERVATION WOOD & support trenches during forenoon & early afternoon. Shelling specially severe near Bn. Headquarters. RAILWAY AVENUE & Brigade (Advanced) Headquarters struck by several shells. One casualty. At 11 pm. gas T.M. attack from 2nd Division drifted over our front line. Helmets had to be put on & enemy retaliation continued for half an hour.	
BUS	29		Wet. Considerable counter artillery activity at 6 am. Battalion relieved during morning by 7/K.S.L.I. & marched to BUS. Billets in huts in BUS wood. Surroundings very muddy.	
	30		Heavy Showers. Bombing practice in the morning. & Heavy rain in afternoon.	
	31		Fine. Bombing practice & arm drill for whole battalion.	

In the field 31/10/16.

S. G. Craufurd Lt. Col.
Commanding 1st Gordon Highlanders.

2449 Wt. W14957/M90 750,000 1/16 J.B.C. & A. Forms/C.2118/12.

1st Battalion The Gordon Highlanders

Roll of Officers serving with Battalion on 31st Oct. 1916.

Lt. Colonel S. G. Craufurd

Major F. R. F. Sworder

Capt. J. M. Cunningham A/Adjt
Capt. G. H. A. Alexander Asst/Adjt
Capt. C. G. C. Davey

Lt. R. J. Giles
Lt. D. McFarlane
Lt. A. M. B. Norman
Lt. D. Buchan
Lt. H. S. Stevens

2/Lt. W. H. Lyell
2/Lt. N. M. Paton
2/Lt. G. M. Berry
2/Lt. T. C. P. Campbell
2/Lt. A. Riddell
2/Lt. J. Lyall
2/Lt. D. Hutton
2/Lt. A. L. Scott
2/Lt. J. Russell
2/Lt. C. C. Thorburn
2/Lt. C. Gemmill
2/Lt. J. McIntosh
2/Lt. H. B. Cook
2/Lt. J. Merrilees
2/Lt. E. L. Mitchell
2/Lt. R. W. Preston
2/Lt. P. J. Pirie
2/Lt. W. G. H. Forbes
2/Lt. W. H. Hendrie
2/Lt. D. G. H. Birnie
2/Lt. R. W. G. Renfrew.

Lieut. & Quarter Master F. W. Clarke
Capt. J. L. Stewart M. O.
Rev. W. H. Leathem C. F.

Details.

Lt. J. Blair At Course of Instruction
Lt. J. Cumming. At Course of Instruction
Capt. H. St. Gammell At F. A.
2/Lt. D. L. Templeton At 13th Corps Hvy. Amm. Park. A. S. C.
2/Lt. R. K. Gordon At Base
2/Lt. G. Ritchie Town Major, Bertrancourt.
2/Lt. T. C. Scoones Brigade Intelligence Officer

Strength of Battalion on 31/10/16

Fighting Strength	O. 39	OR. 931	Total 970.
Detail	O. 6	OR. 106	" 112.

S. G. Craufurd Lt. Colonel.
Commanding 1st Bn The Gordon Highlanders

S E C R ET. Copy No.........

76th INFANTRY BRIGADE OPERATION ORDER No. 54.

17/10/16.

1. All Units and Brigade H.Q. will move today to LOUVENCOURT except the 10th Royal Welch Fusiliers who will move to VAUCHELLES. Water carts, cookers, Maltese and mess carts will accompany units.

2. Starting Point - West exit of BERTRANCOURT.

3. Route - BERTRANCOURT - LOUVENCOURT.

4. Order of March -

	B. S. Point.
Brigade H.Q.	2-19 p.m.
10th Royal Welch Fus	2-20 p.m.
8th K.O.R.L.Regiment	2-30 p.m
2nd Suffolk Regiment	2-30 p.m.
76th Trench Mortar Bty.	2-50 p.m.
76th Machine Gun Coy.	2-51 p.m.

5. 1st Gordon Highlanders will leave North West exit of ACHEUX at 2-15 p.m. and march direct to LOUVENCOURT independantly.

6. Transport lines will not move.

7. Acknowledge.

Issued at ...11 a.m....

[signature] Major,
Brigade Major, 76th Infantry Bde.

Copies to:-

No. 1 8th K. O. R. L. Regiment
2 2nd Suffolk Regiment
3 10th Royal Welch Fusiliers
4 1st Gordon Highlanders
5 76th Machinr Gun Coy.
6 76th Trench Mortar Bty.

SECRET. Copy No.....3.....

76th INFANTRY BRIGADE OPERATION ORDER No. 61.

28/10/16.

1. On 29th instant the 8th Infantry Brigade who are at BUS will relieve the 76th Infantry Brigade. The ~~three Companies of~~ 1st Gordon Highlanders, 1 Coy and 1 company 8th East Yorkshire Regiment will be relieved by 7th King's Shropshire Light Infantry.

The ~~three companies of~~ 1st Northumberland Fusiliers, 1 Coy and two companies of 8th East Yorkshire Regiment will be relieved by 2nd Royal Scots.

The 76th Trench Mortar Battery and attached section of 149th Trench Mortar Battery will be relieved by 8th Brigade Trench Mortar Battery, and attached section of 149th Trench Trench Mortar Battery.

The reliefs will be carried out as per attached table.

The 76th Machine Gun Company and Mhow Machine Gun Squadron will be relieved by 8th Machine Gun Company on 30th instant, details to be arranged between Officer commanding units direct. This relief will be complete by 1 p.m. on 30 instant.

On 29th instant the 2nd Suffolk Regiment and 8th K. O. R. L. Regiment will march to BUS, and their billets at COURCELLES will be taken over by 1st Battalion Scots Fusiliers and 8th East Yorkshire Regiment respectively.

The 10th Royal Welch Fusiliers will remain at BUS.

The 1st Gordon Highlanders and 76th Machine Gun Company when relieved will also proceed to billets at BUS.

2. Troops relieving and relieved from the Right Section will not use that portion of SOUTHERN AVENUE which is west of TAUPIN TRENCH as this portion is shelled. RAILWAY AVENUE and TAUPIN TRENCH will be used instead.

Troops relieving and relieved from the left section will use NORTHERN AVENUE.

3. All Trench Stores, etc., will be properly handed over to relieving units, lists to reach Brigade H.Q. by 4 p.m. on 29th instant.

4. Completion of relief to be reported to 76th Brigade Headquarters.

Code word ---------------- AULIN.

5. Billeting parties will report to Staff Captain at Town Major's office in BUS at 10 a.m. on 29th instant.

6. There will be two busses for the 1st Gordon Highlanders to take men who cannot march, etc., to BUS. Busses will be waiting beyond R.E. Dump in COURCELLES on BERTRANCOURT Road

7. Acknowledge.

T C Leconey

2nd Lt.

Issued to Signals at 7.45 pm For Brigade Major, 76th Infantry Brigade

Copies to :-

No.		No.	
1	8th K.O.R.L.Regiment	8	8th Infantry Brigade.
2	2nd Suffolk Regiment	9	93rd " "
3	10th Royal Welch Fus. ✓	10	3rd Division. "G"
4	1st Gordon Highlanders	11	Town Major, COURCELLES
5	1st Northumberland Fus.	12	76th Machine Gun Coy.
6	8th Infantry Brigade	13	76th Trench Mortar Bty.
7	9th " "	14	War Diary
8		15	Office.

Unit taking over.	Section	Unit handing over	Guides at rate of 1 per platoon 1 per Lewis Gun and 1 per Bn. H.Q.
2nd Bn. The Royal Scots.	Right	1st Northumberland Fus. less 1 company 2 companies of 8th East Yorks. Regiment	Rendezvous – Junction of Railway Avenue with EUSTON DUMP COLINCAMPS ROAD. Guides will be supplied as follows :- Guides for Lewis Gunners of company in front line, Battalion H.Q., and Advanced parties, and 1 guide of right platoon of right company to be at rendezvous at 9-45 a.m. 3 guides for 3 platoons of right Coy.at 10-15 a.m 3 guides for 3 platoons of left Coy.at 11-45 a.m. 1 guide for 1 platoon of left Company, and Lewis gunners of 2 support Coys. at 1-15 p.m. 4 guides of right support Company at 12 noon 4 guides of left support Company at 10-30 p.m.
7th King's O. L. Infantry	Left	1st Gordon Highlanders less 1 company 1 company of 8th East Yorks. Regiment	Rendezvous COLINCAMPS CHURCH. Guides for Lewis Gunners, Signallers, Bn. H.Q., and advanced parties to be at rendezvous at 8-30 a.m. Guides for right company at 9-15 a.m. for left company at 9-35 a.m. for right support company 9-55 a.m. for left support company at 10-15 a.m.
8th Trench Mortar Battery and 1 section of 148th Trench Mortar Bty.		76th Trench Mortar Battery and 1 section of 146th Trench Mortar Battery	8th Trench Mortar Battery will be at COURCELLES at 8 a.m. tomorrow. Guide of 76th Trench Mortar Battery must be there to meet them.

76th Brigade.

3rd Division.

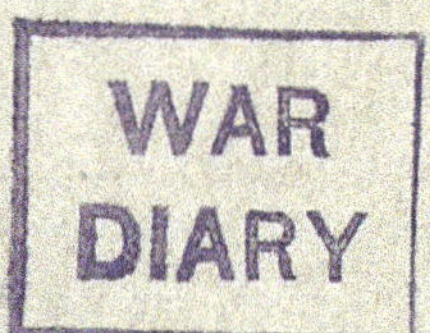

1st BATTALION

GORDON HIGHLANDERS.

NOVEMBER 1 9 1 6

Appendix :- Nominal Roll of Officers.

1st Gordon Highlanders

1 Gordon Hrs. November 1916 Vol 26

Army Form C. 2118

Instructions regarding War Diaries and Intelligence Summaries are contained in F. S. Regs., Part II. and the Staff Manual respectively. Title Pages will be prepared in manuscript.

WAR DIARY

~~or~~

~~INTELLIGENCE SUMMARY~~

(Erase heading not required.)

Place	Date	Hour	Summary of Events and Information	Remarks and references to Appendices
BUS	1		Fine day – Coy parades – Part of 'A' Coy on 30 yards Range in the afternoon.	
	2		Showery – fine in the afternoon – Battalion baths at LOUVENCOURT. Cinematograph entertainment in BUS Y.M.C.A. for the Battalion at 5.0 pm.	
	3		Fine day – Musketry for 'C' & 'D' Coys from 9.0 am to 1.0 pm and 'B' Coy from 3.0 pm to 4.15 pm. The C.O. lectured on the HISTORY of REGIMENT to Officers and NCOs from 2 – 3 pm – Four NCOs joined from Base (reinforcements).	
	4		Fine day – Battalion under Company arrangements (Bombing – Coy drill) Combined Sports in the afternoon with 2nd Suffolks. Ground very wet.	
	5		Fine day – Strong E wind. Church parade in BUS Y.M.C.A. hut at 10.0 am	
	6		Fine day – Strong E wind. Batt. post as it was on – Brigade Concert at 4.0 pm and it was put off during concert.	
	7		Wet day – 1 Coy on the Range.	
	8		Wet day – C.O. – Adjutant – & Coy Commanders went to see ground for laying Cable. This was cancelled in the afternoon.	
	9		Wet – Showery – 300 men on road work – 'D' Coy night marching practice. 2nd Lieut. G.P. Robertson re-joined.	
	10		Fine day – "It" was on again. Coy Commanders went to the trenches in the evening. Lieut. H.G. Stearns left to join M.G. Corps at GRANTHAM.	
	11		Fine day – Battalion resting – A bombing post was made ~~[illegible]~~ for men to practise bomb throwing – Football match Battalion v. BALLOON SECTION R.F.C. Battalion won 3–0. Lieut. J. Cumming re-joined from course.	

1875 Wt. W593/826 1,000,000 4/15 J.B.C. & A. A.D.S.S./Forms/C. 2118.

1st Gordon Highlanders.

Instructions regarding War Diaries and Intelligence Summaries are contained in F. S. Regs., Part II. and the Staff Manual respectively. Title Pages will be prepared in manuscript.

WAR DIARY ~~or~~ ~~INTELLIGENCE SUMMARY~~ November 1916

(*Erase heading not required.*)

Army Form C. 2118

Place	Date	Hour	Summary of Events and Information	Remarks and references to Appendices
BUS	12		Fine day - Church parade in the morning - Battalion paraded at 5.40 pm and moved to Assembly trenches.	
Trenches	13		Fine but misty - At 5.45 am, Battalion attacked the German lines in front of SERRE. The attack was not successful owing to the bad state of the ground, the difficulty of keeping touch + communication owing to the mist, + the heavy Machine Gun fire of the enemy. An isolated party of the Battalion under Capt. Norman + 2nd Lieut Preston held on in the German front line till dark + were the last to leave it, under orders, about 7.0 pm. In the evening the Battalion reorganised behind the front line + ... to hold the trenches - Casualties 141 -	
	14		Fine but cold - Situation fairly quiet throughout the day. The Battalion relieved the 10th ROYAL WELSH FUSILIERS in the front line + ROB ROY at night. Battalion H.Q. moved into advanced Brigade H.Q. + the C.O. took over command of left Subsector. Casualties 2 Killed 3 Wounded.	
	15		Fine + frosty - The day was fairly quiet. Time was spent in improving the position. Wiring of Posts in front line carried out at night. Divisional General visited trenches. Casualties 5 Wounded	
	16		Fine + frosty - Day again fairly quiet. Reconstruction of our line continued. Casualties 1 Killed 3 Wounded.	

1875 Wt. W593/826 1,000,000 4/15 J.B.C. & A. A.D.S.S./Forms/C. 2118.

1st Gordon Highlanders

Instructions regarding War Diaries and Intelligence Summaries are contained in F. S. Regs., Part II. and the Staff Manual respectively. Title Pages will be prepared in manuscript.

WAR DIARY
~~or~~
~~INTELLIGENCE SUMMARY~~
(Erase heading not required.)

November 1916

Army Form C. 2118

Place	Date	Hour	Summary of Events and Information	Remarks and references to Appendices
Trenches	17		Fine & frosty – Day quiet – Battalion relieved at night by 10th R.W.F. and marched to COURCELLES where billeted. Arrived in billets about [illegible]	
COURCELLES	18		Wet day – Sleet & very cold. The Battalion had [illegible]	
VAUCHELLES	19		Fine day. Battalion moved to VAUCHELLES and were billeted in huts. The Officers were billeted in the Village.	
	20		Fine day – The day was given up to Coy Commanders to inspect the men's kits, etc. Draft of 249 O.R. joined. One third had been out before.	
	21		Fine day – Coys under Company arrangements – [illegible] musketry in the afternoon.	
	22		Fine day – Coys under Coy arrangements – 2nd Battalion marched through village. Afternoon passes given to men to visit the 2nd Battalion – Colonel Craufurd received intimation that he was to proceed and take over command of [illegible] Brigade.	
	23		Fine day – 2 Coys did Musketry – remainder under Coy arrangements – Officers & N.C.O's under R.S.M. in the afternoon. [illegible] Draft of 19 O.R. joined from Base.	
	24		Fine day but cold – Battalion received orders to move to [illegible] but it was cancelled later. General Craufurd left to command [illegible] Inf Brigade.	
	25		Wet day – Fatigue party of 150 men at 6.30 a.m. [illegible]	
	26		Very wet – C.O. & O.C. "A" & "C" Coys visited trenches (SERRE SECTOR). Church Parade at 11.30 a.m.	

1875 Wt. W593/826 1,000,000 4/15 J.B.C. & A. A.D.S.S./Forms/C. 2118.

1st Gordon Highlanders

Instructions regarding War Diaries and Intelligence Summaries are contained in F. S. Regs., Part II. and the Staff Manual respectively. Title Pages will be prepared in manuscript.

WAR DIARY
or
~~INTELLIGENCE SUMMARY~~ November 1916
(Erase heading not required.)

Army Form C. 2118.

Place	Date	Hour	Summary of Events and Information	Remarks and references to Appendices
Trenches.	27		Fine – Battalion paraded at 1.15 pm and moved to trenches in SERRE SECTOR and took over from 13th Kings Liverpools. Relief completed at 1.50 am. Trenches very wet & muddy.	
	28		Fine & frosty – Battn working constantly in improving sector as a defensive position. Trenches require a lot of repairing. 1 man wounded. 2nd Lieut Lyall went down with a broken rib –	
	29		Still frosty – a certain amount of mist which enabled wiring to be continued during the morning.	
	30		Frosty – Still misty in the morning & wiring was possible. 2nd Lieut R.K. Gordon re-joined from the Base & took over command of "A" Coy.	

In the Field
3/12/16

[illegible] Major
Commanding 1st Battalion the Gordon Highrs.

1875 Wt. W593/826 1,000,000 4/15 J.B.C. & A. A.D.S.S./Forms/C. 2118.

1st Battalion [illegible] Gordon Highlanders

Roll of Officers [illegible] Battalion [illegible] Nov 1916

Major [illegible]

Capt [illegible]

Lieut [illegible]
[illegible]
[illegible]

2/Lieut [illegible]
" [illegible]
" [illegible] Campbell
" [illegible] Scott
" [illegible]
" C. C. Thorburn
" C. Gemmill
" H. [illegible] Cook
" J. Merrilees
" [illegible] Preston
" [illegible] Pike
" [illegible] Hardie
" [illegible] Burne
" D. R. G. Renfrew
" S. E. Lee
" G. O. Anderson
" G. P. Petrikin
" R. K. Gordon
Lieut & Qr F. W. Clarke
Capt R. Black M.O.
Rev. [illegible] Letham C.F.

Details

2/Lieut D. K. Templeton 18th Corps Heavy Amm Park
" G. Ritchie Town Major at Bertrancourt
" [illegible] Scoones Att 5th Brigade Staff
" W. H. Lyell At F.A.
" D. Hutton do
Lieut R. J. Giles do
Capt C. C. Davey do
" J. M. Cunningham On Leave
" A. N. Brorman do
2/Lt. E. L. Mitchell do

Strength of Battalion 30/11/16 :–		O.	OR.
	Fighting Strength	34	1035
	Details	7	161

[illegible] Lt Col
Commanding 1st Bn the Gordon Highlanders

S E C R E T   Copy No.............3

AMENDMENT No. 4 to 76th Infantry Brigade Operation Order No.37.

Para. 7 Dispositions.

(d) MHOW Machine Gun Squadron (British Section).

2 guns will be in position near West end of JOHN COPSE Tunnel to deal with any of the enemy machine guns or riflemen who may man this front line parapet and oppose our infantry starting for the assault.

These guns will only fire if our infantry is held up whilst emerging from the front trench for the assault.

2 Guns in positions 4 and 5.

These 4 guns will be available to move over to the enemy's lines later in the day if required.

2 Native Sections will be in Brigade Reserve at COURCELLES.

(e) Add to end of para. - and assist 10th Royal Welch Fusiliers to gain Sunken Road. Vide para. 8 (c).

Para. 9.

It is improbable that the "Tanks" will take part in the operations. They will only do so should the ground be considerably drier than at present.

Final decision will be notified later.

Acknowledge

[signature]

Major,
8/11/16. Brigade Major, 76th Infantry Brigade.

Issued at.....3pm.....

Copy No. 1 8th K. O. R. L. Regt.
2 2nd Suffolk Regiment
3 10th Royal Welch Fus.
4 1st Gordon Highlanders
5 76th Machine Gun Coy.
6 76th Trench Mortar Bty.
7 23rd Bde. R.F.A.
8 1/1st East Rdg.Fld.Coy.R.E.
9 & 10 3rd Division. "G".
11 8th Inf. Brigade.
12 92nd Inf. Brigade.
13 Diary
14 Office
15 Bde. Sig. Officer
16 Staff Captain
17
18 Brigade Major.

S E C R E T.   Copy No....3.........

AMENDMENT No. 3 to 76th Infantry Brigade Operation Order No. 57.

The following alterations are made in the objectives of Battalions in 76th Inf.Bde. O.O. 57 dated 24/10/16 para 8 (b) and (c).

(b) <u>1st Gordon Highlanders.</u>

<u>1st Objective.</u>   YELLOW Line from K 0 30 b 6.8 (junction of hedge with SERRE - PUISIEUX Road) to K 0 30 b 2.9 - K 30 a 3.7.

<u>2nd Objective.</u>   As soon as the 10th Bn. Royal Welch Fusiliers have passed through the YELLOW Line, the 1st Bn. Gordon Highlanders will occupy that portion of the BLUE Line from K 30 b 2.9 to K 30 b 6.8 (trench junction inclusive). When these objectives have been gained, the line from K 30 a 3.7 to K 30 b 6.8 will be consolidated to form a defensive flank facing NORTH and strong points 9 and 10 will be constructed and garrisoned.   Also bombing parties accompanied by Lewis Guns will work North East and form blocks up SERRE Trench at K 24 d 5.0 and up BERLIN Trench.   The Battalion will be re-organised, and one company will be held in readiness to support the 10th Royal Welch Fusiliers should they need assistance.

(c) <u>10th Royal Welch Fusiliers.</u>

<u>Objective.</u>   BLUE Line from Trench Junction K 30 b 6.8 exclusive (Junction to 1st Gordon Highlanders) eastward to point where PENDANT TRENCH crosses road at L 25 a 7.5 (L 25 a 7.4 to 8th Infantry Brigade) forming a defensive flank facing North.

On gaining this objective it will be consolidated and strong points 12 and 13 constructed and garrisoned.

The 10th Royal Welch Fusiliers will then push their line forward occupying line of SUNKEN Road L 25 a 6½.5 to L 25 a 3.8½ and then along Sunken Road SERRE - PUISIEUX to L 25 a 0.7.   The original BLUE Line's objective trench from L 25 a 0.7 to L 25 a 6½.5 will form a close support trench.

One Stokes Gun of the two detached in para. 7 (e) will be available to assist with above operation on its arrival near K 30 b 3.7.

Acknowledge.

[signature]

Major,
8/11/16.   Brigade Major, 76th Infantry Brigade.

Issued at ...3pm.......

Copy No.			
1	8th K.O.R.L.Regt.	13	Diary
2	2nd Suffolk Regiment.	14	Office
3	10th Royal Welch Fus.	15	Bde. Sig.Officer
4	1st Gordon Highlanders.	16	Staff Captain
5	76th Machine Gun Coy.	17	
6	76th Trench Mortar Bty.	18	Brigade Major.
7	23rd Bde. R.F.A.		
8	1/1st East Riding Fld. Coy. R.E.		
9 & 10	3rd Division "G".		
11	8th Infantry Brigade.		
12	92nd Inf. Brigade.		

SECRET. Copy No. 3

76th Infantry Brigade Operation Order No. 68

17/11/16.

Trench Map 1/10,000.

1. The 10th Royal Welch Fusiliers will relieve the 1st Gordon Highlanders in the left sub-sector tonight.

2. The detachment 10th Royal Welch Fusiliers now with 2nd Suffolk Regiment will join their battalion in the Left Sub-sector. This detachment will be replaced by details of 2nd Suffolk Regiment being sent from COURCELLES.

3. Guides of the 1st Gordon Highlanders will be at the junction of Railway Avenue with EUSTON HEBUTERNE Road at 4-30 p.m.

4. Detail of relief will be arranged between the O.C. Left sub-sector and O.C. 10th Royal Welch Fusiliers.

5. On completion of relief, Lt.Col. Hunt, 8th K. O. R. L. Regiment, will assume command of the ~~Right~~ Left Sector.

6. On relief the 1st Gordon Highlanders will march to billets at COURCELLES.

7. Completion of relief to be reported to Brigade H.Q.
Code word - WELCH HARP.

8. Acknowledge.

[signature] Capt. for Major,
Brigade Major, 76th Infantry Brigade.

Issued at --------------

Copy No. 1 8th K. O. R. L. Regt.
2 2nd Suffolk Regiment.
3 10th Royal Welch Fus.
4 1st Gordon Highlanders
5 3rd Division. "G".
6 Office.
7 Diary.

SECRET.

Copy No. 3
30/11/16.

76th INFANTRY BRIGADE OPERATION ORDER NO.71.

1. The following relief will take place in the Sector held by the 76th Infantry Brigade on the 1st December.
Relief to be completed by daylight on 2nd December.

2. The 8th Bn. King's Own (R.L.) Regt. will relieve the 1st Bn.Gordon Highlanders in the LEFT Sub-sector.
The 2nd Bn. Suffolk Regt. will relieve the 10th Bn. Royal Welch Fusiliers in the RIGHT Sub-sector.

3. All details of the relief will be arranged between Os.C.Battalions concerned.

4. All movements will, as far as possible, be across the open for parties moving after dark.

5. All trench stores, maps, etc., will be properly handed over. Lists to reach Brigade Head Quarters by noon 2nd December.
Os.C. Sub-sectors will hand over details of work, wiring, and where dumps of wire are situated to incoming battalions to enable the work to be carried on without delay.

6. Completion of relief will be notified to Brigade Head Quarters code word PICCADILLY.

7. 1st Bn. Gordon Highlanders will take over billets of 8th Bn. King's Own (R.L.) Regt. at COURCELLES.

10th Bn. Royal Welch Fusiliers will take over billets of 2nd Bn. Suffolk Regt. at COURCELLES.

Small rear parties should be left behind to hand over billets.

8. Acknowledge.

[signature], Captain,

Issued at 3pm for Brigade Major, 76th Infantry Brigade.

Copies to:-

No.1. 8th K.O.R.L.
2. 2nd Suffolks.
3. 10th R.W.F.
4. 1st Gordon H'ldrs.
5. 76th Coy.M.G.C.
6. 76th T.M.Battery.
7. 8th Infty.Brigade.
8. 94th Infty.Brigade.
9. 3rd Div. G.
10. 3rd Div. Q.
11. Town Major, COURCELLES.
12. War Diary.
13. File.
14. Brigade Major.
15. Staff Captain.

76th Brigade.

3rd Division.

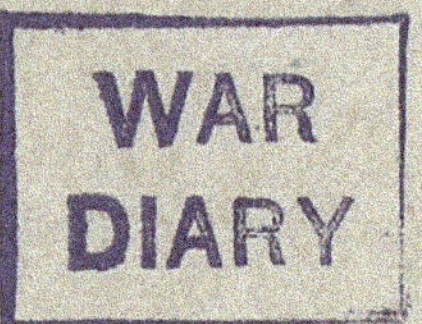

1st BATTALION

GORDON HIGHLANDERS.

DECEMBER 1 9 1 6

Instructions regarding War Diaries and Intelligence Summaries are contained in F. S. Regs., Part II. and the Staff Manual respectively. Title Pages will be prepared in manuscript.

WAR DIARY
or
INTELLIGENCE SUMMARY
(Erase heading not required.)

Army Form C. 2118.

1 Gordon Hrs

Vol 27

Place	Date	Hour	Summary of Events and Information	Remarks and references to Appendices
Trenches	~~1/16~~ 1.12		Hard frost. Wiring continued in morning. Batt" was relieved by 8th K. Own Regt at 8.30 p.m and marched back to huts at COURCELLES.	
COURCELLES	2.12		Fine. Batt" resting. Kit inspection etc	
"	3.12		Fine. Practically whole Batt" on carrying & working fatigues. Bombers were on special training.	
"	4.12		Fine. As yesterday. Special wiring party under 2/Lieut R.T. Peace wire up the wire front line opposite LUKE copse.	
"	5.12		Fine & cold. Batt" moved from COURCELLES at 10.10 a.m. taking over billets from 1/ Northumberland Fusiliers at LOUVENCOURT.	
LOUVENCOURT	6.12		Fine & misty. Over 300 on various working parties. Specialists training carried on. 5 officers reported arrival. 2/Lieut D. Fraser, H.P. Cunton, T.B. Laurence, E.W. Smith, G. Sutherland.	
"	7.12		Dull. 250 on fatigue. Specialists training carried on.	
"	8.12		Wet. Showery. 130 on working parties. Baths for companies. Specialists training carried on. Lt A. Bothwell reported arrival.	
"	9.12		250 on fatigues. Specialists training carried on in billets. 2/Lieut J.D.F. Maclennan reported arrival.	

2449 Wt. W14957/M90 750,000 1/16 J.B.C. & A. Forms/C.2118/12.

Army Form C. 2118.

WAR DIARY
or
INTELLIGENCE SUMMARY
(Erase heading not required.)

Instructions regarding War Diaries and Intelligence Summaries are contained in F. S. Regs., Part II. and the Staff Manual respectively. Title Pages will be prepared in manuscript.

Place	Date	Hour	Summary of Events and Information	Remarks and references to Appendices
	1916			
LOUVENCOURT	10.12		Church parade 10 a.m. 200 on fatigues. Specialists given a rest.	
"	11.12		Rainy. Changeable. 300 on working parties. Batt^n concert in the evening. O C Coys visited line.	
"	12.12		Rainy. Slight snow showers in morning. 200 on working parties. Remainder inspected + fitted out for trenches. Band played round billets.	
"	13.12		Fine cold. Batt^n marched from LOUVENCOURT to trenches (left of SERRE). Men had teas and drew gumboots at COURCELLES on way up. Relief with 13/ Liverpool Regt completed at midnight. Trenches in v. bad condition of mud etc.	
In trenches	14.12		Fine. Cold. Quiet day. Disposition D front line; C + A support, B reserve. No casualties.	
"	15.12		Quiet day " "	
"	16.12		Fine but evening wet. Slight shelling. D Coy relieved by A during night.	
"	17.12		Dull + misty. Quiet day. Batt^n relieved by 8/ King's Own Regt taking over billets in COURCELLES. Relief completed at 8.30 p.m. 2 officers + 50 men left in HITTITE trench for working + carrying [illegible] for King's Own. 2/Lieut W. H. Muir + [illegible] S. S. Fleming reported arrival.	
COURCELLES	18.12		Fine + frosty. Snow in afternoon. Acting Brigadier inspected the Batt^n billets in the morning.	

2449 Wt. W14957/M90 750,000 1/16 J.B.C. & A. Forms/C.2118/12.

Instructions regarding War Diaries and Intelligence Summaries are contained in F. S. Regs., Part II. and the Staff Manual respectively. Title Pages will be prepared in manuscript.

WAR DIARY
or
INTELLIGENCE SUMMARY
(Erase heading not required.)

Place	Date 1916	Hour	Summary of Events and Information	Remarks and references to Appendices
COURCELLES	19 Dec		Snow & rain. 200 on fatigues.	
"	20 Dec		Dull. Rain at intervals. 220 men on carrying parties.	
"	21 Dec		Rain. Batt^n H^d Q^rs + 2 Coys moved to COUIN.	
"	22 Dec		Rain. 1 Coy in COLINCAMPS and 1 Coy in BEAUSSART. 50 men of B Coy in [illegible]	B.W.
COUIN	23 Dec		Rain. Coys in COUIN evening. Officers & NCOs lecture under Bombing & Lewis gun officers.	
			[illegible] Rain at intervals. Parades as yesterday. Lt Col [illegible] to F.A. very dull.	
"	24		Major W. H. K. [illegible] attached to [illegible]. [illegible] COLINCAMPS working till 12 noon.	
"	25		Xmas holidays. Working parties at COLINCAMPS [illegible] 50 men B Coy on carrying party.	
"	26		Dull & cold. Conferences at COUIN [illegible]	
"	27		Frost-bite as usual. Frost in the morning. Work as usual. [illegible]	
"	28		Batt^n to take over command.	
"	29		Heavy rain. Batt^n relieved 13/King's Liverpool Regt in [illegible] sector. Relief complete at 9.20 pm. Enemy shelled [illegible] tramway from 2.15 pm till 8.30 pm. One man wounded in A Coy during relief. One man 13/King's stuck in mud for [illegible] hours [illegible] out [illegible] from [illegible].	

2449 Wt. W14957/M90 750,000 1/16 J.B.C. & A. Forms/C.2118/12.

Instructions regarding War Diaries and Intelligence Summaries are contained in F. S. Regs., Part II. and the Staff Manual respectively. Title Pages will be prepared in manuscript.

[WA]R DIARY
or
INTELLIGENCE SUMMARY
(Erase heading not required.)

Place	Date	Hour	Summary of Events and Information	Remarks and references to Appendices
	1916			
Trenches	Dec 30		Rain morning & evening. Enemy shelled sector from 6 pm to 9 p.m. One 18 pr Batt dropped several shells between our Front & Reserve line trenches. One 18 pr shell entered C.O's dug out who happened to be going round the trenches at the time.	
"	Dec 31		Fine. All our guns opened fire at 11 p.m. on enemy's lines for a few minutes. During day v. quiet.	
	1917		J. S. Burnett Major Cmdg 1/ London [illegible]	
"	Jan 1			

2449 Wt. W14957/M90 750,000 1/16 J.B.C. & A. Forms/C.2118/12.

SECRET. **76TH INFANTRY BRIGADE** Copy No.......3
20/12/16.

OPERATION ORDER NO.75.

1. The 76th Inf.Brigade will be relieved by the 9th Inf.Brigade on December 21st in the SERRE Sector.

2. The 2nd Bn.Suffolk Regt.will be relieved by the 1st Bn.Northumberland Fusiliers in the Right Sub-sector.
The 8th Bn.King's Own(R.L.)Regt.will be relieved by the 12th Bn.West Yorks in the Left Sub-sector.
The Guard of 1 N.C.O. and 3 men on "C" Dump at the junction of NORTHERN and JEREMIAH will be relieved by the 12th Bn.West Yorks.

3. The 76th Coy.M.G.C. will be relieved by the 9th Coy.M.G.C. on December 20th under arrangements to be made by O's C.Companies concerned. Completion of relief to be reported to Brigade Headquarters.

4. One Company of the 10th Bn.Royal Welch Fusiliers will be relieved by one Company of the 4th Bn.Royal Fusiliers in O.P.Dug-outs,SOUTHERN AVENUE. A water guard of 1 N.C.O. and 3 men will be found by this Company.

5. The detachment of 50 men of 1st Bn.Gordon Highlanders will be relieved by 13th Bn.King's(Liverpool)Regt.in HITTITE Dug-outs.

6. GUIDES. For 12th Bn.West Yorks one guide per company for advance
(a) parties to be at the junction of NAIRNE and PAPIN on the EUSTON-HEBUTERNE road at 2 p.m.
Guides at the rate of one per Lewis Gun will be at the same place at 3.45 p.m. and at the rate of one per platoon and one for Battalion Headquarters at 4 p.m.
(b) For 1st Bn.Northumberland Fusiliers one guide per company for advance parties to be at junction of RAILWAY AVE and EUSTON road at 2 p.m. Guides at the rate of one per Lewis Gun will be at the same place at 4.15 p.m. and at the rate of one per platoon at 4.30 pm
(c) The detachment of 1st Bn.Gordon Highlanders in HITTITE will supply two guides for the detachment of the 13th King's(L'pool)Regt. at the junction of NORTHERN AVE and the EUSTON road at 11.30 a.m.
The company of the 10th Bn.Royal Welch Fusiliers will supply four guides for the company of the 4th Bn.Royal Fusiliers at the junction of RAILWAY AVE and EUSTON road at 11 a.m.
An Officer will be in charge of guides at the rendezvous to tell them off for the incoming unit.

7. The C.T's will be RAILWAY AVE and NAIRNE ST. - UP, but all movement after dark will be,as far as possible,over the open. Movement over the top during daylight unless mist is sufficiently thick is forbidden.

8. All trench stores, maps, details of work and position of dumps will be properly handed over. The wire existing in front of the outpost line must be accurately shown to the incoming units by an Officer,but the relief need not be delayed for this purpose. Trench store cards to reach Brigade H.Q. by 10 p.m. one the night of 21st December.
A sufficiency of water for the ensuing 12 hours will be left in the line.
All Gum Boots must be changed in COURCELLES.
The 8th Bn.K.O.R.Lanc.Regt. is allotted billet No.30 and the 2nd Suffolks billet No.8 for this purpose. The gum boots,when changed,must be returned to the Store.
Parties marching back must be in ~~parti~~ formations of about 50 men under an Officer.

9. The 1st Bn.Gordon Highlanders will take over billets at COUIN from the 1st Bn.Northumberland Fusiliers.
The 10th Bn.Royal Welch Fusiliers will take over billets at LOUVENCOURT from ~~13th Bn.King's(L'pool)Regt.~~
The 2nd Suffolk Regt. and 8th K.O.R.L. will take over their usual billets in BUS.
Quartermasters of battalions concerned will make the necessary arrangements.

10. The 10th Bn. Royal Welch Fusiliers will relieve a party of 300 men with Officers of the 12th Bn. West Yorks in LOUVENCOURT on December 30th. This party, which is for work on roads, will leave COURCELLES at 8.30 a. and will be replaced by a similar ~~number~~ party of the 13th Bn. West Yor. A billeting party to proceed beforehand to make necessary arrangements.

11. The usual precautions for marching East of COURCELLES will be observed.

12. Completion of relief will be notified to Brigade H.Q. by the code word "WAILOIL".

13. On completion of relief Brigade Headquarters will move to Billet 101 at BUS.

14. Acknowledge.

Major,

Issued to Signals at 10.30 AM. Brigade Major, 76th Infty. Brigade.

Copies to:-

No.1 8th K.O.R.L.
2 2nd Suffolk Regt.
3 10th R.W.F.
4 1st Gordon Highrs.
5 76th Coy. M.G.C.
6 76th T.M.B.
7 8th Inf. Bde.
8 9th Inf. Bde.
9 3rd Div. G.
10 3rd Div. Q.
11 3rd Div. Arty.
12 Town Major, COURCELLES.
13. " BUS.
14. " LOUVENCOURT.
15. 94th Inf. Bde.
16. Office.
17. Diary.

SECRET.

Ref. Map 1/40000 Sheet 57D.

76TH INFANTRY BRIGADE

OPERATION ORDER NO.77.

Copy No....3..

31/12/16.

1. The following reliefs will be carried out in the sector held by the 76th Infty.Brigade on January 1st.

2. The 8th Bn.KING'S OWN(R.L)Regt.will relieve the 1st BN.GORDON HIGHLANDERS in the left sub-sector.
The 2nd Bn.SUFFOLK Regt. will relieve the 10th Bn.ROYAL WELCH FUSILIERS in the right sub-sector.

3. One company of the 10th Bn.ROYAL WELCH FUSILIERS will relieve the company of 2nd SUFFOLK Regt. in O.P.dugouts, SOUTHERN AVENUE.
One company of the 1st GORDON HIGHLANDERS will relieve the company of 8th KING'S OWN(R.L.)Regt in dugouts in HITTITE and PAPIN.

4. All reliefs will be carried out after dark, and will be over the open as far as possible. RAILWAY and NAIRN C.T's will be available for UP traffic.

5. Details of relief to be made between O's C.Battalions concerned.

6. Trench Store Cards are to reach Brigade Head Quarters by noon on January 2nd.

7. The 10th Bn.ROYAL WELCH FUSILIERS(less 1 company)will take over billets in COURCELLES from 2nd Bn.SUFFOLK Regt. and the 1st GORDON HIGHLANDERS(less 1 company)from the 8th KING'S OWN(R.L.)Regt.

8. Completion of relief will be wired to Brigade Head Quarters by the code word " FAIR " .

9. The usual precautions will be taken for movements East of COURCELLES.

10. Acknowledge.

S. Playfair
Lieutenant,
a/Brigade Major,76th Infantry Brigade.

Issued to Signals at 7.30pm

Copies to:-

No.1. 8th K.O.R.L.
2. 2nd Suffolk Regt.
3. 10th R.W.F.
4. 1st Gordon Highrs.
5. 76th M.G.C.
6. 76th T.M.B.
7. 8th Inf.Bde.
8. 9th Inf.Bde.
9. 3rd Div.G.
10. 3rd Div. Q.
11. 3rd Div.Artillery.
12. 76th Inf.Bde.Signals.
13. 94th Inf.Bde.
14. Town Major,COURCELLES.
15. 40th Bde.R.F.A.
16. Office.
17. War Diary.
18.
19.

S E C R E T

Copy No.........3

76th INFANTRY BRIGADE OPERATION ORDER No. 72.

5/12/16.

1. The 76th Infantry Brigade will be relieved in the SERRE Sector by the 9th Infantry Brigade on the 5th December.

2. The 2nd Suffolk Regiment in the right sub-sector will be relieved by the 1st Northumberland Fusiliers.
The 8th K.O.R.L.Regiment in the left sub-sector will be relieved by the 12th West Yorks Regiment
The guard of 1 N.C.O. and 3 men on "C" Dump at junction of Northern and Jeremiah will be relieved by 12th West Yorks Regiment.

3. 76th Machine Gun Company will be relieved by the 9th Machine Gun Company on 4th December under arrangements to be made between O's C. companies concerned.

4. The 76th Trench Mortar Battery will remain in dugouts North of East of COLINCAMPS and work on new emplacements in conjunction with 9th Trench Mortar Battery until the emplacements are finished.

5. Details of guides both for advanced parties and Lewis Guns, and also for remainder of battalions will be arranged direct between Officers commanding battalions.
An officer from each of the relieving battalions will proceed to the trenches on December 4th to arrange these details.

6. Loading platoon of 1st Northumberland Fusiliers will be at junction of RAILWAY and EUSTON-HEBUTERNE road at 4-15 p.m.
Loading platoon of 12th West Yorks Regiment will be at junction of NORTHERN and EUSTON-HEBUTERNE road at 5 p.m.

7. The following C.T's will be used :-

Right Subsector	UP	- RAILWAY - SACKVILLE - SOUTHERN
	DOWN	- BLENEAU - SACKVILLE - RAILWAY
Left Subsector	UP	- NORTHERN
	DOWN	- CENTRAL

After dark, all movement will be as much as possible over the open.

8. All Trench Stores, maps, details of work and lists of dugouts will be properly handed over. Trench store cards should reach Brigade H.Q. by 12 noon Decr. 6th properly completed and signed. All gum boots to be returned to Brigade gumboot store COURCELLES.

9. Completion of relief to be notified to Brigade H.Q.
Code word - ANGELINA.

10. On completion of relief Brigade H.Q. will move to Billet 101 BUS.

11. ACKNOWLEDGE.

Issued at 8 P.M.
Copies No.

N. Trevor
Captain,
For Brigade Major, 76th Inf. Brigade.

1.	8th K.O.R.L.Regt.	9	3rd Division. "G"
2	2nd Suffolk Regt.	10	" " "Q"
3	10th R.Welch Fus	11	94th Inf.Brigade.
4	1st Gordon Highlanders	12	Town Major, BUS.
5	76th M. G. Coy.	13	" " LOUVENCOURT
6	76th T. M. Bty.	14	Staff Captain.
7	8th Inf. Bde.	15	Office
8	9th Inf. Bde.	16	War Diary

3RD DIVISION
76TH INF. BDE

1ST BATTALION

GORDON HIGHLANDERS.

1917

1st Gordon Highlanders

WAR DIARY
or
~~INTELLIGENCE SUMMARY~~
(Erase heading not required.)

January 1917

Army Form C. 2118

Instructions regarding War Diaries and Intelligence Summaries are contained in F. S. Regs., Part II. and the Staff Manual respectively. Title Pages will be prepared in manuscript.

Place	Date	Hour	Summary of Events and Information	Remarks and references to Appendices
In the trenches "Serre" area	1st		At 5.0 a.m. a prisoner wandered over to our lines captured by Lance Corporal McKenzie (Cromarty). Battalion relieved by 8th K.O.R.L. Relief started at 4.0 p.m. completed at 9.0 p.m., marched back to billets in COURCELLES less one company left in Reserve trenches.	
COURCELLES	2nd		Rested	
	3rd		Relieved 8th K.O.R.L. in same trenches. Relief complete 7.0 p.m. a record	
In trenches	4th		While "D" Company was "standing down" at 5.30 p.m. enemy shelled FORT BRIGGS with H.E. getting two direct hits in the trench casualties 4 killed 2 wounded. Enemy art.y much more active than usual, shelling tramway and C.Ts.	
"	5th		At 5.30 p.m. enemy shelled FORT BRIGGS one direct hit on dug out buried sixteen men of "D" Coy. All dug out with assistance of King's Own by 4.0 a.m. two (wounded) At 10 p.m. relieved by 8th K.O.R.L. Relief completed by 4.30 a.m.	
COURCELLES	6th		Battalion marched to BERTRANCOURT at 6.30 a.m. Played through village by 2nd Battalion The Gordon Highlanders. Proceeding by lorries to RUBEMPRE arriving at 6.0 p.m.	

1875 Wt. W593/826 1,000,000 4/15 J.B.C. & A. A.D.S.S./Forms/C. 2118.

1st Gordon Highlanders

Instructions regarding War Diaries and Intelligence Summaries are contained in F. S. Regs., Part II. and the Staff Manual respectively. Title Pages will be prepared in manuscript.

WAR DIARY
or
~~INTELLIGENCE~~ SUMMARY
(Erase heading not required.)

January 1917
1 Gordon [illegible]

Army Form C. 2118

Vol 28

Place	Date	Hour	Summary of Events and Information	Remarks and references to Appendices
RUBEMPRE	7th		Rested. Sergeant Ross and 23 O.R. arrived from 3rd Battalion.	
	8th		Marched to PERNOIS (12 miles) very bad billets.	
PERNOIS	9th		Rested.	
	10th		Rested and organising companies as follows: Each platoon 1 bombing section 2 rifle (" ") 1 reserve Lewis gun section company 2 Lewis gun teams	
	11th		Ditto	
	12th		Ditto. Training commences. [illegible] the [illegible] in these billets the cold was intense, with [illegible] snow (12° frost)	
	13th		Ditto	
	14th		Following officers arrived from 3rd Battalion Capt. [illegible] (takes over command of "B" Coy) Lieuts. [illegible] (to "C" Coy) 2nd Lieuts. A.A. White and A.S. [illegible]	
	15th		Ditto. Finished up morning's work with a route march.	
	16th		Ditto. Lieut. D.C.D. Munro left to take over command of the HOOD Battalion, Naval Division.	

1875 Wt. W593/826 1,000,000 4/15 J.B.C. & A. A.D.S.S./Forms/C. 2118.

1st Gordon Highlanders

WAR DIARY
or
~~INTELLIGENCE SUMMARY~~
(Erase heading not required.)

Instructions regarding War Diaries and Intelligence Summaries are contained in F. S. Regs., Part II. and the Staff Manual respectively. Title Pages will be prepared in manuscript.

January 1917

Army Form C. 2118

Place	Date	Hour	Summary of Events and Information	Remarks and references to Appendices
PERNOIS	17th		Training	
	18th		Ditto	
	19th		Ditto. Sergeant HAMMOND and 23 O.R. arrived from 3rd Battalion.	
	20th		Ditto. Draft of 26 O.R. from ETAPLES arrived.	
	21st		Sunday.	
	22nd		Training. Battalion soccer team played EAST RIDING R.E. and won (8–1).	
	23rd		Training	
	24th		Training	
	25th		Training. Battalion bombing squad beaten by 2nd Suffolks.	
	26th		Training	
	27th		No training – preparing for move. Football team beaten by 8th R.O.R.L. (3–2).	
	28th		General Craufurd visited the Battalion. At 10.15 am. marched to AMPLIER. (14 miles) arriving 4.0 p.m., very crowded billets in huts	
	29th		at 10.45 am. marched to NEUVILLETTE. (10 miles)	
	30th		At 8.30 am. marched to FLERS (15 miles) arriving 4.0 p.m. 3rd DIVISION transferred to XVII Corps.	

1875 Wt. W593/826 1,000,000 4/15 J.B.C. & A. A.D.S.S./Forms/C. 2118.

1st Gordon Highlanders

WAR DIARY
or
~~INTELLIGENCE SUMMARY~~
(Erase heading not required.)

January 1917

Army Form C. 2118

Instructions regarding War Diaries and Intelligence Summaries are contained in F. S. Regs., Part II. and the Staff Manual respectively. Title Pages will be prepared in manuscript.

Place	Date	Hour	Summary of Events and Information	Remarks and references to Appendices
3	31st		Marched at 11.0 a.m. to PENIN (14 miles) arriving 2.30 p.m.	
			2/2/17 J. S. Burnett Lt Col Commanding 1st Gordon Highlanders	

1875 Wt. W593/826 1,000,000 4/15 J.B.C. & A. A.D.S.S./Forms/C. 2118.

1st Battalion The Gordon Highlanders

Details of Officers serving with Battalion on 31-[illegible]-17

Lt Colonel J. G. Burnett DSO
Major F. K. F. [illegible]
Captain G. W. A. Alexander
Captain J. A. Ross
Captain A. Fraser
Captain J. Lawrence
Lieut D. Buchan
Lieut W. S. Grant
Lieut A. Bathurst
2/Lt W. H. Paton
2/Lt [illegible] Bevir
2/Lt J. C. P. Campbell
2/Lt S. E. Lee
2/Lt J. D. D. MacLennan
2/Lt P. J. Pine
2/Lt E. C. Thorburn
2/Lt E. L. Mitchell
2/Lt A. S. Mackay
2/Lt H. B. Ock
2/Lt J. Sutherland
2/Lt J. G. G. Fleming
2/Lt G. P. Peterkin
2/Lt W. W. Hendrie
2/Lt W. E. Leathem
2/Lt H. F. Purton
2/Lt A. A. White
2/Lt R. K. Gordon
2/Lt W. K. G. Renfrew
2/Lt R. W. Preston
2/Lt D. Hutton
2/Lt J. Russell
2/Lt W. A. Muir

Officers Detached.

Lieut S. C. D. Munro. Temp Comdg "Hood" Battalion
Lieut J. Cumming. 13th Corps Head Quarters
2/Lt D. K. Templeton 13th Corps Hy Amm Park
2/Lt J. C. Seemes 5th Corps Headquarters
2/Lt G. Ritchie Town Major, Bertrancourt
2/Lt D. L. Scott At Field Ambulance
2/Lt C. Gemmill "
2/Lt J. C. Brown "
2/Lt J. Menzies "
2/Lt C. H. Smith "
Captain J. M. Cunningham Attached 76th Brigade

Officers Attached.

Captain J. L. Stewart M. O.
Rev: W. H. Leathem C. F.

Fighting Strength { O. 43 / O.R. 868 } Details O. 7 / O.R. 87

J. G. Burnett Lt Colonel
Commandg 1st Bn The Gordon Highlanders

SECRET.

Ref.Map.
1/40,000 Sheet 37D.

76TH INFANTRY BRIGADE

OPERATION ORDER No. 1.

Copy.No......3

2/1/17.

1. The following reliefs will be carried out in the Sector held by the 76th Infantry Brigade on January ~~2nd.~~ 3rd.

2. The 10th Bn.ROYAL WELCH FUSILIERS will relieve the 2nd Bn.SUFFOLK Regt. in the right sub-sector.
The 1st Bn.GORDON HIGHLANDERS will relieve the 8th Bn.KING'S OWN (R.L.)Regt. in the left sub-sector.

3. One Company of the 2nd SUFFOLK Regt. will relieve the Company of 10th ROYAL WELCH FUSILIERS in O.P.Dugouts in SOUTHERN AVENUE.
One Company of 8th KING'S OWN(R.L.)Regt.will relieve the Company of 1st GORDON HIGHLANDERS in dugouts in HITTITE and PAPIN.

4. Details of relief will be arranged between Os.C. concerned.

5. All reliefs will be carried out after dark and will be over the open as far as possible. RAILWAY and NAIRN C.T's will be available for UP traffic.

6. Trench Store Cards are to reach Brigade Head Quarters by noon on January 4th.

7. The 2nd SUFFOLK Regt.(less one company) will take over billets in COURCELLES from the 10th ROYAL WELCH FUSILIERS; and the 8th KING'S OWN(R.L.)Regt.(less 1 company)from the 1st GORDON HIGHLANDERS.

8. The usual precautions will be taken for movement East of COURCELLES.

9. Completion of relief will be wired to Brigade Head Quarters by the code word BETTER.

10. Acknowledge.

B Playfair
Captain,
a/Brigade Major,76th Infty.Brigade.

Issued to Signals at...8..p.m.

Copies to:-

No.1. 8th K.O.R.L.
2. 2nd Suffolk Regt.
3. 10th R. W. F.
4. 1st Gordon Highrs.
5. 76th M.G.C.
6. 76th T.M.B.
7. 8th Inf.Bde.
8. 9th Inf.Bde.
9. 3rd Div. G.
10. 3rd Div.Q.
11. 3rd Div.Artillery.
12. 76th Inf.Bde.Signals.
13. 94th Inf.Bde.
14. Town Major,COURCELLES.
15. 40th Bde.R.F.A.
16. Office.
17. War Diary.

File.

SECRET. 76th INFANTRY BRIGADE Copy No.......

Ref. Map. 1/40,000 sheet 57D. OPERATION ORDER NO.2. 4/1/17.

1. The following reliefs will be carried out in the sector held by the 76th Infantry Brigade on January 5th.

2. The 8th Bn. KING'S OWN(R.L.)Regt. will relieve the 1st Bn.GORDON HIGHLANDERS in the left sub-sector.
The 2nd Bn. SUFFOLK Regt. will relieve the 10th Bn.ROYAL WELCH FUSILIERS in the right sub-sector.

3. One company of the 10th Bn.ROYAL WELCH FUSILIERS will relieve the company of the 2nd SUFFOLK Regt. in O.P.Dugouts,SOUTHERN AVE.
One company of the 1st GORDON HIGHLANDERS will relieve the company of 8th Bn.KING'S OWN(R.L.)Regt. in dugouts in HITTITE and PAPIN.

4. All reliefs will be carried out after dark and will be over the open as far as possible. RAILWAY and NAIRN C.T's will be available for UP traffic.

5. Details of relief to be made between Os.C.Battalions concerned.

6. Trench Store Cards are to reach Brigade Head Quarters by noon on January 6th.

7. The 10th Bn.ROYAL WELCH FUSILIERS(less 1 company)will take over billets in COURCELLES from 2nd SUFFOLK Regt. and the 1st Bn.GORDON HIGHLANDERS(less 1 company)from 8th KING'S OWN(R.L.) Regiment.

8. Completion of relief will be wired to Brigade Head Quarters. "B.A.B." code will be used.

9. The usual precautions will be taken for movement East of COURCELLES.

10. Acknowledge.

[signature]
Captain,

Issued to Signals at........ a/Brigade Major,76th Infty.Brigade.

Copies to:-

No.1. 8th K.O.R.L.
2. 2nd Suffolk Regt.
3. 10th R.W.F.
4. 1st Gordon Highrs.
5. 76th M.G.C.
6. 76th T.M.B.
7. 8th Inf.Bde.
8. 9th Inf.Bde.
9. 3rd Div.G.
10. 3rd Div.
11. 3rd Div.Artillery.
12. 76th Inf.Bde.Signals.
13. 94th Inf.Bde.
14. Town Major,COURCELLES.
15. 40th Bde.R.F.A.
16. Office.
17. War Diary.

16.(a) Captain H.C.N.TROLLOPE, Suffolk Regt., will be in charge of Infantry guides at COURCELLES for guiding relieving units to where the trench guides meet them. He will be responsible that all parties of relieving battalions are provided with their correct guides.

(b) Captain E.T.WILLIAMS, 2nd Suffolk Regt., will be in charge of the Brigade Embussing arrangements at the embussing points.
1 Officer from each unit will report to him at their embussing point 1 hour before the convoy is due to leave.

17. The 1st Bn.GORDON HIGHLANDERS and 10th Bn.ROYAL WELCH FUSILIERS will take one blanket per man in busses with them: all other blankets will be loaded in the blanket lorries.

18. Destinations in the RUBEMPRE area are as follows:-

Brigade Head H.Q., M.G.Coy., 1/GORDON HIGHRS., 10/R.W.F.	RUBEMPRE.
8/K.O.R.L., 2/SUFFOLKS., 76th T.M.B., No.2 Coy.A.S.C.	PUCHEVILLERS.
7th Field Ambulance.	LE VAL-DE-MAISON.

19. Billeting parties will proceed with the first blanket lorry of their unit and report to the Town Majors concerned.

20. Brigade Head Quarters will close at COURCELLES on completion of reliefs on the night Jan. 7/8th.

21. Acknowledge.

S. Playfair

Captain,
a/Brigade Major, 76th Infty.Brigade.

Issued to Signals at...8p...m

Copies to:-

1. 8th K.O.R.L.
2. 2nd Suffolk Regt.
3. 10th R.W.F.
4. 1st Gordon Highrs.
5. 76th M.G.C.
6. 76th T.M.B.
7. 8th Inf.Bde.
8. 9th Inf.Bde.
9. 3rd Div. G.
10. .. Q.
11. .. Artillery.
12. 76th Inf.Bde.Signals.
13. 94th Inf.Bde.
14. Town Major, COURCELLES.
15. 40th Bde.R.F.A.
16. Office.
17. War Diary.
18. 7th Field Ambulance.
19. No.2 Coy.A.S.C.
20. 97th Inf.Bde.
21. Capt.TROLLOPE, 2nd Suffolks.
22. Capt.WILLIAMS, ...
23. Office.
24. ..

SECRET.

Ref. Maps 57D 1/40000
.. LENS 1/100000

76th INFANTRY BRIGADE

OPERATION ORDER NO.1.

Copy No...3...

5/1/1917.

1. The 3rd Division (less Artillery) will be relieved in the line by the 32nd Division on the 7th and 8th January 1917. On relief the 3rd Division will be withdrawn to the BEAUVAL and MARIEUX areas en route for the CANAPLES training area.

2. The 76th Infty.Brigade will be relieved in the Left Section by the 97th Infty.Brigade and will move to the RUBEMPRE area in accordance with the attached Relief and Embussing Tables.

3. All other details of reliefs will be made between Os.C.battalions concerned.

4. All documents, maps, plans and information relating to the present area will be handed over to relieving units. Trench Store Cards will be sent to Brigade Head Quarters as soon as possible after relief.

5. All reliefs will be overland after dark as far as is possible; there is to be no movement East of the line JEREMIAH-PAPIN before 4.30 p.m.

6. The completion of all reliefs will be wired to 76th Inf.Brigade Head Quarters in "B.A.B." code.

7. One Officer per Company of the 8th KING'S OWN (R.L.)Regt. and 2nd SUFFOLK Regt. well acquainted with the forward area will remain behind for 24 hours with their relieving battalions after relief.

8. The Command of the Brigade Sector will pass to the G.O.C., 97th Infty.Brigade on completion of the reliefs on the night Jan.7/8th.

9. Units of the 97th Infty.Brigade in COURCELLES and in immediate reserve, during the process of relief, will be under the tactical control of the G.O.C., 76th Infty.Brigade.

10. The Transport of the 76th Infty.Brigade (less that of 1st GORDON HIGHLANDERS and 10th ROYAL WELCH FUSILIERS) will move on Jan. 7th under the orders of G.O.C., 9th Infty.Brigade, to the RUBEMPRE - PUCHEVILLERS area.

11. The transport of 10th ROYAL WELCH FUSILIERS will march at 10 a.m. on 6th inst., followed by that of 1st GORDON HIGHLANDERS via AUTHIE-MARIEUX-PUCHEVILLERS to RUBEMPRE, where they will rejoin their battalions.
The BUS-LOUVENCOURT-MARIEUX road will not be used by troops marching, horses or motor transport.

12. The following distances will be maintained between units on the march:-

between companies or similar units - 200 yards.
between battalions - 500 yards.

13. All gum boots will be handed in to Brigade Gum Boot Store, COURCELLES, and a return of the numbers handed in will be sent at once to Brigade Head Quarters.

14. Soup will be available at the Divisional Soup Kitchen, COURCELLES for troops relieved from the line, and arrangements are being made for hot tea at the Embussing Points.

15. The Embussing Point in BUS will be along the LOUVENCOURT Road, the loading bus being at the corner of the LOUVENCOURT Road and the BUS-AUTHIE Road.

The Embussing Point at BERTRANCOURT will be the ACHEUX Road: the tail of the convoy being at the cross roads in BERTRANCOURT.

EMBUSSING TABLE ISSUED WITH 76th INFTY.BRIGADE OPERATION ORDER NO.3 d/d 5/1/17.

Date.	Unit.	Bus convoy serial number.	To march from.	Embus at Time.	Embus at Place.	Destination.	Remarks.
Jan. 6th.	1/GORDON HIGHRS. (less 1 company) 1 Coy. 10/R.W.Fus.	D/76	COURCELLES.	1.30 p.m.	BERTRANCOURT.	RUBEMPRE.	
Jan. 6th.	10/R.W.Fus. (less 2 coys.)	½C/76	COURCELLES.	2 p.m.	BUS.	RUBEMPRE.	
6th.	1 Coy.1/GORDON H. 1 Coy.10/R.W.Fus.	½C/76	Reserve trenches.	10 p.m.	BERTRANCOURT.	RUBEMPRE.	Times of embussing are subject to the completion of reliefs.
7th.	76th T.M.Btty.	C/8	Line.	12.30 p.m.	BUS.	PUCHEVILLERS.	with C/8 battalion (8th Brigade.)
7th.	76th M.G.Coy.	D/8	COURCELLES.	2 p.m.	BERTRANCOURT.	RUBEMPRE.	with D/8 battalion (8th Brigade.)
night 7/8th	8/K.O.R.Lancs. (with 8/M.G.C.)	A/76	Left subsector via COURCELLES.	mid-night.	BERTRANCOURT.	PUCHEVILLERS.	Times of embussing are subject to the
night 7/8th	2/SUFFOLK Regt. (with 8/T.M.B.)	B/76	Right subsector via COURCELLES.	mid-night	BERTRANCOURT.	PUCHEVILLERS.	completion of reliefs.

TIME TABLE OF RELIEFS ISSUED WITH 76th INFTY BRIGADE OPERATION ORDER NO.3. dated 5/1/17.

Date.	Unit.	Location.	Relieved by	Rendezvous for guides from COURCELLES. Place.	Time.	Rendezvous for trench guides. Place.	time.	Remarks.
Jan. 6th.	1/GORDON H. (less 1 coy).	COURCELLES.	16th H.L.I.					
6th.	10/R.W.Fus. (less 1 Coy).	COURCELLES.	17th H.L.I.					
Night of 6/7th.	1 Coy. 10th R.W.Fus.	O.P.Dugouts SOUTHERN AVE.	1 coy. 11th BORDER Regt.	COURCELLES CROSS Roads.	3.30 p.m.	EUSTON K.33.a.2.8	4.45 p.m.	
night of 6/7th.	1 Coy. 1/GORDON H.	Dugouts in PAPIN and HITTITE.	1 coy. 2nd K.O.Y.L.I.	COURCELLES CROSS Roads.	4. p.m.	Junction of EUSTON road & NORTHERN.K.27.a.8.8	5.15 p.m.	
night of 6/7th.	76th M.G.Coy.	LINE.	97th M. G. Coy.	H.Q.,76th M.G.Coy.	2. p.m.			
night of 6/7th.	76th T.M.Btty.	LINE.	97th T. M. Btty.	H.Q.,76th T.M.Btty.	3. p.m.			
night of 7/8th.	2nd Bn. SUFFOLK REGT.	Right Subsector.	17th H.L.I.	COURCELLES CHATEAU.	2.15 p.m.	Junction of RAILWAY AVE & EUSTON Guides for posts at Rt.Subsector H.Q.	4.15 pm 3.45 pm	
night of 7/8th.	8th Bn. K.O.R.LANCS.	Left Subsector.	16th H.L.I.	COURCELLES CHURCH.	2.30 p.m.	Battn.H.Q. Left subsector.	4.45 pm.	Garrisons of posts leave their platoons at CABER TRENCH and pick up 1 guide per post.

AMENDMENT to March Table in 76th Bde. O.O.70.

Guides for Advanced Parties and Lewis Gunners of 1st Gordon Highlanders will meet them at the junction of RAILWAY and HUSTON Road at 2-30 p.m.

Remainder of 1st Gordon Highlanders will go by NORTHERN as ordered, keeping overland as much as possible owing to the bad state of the trench.

Major,
Brigade Major, 76th Infantry Brigade.

SECRET 76th INFANTRY BRIGADE Copy No...3.

Reference LENS 1/100,000. OPERATION ORDER NO.6. 28th Jan.17.

1. The 3rd Division (less Artillery) will come under the orders of the Third Army from midnight January 28/29th.

2. The 76th Infantry Brigade will march on January 29th to the OCCOCHES Area in accordance with the attached march table.
The march will be resumed on January 30th and 31st.

3. Normal distances only will be maintained, and normal halts observed.

4. First line transport and baggage wagons will accompany units.

5. Parties will be detailed to march in rear of the transport, as in to-day's march.

6. Lorries have been asked for on the following scale, and should be at Town Major's Office AMPLIER at 8.15 a.m.

2 per Battalion.
1 for M.G.C.
1 for T.M.B.
1 for E.R.Fd.Coy.R.E.
1 for 7th Field Ambulance.

7. Billeting parties will meet the Staff Captain at the Level Crossing on the DOULLENS-RISQUETOUT road at 10.45 a.m.

8. Reports on the road to the head of the column.

9. Divisional Headquarters after 11 a.m. on January 29th - BOUQUEMAISON.

10. Brigade Headquarters will close at FRESCHEVILLERS at 10.30 a.m. and open at OCCOCHES on arrival.

11. Acknowledge.

/S.C. Langfair

Captain,

Issued to Signals at 11 pm a/Brigade Major, 76th Infantry Brigade.

Copies to:--

1. 8th K.O.R.L.
2. 2nd Suffolk Regt.
3. 10th R.W.F.
4. 1st Gordon H.
5. 76th M.G.C.
6. 76th T.M.B.
7. 8th Inf.Bde.
8. 9th Inf.Bde.
9. 3rd Div.G.
10. 3rd Div. Q.
11. 7th Field Ambulance.
12. 76th Brigade Signals.
13. Staff Captain.
14. No.2 Coy. A.S.C.
15. 1/1st E.R.Fd.Coy.R.E.
16. Town Major, DOULLENS.
17. .. .. AMPLIER.
18. Office.
19. War Diary.
20. Brigade Major.
21. 20th K.R.R.C.
22.

1st Battn The Gordon Highlanders

Instructions regarding War Diaries and Intelligence Summaries are contained in F. S. Regs., Part II. and the Staff Manual respectively. Title pages will be prepared in manuscript.

WAR DIARY
or
~~INTELLIGENCE SUMMARY.~~
(Erase heading not required.)

February 1917

Vol 29

Army Form C. 2118.

Place	Date	Hour	Summary of Events and Information	Remarks and references to Appendices
PENIN ~~[illegible]~~ grad	1st		Battalion rested. Helmet drill with new box respirator	
	2nd		Battalion training continued.	
	3rd		Battalion practised new attack formations.	
	4th		Voluntary Church parade at 11.30 a.m. The [illegible] band attended.	
	5th		Battalion training	
	6th		Battalion had a combined attack practice with 76th Trench Mortar Battery.	
	7th		Battalion training.	
	8th		Battalion marched to WANQUETIN VIA AVESNES LE COMTE — HAUTEVILLE (11 Miles) Billets fair. C.O. – 2nd in command and one company commander went to a Gas lecture.	
WANQUETIN	9th		Battalion rested. Officers visited trenches I 1 Sector East of ARRAS.	
	10th		Parades under Coy. arrangements in preparation for the [illegible]	
	11th		Voluntary church parade at 12.0 noon. Battalion paraded at 4.30 p.m. & marched up to the trenches via WARLUS and DAINVILLE	

A6945 Wt. W11422/M1160 350,000 12/16 D. D. & L. Forms/C./2118/14.

1st Batn The Gordon Highlanders

Instructions regarding War Diaries and Intelligence Summaries are contained in F. S. Regs., Part II. and the Staff Manual respectively. Title pages will be prepared in manuscript.

WAR DIARY
or
~~INTELLIGENCE~~ SUMMARY.
(*Erase heading not required.*)

February 1917

Army Form C. 2118.

Place	Date	Hour	Summary of Events and Information	Remarks and references to Appendices
WANGUETIN	11th (contd)		Halt for teas on the march. Relieved 11th Middlesex Regiment. Relief complete by 11.30 p.m. Situation quiet. Owing to the continuous frost the trenches were in very good condition.	
IN THE LINE	12th		Quiet day. 2 casualties from T. Mortar (slight wounds) in "A" Coy. C, B and A Companies in front line finding their own supports and "D" Coy in reserve	
	13th		Quiet. Work done on Reserve line and wiring of saps in front system. G.O.C. visited the line.	
	14th		Quiet	
	15th		Quiet. Relieved in the afternoon by 10th Royal Welsh Fusiliers, and went into reserve billets in ARRAS.	
ARRAS	16th		Battalion rested. 2Lieuts R. D. Passey and C. L. Maclean reported.	
	17th		Battalion supplied working parties.	
	18th		Ditto. Voluntary church parade at 6.0 p.m.	
	19th		Battalion tested the new box-respirators in a gas room. Relieved 10th Royal Welsh Fusiliers in the afternoon, dispositions	

A6945 Wt. W11422/M1160 350,000 12/16 D. D. & L. Forms/C./2118/14.

1st/4 Battn. The Gordon Highlanders

Instructions regarding War Diaries and Intelligence Summaries are contained in F. S. Regs., Part II, and the Staff Manual respectively. Title pages will be prepared in manuscript.

WAR DIARY
or
~~INTELLIGENCE~~ ~~SUMMARY~~.
(Erase heading not required.)

February 1917

Army Form C. 2118.

Place	Date	Hour	Summary of Events and Information	Remarks and references to Appendices
	19th		Same as the previous tour. 30 other ranks reported and posted to "B" Coy.	
IN THE LINE	20th		Slight trench mortar activity on "A" Coy. casualties 2 killed and 2 wounded.	
			Trenches began to fall in owing to the thaw setting in. 2Lieut L. F. Henry joined	
	21st		Quiet. Rainy trenches got worse	
	22nd		Quiet. Work devoted to support line	
	23rd		Quiet. Battalion relieved by 10th Royal Welsh Fusiliers. "B" Coy took over St Sauveur	
			defences instead of "D" Coy.	
ARRAS	24th		Battalion supplied various working parties. 39 O.Rs (Royal Scots) joined from	
			Camerons and posted to "D" Coy as a platoon.	
	25th		Voluntary church service. "C" Coy practised for the "raid". 28 O.Rs reported	
			from base.	
	26th		Battalion supplied working and carrying parties. Lieut T. C. [illegible] rejoined from Course 2 [illegible]	
	27th		Battalion was relieved by 1st Royal Scots Fusiliers and marched to	
			WANQUETIN. "B" Coy was left in St SAUVEUR defences.	
WANQUETIN	28th		The Battalion marched at 10.30 a.m. en route for HOUVIN-HOUVIGNEUL via [illegible]	
			—AVESNES LE COMTE—ETRÉE WAMIN. (12 miles). Fair billets "A" Coy billeted in	

A6945 Wt. W11422/M1160 350,000 12/16 D. D. & L. Forms/C./2118/14.

1st Battn The Gordon Highlanders

Instructions regarding War Diaries and Intelligence Summaries are contained in F. S. Regs., Part II. and the Staff Manual respectively. Title pages will be prepared in manuscript.

WAR DIARY
or
~~INTELLIGENCE SUMMARY.~~
(Erase heading not required.)

February 1917

Army Form C. 2118.

Place	Date	Hour	Summary of Events and Information	Remarks and references to Appendices
	28th (contd)		BLAVINCOURT for work in wood-cutting. "C" Coy billeted at LIENCOURT in order to practise over the trenches for the raid.	
HOUVIN-HOUVIGNEUL	1st/III		Battalion rested.	

G. W. Alexander Capt. for Lieut. Col.
Commanding 1st Battn The Gordon Highlanders

A6945 Wt. W11422/M1160 350,000 12/16 D. D. & L. Forms/C./2118/14.

S E C R E T. 76th INFANTRY BRIGADE Copy No. 4.

Ref LENS 1/100,000

OPERATION ORDER (Special.) 1/2/17.

1. The 3rd Division is now in XVIIth Corps Reserve.

2. Units of 76th Inf.Bde. will be prepared to move at 2 hours notice, with ammunition and tool wagons, pack animals and L.G. handcarts.

3. Upon receipt of orders, giving the hour of zero, units will march as follows:-

Starting Point. Cross roads ½ mile South of First N in LA MON ROUGE INN, on the AUBIGNY - ARRAS road.

Route. ~~AUBIGNY~~ - HAUTE AVESNES.

Unit.	Time to reach S.P.
10/ R.W.Fus.	Zero
1 Section 76th M.G.Coy.	Zero plus 5 minutes.
8/K.O.R.L.	Zero plus 7 do
1/Gordon Highrs.	Zero plus 12 do
2/Suffolk Regt.	Zero plus 17 do
76th M.G.Coy.(less 1 Section.)	Zero plus 22 do
76th T.M.Bty.	Zero plus 25 do

Routes to the starting Point to be reconnoitred forthwith.

4. Reports after zero to the head of the column. A Brigade H.Q. representative will remain at PENIN.

5. Dress: Marching Order.
120 rounds S.A.A.
Unexpended portion of days ration.
Iron ration.

Water bottles are to be filled every evening.

6. The remainder of the transport will move under the orders of the Staff Captain.

7. Acknowledge.

[signature]
Captain,
a/Brigade Major 76th Inf.Bde.

Issued to Signals at .. P.M. ..

1.	G.O.C.	8.	Brigade Major.
2.	8th K.O.R.L.	9.	Staff Captain,
3.	2nd Suffolk Regt.	10.	76th Bde. Signals.
4.	10th R.W.Fus.	11.	3rd Div. G.
5.	1st Gordon Highrs.	12.	
6.	76th M.G.Coy.	13.	
7.	76th T.M.Bty.	14.	

SECRET. 76TH INFANTRY BRIGADE. Copy N

Ref. ARRAS. 1/10,000 Ed. 6A.

OPERATION ORDER NO. 13. 22nd February 19[illegible]

1. The following reliefs will take place in the Sector held by the 76th Infantry Brigade on the night February 23/24th.

(a) The 10/Rl.Welch Fusiliers will relieve the 1/Gordon Hldrs in the line.

(b) 1 Company 1/Gordon Hldrs will relieve 1 Company 10/Rl.Welch Fusiliers in the ST.SAUVEUR Defences.

2. Details of relief will be made by Os.C. concerned.

3. On relief the 1/Gordon Hldrs (less 1 Company) will take over billets in ARRAS from 10/Rl.Welch Fusiliers (less 1 Company).

4. Trench Store Cards will reach Brigade Head Quarters by noon on February 24th.

5. Acknowledge.

[illegible signature]

Captain,

Issued to Signals at 3.30 p.m. a/Brigade Major, 76th Infantry Brigade.

Copies to:-

No.1. G.O.C.
2. 8/K.O.R.L.Regt.
3. 2/Suffolk Regt.
4. 10/Rl.Welch Fus.
5. 1/Gordon Hldrs.
6. 76/M. G.Company.
7. 76/T. M.Battery.
8. 76/ Bde.Signals.
9. 3rd Division"G".
10. 3rd Division"Q".
11. 36th Infty. Bde.
12. 42nd Infty. Bde.
13. Newzealand Tunnelling Coy.
14. Town Major, ARRAS.
15. WEST Group R.F.A.
16. Brigade Major.
17. Staff Captain.
18. File.
19. War Diary.
20.

SECRET

1st Bn The Gordon Highlanders

Operation Orders by Lt Col. L. G. Burnett D.S.O.
Commanding

22nd Feb, 1917

---

1. The Battalion will be relieved by 10th Bn Royal Welch Fusiliers in the line tomorrow 23rd inst and proceed to the same Billets formerly occupied in Arras.
'B' Coy will garrison ST SAVEUR REDOUBT, 'D' Coy occupying 'B' Coys Billets.
Relief will commence at 3.0 p.m.
2. O.C. 'B' Coy will provide Guides for 'D' Coy and O.C. 'D' Coy will provide Guides to Conduct 'B' Coy to their dispositions in ST SAVEUR REDOUBT. These Guides to be outside 'D' Coys HQrs at 3.0 p.m.
3. ROUTES

"A" Coy IMPERIAL STREET
'B' Coy IODINE and IMPERIAL STREET
'C' Coy ICELAND STREET

A two minute interval will be maintained between platoons.
4. The R.S.M will parade a Carrying Party from the Headquarter Details at 12.0 Noon to carry 'B' Coys Blankets from the Quartermasters Stores and stack them at the Brigade Canteen. One Regimental Police will remain in charge of them till drawn by 'B' Coy
5. Reports to ~~x~~ [relief] Battalion Headquarters
Trench Store Lists will be sent to Headquarters by 11 a.m

G W Alexander

Captain

A/Adjt 1st Bn The Gordon Highlanders

AMENDMENT.

Reference 76th Infantry Brigade O.O. No.14.

para.10. - for WANQUETIN read HAUTEVILLE.

26/2/17.

Distribution. as for O.O.14.

[Signature] Capt
BM 76 Inf Bde

SECRET.
Ref. ARRAS
1/10000 Ed.3A.
LENS.
1/10000 Ed.[illegible]

76th INFANTRY BRIGADE

OPERATION ORDER No.14.

Copy No. 4.

25th February/17.

1. The 76th Infantry Brigade will be relieved by the 8th Infantry Brigade in I 1 Sector on February 27th and 28th and will move to the FOUVIN HOUVIGNEUL and WANQUETIN areas in accordance with the attached table of reliefs.

2. (a) The 10/Rl.Welch Fusiliers will be relieved in the line on 28th Februaryby the 1/Rl.Scot Fusiliers; relief to be completed by 10 a.m.

(b) 1 Company 1/Gordon Hldrs. will be relieved in ST.SAUVEUR Defences by 1 Company 8/E.Yorks.

3. The 76/M.G.C. and 76/T.M.B. will be relieved in the line by the 8/M.G.C. and 8/T.M.B. respectively on February 27th.

4. Details of reliefs will be arranged between Os.C. concerned.

5. (a) The command of the Sector will pass to the G.O.C., 8th Inf.Bde. on completion of the relief of the 10/Rl.Welch Fusiliers by the 1/Rl.Scot Fusiliers on February 28th.

(b) Until the command passes, troops of the 8th Inf.Bde. in ARRAS will come under the tactical control of G.O.C., 76th Inf.Bde.

(c) On assuming command of the Sector the G.O.C., 8th Inf.Bde.will assume tactical control of any units of 76th Inf.Bde. in ARRAS.

6. Trench Store Cards will be sent to Brigade H.Q. as soon as possible after relief.

7. Orders as to Billeting Parties and lorries will be issued separately.

8. 2/Suffolk Regiment and 1/Gordon Hldrs. will continue to provide their usual working parties up to and including all parties who parade for work on February 28th: and the 8/K.O.R.L. will find their usual parties up to and including those who parade for work on Feb.27th.

9. Guides will be provided as follows:-

[illegible]	By.	To meet.	At.	Time	Detail.
Feb.26th	76/T.M.B.	8/T.M.B.	Road junction G.25.b.5.3	7-00 pm	1 guide.
26th	76/M.G.C.	8/M.G.C.	--do--	7-15 pm	do
27th	2/Suffolks.	7/K.S.L.I.	--do--	7-30 pm	1 per Coy.)
27th	1/Gordon H.	1/R.S.F.	--do--	8-15 pm	1 for Bn.H.Q.)
28th	10/R.W.F.	1/R.S.F.	Bn.H.Q.1 Rue des Ganguiors.	6-00 am	1 per Platoon.) 1 for Bn.H.Q.)
28th	8/K.O.R.L.	2/R.Scots.	Road junction G.25.b.5.3	7-00 pm	1 per Coy.) 1 for Bn.H.Q.)
28th	1/Gordon H.	1 Coy. 8/E.Yorks. (for ST.SAUVEUR)	--do--	8-00 pm	1 guide

---

10. Brigade H.Q. will close at ARRAS at 10-30 a.m. on February 28th and open at WANQUETIN on arrival.

11. Acknowledge.

I S C Playfair
Captain,
a/Brigade Major, 76th Infantry Brigade.

Issued to Signals at 3/pm

for distribution P.T.O.

Copies issued to:-

No. 1. G.O.C.
2. 8/K.O.R.L.Regt.
3. 2/Suffolk Regt.
4. 10/Rl.Welch Fus.
5. 1/Gordon Hldrs.
6. 76th M.G.Company.
7. 76th T.M.Battery.
8. 76th Bde.Signals.
9. 3rd Division."G".
10. 3rd Division."Q".
11. 36th Infty Bde.
12. 42nd Infty.Bde.
13. 8th Infty. Bde.
14. 9th Infty. Bde.
15. Newzealand Tunnelling Coy.
16. Town Major,ARRAS.
17. " " WANQUETIN.
18. " " HAUTEVILLE.
19. " " HOUVIN-HOUVIGNEUL.
20. No.2 Co.A.S.C.
21. 7th F.A.
22. 42nd Bde. R.F.A.
23. Brigade Major.
24. Staff Captain.
25. File.
26. War Diary.
27.
28.

Operation Orders

MARCH AND RELIEF TABLE TO ACCOMPANY 76TH INFTY.BRIGADE OPERATION ORDER NO.14 d/- 25/2/17.

Date.	Unit.	Location.	Relieved by.	Destination.	Remarks.
Feb.27th	76th M.G.C.	Line	8th M.G.C.	ARRAS.	By day.
Feb.27th	76th T.M.B	Line	8th T.M.B.	ARRAS	by day.
Night 27/28	2/Suffolk Regt.	ARRAS	7th K.S.L.I.	HAUTEVILLE	To pass AMIENS gate,ARRAS, (G.27.a.2.9) at 6 p.m.
..	76th M.G.C.	..	-	HAUTEVILLE	do do 6.30 p.m.
..	76th T.M.B.	.	-	WANQUETIN	do do 3.45 p.m.
..	1/Gordon H. (less 1 Coy.)	..	1st R.S.F.	WANQUETIN	do do 7.-- p.m.
Feb.28th	10/R.W.F.	Line	1st R.S.F.	ARRAS	By day.
..	2/Suffolk Regt.	HAUTEVILLE.	-	HOUVIN-HOUVIGNEUL.	To march at 10 a.m.
..	1/Gordon H. (less 1 Coy.)	WANQUETIN	-	HOUVIN-HOUVIGNEUL.	.. .. 10-30 a.m.
Night 28/1st	8/K.O.R.L.	ARRAS	2nd R.Scots.	WANQUETIN.	To pass AMIENS gate,ARRAS, (G.27.a.2.9) at 3 p.m.
..	10/R.W.F.	..	-	HAUTEVILLE	do do 6.30 p.m.
..	1 Coy.1st G.H.	ST.SAUVEUR	1 Co.8/E.Yorks.	HAUTEVILLE	To march after relief.
March 1st.	1 Coy.1st G.H.	HAUTEVILLE	-	HOUVIN-HOUVIGNEUL.	To march at 10.30 a.m.

Companies will proceed through ARRAS at 200 yards interval. Normal halts and distances will be observed West of DAINVILLE
Route - DAINVILLE - WARLUS - HAUTEVILLE - LIENCOURT - ETREE WAMIN.

SECRET.
Ref.LENS sheet 11
Ed.2. and
ARRAS 1/10000
Ed.3 A.

76TH INFANTRY BRIGADE

OPERATION ORDER No.10.

Copy No....4...

9th Feby.1917.

1. The 76th Infantry Brigade will relieve the 36th Infantry Brigade in the portion of the line between G.35.b.8.0 and G.30.c.85.20 on the night 11th/12th February.

2. The 1/Gordon Highlanders will relieve the 11/Middlesex Regt. in the line, and 1 company 10/Rl.Welch Fusiliers will relieve 1 company 9/Royal Fusiliers in ST.SAUVEUR defences, in accordance with Relief Table attached.

The 10/Rl.Welch Fusiliers (less 1 company) will take over billets from the 6/Buffs in ARRAS. Billeting party of 10/Rl.Welch Fusiliers will report to Town Major, ARRAS at 2.30 .m. on February 11th.

3. The above reliefs are to be completed by 10 a.m. on February 12th.

4. 76th M.G.C. and 76th T.M.B. will relieve 36th M.G.C. and 36th T.M.B. respectively in the line under arrangements to be made between O's C. concerned.

These reliefs to be completed by 10. a.m. February 11th.

5. The Brigade front will be covered by 1 battery 18 pdrs. and 1 section 4.5 Howitzers of 'I' Group, 12th Divisional Artillery.

6. After relief the boundaries of the Brigade for purposes of defence will be as follows:-

Southern boundary (with 43rd Infty.Brigade) G.35.b.8.0 - G.35.b.20.45-HUNTLE ST.(exclusive) to G.35.a.45.65 - G.35.a.2.9 - G.28.d.15.80.

Northern boundary (with 11/Middlesex Regt) G.30.c.85.20 - G.30.c.25.25 - thence along the road to G.29.c.75.85 thence to G.28.b.65.30.

7. The 10/Rl.Welch Fusiliers will detail a working party of 200 men to work with the NEW ZEALAND Tunnelling Company from February 12th inclusive. Arrangements to be made by O.C., 10/Rl.Welch Fusiliers with O.C., New Zealand Tunnelling Comp.ny.

8. Trench Store Cards will reach Brigade Headquarters by 6 p.m. on February 12th.

9. Transport of units and details will remain as at present.

10. Brigade Headquarters will open at 9 bis RUE CHATEAUDUN, ARRAS at 9 p.m. on February 11th.

11. Acknowledge.

Issued to Signals at..10.20pm..

S.Playfair.
Captain,
a/Brigade Major,76th Infantry Brigade.

Copies to:-

No.1. G.O.C.	10. 8th Inf.Bde.	20. 76th Bde.Signals.
2. 8/K.O.R.L.	11. 9th Inf.Bde.	21. Town Major ARRAS.
3. 2/Suffolks.	12.36th Inf.Bde.	22. File.
4.10/R.W.F.	13.43rd Inf.Bde.	23. War Diary.
5. 1/Gordon H.	14.12th Div.Arty.	24.
6.76/M.G.C.	15. 7th F. A.	25.
7.76/T.M.B.	16.1/1 E.R.Fd.Coy.	26.
8. 3rd Div.G.	17.No.2 Coy.A.S.C.	27.
9. 3rd Div.Q.	18.Bde.Major.	
	19.Staff Captain.	

RELIEF TABLE to accompany 76th INFANTRY BRIGADE OPERATION ORDER NO.10.

Unit.	Date.	From.	To.	In relief of	Guides at Road junction G.25.5.5.3.	Trench guides.	Remarks.
76th T.M.B. (less 2 sections)	Feb.10th	WANQUETIN.	ARRAS & Line.	36/ T.M.B.	7 p.m.		
76th M.G.C. (less 3 sections)	Feb.10th	HAUTEVILLE.	do.	36/ M.G.C.	7 p.m.		
1/Gordon H'ldrs.	Feb.11th	WANQUETIN.	Line.	11/Middlesex Regiment.	1 per coy. and 1 for Battn.Hqrs. at 7 p.m.	1 per platoon & 1 for Bn.Hqrs.at ARRAS STATION at 7.30 p.m.	
10/Rl.Welch Fusiliers.	Feb.11th	HAUTEVILLE.	ARRAS.	6/Buffs.	1 per coy.and 1 for Battn.Hqrs. at 7.30 p.m.		Not to enter WANQUETIN before 4.30pm on Feb.11 th.
1 Coy. 10/R. W. F.	Feb.12th	~~ST.SAUVEUR.~~ ARRAS.	ST.SAUVEUR.	1 coy. 9/R. F.		1 per platoon at 10/R.W.F.Hqrs billet ARRAS at 8 a.m.	

COMPANIES WILL PROCEED THROUGH ARRAS AT 5 MINUTES INTERVAL.

SECRET.
Ref.ARRAS
1/10000
Ed.6A.

76th INFANTRY BRIGADE

OPERATION ORDER No.11.

Copy No 11...

14/2/17.

1. The following reliefs will take place in the Sector held by the 76th Infantry Brigade on the night February 15/16th.

(a) The 10/R.W.F. will relieve the 1/Gordon Highlanders in the line.

(b) 1 Company 1/Gordon Highlanders will relieve 1 Company 10/R.W.F. in the ST.SAUVEUR Defences.

2. Details of relief will be made by Os.C. concerned.

3. On relief the 1/Gordon Highlanders (less 1 Company) will take over billets in ARRAS from the 10/R.W.F. (less 1 Company).

4. Trench store cards will reach Brigade Headquarters by noon on February 16th.

5. Orders as to handing over of work under the O.C., New Zealand Tunnelling Co. will be issued later.

6. Acknowledge.

[signature]

Captain,

Issued to Signals at 8 pm a/Brigade Major, 76th Infantry Brigade.

Copies to:-

No.1 G.O.C.
2. 8th K.O.R.L.
3. 2nd Suffolks.
4. 10th R.W.F.
5. 1st Gordon H.
6. 76th M.G.C.
7. 76th T.M.B.
8. 76th Bde.Signals.
9. 3rd Div.G.
10. 3rd Div.Q.
11. 36th Inf.Bde.
12. 42nd Inf.Bde.
13. Newzealand Tunnelling Coy.
14. Town Major, ARRAS.
15. 'I' Group R.F.A.
16. Brigade Major.
17. Staff Captain.
18. File.
19. War Diary.
20.

OPERATION ORDER No.21.

Ref. Trench Map 1/5000.

by Capt. X.
Commanding 'B' Company.

Copy No....

1. INTENTION.

The intention of the attack tomorrow is to capture the enemy's front and second system of trenches.

2. OBJECTIVE.

The objective allotted for the battalion is to capture a portion of the front system (BLACK LINE on map). The second system will be captured by the supporting battalion.

3. BOUNDARIES.

The Company and Platoon Boundaries are as shown on attached map.

4. FORMATION.

The Company will attack on a 2 Platoon front with 2 Platoons in support.

5 & 6 Platoons in 1st Wave No.5 on right.
7 & 8 Platoons in 2nd Wave No.7 on right.
Waves will be 100 yards distant.
MOPPERS UP will be between the 1st and 2nd Waves.

5. PLACE OF ASSEMBLY.

1st Wave and MOPPERS UP will assemble in our front line trench.
2nd Wave behind parados of our front line trench.

6. ADVANCE & BARRAGE ARRANGEMENTS.

The advance will be by the left. The 1st. and 2nd. Waves will go right through to the objective. At ZERO the barrage will open 50 yards in front of GERMAN front line. At ZERO plus 1 minute the barrage will lift on to German front line when 1st and 2nd Waves will get out of the trenches and form up in NO MAN'S LAND. At ZERO plus 4 minutes the barrage will move forward at the rate of 50 yards every minute until it reaches a line 300 yards in front of BLACK LINE. The barrage must be followed closely by the 1st. Wave.

7. STRONG POINTS.

These are suspected M.G. emplacements at the following points :- A.30.c.75.80, A.30.c.75.60 and A.30.d.40.80.

8. CONSOLIDATION.

The line to be consolidated is the BLACK LINE. The work must be commenced as soon as it is captured. Numbers 5 and 6 Platoons will establish an outpost line 100 to 200 yards in front of BLACK LINE by pushing forward each, 1 N.C.O. and 6 men with a Lewis Gun to occupy suitable shell holes on the Company front.

9. COMPANY H.Qrs.

Up to ZERO minus 10 minutes Coy.H.Qrs.will be in H.Qrs.Dugout in GHOST AVENUE. From ZERO minus 10 minutes until objective is gained Coy.H.Qrs.will be at junction of leading line of Nos.7.&.8. Platoons. On reaching objective Coy.H.Qrs.will be established at A.30.d.40.70.

10. REPORTS.

From ZERO situation reports will be rendered by Platoon Commanders every hour.

11. FLARES.

Platoon Commanders will be prepared to light their flares at ZERO plus 45 minutes. The flares will actually be lit when the contact aeroplane calls for them by sounding a succession of 'As' on the Klaxton Horn or dropping a white light.

12. MOPPERS UP.

The Moppers Up are provided by the supporting battalion. The 2nd. line of Moppers Up will clear GERMAN front line. 1st. line of Moppers Up will clear KOMMANDEUR Trench.

13. DUMPS.

The Battalion Dump is in our front line immediately behind KING Crater. Brigade Dump at Junction of GHOST AVENUE and SPOOK trench.

14. DRESS & EQUIPMENT.

Dress, Fighting Order; 1 Pick or shovel to be carried by every man except 1 and 2 of Lewis gun section, in proportion of 1 pick to 2 shovels. Every man will carry 170 rounds S.A.A. except Signallers, Lewis gunners and Runners who will carry 50 each. Rifle Grenadiers will carry 8 complete rifle grenades and 5 spare rounds of blank ammunition. Bombing sections will carry 5 bombs for each thrower and the remainder 10. Each Officer and N.C.O. will carry 2 Flares. One days rations will be carried in addition to the Iron Ration. Water bottles will be filled.

15. ZERO HOUR & SYNCHRONISATION OF WATCHES.

Zero hour will be at 4.0.am.tomorrow. Platoon Commanders will synchronise watches at 8.pm.and 10.pm.to night and again at Zero minus 30 minutes.

(sgd) X Captain.
Commanding 'B' Coy.

T R E N C H   T O   T R E N C H   A T T A C K.

N A R R A T I V E.

The Division to which you belong has been holding the trenches known as the ROCLINCOURT Sector for the past 3 months. Your battalion has been holding the Sub-Sector as shown on the attached map, approximately 1000 yards of front. A secret Memorandum issued to all Officers has made it plain that an offensive is to take place on a wide front which includes the ROCLINCOURT Sector. With this knowledge the Officers of your battalion have been reconnoitring the system of trenches from which your battalion is to attack, which is of course a much narrower front than that which you have been holding. The boundaries allotted to your battalion in the attack are on the right A.30.c.4.3 to A.30.d.5.3. and on left A.30.c.3.9. to A.30.d.4.9.

Careful reconnaissance has been made of the enemy's trenches opposite this front by observation of all kinds assisted by aeroplanes photos both plan and oblique. The wire in front of enemy's front line has been systematically cut by our T.Ms. for some weeks past and a successful daylight raid carried out by your battalion with a large proportion of officers has not only increased the morale of your battalion but enabled those officers who took part to get a fair idea of the enemy's front and support lines in the neighbourhood.

For the last ten days your Brigade has been out training for this offensive and have practised every phase of the attack on dummy trenches laid out exactly to scale, with names of all trenches, the various dumps HQRS of Units, etc., carefully marked.

Thus every Officer, N.C.O. and man is acquainted with his duties in the coming offensive as far as it is possible to be under practice conditions. Your battalion together with the 1st Blankshires is detailed to take the first objective or BLACK LINE as marked on the attached map, the remaining 2 battalions providing the MOPPING UP parties in this first attack. After the taking of the BLACK LINE these 2 RESERVE BATTALIONS will advance through the BLACK and proceed to the second objective (not shown on the map) and your battalion and 1st BLANKSHIRES provide the MOPPERS UP.

Your battalion is attacking with 2 Coys. in front line and 2 in Reserve, 'A' on the right, 'B' on left, with 'C' and 'D' in reserve 'C' on right, 'D' on left. The frontage of your Company which is 'B' Company is from KING Crater inclusive to the left of the Battalion boundary.

Your Platoon (No.8) forms part of the 1st wave and your frontage is as shown on attached map.

ZERO hour in the offensive has been fixed at 4.am tomorrow. Your battalion which is now in ARRAS leaves its billets at 11.pm tonight to get into its allotted position by 3.am.

Although every detail has been practised and all instructions are known, the following orders have been issued by your Company Commander -

P.T.O.

O.C. A Coy.

(i). please distribute to offrs of your coy.
(ii). map referred to may be seen in O.R.
(iii). C.O. is liable to ask questions

E. Chase 2/6

QUESTIONS.

1. You are in charge of the platoon. What do you see to as regards your men before the attack takes place ? Time limit 5 minutes.

2. What steps have you taken to ensure that all your men know where to obtain material and where to deliver messages after they have started on the attack.
Time limit 5 minutes.

3. A Machine gun is holding up your platoon at the position indicated to you - the platoon on your left is also held up - the platoon on your right continues to advance. State briefly what action you take.
Time limit 5 minutes.

4. Having captured the Machine gun and the barrage having in the meantime advanced some distance ahead of you. Describe briefly how you would advance, the enemy having opened rifle fire and machine gun fire on you from objective.
Time limit 5 minutes.

5. The objective having been captured what action do you now take ?

Time allowed 10 minutes.

****

1st Battn The Gordon Highlanders

WAR DIARY

or

~~INTELLIGENCE SUMMARY.~~

(*Erase heading not required.*)

March 1917

Vol 20

Sheet 1

Army Form C. 2118.

Instructions regarding War Diaries and Intelligence Summaries are contained in F. S. Regs., Part II. and the Staff Manual respectively. Title pages will be prepared in manuscript.

Place	Date	Hour	Summary of Events and Information	Remarks and references to Appendices
HOUVIN-HOUVIGNEUIL	March 1		Cleaning up. B + A Coys rejoined from detachment	
	2		Training. C.O took over command of Bde, Brigadier being on leave. Capt Cross took over command of Bn	
	3		Training.	
	4		Church voluntary service. C. Coy. left ~~LIGNEREUIL~~ LIENCOURT for ARRAS to carry out raid.	
	5		Successful raid carried out by 'C' Coy under Capt. W.H.S. GRANT in snowstorm 21 prisoners and 1 m.g. captured 11 Germans killed. Casualties Capt GRANT 4 O.R. slightly wounded.	
	6		C Coy rejoined	
	7		Training. Draft 26. O.R from ETAPLES	
	8		Snow.	
MAGNICOURT	9		March to MAGNICOURT 1 mile Billets fair.	
	10		Route march. Draft 23 O.R from ETAPLES.	
	11		Rain. Church voluntary service.	
	12		Training. Lt Colonel J. G. BURNETT D.S.O. resumed command.	

A6945 Wt. W11422/M1160 350,000 12/16 D. D. & L. Forms/C./2118/14.

1st Batt: The Gordon Highlanders

WAR DIARY
or
~~INTELLIGENCE~~ SUMMARY.
(*Erase heading not required.*)

March 1917

Army Form C. 2118.

Sheet 2

Instructions regarding War Diaries and Intelligence Summaries are contained in F. S. Regs., Part II. and the Staff Manual respectively. Title pages will be prepared in manuscript.

Place	Date	Hour	Summary of Events and Information	Remarks and references to Appendices
MAGNICOURT	13		Training	
	14		Lt Gen HALDANE commanding 6th Corps inspected battalion and complimented them on their smart appearance. He presented the undermentioned with Military Medals for gallantry during recent raid	
			L/Cpl CHRISTIE Ptes BLACK, LAMBIE & GARSIDE	
	15		Officers watch 9th Bde attack over practice trenches.	
	16		Training	
	17		Do.	
LIENCOURT	18		Bn marches to billets in LIENCOURT. Draft 51 O.R.	
	19		Very cold Training	
	20		Do	
	21		Attack practice	
	22		Bde. do. Afternoon baths at BERLENCOURT	
	23		Bde attack practice	
	24		do	
	25		Church voluntary service	

A6945 Wt. W11422/M1160 350,000 12/16 D. D. & L. Forms/C./2118/14.

1st Battn The Gordon Highlanders

Instructions regarding War Diaries and Intelligence Summaries are contained in F. S. Regs., Part II. and the Staff Manual respectively. Title pages will be prepared in manuscript.

WAR DIARY
or
~~INTELLIGENCE SUMMARY.~~
(Erase heading not required.)

March 1917

Sheet 3

Army Form C. 2118.

Place	Date	Hour	Summary of Events and Information	Remarks and references to Appendices
LIENCOURT	26		Heavy rain. Bde attack practice	
	27		Rain & snow. Following officer joined Capt. W.P.M RUSSELL M.C. LE FIENNES	
	~~28~~		Rugby football match v. 8th K.O.R.L. Beaten 15 - nil	
	28		Training	
	29		Heavy rain	
	30		Training	
	31		Demonstration by 1 Platoon B Coy. of capture of strong point with live grenades & bombs	

2/4/17

J S Burnett Lt Col
Cmdg Gordon Highrs

A6945 Wt. W11422/M1160 350,000 12/16 D. D. & L. Forms/C./2118/14.

1st Battn. The Gordon Highlanders

Roll of Officers serving with Battalion on 31-3-17

Lt. Colonel J. L. G. Burnett D.S.O. Commanding

Capt. H. P. M. Russell M.C. — Second in Command
" G. W. A. Alexander — Adjutant
2/Lt. W. L. G. Renfrew — Transport Officer
Lt. P. J. Pirie — Asst Adjt.

A Coy

Capt. N. Fraser (Commanding)
Lt. D. Buchan
2/Lt. R. K. Gordon
" J. O. F. McLennan
" D. L. Scott
" C. L. McLean

B Coy

Capt. A. R. Cross (Commanding)
Lt. J. G. Fiennes
2/Lt. R. W. Preston
" J. Russell
" C. C. Thorburn
" J. H. Muir
" A. S. McKay

C Coy

Capt. A. Bothwell M.C. (Commanding)
2/Lt. D. C. Scoones M.C.
" G. Sutherland
" R. D. Passey
" H. B. Cook
" J. C. P. Campbell

D Coy

Capt. J. B. Lawrence M.C. (Commdg)
2/Lt. H. J. Paintan
" W. M. Hendrie
" W. G. Leatham
" J. G. S. Fleming
" G. M. Berry

2/Lt. N. M. Paton — Signalling Officer
" S. E. Lee — Bombing Officer

Officers Detached

Lt. J. Cumming — 13th Corps H.Q.
2/Lt. D. K. Templeton — 13th Corps H.Q. Amm Park
2/Lt. J. M. Cunningham — 76th Bde H.Q.
" A. A. White — 76th T.M. Battery
" G. Ritchie — Town Major Berlencourt
" J. McWilliam — At F.A.
" D. Hutton — On Leave
" L. F. Humbly — On Leave

Officers Attached

Capt. J. L. Stewart — M.O.
Rev. W. A. Leathem — C.F.

	O.	O.R.
Strength	40	1021
Details	3	40

J. L. G. Burnett

Lt. Colonel
Commanding 1st Bn The Gordon Highlanders

1st Bn. The Gordon Highlanders

WAR DIARY
or
~~INTELLIGENCE SUMMARY.~~
(Erase heading not required.)

April 1917. 76/3 Army Form C. 2118.

Instructions regarding War Diaries and Intelligence Summaries are contained in F. S. Regs., Part II. and the Staff Manual respectively. Title pages will be prepared in manuscript.

Sheet 1.

Vol 31

Place	Date	Hour	Summary of Events and Information	Remarks and references to Appendices
	April			
LIENCOURT	1st		Voluntary church parade 11.0am. Cold + showery	
— " —	2nd		Windy, cold. Bde. practise attack over trenches at LIENCOURT	
	3rd		Cold + snow. Battn. to baths at BERLENCOURT.	
	4th		Cold. Battn. rested + prepared for move. Battn. paraded at 5.30 pm. and marched to WANQUETIN. Major A de R LONG and Capt. R.A. WOLFE MURRAY joind Battn.	
WANQUETIN	5th		Fine. Battn rested + prepared for operations, spare kits being dumped. Move at 6.30pm. postponed 24 hrs.	
	6th		Battn. rested.	
	7th		Battn. paraded at 6.30 pm. for ARRAS. Billeted in cellars and H.Q. in a ~~house~~ in Rue Pastour.	
ARRAS.	8th		Battn. prepared for move to assembly positions, bombs, shovels flares etc being drawn. At 6.0 pm. first Coy. moved via tunnel to assembly position. No casualties. O.C. Coy + 2nd in command	
	~~9th~~		of 8th K.O.R.L. Coy attached, killed in ARRAS while parading for assembly positions.	

A6945 Wt. W11422/M1160 350,000 12/16 D. D. & L. Forms/C./2118/14.

1st Batt. The Gordon Highlanders

Instructions regarding War Diaries and Intelligence Summaries are contained in F. S. Regs., Part II. and the Staff Manual respectively. Title pages will be prepared in manuscript.

WAR DIARY
or
~~INTELLIGENCE SUMMARY.~~
(Erase heading not required.)

~~March~~ April 1917.

Army Form C. 2118.

Sheet 2.

Place	Date	Hour	Summary of Events and Information	Remarks and references to Appendices
ARRAS (TRENCHES)	9th		Fine. Zero hour 5.30 am. and Battn attacked (See O. Os.)	
	10th		(See O. Os).	
	11th		(See O. Os).	
	12th		Battn. in tunnel having arrived at about 8.0 am.	
	13th		Battn. left tunnel at 8.30 pm. to take over billets in ARRAS.	
ARRAS.	14th		Battn. rested and cleaned up	
	15th		Battn rested kit inspections etc.	
	16th		Raining. Coys under Coy arrangements in billets.	
	17th		Battn. paraded + cards for recognition given out by C.O.. G.O.C. Brigade spoke to Battn. Moved billets to Rue Pasteur.	
	18th		Rained heavily. Coys under O.C. Coys in billets	
	19th		Batt. went out to practise wiring. Armourer Sgt. inspected rifles.	
	20th		Battn. prepared to move. G.O.C., C.O. Adjt. and Coy. Commdrs went out to reconnoitre routes to VIth Corps front. Move put off till 22nd. Accident. Sgt Manson and 2 O.R. wounded while	

A6945 Wt. W11422/M1160 350,000 12/16 D. D. & L. Forms/C./2118/14.

1st Batt. The Gordon Highlanders

Instructions regarding War Diaries and Intelligence Summaries are contained in F. S. Regs., Part II. and the Staff Manual respectively. Title pages will be prepared in manuscript.

WAR DIARY

or

~~INTELLIGENCE SUMMARY.~~

(Erase heading not required.)

~~March~~ April 1917.

Army Form C. 2118.

Sheet - 3.

Place	Date	Hour	Summary of Events and Information	Remarks and references to Appendices
ARRAS.	20th		while extracting bullets for firing Rifle Grenades.	
	21st		Battn. training. A + B. C + D Coys. practised attack. Massed bands 1st, 6th, 8/10th + 9th Battns. played in Barbed wire Square.	
	22nd		Battn. prepared for move. Voluntary church parade 11.45 am in Salle des Concerts.	
	23rd		Battn. moved to trenches W. of BOIS DES BOEUF at 6.0 pm. Fine day. Divn in Corps Reserve.	
MONCHY LEPREUX	24th		Bde. took over line E of MONCHY LEPREUX from 86th Bde of 29th Divn at 3.0 am. during relief hostile art. opened fire result 35 casualties.	
	25th		Intermittent shelling. No C.Ts. Battn. H.Q. very heavily shelled and practically blown in.	
	26th		Bn. H.Q. moved to dugout occupied by H.Q. of R.W.F., K.O.R.L. + K.S.L.I. Heavy shelling by day + much sniping by night.	
	27th		Heavy shelling. Hostile aeroplane brought down in our lines by 8th K.O.R.L. 9.15 pm enemy attacked K.O.R.L. + "B" Coy + were	

A6945 Wt. W11422/M1160 350,000 12/16 D. D. & L. Forms/C./2118/14.

1st Batt. The Gordon Highlanders

WAR DIARY
or
~~INTELLIGENCE SUMMARY.~~
(Erase heading not required.)

~~March~~ April 1917.

Army Form C. 2118.

Sheet 4.

Instructions regarding War Diaries and Intelligence Summaries are contained in F. S. Regs., Part II. and the Staff Manual respectively. Title pages will be prepared in manuscript.

Place	Date	Hour	Summary of Events and Information	Remarks and references to Appendices
MONCHY	27th		were repulsed, 4 prisoners captured casualties 3 O.R.	
LEPREUX.	28th		Front + support lines shelled Capt. BOTHWELL + 2nd Lieut. HUNTLEY killed. Sniping worse	
	29th		Intermittent shelling. Snipers got 5 men. Men detailed in each Platoon to fire at ground level much reduced sniping.	
	30th		Still in trenches.	

R. A. Wolfe-Murray Major
for Lt. Colonel
Commdg. 1st Bn. The Gordon Highlrs.

A6945 Wt. W11422/M1160 350,000 12/16 D. D. & L. Forms/C./2118/14.

1st Battalion The Gordon Highlanders

Roll of Officers serving with Battalion on 30/4/17.

Lt Col J.L.G. Burnett D.S.O. Commanding
Major A de L. Long Second in Command
Capt C.W.A. Alexander Adjutant
Lt. D.Y. Pirie Asst Adjt
2/Lt D.R.G. Renfrew Transport Officer

A Coy
Capt R.A. Wolfe Murray (Comdg)
2/Lt. R.K. Gordon
" D. Hutton
" J. Russell
" A.G. McLennan

B. Coy
Lt J.G. Fiennes (Comdg)
2/Lt. C.C. Leatham
" J.A. Muir

C. Coy
2/Lt. A.A. White
" H.B. Cook
" J.C.P. Campbell

D. Coy
Capt. J.B. Lawrence M.C (Comdg)
2/Lt J.G.G. Fleming
" A.S. McKay
" J. Mcniven
" R.W. Preston

2/Lt N.M. Paton Signalling Officer
" R.D. Passey Bombing Officer

Officers Detached.

Capt W.P.M. Russell M.C 76th Brigade H.Q.
2/Lt. J.M. Cunningham " "
" D.A. Templeton
" G. Ritchie 13th Corps Hq. Amm. Park A.S.C
" C.L. McLean Town Major Berlincourt
At. F.A.

Officers Attached

Capt J.L. Stewart M.O.
Rev W.H. Leathem C.F.

Strength {Officers - 28 / Other Ranks - 755} Details {Officers - 3 / Other Ranks - 46}

R.A. Wolfe Murray Major
for Lt Colonel
Commanding 1st Gordon Highlanders

30/4/17.

Report on Operations at Arras
9th to 11th April 1917.

The Battalion having received orders from the Brigade to take part in the assault on the first four German Lines of Trenches, proceeded to ARRAS on the 6th April and went into caves.

8th At 6.0 p.m. the Battalion plus one Company H.O.R.L. Regiment proceeded to the Assembly Trenches via the Tunnel in the following order:-

1st Line:- C Coy under 2/Lt J.C. [illegible], M.C.
B Coy under Captain A.R. Cross
Support Line:- D Coy under 2/Lt H.A. Paxton
A Coy under Captain W. Fraser
3rd Line:- B Coy 5th H.O.R.L. Regiment. Captain Fiddes having been killed on the way to the Assembly Trenches, this company was taken over by Lieut Young H.O.R.L.

Total Frontage - TWENTY STREET to SAP 56, about 490 yards.

9th At 5.30 a.m. - zero hour - the heavy bombardment started and the Battalion advanced in the following formation:-

Two waves of two companies each; each Company on a two platoon frontage.

Little opposition was encountered, the wire was reported well cut and the fourth objective (GLASGOW and GATESHEAD Trenches from NEW GERMAN TRENCH to 76) was reached at the scheduled time 5.50 a.m. Consolidation was proceeded with, strong points being formed at B - C - and D.

The approximate casualties up to this point were 60.

The two front Coys Headquarters were established at the ruin in centre of GLASGOW Trench and the 4th GERMAN LINE south of TILLOY Road.

By this time the Kings Own had cleared and formed a garrison in trenches X and Y facing south. The 10th Royal Welsh Fusiliers passed through 1st Gordon Highlanders and made good the far edge of DEVILS WOOD. The slight casualties experienced are attributable to the fact that all the waves were clear of our front line trenches before the German barrage came down. Touch was maintained on the left with the 6th Queens throughout.

No machine gun fire was encountered until reaching the second line. Battalion Headquarters remained in the tunnel.

The fact that the communication between Companies Battalion and Brigade was never lost is attributed to the fact that the Battalion Headquarters were not moved but that a Report Centre was established by [illegible] in Y Trench in the German third line, with telephone communication to Battalion Headquarters.

About 11.30 a.m. the 1st Gordon Highlanders were placed under the orders of the G.O.C. 8th Infantry Brigade.

At 12.40 p.m. the following message was received "1st Gordons will move forward to BOIS-DES-BOEUFS and secure left flank of 8th Infantry Brigade. They will get into touch with the 7th KSLI and 8th East Yorks. and support them if necessary. 1st R.S.F. and 8th KORL are in reserve"

The Battalion Headquarters which had been moved forward to the third German Line at 1 p.m. was further advanced to "NOISY REDOUBT" about 3 p.m. and was again moved to a point on the TILLOY Road South of BOIS-DES-BOEUFS at 4.30 p.m.

The attack of the 8th Infantry Brigade on the Brown Line having failed, an order by telephone was received at 6.25 p.m. that the 1st Gordon Highlanders with the 8th KORL Regt on their right would attack the Brown Line at 7 pm and with the information that the 12th Infantry Division had taken FEUCHY CHAPELLE and the Grid south of the CAMBRAI ROAD. This information proved to be incorrect.

The 8th Kings Own did not receive their orders until 6.50 pm with the result that the Battalion attacked the Brown Line alone and was enfiladed from FEUCHY CHAPELLE with Machine Gun fire. The Battalion had to fall back to the neighbourhood of the FEUCHY CHAPELLE Road where they dug themselves in.

At a conference of Commanding Officers at 12 Mid-night, the GOC 8th Infantry Brigade decided that the Gordon Highrs and Kings Own should be withdrawn in Reserve to a trench running north and south in front of BOIS DES BOEUFS and that the Brigade should take the Brown Line at 12.15 am on the 10th.

10th The attack on the Brown Line having proved successful the Battalion was replaced under the command of the G.O.C 76th Brigade.

11th At 5.25 am an order was received that the Brigade would attack GUEMAPPE at 6.30 am. The 8th KORL on the left, 2nd Suffolks on the right, 10th Royal Welsh in Support and 1st Gordon Highlanders in Reserve. The 14th Division were reported to be attacking WORNCOURT at 6 am; zero hour was subsequently altered to 7 am.

The Battalion in due course moved up as far as the Brown Line with Headquarters in German Artillery Dugouts 200 yards in front.

The situation now became rather obscured and it was finally ascertained that the firing line was held up by Machine Gun Fire south of LA FOSSES FARM; the men were sheltered in shell holes.

The Suffolk Headquarters were moved to our H'qrs. An advanced Observation post with telephonic communication was set up on a Ridge and the Battalion was in communication with the Kings Own

4

and Brigade.

At 1.45 pm the Commanding Officer received instructions from Brigade by telephone that the Gordons and Kings Own would attack GUEMAPPE at 3.0 pm, the Kings Own to [illegible] the assault [illegible] on the left of the Gordons [illegible] with them. [illegible] that our flanks were [illegible] at WANCOURT. This information proved to be incorrect. The Kings Own [illegible] were scattered [illegible] still [illegible] unable to [illegible] the orders in time and the attack was held up after heavy casualties by the enemy machine gun fire from the village of GUEMAPPE and from both flanks.

Reorganisation or withdrawal was impossible during daylight. Heavy snowfall set in. The Battalion dug itself in and was finally relieved by the 11 Northumberland Fusiliers about 2 am. All the available tools were handed over to this unit to allow them to consolidate the position.

The Battalion marched back to the ARRAS [illegible] where it arrived at 8 am in an exhausted state.

Total Casualties during the whole operations were 13 Officers 263 other ranks.

R. A. Wolfe Murray Major
for
Lieut Colonel
Comdg. 1 Bn. The Gordon Highlanders

WAR DIARY

SECRET.

OPERATION ORDERS by Lieut-Col. J.G. Burnett, D.S.O.

Commanding 1st. Battalion The Gordon Highlanders.

1. On Z day at zero hour, the Battalion will attack and consolidate GATESHEAD and GLASGOW Trenches from the junction of GATESHEAD with the NEW GERMAN TRENCH which runs from the southwest of TILLOY village to SAP W. 10 inclusive to .16 north of the CAMBRAI ROAD exclusive.

2. The 37th. Infantry Brigade of the 12th. Division is attacking on our left.

The 10th. Royal Welch Fusiliers will pass through us and capture the DEVILS WOOD. The 8th. K.O.R.L. Regt. will eventually consolidate GARELOCH and GATESHEAD Trenches on our right.

3. The Attack will be on a front of two companies, each on a front of two platoons.

The advance will be in four waves.

1st and 2nd Waves "C" Coy. on right) Objectives :- 1st & 2nd.German
"B" Coy. on left,) Lines.

3rd and 4th Waves "D" Coy. on right) Objectives :- 3rd & 4th German
"A" Coy. on left) Lines (GILLINGHAM and GLASGOW Trenches)

Distance between waves 30 yards. The second wave to leave Assembly Trenches simultaneously with first.

The attached company of 8th. K.O.R.L. Regt will follow immediately behind the 3rd and 4th. wave in rear of "D" Coy.

FRONTAGES. Right Companies from NEW GERMAN Trench to SAP W.12 both inclusive.

Left Companies from TILLOY ROAD exclusive to .30 inclusive.

4. ASSEMBLY TRENCHES.

Front Line North of TWENTY STREET - "C" and "B" Coy's.

Support Line North of TWENTY STREET - "D" and "A" Coy's with attached Company of 8th. K.O.R.L. Regt.

Boards have been placed in Assembly Trenches marking the right and left of each platoon with company letters.

5 LEWIS GUNS

O.C. "B" and "C" Coy's will place two Lewis Guns each in shell holes in front of our barbed wire at zero minus 30 minutes to engage enemy machine guns and riflemen firing from the front line or shell holes. They will rejoin their platoons as the latter pass them.

6. In the event of a hold-up occurring to the 12th. Division on our left, "A" and "D" Coys. will push on to their original objectives and will not form a defensive flank to the left. A defensive flank to the left will be formed by the 10th. Royal Welch Fusiliers.

7. INSTRUCTIONS ON REACHING OBJECTIVES COMPANIES CONSOLIDATE AS UNDER.

"D" Coy. 4th. and 3rd. Lines from NEW GERMAN Trench to Road running south of DEVILS WOOD inclusive.

"A" Coy. 4th. and 3rd. Lines from Road to Trench Junction at .16 and G.36 b.8.8 both inclusive.

O.C., "A" Coy will immediately make good the house on N.west edge of DEVILS WOOD on reaching the fourth line.

"C" Coy. 1st and 2nd Lines from NEW GERMAN Trench to Road both inclusive.

"B" Coy. from Road exclusive to .30 and along Trench running to .78 both inclusive.

Attached Coy. The attached Coy. of the 8th. K.O.R.L. Regt will mop up and form garrison of trenches facing south as under:-

(1) Right two platoons - Trench Junction NEW GERMAN Trench and second line to point about G.36.d.5.6 both inclusive.

(2) Left two platoons - Trench junction G.36 b.4.5 on German second line to a point about G.36.d.8.8 both inclusive.
O.C. this company will establish his Headquarters with that of "D" Coy. 1st. Gordon Highlanders.

STRONG POINTS.

"D" Coy. (1) Junction of NEW GERMAN Trench and GATESHEAD Trench (G.36 d 4.9.)

(2) about G.36 b 4.5.

"A" Coy. About junction of GILLINGHAM Trench and the CAMBRAI ROAD.

A Party of R.E's with material have been detailed to assist in the construction of these points.
Coy's will place Lewis Guns in them until the arrival of the 76th, Machine Gun Coy, Guns.

8. DUMPS BRIGADE.

S.A.A.: BOMBS. (1) Tunnel G.36.a.1.3 off EIGHTEEN STREET.
(2) Tunnel G,36.a.4.6 off TWENTY STREET.
(3) Tunnel G.36.a.2.9 off IMPERIAL STREET.
R,E.STORES. (1) FIFTEEN STREET and Craters north of it at G,35,b.7.2.
(2) South of IMPERIAL STREET and west of STRAFE WOOD at G,30.c.1.2.
RATIONS AND WATER. 76th, Brigade Dump in Tunnel off EIGHTEEN ST.

DUMPS - FORWARD REGIMENTAL. Forward Dumps for S.A.A. and Bombs Grenades, and R,E, Stores will be placed as under.

(a) By No.1 and 3 Carrying Parties and centre of second objective (about G,36.b.4.5)
(b) By No,2 and 4 Carrying Parties at about G,36.b.60.35 centre of third objective.

Two Lewis Gunners from "A" and "D" Coys will remain at Dump B and two from "B" and "C" Coys. at Dump A for the purpose of charging Lewis Gun Magazines. A proportion of Regimental Bombers for looking after the bombs will also be at these two points.
2/Lt. Lee will appoint a man in charge of each dump who will acquaint "C" and "B" Coys Headquarters in the case of Dump A and "A" and "D" Coys Headquarters in the case of Dump "B" when the stores arrive.

9. CHARGING OF LEWIS GUN MAGAZINES.
Coys, will send all empty Lewis Gun Magazines to either Dump "A" or Dump "B" for re-charging. The eight Lewis Gunners for these dumps will report to 2/Lt. Lee at Battalion Headquarters at zero minus 60.

10. CARRYING PARTIES.
No. 1 Party (No, 1 Platoon 8th. K.O.R.L.) to carry wiring material Guides, three Pioneers 1st Gordon Highlanders.
No. 2 Party (No. 2 Platoon 8th. K.O.R.L.) to carry wiring material Guides, three Pioneers 1st Gordon Highlanders.
No, 3 Party (No. 3 Platoon 8th, K.O.R.L.) to carry S.A.A., Rifle Grenades and Bombs; Guides three Bombers 1st Gordon Highrs,
2/Lt, Lee will be responsible for detailing guides and dispatching of all carrying parties. He will remain at the S.A.A.Dump in the mouth of EIGHTEEN STREET Tunnel. Guides will report to him there on return from each journey.

11. S.O.S. SIGNALS.
To be kept at Coy, Headquarters and only to be used on the order of a Company Commander.

12. PRISONERS.
All Prisoners to be sent to Battalion Headquarters.

13. POLICE.

The Police will be under the Regimental Sergeant Major, who will provide escorts to take Prisoners to Brigade Headquarters and furnish two control posts at mouths of Tunnels (a) in TWENTY S.. and (b) in Support Line near IODINE STREET.

14. DRESS - EQUIPMENT.

As in S.S. 135 Section 31. Great coats will not be worn Shovels will be carried as under:-
Rifle Sections:- 1 per man, Lewis Gun Sections:- 2 per team.
Bombing Sections:- 2 per section. Grenade Sections:- 1 per man.
Bombing and Rifle Grenade Sections will be equipped as per previous instructions.

15. MEDICAL.

The Regimental Aid Post will be at G.3[illegible].a.5.8. in IODINE STREET.

16. RATIONS.

One Iron Ration plus the unexpended portion of the current days ration will be carried. On the evening of Z day, one Iron Ration per man will be issued under arrangements which will be notified for consumption on Z plus one day.

17. SIGNALS.

Signallers will not accompany companies in the assault. As soon as objective is reached, a Signalling Station will be established in a convenient dugout in German second or third line near CAMBRAI ROAD. This will be used as a Report Centre and will be in Signal Communication with Battalion Headquarters. As soon as this Report Centre is established four Orderlies from Battalion Headquarters will report to Signal Officer there who will inform the Companies of its position. The dugout will be marked by a "Signallers White Flag".

All written messages as well as signal messages should be sent here by Company Commanders and these will be sent on to Battalion Headquarters as soon as possible.

18. HEADQUARTERS.

BRIGADE. At EIGHTEEN STREET Branch of Tunnel behind the Support Line.

BATTALION. TWENTY STREET Tunnel. Entrances (a) TWENTY STREET in Support Line (b) in NO MANS LAND which will be marked by flags.

6/4/17

(sgd) [illegible].W.A. Alexander, Captain,
A/Adjutant 1st Bn. The Gordon Highlanders.

1st Battalion The Gordon Highlanders

26/5

1 Gordon Hrs

Vol 32

WAR DIARY
or
INTELLIGENCE SUMMARY.
(Erase heading not required.)

Army Form C. 2118.

Instructions regarding War Diaries and Intelligence Summaries are contained in F. S. Regs., Part II. and the Staff Manual respectively. Title pages will be prepared in manuscript.

Place	Date	Hour	Summary of Events and Information	Remarks and references to Appendices
	May		Bn. was relieved by 1st R.S.F. and moved into [illegible] N of TILLOY.	
TILLOY	1st		Captain W. J. Graham joined the Battalion	
—	2nd		Battalion rested in trenches north of TILLOY.	
—	3rd		Battalion moved to the BROWN LINE in relief of the 1st R.S.F.	
—	4th		In BROWN LINE resting	
—	5th		— ditto —	
—	6th		— ditto — Working Parties of [illegible] Companies [illegible]	
—			of MONCHY in conjunction with R.O.R.E. [illegible]	
—	7th		BROWN LINE. Work as 6th, 1420 [illegible]	
—	8th		Orders for relief of 9th Brigade received and put off. [illegible] and	
—			[illegible] Lieuts [illegible] Wilson, [illegible] and [illegible] joined Battalion [illegible]	
—	9th		BROWN LINE. Relief again put off.	
MONCHY-LE-PREUX	10th		Battalion relieved 9th Brigade (R.[illegible] [illegible]). [illegible]	
			Coy. and "A" Coy. in support	
—	11th		Captain Davey and 2/Lt F. W. Broadhurst [illegible]	
			Fairly quiet — MONCHY [illegible] shelled in the evening.	
—	12th		Fairly quiet. London [illegible] attacked and captured [illegible]	

A6945 Wt. W11422/M1160 350,000 12/16 D. D. & L. Forms/C./2118/14.

1st Bn The Gordon Highlanders

Instructions regarding War Diaries and Intelligence Summaries are contained in F. S. Regs., Part II. and the Staff Manual respectively. Title pages will be prepared in manuscript.

WAR DIARY
or
~~INTELLIGENCE~~ SUMMARY.
(Erase heading not required.)

May 1917.
Sheet 2.

Army Form C. 2118.

Place	Date	Hour	Summary of Events and Information	Remarks and references to Appendices
MONCHY-LE-PREUX	12th	(Contd)	Enemy retaliated heavily on MONCHY Defences and VINE LANE. A 9.2 of	
—			ours was dropping short on our front line. Casualties 2/Lt J.D.F. MacLennan	
—			killed and 6 O.R. casualties.	
—	13th		Enemy shelled front and support system intermittently – 8 Casualties.	
—	14th		Battalion relieved by Inniskillings. Relief was delayed by [illegible] crossing	
			Bridge Way [illegible] C.T. and relief was not completed till 4.0 a.m. A	
			mist being prevalent during the morning saved the Battalion from having heavy	
			casualties – Casualties 6 OR.	
DUISANS	15th		Battn had tea at TILLOY and then embussed for DUISANS by Companies	
			and slept rest of day. This concluded a tour of 23 days in the trenches,	
			the longest done by the Bn since 1915. Total Casualties 5 Officers (all killed) & 89 O.R.	
—	16th		Battn cleaned up and rested. Bath Parade at 5 p.m. postponed owing to heavy rain.	
NOYELLETTE	17th		Battn moved to NOYELLETTE and arrived at 1 p.m. Men and Officers in	
			Nissen Huts – [illegible] comfortable.	
AMBRINES	18th		Battn moved to AMBRINES at 5 p.m. Coys at disposal of Coy Commanders	
			in morning. Billets poor but cramped.	

A6945 Wt. W11422/M1160 350,000 12/16 D. D. & L. Forms/C./2118/14.

1st Bn The Gordon Highlanders

Instructions regarding War Diaries and Intelligence Summaries are contained in F. S. Regs., Part II. and the Staff Manual respectively. Title pages will be prepared in manuscript.

WAR DIARY
or
~~INTELLIGENCE SUMMARY.~~
(*Erase heading not required.*)

May 1917

Vol 3

Army Form C. 2118.

Place	Date	Hour	Summary of Events and Information	Remarks and references to Appendices
AMBRINES	19th		Lieut L. G. D. Mann M.C. joined from England. Coys at disposal of Coy Commanders	
"	20th		Voluntary Church Parade 12 Midday	
"	21st		Coy training – "A" Coy Range. Medal Parade at DENIER at [illegible]	
"	22nd		Coy training. Rain interfered with training. Lieut Mann [illegible]	
			as 2nd in Command. A – B – C and D Coys [illegible] O.R. [illegible]	
"	23rd		10-30 to 11-30 am Lecture by Captain [illegible] [illegible] – [illegible]	
			Demonstration to Officers and N.C.O.s 2-15 pm	
			The G.O.C. visited the Battalion at training. Commanding Officer [illegible]	
"	24th		Platoon training – Shooting Drill for Officers and N.C.O.s [illegible]	
"	25th		Platoon training.	
"	26th		Platoon training.	
"	27th		Voluntary Church Parade 12 Noon. Football Match with [illegible] [illegible] – Won 4-0.	
"	28th		Tactical training – C Coy [illegible] [illegible] [illegible] and [illegible]	
			morning. Football Match with 2nd Buffs – Won 4-0.	
"	29th		Platoon training – B Coy [illegible] [illegible]	

A6945 Wt. W11422/M1160 350,000 12/16 D. D. & L. Forms/C./2118/14.

1st Bn The Gordon Highlanders

Army Form C. 2118.

Instructions regarding War Diaries and Intelligence Summaries are contained in F. S. Regs., Part II. and the Staff Manual respectively. Title pages will be prepared in manuscript.

WAR DIARY
or
INTELLIGENCE SUMMARY.
(*Erase heading not required.*)

May 1917

Sheet 4.

Place	Date	Hour	Summary of Events and Information	Remarks and references to Appendices
AMBRINES	30th		Platoon training	
—	31st		Platoon training	

J. Burnett Lieut Colonel
Commanding 1st Bn The Gordon Highlanders

A6945 Wt. W11422/M1160 350,000 12/16 D. D. & L. Forms/C./2118/14.

1st Battalion The Gordon Highlanders

Roll of Officers serving with Battalion on 31st May 1917.

Lieut Col J. R. G. Burnett D.S.O. Commanding.

Major R. A. Wolfe Murray 2nd in Command
Lieut R. J. Pirie Assistant Adjutant
2/Lt D. R. G. Renfrew Transport Officer
" G. Ritchie A/Quartermaster

"A" Coy.

Capt W. J. Graham (Commanding)
2/Lt J. Hutton
" J. Russell
" R. K. Gordon
" W. R. Broadhurst
" J. Merrilees.

"B" Coy.

Capt J. E. Fenner (Commdg)
2/Lt C. C. Heathcote
" A. D. Mackay.

"C" Coy.

Lieut A. K. Davidson (Commanding)
" O. Horsley
2/Lt H. B. Cook
" R. G. Roe
" R. D. Passey.
" J. C. P. Campbell.
" P. E. Dove

"D" Coy.

2/Lt R. W. Preston (Commdg)
" A. McKie
" H. J. Wilson

Officers Detached

Capt	W. P. M. Russell M.C.	76th Bde HQ
Lieut	J. M. Cunningham	do.
2/Lt	D. K. Templeton	13th Corps Heavy Arty Park A.C.
"	C. Sanderson D.S.O.	Royal Welsh Fusiliers
Capt	C. G. C. Davey.	At F.A.
"	G. W. McAlexander M.C.	On Leave
2/Lt	N. M. Paton	"
"	J. H. Muir	"
Capt	J. B. Lawrence M.C.	"
2/Lt	J. G. J. Fleming M.C.	"
Lieut	D. D. A. Lockhart	On Course

Officers Attached

Capt.	J. L. Stewart	M.O.
Rev.	A. M. McIver.	C.F.

	O.	O.R.
Strength	35	809
Details	3	41

J. R. G. Burnett
Lieut Colonel
Commanding 1st Bn The Gordon Highlanders

1st Battalion The Gordon Highrs.

Instructions regarding War Diaries and Intelligence Summaries are contained in F. S. Regs., Part II. and the Staff Manual respectively. Title pages will be prepared in manuscript.

WAR DIARY
or
~~INTELLIGENCE SUMMARY.~~

(Erase heading not required.)

76/3

June 1917

Vol 33

Army Form C. 2118.

Place	Date 1917	Hour	Summary of Events and Information	Remarks and references to Appendices
AMBRINES	1st June		Battalion prepared for move to ARRAS. Colonel Burnett DSO. returned off leave ~~and~~ gave ~~took~~ Battalion boxing competition	
ARRAS	2nd "		Battalion paraded at 6.55 am and embussed ~~for~~ on MAGNICOURT road for ARRAS, reached ARRAS about 10.30 a.m. and were billeted in Levis Barracks. Good billets – Offrs – Rue-pasteur.	
"	3rd		Slight bombing from planes during night 2/3rd. Voluntary Church parade 12.0 NOON.	
"	4th		Battalion training for coming operations. Moved billets to GRANDE and PETITE PLACE owing to shelling.	
"	5th		Training as on 4th	
"	6th		ditto	
"	7th		ditto	
"	8th		Assault practise in conjunction with 2nd Bn The Suffolk Regiment.	
"	9th		ditto	
"	10th		Voluntary Church parade at 11.0 a.m.	
"	11th		Heavy rain in morning, assault practise postponed till 4.0 pm.	

A6945 Wt. W11422/M1160 350,000 12/16 D. D. & L. Forms/C./2118/14.

2 1st Batt. The Gordon Highlanders

Instructions regarding War Diaries and Intelligence Summaries are contained in F. S. Regs., Part II, and the Staff Manual respectively. Title pages will be prepared in manuscript.

WAR DIARY
or
~~INTELLIGENCE SUMMARY.~~
(Erase heading not required.)

June 1917

Army Form C. 2118.

Place	Date 1917	Hour	Summary of Events and Information	Remarks and references to Appendices
ARRAS	11th (contd)		G.O.C. 3rd Div: present. Capt. G. E. Malcolm M.C. reported	
"	12th		Assault practise in conjunction with ~~VI Corps~~ 2nd Suffolks before VIth Corps Commander (General Byng) Battalion marched past. ARRAS shelled with 12". German plane brought down over ARRAS. Battalion relieved 1st R.S.F. in HILL trench E. of MONCHY during night 12/13th	
In the Line	13th		Battalion in Trenches very wet but dried up during the day.	
"	14th		Moved into assembly positions by 2.0 a.m. Battalion attacked at 7.20 a.m. took HOOK TRENCH and established posts on the MOUND and HIGH ground. Attached is the account of operations from 14th – 19th.	
ARRAS.	20th		Battalion embussed at 3.45 p.m. and arrived at GRENAS at 5.30 p.m. Good billets. Draft of 65 O.R. joined	
GRENAS	21st		Battalion resting & cleaning up	
"	22nd		ditto	
"	23rd		ditto	

A6945 Wt. W11422/M1160 350,000 12/16 D. D. & L. Forms/C./2118/14.

3. 1st Battalion The Gordon Highrs.

Instructions regarding War Diaries and Intelligence Summaries are contained in F. S. Regs., Part II. and the Staff Manual respectively. Title pages will be prepared in manuscript.

WAR DIARY
or
INTELLIGENCE SUMMARY.
(*Erase heading not required.*)

June 1917

Army Form C. 2118.

Place	Date 1917	Hour	Summary of Events and Information	Remarks and references to Appendices
GRENAS	24th		Voluntary church parade	
"	25th		Battalion commenced platoon training. Brigadier inspected	
			transport. Lieuts F.S. Gammell, D.E. Bucher, A.J. Grant, J. Ballantine and	
			J.A. Fleming joined	
	26th		Battalion training. Played East Riding R.E. at cricket & won	
	27th		Training continued. Draft of 331 reported	
	28th		Training	
	29th		Medal presentation by Corps Commander, address congratulating	
			Battalion on operations against INFANTRY HILL and of its smart	
			turn out after such trying times	
	30th		Prepared for move to BIHUCOURT AREA.	
			Attached is the roll of officers for the month	

1st BATTALION No. ..... Date 2/7/17 GORDON HIGHLANDERS

R.A. [illegible] Major
Commanding 1st Bn The Gordon Highrs.

A6945 Wt. W11422/M1160 350,000 12/16 D. D. & L. Forms/C./2118/14.

NOMINAL ROLL OF OFFICERS SERVING WITH BATTALION
ON 30TH. JUNE 1917.

Lieut.Col. J.L.G. Burnett D.S.O.
Major R.A. Wolfe Murray.
Captain & A/Adjt G.W.A. Alexander. M.C.
Lieut & Asst/Adjt P.T. Pirie.
2/Lieut. D.R.G. Renfrew.
" N.M. Paton
" T.C. P. Campbell. M.C.
" R.D. Passey.
" G. Ritchie.
Captain W.J. Graham.
2/Lieut. D. Hutton.
" R.K. Gordon.
" J. Merrilees.
" D.E. Bucher.
Lieut. H.S. Gammell. M.C.
2/Lieut. A.S. Mackay.
" J.H. Muir.
" A.J. Grant.
Capt. G.E. Malcolm.
Lieut. O. Horsley. M.C.
2/Lieut. H.B. Cook.
" J.A. Fleming.
Captain T.B. Lawrence M.C.
2/Lieut. R.W. Preston.
" J.G.G. Fleming. M.C.
" J. Ballantine.
Lieut & Quartermaster G.H.G. Farrant.

ATTACHED. Captain J.L. Stewart M.O.
Rev. I.M. McIver. Chaplain.

DETAILS. Captain W.P.M. Russell Attd 76th. Brigade.
Lieut J.M. Cunningham. "
2/Liwut. D.K. Templeton. 13th. Corps H.A.P. ASC.
Captain C.G.C. Davey. In Hospital.
2/Lieut. R.G. Rose. Wirless Depot Coy.WARLUS.

Total Strength of Battalion. 32 Offs. 983 O.R. = 1015
Details. 3 Offs. 42 O.R. = 45

ACCOUNT OF OPERATIONS AGAINST INFANTRY HILL - EAST OF MONCHY.

14th. to 19th. June 1917.

14th. At 7-20 A.M. the Battalion assaulted in conjunction with the 2nd. Suffolk Regiment in three waves:-

1st. wave = Lightly armed men distributed along the front.
2nd. wave = Two companies.
3rd. wave = ~~Two~~ companies.

The 1st. objective was reached in 28 seconds, hardly a shot being fired until the trench was entered; the Germans kept a very poor lookout. There was a considerable amount of bombing especially on the right, through a gap having occurred between our right and the Suffolks. A nest of about 30 Germans held out under an Officer and on the Officer being killed they surrendered.

The first message was received at 7-45 A.M. by pigeons.

At 8-10 A.M. a message was received by runner "Mound occupied with little opposition".

The Battalion was now holding Hook Trench with five posts in front, holding line from Suffolks ~~on~~ left in Long Trench across the Mound to a point 150 yards in front of left end of Hook Trench. The Germans were holding a trench 200 yards down the slope beyond the Mound.

At 9-30 A.M. Message as follows from O.C. "D" Coy, holding sector north of Hook begins "Enemy holding shell holes and a small piece of detached trench on my left. Snipers and Machine Gun firing from left front. Am organising bombing attack with rifle grenade barrage about 11 A.M. Can artillery cooperate" message ends. This was done and the trench was taken by 12 Noon. A strong point was now formed at the north end of Hook with an advanced bombing post in the new piece of trench which was taken.

At 5-30 P.M. enemy counter-attacked from trench beyond Mound from the direction of BOIS DE AUBERPINES after a bombardment. Our artillery inflicted very severe casualties as they deployed from the village. The enemy advanced to within 200 yards to the north end of Hook Trench and within 40 yards of the posts. They were everywhere driven off.

At 5-40 P.M. one of our 18 pounder batteries shelled our posts on the Mound Ridge. 2 Officers and about half the men became casualties and the posts fell back.

At 10-50 P.M. posts reported re-established in their original positions. This transpired afterwards to be inaccurate in the case of the two posts which should have been on the high ground near the Mound and which had not advanced quite up to the crest. Hook Trench was fairly heavily shelled in the centre. Casualties in Officers to date were 4 Killed and 3 Wounded. This only left 3 Officers and 2 more Company Commanders were sent for from the Details.

15th. 2 A.M. New Company Commanders arrived.

The enemy were quiet throughout the day except for heavy sniping. Much execution was done by rifle grenades which flashed the Germans from shell holes while the riflemen picked them off.

Very good practice was done throughout the day by the Stokes Guns which registered many hits in the German Trench, beyond the Mound and which could be seen from our No. 1 Post.

16th. 2-30 A.M. Shrapnel Trench heavily barraged. Enemy attacked at 3 A.M. driving in posts except Nos. 1 and 2. and approaching to within a few yards of Hook Trench. Bombs got very low and at one point men were throwing Hales Grenades after pulling down the vane. The attack was beaten off but enemy remained in possession of the Mound.
10 A.M. Bombing attack organised by the right centre Coy. to drive out a portion of the enemy which had established a post 100 yards in front of our centre. Two further attempts were made and they were finally driven out by rifle grenades, the whole lot (consisting of about 16) being killed.

17th. 1-45 A.M. The Battalion attacked in accordance with orders from Brigade. The scheme was to attack in one wave advancing half left, the right of the Battalion making for a point on the ridge 100 yards to the right of the Mound. The whole Battalion to occupy the high ground on this line which in conjunction with the twoposts Nos. 1 and 2 still in our possession would give a continuous line along Hook Trench. The artillery barrage opened five minutes after zero and the Welch Fusiliers occupied Hook Trench.
The enemy were in no way surprised and it is probable that they were organising an attack themselves as they were standing in the north part of Hook Trench with one foot on theparapet. The lines fell back with the exception of the left company, leaving four small posts 100 yards in advance of the centre of the line. The left company dug itself in 100 yards in advance of the north end of Hook and this trench was next morning sapped through to Hook.
Quiet throughout the day except that sniping had increased owing to the enemy being in possession of the Mound.
Work of driving Germans from shell holes by rifle grenades continued..

18th. Orders having been received for the Kings Own Regiment to relieve Battalion in Hook Trench, the relief was in progress when at 1-30 A.M. enemy opened a very heavy bombardment on Hook and Hill Trenches followed by an Infantry Attack in force at 3-30 A.M. Nos. 1 and 2 posts were driven in after both the Lewis Guns had been knocked out of action, and ¾ of the men wounded or killed.
2/Lt. Merrilees in charge of No. 1 post failed to get back and appeared two days later having been out in a shell hole.
The infantry attack was beaten off after it had advanced to within 50 yards of Hook. All the men in Nos. 4,5,6and 7 posts are missing or killed. Casualties were particularly heavy in Hill Trench near the willows.
The relief was completed by 5 A.M. ¾ of the Battalion being placed in Hill and the remainder in Dale Trenches.
During this bombardment 2/Lt. Sanderson D.S.O. was killed and Capt. Fiennes and Lieut. Lockhart had become casualties. This left only two officers in the firing line.

19th. Battalion relieved by "C" Coy. Royal Fusiliers.

REMARKS.

(1) It is deduced from these operations that the posts in front unless very strong indeed, which in this case weakened the front line too much, form no protection against an infantry attack.

(2) That the centre post was not as far forward as they thought which enabled the enemy to mass under cover of the Mound. All the Officers of this company had been killed or wounded and when their substitutes arrived, it was too light to visit the posts.

(3) The use of the Stokes Mortars was exemplified by the fact that they reached the German Trench beyond Hook Trench, over which most of the artillery shells went. They had however a rather large percentage of duds, in one case 7 out of 15

(4) There is no doubt that about ⅔ of the casualties inflicted on the enemy after the objectives had been taken in the immediate neighbourhood of the trenches were inflicted by rifle grenades, directly or indirectly, by making the enemy break cover when they afforded an easy mark to a rifle.

(5) That the use of lights in cooperation with the artillery should be more encouraged, as cases of the artillery firing short were frequent during these operations and the telephone lines were in an almost constant state of disrepair. In one case also there was the greatest difficulty from this cause in getting our barrage down, and the lights not being [illegible]

(6) That the pigeon service proved of the greatest value. Only on one occasion was there any delay when owing to the dust caused by the shells, the birds refused to fly.

TOTAL CASUALTIES = Killed 70
Wounded. 162
Missing -27. } includes officers named below.

OFFICERS CASUALTIES.

KILLED:- Lieut. A.R. Davidson 14/6/17. 2/Lt. C.C. Thorburn 14/6/17
2/Lt. P.E. Dove 14/6/17 2/Lt. H.Y. Wilson 14/6/17. 6/17
2/Lt. C. Sanderson D.S.O. 18/6/17. Capt J.E. Fiennes 18/6/17

WOUNDED:-Lieut. D.D.A. Lockhart 18/6/17. 2/Lt. J.Russell 14/6/17
2/Lt. W.R. Broadhurst 14/6/17 2/Lt. A.A. White 14/6/17.

Lieut. Colonel.

Commanding 1st Bn. The Gordon Highlanders.

In the Field.
24/6/17.

1st Battalion The Gordon Highlanders

Instructions regarding War Diaries and Intelligence Summaries are contained in F. S. Regs., Part II. and the Staff Manual respectively. Title pages will be prepared in manuscript.

SECRET / CONFIDENTIAL

WAR DIARY
or
~~INTELLIGENCE SUMMARY.~~
(*Erase heading not required.*)

1 Gordon Hi
July 1917
Vol 34

Army Form C. 2118.

Place	Date	Hour	Summary of Events and Information	Remarks and references to Appendices
GRENAS	1st		Battalion paraded at 10.5 am. and marched to DOULLENS. Entrained at 12.10 pm. and arrived at ACHIET LE GRAND at 4.15 pm. Transport trekked by road. The 2nd Battalion was billeted at MORY and a number of their officers and men met the battalion at the station and the camp in which we bivouacked. Pipes & drums of 2nd Batt. played us over.	
BIHUCOURT	2nd		Specialist training carried on in morning. Football match v. 2nd Batt. in afternoon (Result lost 3–0). The pipes and drums of both battalions massed bands and played.	
	3rd		Battalion paraded at 4.0 pm. and marched to BEUGNY into bivouacs. Officers in tents.	
BEUGNY	4th		Training continued. 2nd Battalion sent over their football team to play return match. (Result 3–1 win for 2nd Batt.)	
	5th		Training continued. Relay race and tug-o'-war v. 2nd Batt. on their ground both of which they won.	
	6th		Training contd. Rugby match v. Australian gunners (lost)	

A6945 Wt. W11422/M1160 350,000 12/16 D. D. & L. Forms/C./2118/14.

1st Battalion The Gordon Highlanders

Instructions regarding War Diaries and Intelligence Summaries are contained in F. S. Regs., Part II. and the Staff Manual respectively. Title pages will be prepared in manuscript.

WAR DIARY
or
~~INTELLIGENCE SUMMARY~~.
(*Erase heading not required.*)

July 1917

Army Form C. 2118.

Place	Date	Hour	Summary of Events and Information	Remarks and references to Appendices
BEUGNY	7th		Battalion inspected by G.O.C. IV Corps (Genl. Woollcombe)	
"	8th		Church parade cancelled owing to rain. 2Lieut C.H. LEE M.C. joined	
"	9th		Coy under company arrangements for parade. Draft of 19 pipers and drummers reported from 3rd battalion.	
"	10th		Battalion relieved 1st Royal Scots Fusiliers in the line. A and B Coys in front line and C and D Coys in support. The line both front and support consisted of posts. No communication trenches existed either	
In the line	11th		Quiet day. Fighting patrol sent out at night from "C" Coy along right Coy front. Enemy encountered holding a strong post which was not known after suffering 2 casualties our patrol returned. 2Lieut V.M. Paton and C.H. LEE were wounded in B Coys H.Q. as the enemy bombarded our front line in response to the bombing of their post. 2Lieut Paton died of wounds on 16th (casualties 2 offrs wd other ranks 1 killed 7 wd)	
	12th		Quiet day. Work commenced in connecting up and widening front line posts. 4 O.R. casualties	

A6945 Wt. W11422/M1160 350,000 12/16 D. D. & L. Forms/C./2118/14.

1st Battalion The Gordon Highlanders

Instructions regarding War Diaries and Intelligence Summaries are contained in F. S. Regs., Part II. and the Staff Manual respectively. Title pages will be prepared in manuscript.

WAR DIARY
or
~~INTELLIGENCE SUMMARY.~~
(*Erase heading not required.*)

July 1917

Army Form C. 2118.

Place	Date	Hour	Summary of Events and Information	Remarks and references to Appendices
In the line	13th		Quiet day. Much aeroplane activity. Wak continues.	[illegible] casualties
	14th		Quiet.	
	15th		ditto 1 O.R. casualty	
	16th		Quiet day. Slight shelling at about 4.0 p.m.	
	17th		Quiet. Pioneers (K.R.R.) wired in front of Rt Coy. 2	[illegible]
	18th		Quiet day. Brigade front shortened by side slip to the left.	
	19th		Battalion relieved by 2nd Suffolk regiment, relief completed by 1.10 a.m. 1 casualty	
BEUGNY	20th		Battalion rested, cleaned up [illegible]	
	21st		Resting.	
	22nd		Church Parade.	
	23rd		Battalion [illegible] — march past etc.	
	24th		Guard competition - won by No 15 platoon - [illegible] No 4 [illegible]	
	25th		Battalion relieves 2nd SUFFOLK regiment in the [illegible] front and Aasd B. C. [illegible] Support [illegible] [illegible]	

A6945 Wt. W11422/M1160 350,000 12/16 D. D. & L. Forms/C./2118/14.

1st Battalion The Gordon Highlanders

WAR DIARY
or
~~INTELLIGENCE SUMMARY~~
(Erase heading not required.)

July 1917

Army Form C. 2118

Instructions regarding War Diaries and Intelligence Summaries are contained in F. S. Regs., Part II. and the Staff Manual respectively. Title Pages will be prepared in manuscript.

Place	Date	Hour	Summary of Events and Information	Remarks and references to Appendices
In the line	26th		Quiet. Pioneers wiring R. Company front. Slight trench	
"			mortaring from the enemy. 1 O.R. killed and 1 wounded.	
"	27th		Quiet. Wiring continued. 2 O.R. wounded. Draft of 30 O.R. joined	
"	28th		Quiet wiring continued 3 O.R. wounded	
	29th		Quiet day. At 7.30 am enemy attempted a raid on "C" Coys right but was driven off. 1 O.R. was killed and 1 wounded by enemy trench mortar barrage.	
	30th		Quiet wiring and widening of trenches continued. 3 O.R. wounded	
	31st		Quiet day 1 other rank wounded.	
			The undermentioned officers joined on dates as stated.	
			2/Lieut F. Davison, " R. Reid, B.J. Pendlebury, F. Douglas } 16/7/17; 2/Lieut A.K. White 13/7/17; " J.R. Newlands 26/7/17	
			Attached is the roll of officers for the month.	

4/8/17

J. S. Burnett Lieut Col
Commanding 1st Batt. The Gordon Highlanders

1875 Wt. W593/826 1,000,000 4/15 J.B.C. & A. A.D.S.S./Forms/C. 2118.

1st. Battn. The Gordon Highlanders.

Roll of Officers on strength of Battalion at 31/7/17.

Lieut. Col. J.L.G. Burnett D.S.O.
Major R.A. Wolfe Murray.
Capt. G.W.A. Alexander M.C. A/Adjutant.
Lieut. P.T. Pirie. Asst /Adjutant.
" G.H.G. Farrant Quartermaster.
2/Lt. D.R.G. Renfrew Transport Officer.
" T.C.P. Campbell M.C. Sniping Officer.
" G. Ritchie.

"A" Coy.

2/Lieut. H.B. Cook (Commanding)
" D. Hutton.
" R.K. Gordon.
" J. Merrilees.
" D.E. Bucher.

"B" Coy.

Captain H.S. Gammell M.C. (Commdg)
2/Lieut. B. Pendlebury.
" A.K. White.

"C" Coy.

Captain G.E. Malcolm M.C. (Commanding)
2/Lieut. F. Douglas.
" R. Reid.
" J.S. Fleming.

"D" Coy.

2/Lieut. J.H. Muir (Commanding)
" J. Ballantine.
" F.H. Davison.
" J.R. Newland.

Captain J.L. Stewart M.O.
Rev. I.M. McIver C.F.

Captain W.P.M. Russell M.C. Attd 76th. Bde.
Lieut. J.M. Cunningham "
2/Lt. R.G. Ree, Wireless Depot Coy. Warlus.
" R.W. Preston. Base Training Camp.
" A.S. Mackay. "
" A.J. Grant. Field Ambulance.
" J.G. Fleming D.S.O. M.C. "

1st Bn The Gordon Highlanders

Army Form C. 2118.

WAR DIARY
or
~~INTELLIGENCE SUMMARY.~~
(Erase heading not required.)

Sheet 1 Vol 35

Instructions regarding War Diaries and Intelligence Summaries are contained in F. S. Regs., Part II. and the Staff Manual respectively. Title pages will be prepared in manuscript.

Place	Date	Hour	Summary of Events and Information	Remarks and references to Appendices
	August			
In the Field	1st		Quiet. Improving Posts.	
"	2nd		Relieved by 2nd Suffolk Regt. Relief complete 12.30 am. 1 OR Wounded	
			Marched to BEUGNY.	
BEUGNY	3rd		Rested.	
"	4th		Training	
"	5th		Church Parade with Divisional Band	
"	6th		Training	
"	7th		Training	
"	8th		Training - The following Officers reported for duty:- Lieut CM Brown	
			takes over Command D Coy. Lieut JC Watson takes over Command A Coy	
			2/Lt W H Lydell and 2/Lt H J Walker.	
	9th		Training 2/Lieut J C Clark joined Battalion	
	10th		2/Lieut A W Annand joined Battalion	
	11th		Took over the line from 2nd Suffolk Regt. Relief complete 12.50 am	
In the field	12th		Worked at joining up Posts. 3 OR wounded by shellfire	
	13th		Quiet.	

A6945 Wt. W11422/M1160 350,000 12/16 D. D. & L. Forms/C./2118/14.

1st Bn Gordon Highlanders

Instructions regarding War Diaries and Intelligence Summaries are contained in F. S. Regs., Part II. and the Staff Manual respectively. Title pages will be prepared in manuscript.

WAR DIARY
for
~~INTELLIGENCE~~ SUMMARY.
(Erase heading not required.)

August 1917

Sheet 2.

Army Form C. 2118.

Place	Date	Hour	Summary of Events and Information	Remarks and references to Appendices
	August			
In Mayfield	14th		Quiet	
	15th		Slight shelling by night.	
	16th		Quiet.	
	17th		Gas Projectiles were sent over at 11 pm from the 9th Brigade front on our left. 1 OR wounded in resulting retaliation.	
	18		Battalion relieved by 2nd Suffolk Regt. Relief complete at 1.30 am. C Coy left in Reserve Dugouts.	
BEUGNY	19th		Rested	
	20th		Baths.	
	21st		Adjutants Parade and Coy Training	
	22nd		Reserve Coy relieved. Erection of Huts begun	
	23rd		Battalion Parade	
	24th		Drill Demonstration by Platoon under Lieut J.C. Watson before the Corps, Divisional and Brigade Commanders. It was most unfortunate that the day was windy, the result being that the drill was not nearly as satisfactory as it was in practise	

A6945 Wt. W11422/M1160 350,000 12/16 D. D. & L. Forms/C./2118/14.

1st Bn The Gordon Highlanders

Instructions regarding War Diaries and Intelligence Summaries are contained in F. S. Regs., Part II. and the Staff Manual respectively. Title pages will be prepared in manuscript.

WAR DIARY
for
~~INTELLIGENCE~~ SUMMARY.
(*Erase heading not required.*)

August 1917

Army Form C. 2118.

Sheet 3

Place	Date	Hour	Summary of Events and Information	Remarks and references to Appendices
	August			
REUGNY	25th		Training	
	26th		Relieved 2nd Suffolk Regt in the Line. Relief complete 1.30am	
			1 OR wounded 2/Lieut C.H. Howard joined Battalion	
[illegible]	27th		Raid Lord	
	28th		Worked between Posts.	
	29th		ditto 1 OR wounded	
	30th		No 37 Post shelled at 3 pm. 1 OR Killed 2 OR wounded.	
	31st		Worked between Posts.	
			Total Strength Officers 36 OR 991	

A6945 Wt. W11422/M1160 350,000 12/16 D. D. & L. Forms/C./2118/14.

1st Battalion The Gordon Highlanders
Nominal Roll of Officers

Lieut Colonel	J. G. Burnett DSO	Commanding
Major	[illegible]	2nd in Command
Capt	[illegible] MC	Adjutant
Capt	[illegible]	Asst Adjutant
	[illegible]	Transport Officer
Lieut	[illegible]	[illegible]

A Coy

Capt J C Watson (Comdg)
2/Lieut A R Cook
" [illegible]
" R K Gordon
" J [illegible]
" [illegible]
" A W Annand

B Coy

Capt H S [illegible] MC Comdg
2/Lieut [illegible]
" [illegible]
" [illegible]
" [illegible]
" [illegible] MC

C Coy

Capt G E Malcolm MC (Comdg)
2/Lieut A J Walker
" F Douglas
" R Reid
" J S Fleming
" G Ritchie

D Coy

Capt C M Brown Comdg
2/Lieut J M Muir
" J M Davidson
" J R Newland
" J Ballantyne

Attached

Lieut F. A. Evans Medical Officer USR
Revd A M McTart Chaplain

Detached

Capt	W P M Russell MC	3rd Div Reinforcing Camp
	J M Cunningham	76th Bde HQ
2/Lieut	R G Keb	Wireless Depot Coy [illegible]
	R W Presley MC	Base Training Camp
"	A S McKay	do
	~~A K White~~	~~76th T M B~~
	J G G Fleming DSO MC	Field Ambulance

	O.	O R	Total
Strength	36	991	1027
Details	11	133	144

J. G. Burnett

Lieut Colonel
Comdg 1st Bn The Gordon Highrs

1st Battalion The Gordon Highlanders

76/3

Instructions regarding War Diaries and Intelligence Summaries are contained in F. S. Regs., Part II, and the Staff Manual respectively. Title pages will be prepared in manuscript.

WAR DIARY
or
~~INTELLIGENCE SUMMARY.~~
(Erase heading not required.)

Army Form C. 2118.

September 1917

Vol 36

Place	Date	Hour	Summary of Events and Information	Remarks and references to Appendices
In the line	1st		Very quiet no casualties	
	2nd		ditto	
	3rd		Relieved by 2nd Suffolk Regiment Relief complete 10.30pm This finished the battalion tour in this sector. When the trenches were taken over they consisted of isolated posts, indifferently wired and no communication trenches. When handed over all posts were improved and joined up by trenches 7' deep duckboarded for almost the whole length. A C.T. 1200 yards long was made up to the right of the position and the Left Coy Hd Qrs was also joined up to the line by a CT	
			The wire was in excellent condition and constantly improved by the system of each man in the battalion whenever practicable being made to make 2 gooseberries per day. The battalion was complimented on the work done by the Divisional and Brigade commanders	
BEUGNY	4th		Rested. Baths for companies	

A6945 Wt. W11422/M1160 350,000 12/16 D. D. & L. Forms/C./2118/14.

1st Bn The Gordon Highlanders [illegible]

Army Form C. 2118.

WAR DIARY
or
~~INTELLIGENCE~~ SUMMARY.
(Erase heading not required.)

Instructions regarding War Diaries and Intelligence Summaries are contained in F. S. Regs., Part II. and the Staff Manual respectively. Title pages will be prepared in manuscript.

Place	Date	Hour	Summary of Events and Information	Remarks and references to Appendices
BEUGNY	5th		Battalion went through Gas Chamber at FREMICOURT. Moved to	
			BARASTRE area at 9.0 pm after being relieved by	
			Londons. "B" Coy who were in Beugny [illegible]	
			dugouts rejoined the battalion	
BARASTRE	6th		Bn training	
	7th		ditto	
	8th		ditto a New practise attack.	
	9th		Battalion training in conjunction with 8th KORL on practise area.	
	10th		Battalion training. Lecture by the Divisional Commander to all	
			officers of division on "coming operations"	
	11th		Battalion training Attack practise.	
	12th		ditto	
	13th		76th Bde attack practise witnessed by Army Commander (Gen Gough)	
	14th		Training. Bde boxing competition commenced.	
	15th		Battalion on long range at LE TRANSLOY. "B" Coy went through Gas Chamber. Col.	
			C.G. Burnett DSO went to Field Ambulance and Major [illegible] Murray took over command	

A6945 Wt. W11422/M1160 350,000 12/16 D. D. & L. Forms/C./2118/14.

1st Bn The Gordon Highlanders

Instructions regarding War Diaries and Intelligence Summaries are contained in F. S. Regs., Part II. and the Staff Manual respectively. Title pages will be prepared in manuscript.

WAR DIARY
or
~~INTELLIGENCE SUMMARY.~~
(Erase heading not required.)

September 1917

Army Form C. 2118.

Place	Date	Hour	Summary of Events and Information	Remarks and references to Appendices
BARASTRE	16th		Church parade under Bishop of Khartoum G.O.Cs Corps Div & Bde attended	
	17th		Prepared for move	
"MOVE"	18th		Battalion parade at 5-35 am and marched to BAPAUME Train left at 9-30 am arrived at GOODERSVELTE at 6-30 pm and battalion reached billets near WATOU at 10-0 pm (camp very crowded). "A" Coy was detailed as brigade loading party so remained at BAPAUME till 1-30 am 19/9/17	
WATOU	19th		Battalion rested and under 1 hours notice being in CORPS reserve	
	20th		ditto Inter-platoon tug-of-war.	
	21st		Battalion training CO Adj and Company Commanders went to Corps Hd Qrs to see a "MODEL" of the area of operations.	
	22nd		Battalion moved at 3-15 pm and marched to BRANDHOEK and arrived at 7-0 pm O.C. Coys went up to visit the line.	
	23rd		Battalion rested. Another detachment went up to the line.	
	24th		Battalion paraded at 5-30 pm and entrained for YPRES, marched to EAST of YPRES and bivouacked under hedges for the night	

A6945 Wt. W11422/M1160 350,000 12/16 D. D. & L. Forms/C./2118/14.

1st Bn The Gordon Highlanders   September 1917

Instructions regarding War Diaries and Intelligence Summaries are contained in F. S. Regs., Part II. and the Staff Manual respectively. Title pages will be prepared in manuscript.

WAR DIARY
or
INTELLIGENCE SUMMARY.
(Erase heading not required.)

Army Form C. 2118.

Place	Date	Hour	Summary of Events and Information	Remarks and references to Appendices
YPRES	25th		Bivouacked in open and prepared for move into [illegible] positions	
	26th		ZERO hour 5-50 am and battalion attacked. Battalion [illegible] and came out of action on night of 29/30th and [illegible] near VLAMERTINGHE. Operation orders and report on operations attached	
VLAMERTINGHE	30th		Moved to WINNEZEELE by bus at [illegible] pm and arrived at about 10-0 pm	
			Roll of Officers is attached.	

R. H. [illegible] Major
Commanding 1st Gordon Highlanders

1st BATTALION
No.........
Date.........
GORDON HIGHLANDERS

A6945 Wt. W11422/M1160 350,000 12/16 D. D. & L. Forms/C./2118/14.

1st Battalion The Gordon Highlanders

List of Officers serving with the Battalion on 30th September 1917

Major R.A. Wolfe Murray
Capt G.W.A. Alexander Adj
" P.T. Pirie Asst Adj
Lieut G.H.S. Farrant Q.M.
Capt R.R.G. Renfrew Transport Officer
2/Lieut G. Ritchie
2/Lieut. T.C.R. Campbell, Intelligence Officer

A Coy

2/Lt A.W. Annand
" R.K. Gordon
" J. Morrilees
" R.E. Bucher

B Coy

2/Lt J.B. Elliot
S.C. Clark

C Coy

Capt G.E. Malcolm M.C.
2/Lt H.B. Cook
" H.J. Walker
" R. Reid

D Coy

Capt T.B. Lawrence M.C.
Lieut S.P. Gillespie
2/Lt J.K. Newland
J.H. Davidson

Attached

Lieut J.A. Evans M.C.
Revd A.M. McIver C.F.
Monsieur A. Calans Interpreter

Detached

Capt W.P.M. Russell M.C. 19th Corps Reinforcing Camp
2/Lieut R.W. Preston M.C. do
" R.G. Ree Army Signal Coy
" A.S. Mackay Base Training Camp
Lieut Col J.R.G. Burnett D.S.O. At Hospital
2/Lieut B.J. Pendlebury At P.A.
" C.H. Horswell At P.A.
" D. Hutton At P.A.
" J.G.G. Fleming D.S.O. M.C. At 15th I.B.D.
Lieut J.M. Cunningham Attd 76th Bde

Strength of Battalion

	O.	O.R.	Total
Fighting Strength	30	717	747
Details	10	62	72

REPORT ON THE RECENT OPERATIONS AT ZONNEBEKE.

25TH. TO 29TH. SEPTEMBER 1917.

25TH. At dusk on the evening of the 25th, September, the Battalion marched from bivouacs east of YPRES, up "F" Track, past the Railway Dump and assembled on tapes in the front line, South of the YPRES-ROULERS Railway Line; the Battalion occupying a frontage of 400 yards.

The 8th. Kings Own were on the right of the Battalion in the front line, with the 10th. Royal Welch Fusiliers and the 2nd. Suffolks in the supporting line.

The 8th. Infantry Brigade were attacking on our left.

26TH. Zero hour was at 5-50 A.M.

Previous to this, one company - "B" Coy - crossed ZONNEBEKE BOG in front of the assembly line so as to avoid delay.

At zero hour the Battalion advanced "A" and "B" Companies establishing themselves in the first objective - the GREEN LINE - in ten minutes time, "C" and "D" Companies passing through them and capturing the final objective - the BLUE LINE - in about twenty-five minutes.

The two Supporting Battalions now passed through the 1st Gordon Highlanders, and 8th. Kings Own and captured the RED LINE the final objective of the Brigade at about 8 A.M.

The German barrage opened fire at about 6-10 A.M. on the original front line and the ZONNEBEKE RIDGE. The enemy continued to shell this ground throughout the day, with a slight lull between the hours of 10 A. M. and 3 P.M. when the shelling was not so heavy.

At about 10 A.M. the 10th. Royal Welch Fusiliers, reporting that they were holding the front line very weakly, the Battalion moved forward at 10-30 A.M. at a distance of about 400 yards, in order to be in closer support to them.

From 3 P.M. to 6 P.M. the enemy shelling became intense.

The German counter-attack was launched at about 6-30 P.M. but was successfully beaten off, some of the troops on our left withdrawing. All the 76th. Brigade stood fast.

The troops on our left were eventually rallied with the assistance of Captain G.W.A. Alexander M.C. 2/Lieut. T.C.P. Campbell M.C. and No. 10286 L/Cpl D. Blair and re-established themselves on their objectives.

About 7-30 P.M. one company - "D" Coy - lined the YPRES-ROULERS Railway Embankment to form a protective flank on our left as the situation on the left was doubtful.

The night 26/27th. was very quiet.

27TH. Throughout the day fairly heavy shelling and sniping were encountered.

A 3rd. Divisional Aeroplane dropped a message about 4 P.M. giving information that the enemy was massing for a counter-attack behind HILL 40 and STATION BUILDINGS; this message was transmitted to companies.

The enemy counter-attack was launched, preceded by heavy shelling at about 6 P.M. This was successfully beaten off by our artillery barrage and rifle and lewis gun fire.

During the night 27/28th, the situation was very quiet.

28TH. The day passed without incident other than an attack arranged on STATION BUILDINGS and HILL 40 (on our left) which was eventually cancelled.

Throughout the night 28/29th, a few gas shells were sent over.

29TH. The day passed without incident.

The Battalion was relieved during the night by "B" Company 33rd. Australian Infantry and "B" Company 34th. Australian Infantry. This took place in broad moonlight and was spotted by the enemy who commenced shelling and opened fire with machine guns inflicting a few casualties.

The total casualties during the whole operations were:-
Officers. One killed, One Died of Wounds, One Missing and seven wounded (two of whom remained at duty).

Other Ranks. Killed 37.
Wounded 203
Missing 10
250

(Sgd) R.A. Wolfe Murray, Major.
Commanding 1st Bn. The Gordon Highlanders.

In the field.
4/10/17.

1st Battalion The Gordon Highlanders.

OPERATION ORDERS BY MAJOR R.A. WOLFE MURRAY,
COMMANDING, 25TH SEMPEMBER 1917.

GRAVENSTAPEL (1/10.000)
Sheet 28 N.W. (Ed.6A) and 28 N.E. (Ed.7A) 1:20.000.

The 76th Brigade will attack and consolidate the BLUE LINE on "Z" day at an hour "Zero" to be notified later.

The 8th Bridage will be on the left and the 4th Australian Division on the right.

The Brigade will attack on a two Battalion frontage, the 8th K.O.R.L. Regiment on the right and the 1st Gordon Highlanders on the left.

The 2nd Suffolks will pass through the 8th K.O.R.L. and the 10th Royal Welch Fusiliers will pass through the 1st Gordon Highlanders, and capture the final objective - the BLUE LINE.

<u>OBJECTIVE</u>. The Battalion will capture and consolidate the line D27a9.2 in touch with the 8th K.O.R.L. - ST. JOSEPH INSTITUTE - thence due north to railway at D27a7.8 (railway inclusive) in touch with the 2nd Royal Scots.

O.C. "B" and "C" Coys. will detail special platoons to capture and garrison ST. JOSEPHS INSTITUTE and CHARING CROSS respectively (level crossing D26b9.4).

<u>DISPOSITIONS</u>. The assualt will be in two waves,
<u>1st wave</u> "A" and "B" Coys, each on a two platoon frontage.
<u>2nd wave</u> "C" and "D" Coys, each on a two platoon frontage.

The Battalion frontage will be divided into Company frontages as under:-

<u>Left Coy</u>. D26d4.7 to ~~XXXXX~~ YPRES-ROULERS Railway inclusive D26d20.10.

<u>Right Coy</u>. From D26d5.3 to D26d4.7.

<u>ASSEMBLY</u>. In getting into the Assembly Positions, "C" and "D" Coys. will cover off "A" and "B" Coys. respectively, at a distance of 30 yards.

"B" Coy. will assemble across the STEENBEKE STREAM.

Lieut. S.P. Gillispie and 2/Lieut. T.C.P. Campbell M.C. with 4 Snipers will mark out the assembly positions with boards on "Y" night.

The 76th Machine Gun Coy. will place guns at the following points as soon as they have been taken:-
(a) One gun by vicinity of ST. JOSEPHS INSTITUTE.
(b) One gun to cover railway in vicinity of CHARING CROSS.

<u>ARTILLERY</u>.

The attack will be immediately preceded by a bombardment lasting two hours.

The Battalion will advance under a creeping field artillery barrage which will move as follows:-

Open 150 yards from the front position and lift at zero plus five minutes. Thence for 200 yards at the rate of 100 yards in four minutes - thence to RED LINE at the rate of 100 yards in six minutes.x All lifts will be 50 yards.
thence to final objective at the rate of 100 yards in eight minutes

<u>DRESS</u>. Fighting order.
Lewis Gun Sections - 20 Magazines.
Rifle Grenade Squads - 16 Rifle Grenades (No.24 and 23)
Aeroplane flares - "A" and "B" Coys. 50 each.
One bomb per man will be carried in the pocket, except rifle grenade squads.
Shovels 150 each to "A" and "B" Coys.
" 100 each to "C" and "D" Coys.

<u>DUMPS.</u> Dumps of water, bombs, S.A.A. etc will be as under:-
<u>Right Battalion</u> at HONNEBEKE WOOD (J26c35.15)
<u>Left Battalion</u> at railway D26c1.4.

<u>DRESSING STATION</u> Dressing Station will be in Pill Box at D26c35.15.

<u>PRISONERS.</u> All prisoners will be sent down to the Dressing Station to be used as Stretcher Bearers under escort of not more than 1 for every 10 Prisoners.

<u>REPORTS.</u> Battalion Headquarters will be at D26d4.5.

(Sgd) G.W.A. Alexander, Captain.
Adjutant 1st Battn. The Gordon Highlanders.

1st Bn The Gordon Highlanders

Instructions regarding War Diaries and Intelligence Summaries are contained in F. S. Regs., Part II. and the Staff Manual respectively. Title pages will be prepared in manuscript.

WAR DIARY
or
INTELLIGENCE SUMMARY.

(Erase heading not required.)

October 1917

76/3

Army Form C. 2118.

WO 95/1437

Place	Date	Hour	Summary of Events and Information	Remarks and references to Appendices
WINNEZEELE	1st		Battalion rested and cleaned up.	
	2nd		Battalion paraded at 11.0 a.m. for [illegible]	
	3rd		Battalion paraded at 11.0 a.m. for address by G.O.C. [illegible] Division. Capt A.M.P. Norman, 2Lieut Chedburn, 2Lt [illegible] MacGregor and [illegible] also 265 other ranks [illegible]	
	4th		Battalion marched to CHAMPAGNE [illegible] miles [illegible] in billets by 7.0 p.m.	
	5th		Battalion rested and marched to WIZERNE and entrained at 9.30 p.m. for BAPAUME.	
	6th		Arrived BAPAUME at 8.0 a.m. and marched to Camp at [illegible]. Camp fairly comfortable	
	7th		Battalion paraded at 11.15 a.m. for [illegible]. 2Lieut [illegible] joined	
	8th		Battalion training. Capt H.S. [illegible] M.C., 2Lt Johnston joined	
	9th		Battalion training. Draft of 140 O.R. joined (46 from [illegible] from 9th [illegible])	
	10th		Battalion prepared for move to Trenches.	
	11th		Battalion embussed for move to Trenches [illegible] had dinners and [illegible] relieved 2/5 West Yorks 185 Bde, 62 Div in BULLECOURT [illegible] complete by midnight. Front line [illegible] and [illegible] Support [illegible] Drafts [illegible] for working parties. [illegible]	

D. D. & L., London, E.C.
(A8001) Wt. W1771/M2031 750,000 5/17 Sch. 52 Forms/C2118/14

1st Bn. The Gordon Highlanders October 1917

WAR DIARY
or
INTELLIGENCE SUMMARY.
(Erase heading not required.)

Army Form C. 2118.

Instructions regarding War Diaries and Intelligence Summaries are contained in F. S. Regs., Part II. and the Staff Manual respectively. Title pages will be prepared in manuscript.

Place	Date	Hour	Summary of Events and Information	Remarks and references to Appendices
IN THE LINE	12th		Quiet. Trenches bad and sides falling in. Work on wiring. Casualties nil.	
	13th		Quiet. Work continued on trenches and wiring. No casualties.	
	14th		Quiet. 1 O.R. attached R.E. killed. Lt. HORSWELL rejoined from F.A.	
	15th		Quiet. Inter Coy relief. No casualties.	
	16th		Quiet. Work started by day. Wiring at night. 2Lieut Angus McConnachie, Henderson, Kennedy and Goldfinch joined.	
	17th		Quiet. 5 O.R. attached R.E. wounded.	
	18th		Battalion relieved by 2nd Suffolks. Relief complete by 11 o.p.m.	
MORAY	19th		Battalion rested and cleaned up. Col. Burnett returned from F.A.	
	20th		Coys at disposal of O.C. Coys for Routine inspections. 2Lieuts Wilson, Donald and Thomson joined	
	21st		Voluntary Church Parade at 11 a.m.	
	22nd		Battalion training. Specialist instruction	
	23rd		Battalion training.	
	24th		ditto	
	25th		Overwhelming gale no training. Working party of 50 O.R. for work in Abbaye MORAY (new Billets)	

D. D. & L., London, E.C. (A8001) Wt. W1771/M2031 750,000 5/17 Sch. 52 Forms/C2118/14

1st Bn The Gordon Highlanders

Instructions regarding War Diaries and Intelligence Summaries are contained in F. S. Regs., Part II. and the Staff Manual respectively. Title pages will be prepared in manuscript.

WAR DIARY
or
INTELLIGENCE SUMMARY.
(Erase heading not required.)

October 1917

Army Form C. 2118.

Place	Date	Hour	Summary of Events and Information	Remarks and references to Appendices
MORAY	26th		Battalion relieved 2nd Suffolks in BULLECOURT Sector. [illegible] A and B, support C and reserve D. No casualties. Battalion on our left ejected gas projectiles at 1.0 a.m.	
BULLECOURT	27th		At 3.0 a.m. gas projectiles again ejected [illegible] M.G activity. Quiet [illegible] Casualties [illegible] and 1 wd (shell shock)	
	28th		Quiet day. Slight T.M. and [illegible] activity [illegible] Work continued on trenches and wire.	
	29th		Quiet day no casualties. Work continued and [illegible] front line	
	30th		Quiet day. No casualties. Work continued	
	31st		Quiet day. Work continued. Slight T.M. activity	
			Roll of officers is attached.	
			[signature] Major Commanding 1st Bn The Gordon Highlanders	

D. D. & L., London, E.C. (A8001) Wt. W1771/M2031 750,000 5/17 Sch. 52 Forms/C2118/14

Nominal Roll of Officers serving with Battalion
on 31/10/17.

Lieut. Col. J.L.G. Burnett. DSO.
Major R.A. Wolfe Murray MC.
Capt & Adjt, G.W.A. Alexander MC.
Capt & Asst/Adjt P.T. Pirie.
Capt D.R.G. Renfrew Transport Officer.
Lieut & QM. G.H.G. Farrant.
" T.C.P. Campbell. MC.
" G. Ritchie.
" J.R. Newland. L.G. & Bombing Officer.
2/Lieut. H.J. Walker. Signalling Officer.

"A" Coy.
Capt A.M.B. Norman (Commdg)
Lieut. D. Hutton.
" J. Merrilees.
2/Lieut. D.E. Bucher.
" W.G. Henderson.
"

"B" Coy.
Capt H.S. Gammell MC (Commdg)
Lieut. C.H. Horswell.
2/Lieut. S.C. Clarke.
" J.J. Ogston.
" ~~A.M. Angus~~.
" E.A.H. Goldfinch.
" A.M. Angus.

"C" Coy.
Capt G.E. Malcolm M.C. (Commdg)
Lieut. H.B. Cook.
" W.A. Johnston.
" B.S. Chedburn.
2/Lieut. R. Reid.
" D. Kennedy.
" J.K. Donald.
" A. Thomson.

"D" Coy.
Lieut. A.W. Annand MC (Commdg)
2/Lieut. M.W. Penman.
" D.H. McGregor.
" F.W. Davitt.
" J. Wilson.
"

ATTACHED.

Capt F.A. Evans. Medical Officer.
Rev. A.M. McIver. Chaplain.

DETACHED.

Capt W.P.M. Russell MC. Attd 3rd. Div. Depot Battn.
" T.B. Lawrence MC. do.
2/Lieut. A.G. ~~Angus~~ Moffat. do.
Lieut. R.G. Roe, Army Signal Coy.
" S.P. Gillespie. At Field Ambulance.
" J.B. Elliot. do.
" J.G.G. Fleming DSO MC. 18th. I.B.D.
" J.M. Cunningham Attd 76th. Bde.
2/Lieut. C.M.V. McConnachie. Attd 76th. T.M.B.

Strength of Battalion	Officers.	O.R.
Fighting Strength.	45	1087.
Details.	16	147.

P. T Pirie Capt for Major.
Commdg. 1st Bn. The Gordon Highlanders.

In the field.
31/10/17.

1st Battn Gordon Highlanders.

1 Gordon Hrs
November 1917
Sheet I
Vol 38

Instructions regarding War Diaries and Intelligence Summaries are contained in F. S. Regs., Part II. and the Staff Manual respectively. Title pages will be prepared in manuscript.

Army Form C. 2118.

WAR DIARY
or
~~INTELLIGENCE SUMMARY~~.
(Erase heading not required.)

Place	Date	Hour	Summary of Events and Information	Remarks and references to Appendices
	NOV.			
BULLECOURT	1st		Quiet day work on the trenches was continued as usual no casualties	
	2nd		Quiet. Enemy shelled TOWER SUPPORT Work as usual on the trenches	
	3rd		Slight shelling round about BULLECOURT AVENUE in the morning. The Battn was relieved by 2nd SUFFOLK REGT in the evening. Relief complete by 9.15 pm no casualties	
MORY	4th		The Battn rested. Baths in MORY. Voluntary church parade	
	5th		Battn training Football team beat K.O.R.L 2-1 in the afternoon	
	6th		Bad weather no training done.	
	7th		A and B Coys moved into the ABBAYE. MORY also HQ. The ABBAYE was in an unfinished condition	
	8th		Heavy Rain no training Beat R.W.F. 7-0 at football	
	9th		Rain no training	
	10th		Rain – no training	
BULLECOURT.	11th		Battn relieved the 2nd Suffolk Regt in the line. Dispositions D Coy right front C Coy left front A Coy in TIGER TRENCH B Coy	

A6945 Wt. W11422/M1160 350,000 12/16 D. D. & L. Forms/C./2118/14.

1st Bn The Gordon Highlanders

WAR DIARY
or
~~INTELLIGENCE SUMMARY.~~
(Erase heading not required.)

Army Form C. 2118.

November 1917.

Sheet II

Instructions regarding War Diaries and Intelligence Summaries are contained in F. S. Regs., Part II. and the Staff Manual respectively. Title pages will be prepared in manuscript.

Place	Date	Hour	Summary of Events and Information	Remarks and references to Appendices
BULLECOURT	Nov 11th		in RAILWAY EMBANKMENT. Relief was complete by 9·20 pm. There were no casualties	
	12th		Gas projectiles were fired from the Brigade front on our left at 7am in the morning. There was no retaliation. Remainder of day quiet. At night the usual working parties were detailed. No casualties	
	13th		Very quiet day. Visibility was very bad owing to mist until 1 pm. We carried out trench mortar bombardments during the day. There was very little retaliation. There were no casualties	
	14th		During the afternoon and evening the enemy shelled TOWER SUPPORT heavily with 5·9 shells. Two men were killed and 3 others wounded. Shelling ceased about 8·30 pm. During the night both support companies were carrying up trench mortar amm. etc for the 9th Brigade. There were no wiring parties or patrols in order to let our guns break the enemy wire. During the night 13/14th our patrols were out from 12·30 pm till 2am examining the enemy front line wire	

D. D. & L., London, E.C.
(A8004) Wt. W1771/M2731 750,000 5/17 Sch. 52 Forms/C2118/14

1st Bn Gordon Highlanders

WAR DIARY
or
~~INTELLIGENCE SUMMARY.~~
(Erase heading not required.)

Instructions regarding War Diaries and Intelligence Summaries are contained in F. S. Regs., Part II. and the Staff Manual respectively. Title pages will be prepared in manuscript.

Army Form C. 2118.

November 1917

Sheet III

Place	Date	Hour	Summary of Events and Information	Remarks and references to Appendices
BULLECOURT	15th		Quiet day. In the evening the Battn was relieved by the	
"	"	9pm	2nd Suffolk Regt. The relief was complete by 8.45 pm	
			All the battalion went into rest billets in the ABBAYE. MORY	
MORY	16th		Battn rested and cleaned up	
"	17th		Battn was medically inspected by the M.O. and had baths in MORY	
	18th		Usual voluntary church parades. C.O attended conference at Bde HQ	
	19th		Battn practised "advanced guard" ~~the~~ scheme in the morning between MORY and BEHAGNIES. The G.O.C 76th Brigade was present. Battn also practised artillery fo[rmation]	
	20th		9th Brigade attacked German front line near BULLECOURT. Battn under orders to move at [1?] hours notice. Col Burnett saw all officers at a conference and explained scheme.	
	21st		Quiet day. Brigade boxing contest at ABBAYE in the afternoon	
	22nd		Quiet day. Companies at the disposal of Coy Commanders.	

D. D. & L., London, E.C.
(A8004) Wt. W1771/M2031 750,000 5/17 Sch. 52 Forms/C2118/14

1st Bn Gordon Highlanders

WAR DIARY
or
~~INTELLIGENCE SUMMARY~~.
(Erase heading not required.)

Army Form C. 2118.

Instructions regarding War Diaries and Intelligence Summaries are contained in F. S. Regs., Part II. and the Staff Manual respectively. Title pages will be prepared in manuscript.

November. 1917
Sheet IV

Place	Date	Hour	Summary of Events and Information	Remarks and references to Appendices
~~[illegible]~~ MORY	Nov 23rd		Battn paraded at 10.30 am. Col Burnett attended a conference at Brigade H.Q.	
	24th		Battn paraded at 10.30 am. to practise scheme for following up the enemy in case of retreat. Scheme was carried out very successfully by all Coys.	
	25th		Sunday. Voluntary church service at 11 am	
BULLECOURT	26th		Battn relieved the 1st NORTHUMBERLAND FUSILIERS and 2 coys of the 4th ROYAL FUSILIERS in the BULLECOURT SECTOR. We took over the newly captured HUN trenches on that front. A Coy right FRONT. B Coy CENTRE FRONT. C Coy LEFT FRONT. 2 platoons D in TIGER TRENCH. 2 platoons in TOWER SUPPORT. Relief completed by 9.25 pm. B Coy captured a prisoner. No casualties	
	27th		Quiet day. Slight T.M. activity. Captured trenches very muddy. Battn worked in clearing and improving trenches. B Coy captured another prisoner 469th Regt. Casualties 4 OR's wounded. 1 Officer and 3 o.r. went on patrol. Found German front line held.	
	28th		Quiet day. Work on trenches continued. Casualties ~~[illegible]~~ ~~killed~~. nil	
	29th		Enemy barraged for one hour on our trenches at "stand too" Artillery more active all day	

D. D. & L., London, E.C. (A8004) Wt. W1771/M2731 750,000 5/17 Sch. 52 Forms/C2118/14

1st Battn Gordon Highlanders

WAR DIARY
or
~~INTELLIGENCE~~ SUMMARY.
(Erase heading not required.)

Army Form C. 2118.

Instructions regarding War Diaries and Intelligence Summaries are contained in F. S. Regs., Part II. and the Staff Manual respectively. Title pages will be prepared in manuscript.

November 1917
Sheet V

Place	Date	Hour	Summary of Events and Information	Remarks and references to Appendices
BULLECOURT	29th (cont'd)		Casualties 1 man killed 1 wounded. 2 platoons of C Coy were relieved by the 1st Batt Royal MUNSTER FUSILIERS 16 Division	
MORY	30th		Battn was relieved by the 2nd SUFFOLK REGT in the BULLECOURT SECTOR. Relief complete by There was 1 man killed and one wounded. The Battn went into Billets at the ABBAYE MORY	
			Nominal Roll of Officers in the Battalion during the month is attached.	
			R. A. Wolfe-Murray. Major Commdg 1st Batt. The Gordon Highlanders	

D. D. & L., London, E.C. (A8004) Wt. W1771/M2031 750,000 5/17 Sch. 52 Forms/C2118/14

Roll of Officers on Strength of Battalion on 30th. November 1917.

Lieut. Col. J.L.G. Burnett D.S.O.
Major R.A. Wolfe Murray. M.C.
Capt & Adjt, G.W.A. Alexander MC.
Lieut & A/Adjt, W.H. Lyell.
Captain D.R.G. Renfrew T.O.
Lieut. G.H.G. Farrant QM.
" T.C.P. Campbell M.C. Intell. Officer.
" J.R. Newland. L.G. & Bombing "
" G. Ritchie.
2/Lieut. H.J. Walker. Signalling Officer.

"A" Coy.
Capt A.M.B. Norman.
Lieut. D. Hutton.
" J. Merrilees.
2/Lieut. D.E. Bucher.
" W.G. Henderson.
" A.S. Anderson.

"B" Coy.
Capt H.S. Gammell M.C.
2/Lieut. S.C. Clarke.
" J.J. Ogston.
" A.M. Angus.
" E.A.H. Goldfinch.
" P. Cairns.

"C" Coy.
Capt G.E. Malcolm. M.C.
Lieut. C.H. Horswell
" W.A. Johnston.
2/Lieut. R. Reid.
" D. Kennedy.
" J.K. Donald.
" A.Thomson.

"D" Coy.
Lieut. A.W. Annand. M.C.
2/Lieut. M.W. Penman.
" D.H. McGregor.
" F.W. Davitt.
" J. Wilson.
" W.O. Caldicott.

A T T A C H E D.

Capt F.A. Evans. Medical Officer.
Rev. A.M. McIver. Chaplain.

D E T A C H E D.

Capt. W.P.M. Russell MC. Attd 3rd. Div. Depot Bn.
" T.B. Lawrence. M.C. do.
2/Lieut. A.G. Moffatt. do.
Lieut. R.G. Rose Army Signal Coy.
Capt. P.T. Pirie. At Field Ambulance.
Lieut. H.B. Cook. do.
" B.S. Chedburn. do.
" J.G.G. Fleming DSO.MC. 18th. I.B. Depot.
" ~~S.P. Gillespie~~ J.M. Cunningham 76th. Bde HQ.
" S.P. Gillespie. Field Ambulance.

Strength of Battalion.

	O.	O.R.	Total.
Fighting Strength.	45	1035	1080
Details	14	105	119.

R.A. Wolfe Murray
Major.
Commanding 1st Bn. The Gordon Highlanders.

1st Gordon Highlanders

GH 22/1

Vol 34

Army Form C. 2118.

Instructions regarding War Diaries and Intelligence Summaries are contained in F. S. Regs., Part II. and the Staff Manual respectively. Title pages will be prepared in manuscript.

WAR DIARY
or
INTELLIGENCE SUMMARY.

(*Erase heading not required.*)

Place	Date	Hour	Summary of Events and Information	Remarks and references to Appendices
ABBAYE MORY	1.		Battalion rested and cleaned up. Lt Col BURNETT [illegible] to proceed to take over the 18th Inf Bde [illegible] rank of temp. Brigadier General	
	2		GENERAL BURNETT left the Battn for the [illegible] Bde [illegible] and J. G FLEMING. DSO. MC [illegible]	
	3.		Quiet day	
BULLECOURT	4.		The Battn relieved the 2nd SUFFOLK REGT in the BULLECOURT sector in the line. Dispositions [illegible] front. B Coy + 2 platoons X of C Coy in [illegible] SUPPORT [illegible] JOY RIDE LEFT. Remainder of C Coy in TIGER TRENCH. Relief Complete by 9.20 pm. No casualties	
	5		Quiet day. Working parties at night on the [illegible] and support lines. No casualties [illegible]	
	6		Notice came from Division that an enemy attack was impending. It did not come off however!	
	6.		Quiet day. Division ordered special [illegible] news had been received of an [illegible] did not come off	
	7.		Quiet day except for [illegible] Coy relief [illegible]	

D. D. & L., London, E.C.
(A8001) Wt. W1771/M2031 750,000 5/17 Sch. 52 Forms C2118/14

1st Batt Gordon Hghrs.

Instructions regarding War Diaries and Intelligence Summaries are contained in F. S. Regs., Part II. and the Staff Manual respectively. Title pages will be prepared in manuscript.

WAR DIARY
or
INTELLIGENCE SUMMARY.
(Erase heading not required.)

December. Sheet II

Army Form C. 2118.

Place	Date	Hour	Summary of Events and Information	Remarks and references to Appendices
BULLECOURT	7		left Coy sector and B relieved A in right Coy sector. Casualties nil	
	8		Quiet day. The frost which had held since the 5th started thaw and the trenches began to cave in especially in the new front line (BOVIS and TUNNEL TRENCHES) Casualties 1 man wounded.	
	9		Quiet day. Work on strengthening wire continued. Attack by enemy still expected.	
	10		Enemy shelled Battn Hq in the morning in RAILWAY RESERVE otherwise a quiet day. Battn was relieved by the 2nd SUFFOLK REGT. Relief complete 9.30pm. No casualties. Battn went into close support at ECOUST. Dispositions: Battn Hq, B, & C Coys in RAILWAY EMBANKMENT. A Coy in dugouts in ECOUST – MOREUIL Road. D Coy in TIGER TRENCH. The Coys in the EMBANKMENT were very crowded.	
RAILWAY EMBANKMENT ECOUST	11th		Whole Battn "stood too" from 6.30am till 8am on a warning from Brigade. Nothing occurred. Battn was employed on improving shelters and accomodation in their alarm posts at EMBANKMENT. A & D Coys improved	

D. D. & L., London, E.C.
(A8004) Wt. W1771/M2-31 750,000 5/17 Sch. 52 Forms/C2118/14

1st Gordon Highlanders

WAR DIARY
or
INTELLIGENCE SUMMARY.
(Erase heading not required.)

December Sheet III

Army Form C. 2118.

Instructions regarding War Diaries and Intelligence Summaries are contained in F. S. Regs., Part II. and the Staff Manual respectively. Title pages will be prepared in manuscript.

Place	Date	Hour	Summary of Events and Information	Remarks and references to Appendices
~~[illegible]~~ RAILWAY EMBANKMENT.	11		to the 8 KORL and 2nd Suffolks [illegible] C Coy supplies 1 off and 50 or [illegible] 56th Field Coy. RE	
	12		Battn was warned by Brigade of an impending enemy attack. Battn stood too at 6 am [illegible] barrage on 8 KORL on [illegible] 9th Bde front. At 7 am the infantry attack [illegible] against 9th Bde front on our right. [illegible] line between BUNNY HUT [illegible] very vague. Battn stood too [illegible] till stand too next morning. Casualties 9 wounded.	
	13		Battn stood down about 8 am [illegible] working parties at night [illegible] to 2nd Suffolks [illegible]	
	14		Quiet day. During [illegible] positions in the Embankment [illegible] and usual working parties at night [illegible] was killed outside the [illegible] [illegible] One man was wounded.	

(A8004) D. D. & L., London, E.C. Wt. W1771/M2 31 750,000 5/17 Sch. 52 Forms/C2118/14

1st Gordon Highlanders

WAR DIARY
or
INTELLIGENCE SUMMARY.
(Erase heading not required.)

Army Form C. 2118.

Instructions regarding War Diaries and Intelligence Summaries are contained in F. S. Regs., Part II. and the Staff Manual respectively. Title pages will be prepared in manuscript.

December Sheet IV

Place	Date	Hour	Summary of Events and Information	Remarks and references to Appendices
EMBANKMENT	15		Quiet day. In the afternoon 1 batt of the Brigade on our left (119) 19 RWF made a raid on NEPTUNE with artillery support. Believed to have been successful very slight retaliation GENERAL CRAUFURD looked in to see the Battn at lunch time	
	16		Work on the shelters by day	
BULLECOURT		5.30	The Battn relieved the 2nd SUFFOLK RGT in the line in the evening at 5.30 pm Dispositions C & B Coys front line ½ D Coy and A Coy in TOWER TRENCH and JOY RIDE LEFT. ½ D in STATION REDOUBT Relief not complete till 10.30 pm no casualties	
	17		A few shells fell on RAILWAY RESERVE otherwise a quiet day. About 8 pm C Coy reported 18 pdrs firing short. 1 Cpl killed and 2 men wounded MG fire was also reported to be falling short.	
	18		Quiet day. Work as usual during the night. Support coys wiring front line and JOY RIDE. 1 Coy of 2/Suffolks was carrying for us. Again trouble over short shooting of 18 pdrs no casualties Hard frost.	
	19		Internal relief at dusk. No carrying parties from Suffolks no casualties Hard frost	
	20		Frost held all day and no work could be done in the hard ground. Wiring was done on existing stakes in front of the support line under cover of a thick mist in the afternoon no short shooting during the night.	
	21		Frost still holding. Some snow. Wiring in the afternoon had to be curtailed owing to MG being opened on the party	

D. D. & L., London, E.C. (A8004) Wt. W1771/M2 31 750,000 5/17 Sch. 52 Forms/C2118/14

1st Gordon Highlanders

Instructions regarding War Diaries and Intelligence Summaries are contained in F. S. Regs., Part II. and the Staff Manual respectively. Title pages will be prepared in manuscript.

WAR DIARY
or
INTELLIGENCE SUMMARY.
(Erase heading not required.)

Army Form C. 2118.

Place	Date	Hour	Summary of Events and Information	Remarks and references to Appendices
BULLECOURT	22		Quiet day.	
ABBOYE [illegible] MORY		7.30	The Batt was relieved in the line by the [illegible] Reserve relief. Relief complete 7.30 pm [illegible]	
	23.		Batt rested and cleaned up [illegible] [illegible] billeting	
	24		Batt under Coy arrangements [illegible] Armourer Sgt. started inspection of rifles	
	25		Christmas Day. Coys inspected by the C.O. [illegible] parade grounds [illegible]	
		2.30	Concert in MORY THEATRE for Batt in the afternoon. [illegible] issue of beer to the Batt also plum puddings.	
	26.		Quiet day. CO inspected D Coy in the morning [illegible] held in our billets. GEN. CAMERON [illegible] with Batt	
	27.		Batt paraded under Coy arrangements [illegible] intensely cold. Coys did some marching and [illegible]	
		12 noon	R.S.M.'s parade for drill. C.O. [illegible] the officers [illegible]	
	28.		Quiet day. Batt was visited by the C.O. of the 19th Middlesex Regt. who relieved us in Brigade Reserve on the 28th inst. Batt prepared to move on the 29th.	

D. D. & L., London, E.C.
(A8004) Wt. W1771/M2731 750,000 5/17 Sch. 52 Forms/C2118/14

Instructions regarding War Diaries and Intelligence Summaries are contained in F. S. Regs., Part II. and the Staff Manual respectively. Title pages will be prepared in manuscript.

WAR DIARY
or
INTELLIGENCE SUMMARY.
(Erase heading not required.)

Army Form C. 2118.

Place	Date	Hour	Summary of Events and Information	Remarks and references to Appendices
MORY ABBAYE	29		Reveille 7 am. Batt[n] paraded to move off to new area at 9.40 pm. Transport following 200 yds in rear of Batt[n].	
HENDECOURT.			Batt arrived in No 5 Camp at 2 30 pm. Camp all Missen Huts in rather a bad condition	
	30.		Battalion was employed in cleaning up and improving the Camp generally. Coys Commanders conference in the evening	
	31.		Battalion paraded by Companys at 9 30 pm for rapid running and marching. RSM's parade at 12 midday officers under the Commanding Officer. Being HOGMANAY the officers had a dinner at which GOC 76 BRIGADE attended also Capt. W G GRAHAM and the BM 76th Bde. The Sergeants Mess held a Smoking Concert at 9.30 pm which was attended by the GOC 76th Inf Bde and other guests also the Commanding Officer 2nd in command, adjutant and Coy commanders of the Battalion	

R A Bagge Murray Lt Col
Comdg 1st Gordon Highlanders

D. D. & L., London, E.C.
(A8004) Wt. W1771/M2931 750,000 5/17 Sch. 52 Forms/C2118/14

1st. Battalion The Gordon Highlanders.

Roll of Officers on strength of Battalion on 31/1[illegible]

Lieut. Col. R.A. Wolfe Murray. D.C.
Major G.E. Malcolm. M.C.
Capt & A/Adjt, H.S. Gemmell M.C.
Lieut & Asst/Adjt, A.H. Lyell.
Captain D.R.G. Renfrew, T.O.
Lieut. D. Hutton A/W.O.
Lieut. T.C.P. Campbell M.C. I.O.
Lieut. J.R. McLinnc.
Lieut. G. Ritchie.
2/Lieut. H.C. Salter, Signalling Officer.

"A" Coy.
Capt A.C.B. Morgan. (Commanding)
Lieut. A.S. Harvey.
" J. Merrilees.
2/Lieut. P.K. Bucher.
" A.G. Henderson.
" A.S. Anderson.
" C. Hutchins.

"B" Coy.
Lieut. C.H. Horswell (Commdg)
2/Lieut. S.C. Clarke.
" A.A. Angus.
" [illegible].A.H. Goldfinch.
" J.J. Ogston.
" P. Cairns.
" G. Murray.

"C" Coy.
2/Lieut. J. Wilson (Commdg)
Lieut. A.McL. Bell.
2/Lieut. R. Reid.
" D. Kennedy.
" A. Thomson.
" J.F. Donald.
Lieut. W.A. Johnston.

"D" Coy.
Captain A.W. Annand. M.C. (Commdg)
Lieut. H.B. Cook.
2/Lieut. E.W. Penman.
" D.H. McGregor.
" F.W. Davitt.
" W.O. Caldicott.
" A.G. Moffat.

A T T A C H E D.

Captain F.A. Evans, Medical Officer.
Rev. A.M. McIver. Chaplain.

D E T A C H E D.

Captain W.A.M. Russell. M.C. Attd 3rd. Div. Depot Bn.
Lieut. R.G. Roe, Army Signal Coy.
Captain P.T. Pirie, Field Ambulance.
Lieut. J.G.G. Fleming D.S.O. M.C. Interview at War Office.

Strength of Battalion.	O.	O.R.	Total.
Fighting Strength.	42	977	1019.
Details.	1[illegible]	115	129.

Lieut. Col.
Commanding 1st Bn. The Gordon Highlanders.

2nd Division

War Diaries

1st Gordon Highlanders

January To 21st ~~July~~ ~~August~~ December

1918

76th Brigade.

3rd Division.

1st BATTALION GORDON HIGHLANDERS::: JANUARY 1918.

WAR DIARY
for January 1918 1 Gordon Hrs
~~INTELLIGENCE SUMMARY.~~
(Erase heading not required.)

Army Form C. 2118.

Vol 46

Instructions regarding War Diaries and Intelligence Summaries are contained in F. S. Regs., Part II. and the Staff Manual respectively. Title pages will be prepared in manuscript.

Place	Date	Hour	Summary of Events and Information	Remarks and references to Appendices
S. Mefield	1st		A whole holiday according to Brigadier's Instructions	
—do—	2nd		Training started in earnest. There was an excellent Parade Ground just outside the Camp; quite sufficient for all 4 Companies to parade without interfering with one another. Very cold and training difficult in consequence	
—do—	3rd		Still no sign of a break in the frost. Usual training parades. Considerable difficulty was experienced in getting wood to keep the Stoves going.	
—do—	4th		Usual training parades. Certain Officers proceeded in a Lorry to reconnoitre Corps Second Line about CROISILLES.	
—do—	5th		Inspection of Companies by Commanding Officer. Hut competition in afternoon. Lecture to Officers by Comdg Off. on Ceremonial Drill	
—do—	6th		Church Parade in Coy. Officers Mess Hut. Padre McIvers farewell sermon	
—do—	7th		Usual platoon training till 12 Noon, after C.O's parade, practice of March Past etc for G.O.C's Inspection next day Our American Doctor Evans left.	

A6945 Wt. W11422/M1160 350,000 12/16 D. D. & L. Forms/C./2118/14.

Army Form C. 2118.

Instructions regarding War Diaries and Intelligence Summaries are contained in F. S. Regs., Part II. and the Staff Manual respectively. Title pages will be prepared in manuscript.

WAR DIARY or INTELLIGENCE SUMMARY.

for January 1918

(*Erase heading not required.*)

Place	Date	Hour	Summary of Events and Information	Remarks and references to Appendices
In the field	8th		Inspection by G.O.C. 76th Brigade at [illegible] [illegible] just as he was coming on to parade when [illegible] all day. March Past in the [illegible] and [illegible] Clearing Scheme. Lewis Guns on the Range to be cancelled [illegible] very pleased with the Battalion's Turnout [illegible]	
— do —	9th		Usual training parades. [illegible] in the afternoon.	
— do —	10th		Everything quite soft and very muddy. [illegible] the Corps Commander's Inspection at 2 pm. The [illegible] after the March Past.	
— do —	11th		Usual training parades. [illegible] Coy training.	
— do —	12th		Thaw continued. Battalion training. Coy [illegible] Lieut [illegible] reported. Brigadier General Crawford [illegible] the Battalion.	[illegible] U.S. Army
— do —	13th		Frosty weather. Church Service in the Officers' [illegible] Coy. Major J. J. Pryde C.B.	
— do —	14th		Frost continued but thaw set in in the evening.	

A6945 Wt. W11422/M1160 350,000 12/16 D. D. & L. Forms/C./2118/14.

Instructions regarding War Diaries and Intelligence Summaries are contained in F. S. Regs., Part II. and the Staff Manual respectively. Title pages will be prepared in manuscript.

Army Form C. 2118.

WAR DIARY
or
INTELLIGENCE SUMMARY.
(*Erase heading not required.*)

January 1918

Place	Date	Hour	Summary of Events and Information	Remarks and references to Appendices
In the field	14th	(contd)	Battalion training, 1 Coy on Range, 1 Coy Wiring, 2 Companies Coy training	
-do-	15th		Raining and everything quite soft. Battalion training as 14th	
			Visit from General Craufurd	
-do-	16th		Training as on 15th. General P.W. Brown visited the Battalion.	
			Weather still continues wet but mild.	
-do-	17th		Battalion was to practice counter attack in conjunction with	
			aeroplanes owing to weather conditions it was postponed.	
-do-	18th		[illegible] still continued. In the morning – 1 Coy on Range, remainder Coy	
			training. At 2.30 pm the Battalion marched to see demonstration	
			by 76th T.M.B.	
-do-	19th		3 Coys practised counter attack in conjunction with aeroplanes.	
			B Coy on Range in morning.	
-do-	20th		Weather still continued fine. Divine Service held in Officers	
			Mess by Captain Burke C.F., who had arrived the day before.	
-do-	21st		Weather continues fine. Ground very wet. Battalion training.	
-do-	22nd		Battalion training 1 Coy on Range. B Coy practising field firing,	

A6945 Wt. W11422/M1160 350,000 12/16 D. D. & L. Forms/C./2118/14.

Instructions regarding War Diaries and Intelligence Summaries are contained in F. S. Regs., Part II. and the Staff Manual respectively. Title pages will be prepared in manuscript.

WAR DIARY
or
INTELLIGENCE SUMMARY.
(*Erase heading not required.*)

January 1918

Army Form C. 2118.

Place	Date	Hour	Summary of Events and Information	Remarks and references to Appendices
In the field	23rd		Weather still continues fine. 2Lt J. Thomson [illegible]	
			Coy training, 1 Coy on Range 1 Coy firing [illegible]	
-do-	24th		Battalion paraded as strong as possible and [illegible]	
			Line [illegible] WAILLY. B Coy [illegible]	
			carried out demonstration [illegible]	
			and NCOs of 3rd Division. [illegible]	
-do-	25th		Battalion moved from [illegible] CARLISLE LINE ([illegible]	
			BEAURAINS)	
-do-	26th		Battalion moved to trenches and relieved [illegible]	
			Fusiliers 34th Division [illegible] WANCOURT-	
			GUEMAPPE Sector. Relief completed 9.45 pm. No casualties	
-do-	27th		Very clean trenches though rather shallow in places [illegible]	
			not revetted. Line quiet [illegible] very good [illegible]	
-do-	28th		Misty in morning but cleared later. B Coy [illegible]	
			in the afternoon in a [illegible]	
			the enemy; 1 man killed [illegible]	

A6945 Wt. W11422/M1160 350,000 12/16 D. D. & L. Forms/C./2118/14.

Instructions regarding War Diaries and Intelligence Summaries are contained in F. S. Regs., Part II. and the Staff Manual respectively. Title pages will be prepared in manuscript.

WAR DIARY
for
INTELLIGENCE SUMMARY.

January 1918

(*Erase heading not required.*)

Army Form C. 2118.

Place	Date	Hour	Summary of Events and Information	Remarks and references to Appendices
In the field	28th		alteration of dispositions to 2 Coys in front line. After dark the Coys moved A Coy going back to MARLIERES caves (North east of WANCOURT)	
-do-	29th		Divisional Commander round the line in the morning and gave instructions for change back to the old disposition with 3 Coys in the front line. A Coy right front beyond COJEUL River 'C' Coy centre front – D Coy left front and B Coy in Support. Changed round after dark. All this greatly upset work only Support Coy (B) being able to do full nights work. In 2 nights about 400 yards of thick Concertina entanglement put out with loose wire as well. Captain C.G.C. [illegible], Lieut D.R.A. [illegible] & Lieut 2/Lt N.J.P. Allison and Lieut C.P. Brown joined from England	
-do-	30th		Beautiful day. 2 OR wounded. Relieved by 10th R.W.F. in evening. A few gas shells over during relief. Relief complete. Battalion back to Support in WANCOURT area with 1 Coy in EGRET Trench (on right bank of COJEUL) and 1 in MARLIERES Caves	

A6945 Wt. W11422/M1160 350,000 12/16 D. D. & L. Forms/C./2118/14.

Instructions regarding War Diaries and Intelligence Summaries are contained in F. S. Regs., Part II. and the Staff Manual respectively. Title pages will be prepared in manuscript.

WAR DIARY
or
INTELLIGENCE SUMMARY.

(*Erase heading not required.*)

for January 1918

Army Form C. 2118.

Place	Date	Hour	Summary of Events and Information	Remarks and references to Appendices
In Reserve	31st		Fatigue Parties in the line and on the [illegible] [illegible] [illegible] under construction	
			G. S. Malcolm Major	
			(Comdg 1st Bn [illegible] [illegible])	

A6945 Wt. W11422/M1160 350,000 12/16 D. D. & L. Forms/C./2118/14.

1st. Battalion The Gordon Highlanders.

Roll of Officers on strength of Battalion at 31/1/18.

Lieut. Col. R.A. Wolfe Murray M.C.
Major G.E. Malcolm. M.C
Captain and A/Adjutant H.S. Gammell M.C.
Captain and Asst/Adjt, W.A. Dyke.
Captain D.R.G. Renfrew. Transport Officer.
Lieut D. Hutton, Quartermaster.
Lieut. T.C.P. Campbell M.C. Intell. Officer.
Lieut. J.R. Newland. Lewis Gun Officer.
2/Lieut. H.J. Walker Signalling Officer
Lieut. G. Ritchie.

"A" Coy.

Captain A.M.B. Norman (Commdg)
Lieut. A.S. Harvey.
" D.D.A. Lockhart.
2/Lieut. D.E. Bucher.
" W.G. Henderson.
" A.S. Anderson.
" C.D.M. Hutchins.
" W.H. Gunn.
Lieut. J. Merrilees.

"B" Coy.

Captain C.H. Horswell (Commdg)
Lieut. W.H. Lyell.
2/Lieut. S.C. Clarke.
" A.M. Angus.
" E.A.H. Goldfinch.
" J.J. Ogston.
" P. Cairns.
" G. Murray.
" J. Thomson.
" C.P. Drover.

"C" Coy.

Captain C.G.C. Davey. (Commdg)
Lieut. A McL. Bell.
2/Lieut. J. Wilson.
" R. Reid.
" D. Kennedy.
" A. Thomson.
" J.K. Donald.
Lieut. W.A. Johnston.

"D" Coy.

Captain A.W. Annand MC. (Commdg)
Lieut. H.B. Cook.
2/Lieut. M.W. Penman.
" D.H. McGregor.
" F.W. Davitt.
" W.O. Caldecott.
" A.G. Moffatt
" A.D. Scarth.
Lieut. H.J.N.P. Allison.

A T T A C H E D.

Lieut. C.A. Bardsley Medical Officer.
Rev. E.H. Duke. Chaplain.

D E T A C H E D.

Captain W.P.M. Russell M.C. Attd 3rd. Div. Depot Bn.
Lieut. R G. Roe, Attached Army Signal Coy.
Captain P.T. Pirie Field Ambulance.

Strength of Battalion.

	Off.	O.R	Total.
Fighting Strength.	49	955	1004.
Details.	1[illegible]	130	14[illegible].

Lieut. Col.
Commanding 1st Bn. The Gordon Highlanders.

31 -1- 18.

76th Brigade.

3rd Division.

<u>1st BATTALION GORDON HIGHLANDERS :: FEBRUARY 1918.</u>

Instructions regarding War Diaries and Intelligence Summaries are contained in F. S. Regs., Part II. and the Staff Manual respectively. Title pages will be prepared in manuscript.

WAR DIARY

~~or INTELLIGENCE SUMMARY.~~

(*Erase heading not required.*)

Army Form C. 2118.

Place	Date	Hour	Summary of Events and Information	Remarks and references to Appendices
WANCOURT GUEMAPPE	1/2/18		Heard of proposed disbanding of 10th R.W.F. and our relief of them in front line that night. All quiet, and relief complete 8.25 p.m. No casualties.	
	2/2/18		Col. Wolfe Murray left the line early to go on leave. Raid at 8.30 am by Bn on our left (4th Worc). Slight retaliation on our front. 2 killed.	
	3rd		Hostile artillery rather active at intervals during the day gas and H.E. Casualties 1 killed. Div. on our left carried out a gas bombardment in the evening, which produced some retaliation on our sector. Work on improvement of trenches.	
	4th		Quieter. Fine weather still held. Trenches dry. Usual work. No casualties.	
	5th		Usual work. No casualties	
	6th		Quiet day. Relief in evening by ~~[illegible]~~ 8th K.O.R.L. Relief complete 7.10 pm. No casualties. Back to support just behind WANCOURT.	
	7th		Baths at NEUVILLE VITASSE. Work on the new support Bn HQ. under construction. Fatigues in the line at night.	
	8th		As 7th. Weather fine & dry.	
	9th		Attempted hostile raid to right of Bde sector during morning stand-to. Artillery active for about half an hour but nothing anywhere near our position in support. Bn relieved 2/Suffolk Regt in Right Subsection. All quiet. Relief complete 9.15 pm.	

B. (A8004) Wt. W1771/M2031 750,000 5/17 Sch. 52 Forms/C2118/14 D. D. & L., London, E.C.

Instructions regarding War Diaries and Intelligence Summaries are contained in F. S. Regs., Part II. and the Staff Manual respectively. Title pages will be prepared in manuscript.

WAR DIARY
or
INTELLIGENCE SUMMARY.
(Erase heading not required.)

Army Form C. 2118.

Place	Date	Hour	Summary of Events and Information	Remarks and references to Appendices
WANCOURT–GUEMAPPE	Feb. 10th		Some gas shells round Bn H.Q. at morning stand-to. Otherwise quiet.	
	11th		Quiet day. Our snipers very active against individual movement behind enemy's line. No retaliation. Major G.E. Malcolm went off for the day to a tank demonstration and Capt. C.G.C. Davey in command.	
	12th		Everything as usual.	
	13th		Slight shelling round Bn H.Q. and SHIKAR AVENUE during the day. Usual work.	
	14th		Very clear day, and our snipers active again. Work as usual. Still no signs of break in the weather.	
	15th		Relief by 8th K.O.R.L. who moved into the new Bn H.Q. in EGRET TRENCH, barely completed. The Bn back to support.	
	16th		Baths at NEUVILLE VITASSE. Usual work on new H.Q. and wire-carrying in the line for K.R.R.C.	
	17th		Same as 16th.	
	18th		Relief of 2nd Suffolk Regt. in left subsection. Relief complete 8.30 p.m. No casualties, but gas shells round Bn H.Q. between 9 and 10 pm.	
	19th		Trenches dry as ever. Quiet day. No casualties.	
	20th		Quiet during day. Some T.M.s on EE post ('C' coy) about 9 pm. Successful retaliation by our 4.5" hows.	
	21st		T.M.s on 'C' coy again during morning stand-to. Retaliation again. Several artillery officers up during morning to ~~[illegible]~~ locate it. Visibility very good. Much sniping by our 18 pdrs on individual movement behind enemy's lines.	

D. D. & L., London, E.C. (A8001) Wt. W1771/M2031 750,000 5/17 Sch. 52 Forms/C2118/14

Army Form C. 2118.

WAR DIARY
or
~~INTELLIGENCE SUMMARY.~~

(Erase heading not required.)

Instructions regarding War Diaries and Intelligence Summaries are contained in F. S. Regs., Part II. and the Staff Manual respectively. Title pages will be prepared in manuscript.

Place	Date	Hour	Summary of Events and Information	Remarks and references to Appendices
WANCOURT–GUÉMAPPE	Feb 22nd		A slight drizzle, the first rain for a long time. Quiet as usual. Work on KEY and CAVALRY TRENCHES (the new RESERVE LINE)	
	23rd		~~[illegible] no casualties~~ Raid by 7th Cameron Highlanders (15th Divn) on our left 3.30 am. Retaliation slight, but 1 killed & 2 wounded. Quiet during day	
	24th		Relief by 8th K.O.S.L., complete 8 pm. No casualties. Back to support.	
	25th		Baths work on new H.Q. and fatigues in the line as usual. Col. Wolfe-Murray back from leave.	
	26th		As 25th	
	27th		Relief of 2nd Suffolk Regt. in right subsection. New dispositions, 2 coys in front line, 2 in support instead of 3 in front line & 1 in support. Relief complete 8.10 pm. Casualties nil.	
	28th		Work on digging new trench on both sides of KESTREL AVENUE, and wiring APE SUPPORT. Casualties 2 wounded.	

R. A. Wolfe-Murray Lieut-Col
cmdg 1st Bn The Gordon Highlanders

D. D. & L., London, E.C.
(A8001) Wt. W1771/M2031 750,000 5/17 Sch. 52 Forms/C2118/14

1st. Battalion The Gordon Highlanders.

Roll of Officers on strength of Battalion at 28/2/18.

Lieut.Col. R.A. Wolfe Murray M.C.
Major G.E. Malcolm M.C.
Capt & A/Adjt, H.S. Gammell M.C.
Capt & Asst/Adjt, W.A. Dyke.
Lieut. T.C.P. Campbell M.C. Int. Officer.
Captain D.R.G. Renfrew, Transport "
Lieut. J.R.Newland L.G. Officer.
Lieut. D. Hutton A/QM.
2/Lieut. H.J. Walker Signalling Officer.

"A" Coy.

Capt A.M.B.Norman (Commdg)
Lieut. A.S. Harvey.
2/Lieut. D.F.Bucher.
" W.G. Henderson.
" C.D.M. Hutchins.

"B" Coy.

Capt C.H.Horswell (Commdg)
2/Lieut. S.C. Clarke.
" A.M. Angus.
" W. Murray.
" J. Thomson.
" P. Cairns.
Lieut. C.P. Drover.

"C" Coy.

Capt C.G.C. Davey (Commdg)
Lieut. A.McL. Bell
Lieut. W.A. Johnston.
2/Lieut. R. Reid.
" D. Kennedy.
" A. Thomson.
" J.K. Donald.

"D" Coy.

2/Lieut. J. Wilson (Commdg)
" D. McGregor.
" F.W. Davitt.
" A.G. Moffat.
" A.D. Scarth.

A T T A C H E D.

Lieut. C.A. Bardsley.	Medical Officer.
Rev. E.H. Duke.	Chaplain.

D E T A C H E D.

Capt W.P.M. Russell M.C.	3rd. Div Depot Battn.
Lieut. R.G. Ree,	Army Signal Coy.
Capt A.W. Annand M.C.	Hospital.
Lieut. H.J.N.P. Allison.	"
Lieut. G. Ritchie.	"
Lieut. D.D.A. Lockhart.	"
Lieut. W.S.Hastings ,	"
2/Lieut. W.H. Gunn.	"
" M.W. Penman.	"
" J.J.Ogston.	"

STRENGTH OF BATTALION.

	Officers.	O.R.	Total.
Fighting Strength.	43	905	948
Details.	18	87	105

Lieut. Col.
Commanding 1st Bn. The Gordon Highlanders.

Copy.

To. Officer Commanding
1st Bn. The Gordon Highlanders.

On behalf of all ranks of the 10th. Battalion Royal Welch Fusiliers, I desire to thank you for your very friendly message on the breaking up of this Battalion.

This unit heard of its disruption and consequent severance from the 1st Bn. Gordon Highlanders and other units of the 76th. Infantry Brigade with keen regret.

We shall always cherish both the memory of our rivalry on the playing field and our emulation of the 1st Gordons on the field of Battle. We are not without hope that in our new sphere we may still be associated with the 75th. Regiment.

(Sgd) R.A. Anderson Major.
Commanding 10th. Battalion Royal Welch Fusiliers

Carlisle Lines.

France.
3/2/18.

To Major R.A. Anderson, Officers and Men of
10th. Battn./Welch. Fusiliers.
Royal

The Commanding Officer, Officers and men of the 1st Bn. The Gordon Highlanders wish to express their great regret at bidding you farewell.

We have played against you and fought alongside you, and have always found you the best of friends.

May you have the best of luck always wherever you may be; we will never forget you.

(Sgd) G.E. Malcolm Major.
Commanding 1st Bn. The Gordon Highlanders

76th Brigade.

3rd Division.

1st BATTALION

GORDON HIGHLANDERS

MARCH 1918

Instructions regarding War Diaries and Intelligence Summaries are contained in F. S. Regs., Part II. and the Staff Manual respectively. Title pages will be prepared in manuscript.

76/13

WAR DIARY
or
INTELLIGENCE SUMMARY.
(Erase heading not required.)

1 Gordon H.

8/A 42

Army Form C. 2118.

Place	Date	Hour	Summary of Events and Information	Remarks and references to Appendices
WANCOURT Sector Right	1.3.18		Light shelling quiet day Bright in the morning but began snowing hard in the afternoon Work digging new trench (both sides of Rutted Avenue & Wiring Casualties nil	
	2.3.18		Quiet day Dull & cold, began snowing about 1.20 pm Work clearing up trenches Relieved by 8th Battn KSLI & 2 platoons W Company 2nd Suffolk Regt Relief complete 9.5 pm Battn moved back to support dugouts. Casualties 1 wounded	
Support dugouts	3.3.18		Quiet day cold & sky cloudy Casualties nil	
	4/3/18		Quiet day cold wind blowing sky overcast A Coy worked on new trench in front of Buzzard work had to be discontinued on account of darkness worked resumed at 5 AM morning of 5th Casualties nil	
	5/3/18		Quiet day Fairly bright sunshine Work on Signals cable & new trench in front of Buzzard C Coy relieved W Coy 2nd Suffolks in RAKE Trench Relief complete 9.15 PM Battn HQ moved into new head quarters A: D Coys Battled Casualties nil	
	6.3.18		Quiet day Sun shining brightly. Work on new Battn HQ. 2nd Lieut J Clarke reported from RMUR and was posted to A Coy Casualties nil	
Left Sector WANCOURT	7.3.18		Quiet day sun shining brightly work on support dugouts Relieved 2nd Suffolk Regt in Left WANCOURT Sector Relief complete 6.30 pm Casualties nil Relieved by 8th KORLR in support dugouts.	
	8.3.18		Quiet day Sun shining brightly work digging of new trench and U bays in RAKE Trench Casualties 1 Killed 1 wounded	
	9.3.18		Quiet sunny day Few shells fell near Battn HQ from 7 to 9 pm work on RAKE Trench Casualties Capt C H HORSWELL & 5 O.R wounded.	
	10.3.18		Sunny quiet day work on RAKE still continues also work on SHOVEL. C Coy HQ moved from RAKE to KEY SUPPORT. D Coy from CAVALRY Trench to NEW BISON. Casualties 1 O R wounded	
	11.3.18		Very quiet day Sun shining brightly usual work on RAKE & SHOVEL Trenches Casualties nil	
	12.3.18		Sun shining brightly Quiet day. Battn Relieved by 8th King Own RL Regt after relief dispositions were as follows A Coy RAKE. D Coy SHOVEL & NORTHERN Trench B.C & Battn HQ Support dugouts Relief complete 9.15 pm Casualties nil	

D. D. & L., London, E.C.
(A8001) Wt. W1771/M2031 750,000 5/17 Sch. 52 Forms/C2118/14

Instructions regarding War Diaries and Intelligence Summaries are contained in F. S. Regs., Part II. and the Staff Manual respectively. Title pages will be prepared in manuscript.

WAR DIARY
or
INTELLIGENCE SUMMARY.
(Erase heading not required.)

Army Form C. 2118.

Place	Date	Hour	Summary of Events and Information	Remarks and references to Appendices
WANCOURT SECTOR Support Trenches	13.3.18		Quiet day. Our artillery commence harrassing fire on enemy's positions. Casualties nil	
	14.3.18		Fairly dull day but brightened towards noon. 7.30 p.m C Coy relieved D in SHOVEL & NORTHERN TRENCH. Nightly harrassing fire of our artillery on enemy's lines still continues. Casualties nil	
	15.3.18		Quiet day sunny but chilly north easterly wind blowing. Harrassing fire still continues. Casualties 1 OR wounded.	
	16.3.18		Quiet day. Enemy shell front slightly in retaliation to our harrassing bombardment. B Coy relieved C Coy in SHOVEL & NORTHERN Trenches. Casualties 1 OR wounded	
	17.3.18		Quiet day weather threatening. Casualties 1 OR wounded	
	18.3.18		Weather fine slightly cloudy. Quiet day. C Coy relieved B in SHOVEL & NORTHERN Trenches. D Coy relieved A in RAKE. Relief complete 9.30 p.m 2 OR wounded	
	19.3.18		Quiet day Raining. Casualties nil.	
	20.3.18		Quiet & misty day cloudy in the morning but brightened in the afternoon. B Coy relieved C in SHOVEL & NORTHERN Trenches relief complete 9.45 p.m Casualties nil	
	21.3.18		Misty day till 10 AM afterwards weather fine & sunny. Great enemy offensive began on our Right. Our front quiet except for heavy enemy barrage	
			21st to 29th Already recorded	
	30.3.18		Battalion after being relieved from NEUVILLE VITASSE by 31st Battn Canadian Inf marched to RIVIERE. Every one was in their billets by 8.20 A.M. After a hot breakfast all Ranks slept till 1.30 pm then had dinner at 2.30 pm. Battn marched off for WARLUZEL Route BEAMETZ-R, [illegible], Gouy en Artois, Sombrin. Although it rained all the time and the roads were heavy the distance about 18 Kilometres the men marched well and were in good spirits. Only 5 men fell out. Battn Reached WARLUZEL at 7.30 p.m. A draft of 63 OR joined here. The total distance that day was about 29 kilometres and this after 7 days continuous fighting & 52 days in the trenches.	
	31.3.18		Day of Resting & getting cleaned up.	

D. D. & L., London, E.C. (A8001) Wt. W1771/M2031 750,000 5/17 Sch. 52 Forms/C2118/14

The Boche Offensive
(March 1918)
in so far as it concerned me.

Written by:- Lieutenant D.D.A.Lockhart, 1st Gordon Highlanders, (3rd Division, VI Corps, Third Army.).

- - - - - - - - - - - - - - -

Written in hospital in Mount Street, London.

About the middle of March, I came back from hospital after trench fever and duly reported at Battalion Headquarters. Here I was told that I might go back to "Details", and live peacefully there for a few days, in order to get fit again. Accordingly I went back and, sharing a Nissen hut with the Padre and Cabane, the interpreter, I lived in the height of comfort for a few days.

I am rather hazy about exact dates but it must have been the night of the 20th-21st that we were aroused by the most terrific barrage opening. It sounded at first as if it came from our part of the line, but after close investigation, we decided that it was further slightly south. We all said to each other at Details-"This is the beginning of the offensive".

The shelling had undoubtedly increased even in front of us, and the whole of the following day, the Boche was sending shells right over into our back areas, including the Arras-Bapaume Road, and even Boisleux-au Mont, where Divisional Headquarters was situated, a thing quite unprecedented, and very startling to the various military inhabitants of the said back areas!

All that day, varied and wild rumours kept filtering in. We heard pretty authoritatively that Bullecourt had been taken and also Croisilles, but not even the most imaginative rumour-monger of a quartermaster sergeant dreamt that the offensive had been launched on such a wide frontage as it actually was. We all of us regretted the loss of Bullecourt, but fully imagined that the Guards or some other Division would promptly do a counter-attack and find not much difficulty in ejecting the invader once again.

That night (the 21st-22nd, I imagine) the shelling intensified into another barrage, but luckily it failed to keep us from sleep, and in fact we all of us slept at least eleven hours, which was as well, considering what was to follow. March 22nd I was just sitting down to breakfast at about 10.30, when R. the Transport Officer, came in and announced that he had got a telephone message from Battalion Headquarters saying that Harvey (who had also been having a rest at Details) and I were both to report there by lunch time. It came as rather a shock to both of us, after our peaceful time at Details, but anyway rumour was current that the Division was to be relieved any day, after its long spell of sixty days in the line. So at noon, we said goodbye to the Padre and started out.

We found Battalion Headquarters just sitting down to lunch, and after reporting, we sought out A Coy., which was stationed at the old Battalion Headquarters on the Wancourt - Tilloy road.

H..relieved N..of the command of the Company, the latter returning to Details. The only other officers were H.. and C.. a full Lieutenant newly transferred from the Naval Division.

We whiled away that day fairly peacefully, reading and writing letters, but we could not but notice the increase in shelling. When I had been there before, a shell on that side of Wancourt was almost unheard of, and now they were constantly dropping into the valley all round.

At about 9.30 p.m., we retired to bed, in the dugout, and about 10 o'clock we were just dropping off to sleep, when suddenly a Battalion Orderly came in with a message for Harvey.

"Pack up everything and stand to on the road", was the gist of the order, and we dragged ourselves from our beds, got our things together, and went up on to the road to collect our platoons; no one knew what was happening, but the rumour went round that we were going to retreat, a rumour which seemed confirmed by the tremendous bustle and activity which was going on along the road. Motor lorries, never before seen so near to the line in that part, were trundling along in the direction of Wancourt, limbers, drawn by horses and mules, were constantly moving along the road, and one great tractor with caterpillar wheels was preparing to take back a six inch gun from the battery situated just behind us.

I collected my platoon - No.1 - on to the road and introduced myself to the platoon sergeant B., new since I was with the Company before, he had been Transport Sergeant at Aberdeen since the beginning of the war, and had only been out three or four days.

The men's great coats were now collected and put on a lorry, and bombs were issued out to every man. We were then sent along to a dump to draw picks and shovels, and after that were allotted a length of trench to dig. It took some time to get to our places and start digging, and we had no sooner done so than we got the order to close on the road again. There I found Major M..the second in command. He told me that I was to take No.1 and 2 Platoons along to dig under Captain D.. who was in command of C Coy., and that I was to come along with him then and see the place.

On the way I sounded him as to what was happening, and he told me that we were withdrawing from the present front line, 1½ miles away, and that the trench we were going to dig was thenceforth to be the front line; this was owing to the advance of the Boche further south. The Suffolks who were in the front line were to remain there until just before dawn, when they would withdraw, leaving one platoon to keep up the fiction as long as possible. He said that when the Boche found out what had happened, anything might be expected - cavalry down the Tilloy road etc. He also said that we had the Guards Division and a lot of Tanks behind us, a rumour which I afterwards discovered to be mostly false (<u>some</u> of the Guards were digging the Army line by Neuville Vitasse, that was all).

When we got to the place, M..detailed a C Coy. sergeant to guide me and my platoons along to Captain D.. After plodding along for about 200 yards over difficult ground, the sergeant said feebly that he must have lost his way and that he would go on and find out whether that were the right trench. He disappeared, and after we had waited some time, we heard someone shouting for us from away in front of the trench we were standing by. We at once moved across to where the shouting came from and discovered the real trench there. After much wandering, I found D.. also, who was in conversation with the C.O. They instructed me as to where my men were to dig, and at length after a long period of indescribable annoynace to myself, during which I lost men and found them again, lost both breath and temper trying to get D..'s men out of the trench that we were to dig, and nearly lost patience with honest but inefficient Sergeant B. After a long time, as I have said, I at last got the men working in their appointed places. The trench was the most wretched one; part of it was an old trench, very wide and mostly fallen in - the rest was new enough, but had been dug a foot deep or more already, and wide enough for a motor car to drive along it. This was to prove a great annoyance in the days to come.

All night the road was thronged with traffic-limbers, lorries, field guns moving backwards and forwards along the road(the field guns of course were moving backwards). Towards dawn, we struck work and moved to the right, to the trenches we were really to occupy. No.2 platoon was just to the right of the Wancourt-Tilloy road. No.1 platoon to the left. By and By the Suffolks who had been occupying the front line passed along the road to the rear, and we then blocked the roads with knife-rests and the railway line also.

<u>March 23rd.</u> At 5 o'clock we stood to till 7 a.m., but before that time I had my scrappy breakfast, which consisted of tea, melted cheese spread on bread and euphemistically styled "Welsh Rabbit" by my servant (Wilson) and then I was given some bread, butter and marmalade by a private in my platoon who had compassion on me. This breakfast I ate in Platoon Headquarters, which was quite a respectable "elephant" hut covered with earth and containing seven wire beds, a stove and a bench (It is marked "Shelter" in Map 1). Company Headquarters was situated where the sunken road to the right of the

Cemetery crosses the trench.

I now arranged alternate tours of duty of three hours duration, throughout the day, with Sergeant B.. Of course, being newly out, he could not be persuaded to sleep during his off duty hours, but ran about like a child with a new toy, drinking in the atmosphere of war!

About 9 o'clock, or thereabouts, the first Germans appeared - remarkably quickly, considering everything. These consisted of single men on foot and occasional cyclist who appeared dimly behind some camouflage on a road on the rising ground to the right of the road where Coy.Hqrs.were situated. These men were promptly fired on, and thereafter took more care not to show themselves.

That was all we personally saw that day of the Boche, though further along, I believe, they caught quite a large body advancing carelessly. Of course, with us, the reason probably was that they did not dare to advance up the much exposed Wancourt "valley", but contented themselves with remaining in the obscurity of the trees in Wancourt itself; indeed, we caught a glimpse of a figure now and then amongst the trees.

For the rest of the day, there were only two events worthy of note,one was that to my intense annoyance, someone stole all my rations from my hut, so that until dinner time I had to subsist on strips of concentrated meat, and the charity of Sergeant B..

The other was a much more serious event. Just in front of our trenches there was an old artillery canteen, and more important an abandoned barrel of beer.

The first I knew of the matter was finding a man in No.1 Lewis Gun Team lying on the ground. On investigation, I discovered him to be dead drunk. Near by was an old rum jar, which I found to be half full of beer and I emptied it into the trench. I took the man's name and went on up the trench and, to my horror, found my only full corporal with any experience lying on the ground in the same state.

I turned to Platoon Hqrs. and almost ran into a stretcher-bearer reeling out in a great hurry, also drunk as could be. The other stretcher- bearer was nowhere to be found. By-and-by the chief stretcher-bearer of the Company came along, and I noticed something strange in his manner. On my telling him about my stretcher-bearer, he calmly confessed that he himself had just been put on report for the same offence.

He then went into Platoon Hqrs. shook my stretcher-bearer, who by now was helpless, and coming out, coolly proceeded in the direction of the canteen. I called him back, and on his hesitating to obey, I produced my revolver, which had the desired effect. I then sent Sergeant Barber, Donald Stewart (a most reliable old soldier, whom I could trust) and another man out to fetch in the missing stretcher-bearer (who presumably was in the canteen) and to empty away the beer barrel. They came back shortly afterwards and Sergeant B.. reported that the beer barrel had only a pint left in it - this I presume he and the other two drank - and that the stretcher-bearer was being sobered up by Donald Stewart, who had remained behind in the canteen. These two turned up shortly afterwards, and I appointed Stewart and another man as stretcher-bearers until the real ones were sober.

That was the end of the "beer incident", except that a short time after, while passing up the trench, I saw one of the men dip a cup in a huge kind of canister for carrying shells, and drink. I at once had my suspicions and, looking into the canister, found it half full of beer; this I emptied over the parades, and I think that was all the remainder of the beer.

The names of the men I sent in to H..but I dont think anything happened to them in the end. It is only fair to the stretcher-bearers to say that they did excellent work in the succeeding days.

That morning, B.Coy.who were on the extreme right came in for some trouble.

They had mistaken the trenches that they were to

dig; when the Germans arrived in the morning, they had only got on a little way with the right trenches. Several. including Drover (the Company Commander) were sniped and the Germans occupied the trenches they were holding; they were, however, immediately ejected by a counter-attack on the part of B.Coy. and also by D.Coy.under Campbell who bombed along. Still B.Coy. had a fair number of casualties. Moffat also was very seriously wounded and only just lived.

That night (the 23rd-24th), my Lewis Gun Team were sent out to the wire, to stay out for the night; everyone was warned about them, of course, but suddenly, without warning, and I presume owing to the beginning of an attack, probably to the right, our guns opened a tremendous barrage, of which many shells dropped a bit short - just in front of our wire. All at once, several black figures came running wildly towards our trenches. Some idiots opened fire, but luckily without any success, as it turned out to be my unfortunate Lewis Gun Team!

Later that night, I was sent out on patrol; I took Corporal Boyle, Donald Stewart and two or three other men, we had orders though, to go only just beyond the wire, in case of enemy fighting patrols. So we went out and squatted in a large shell-hole.

It was brilliant moonlight. We could hear the Germans talking and shouting orders quite distinctly, and occasionally a thumping noise from which we concluded that there was an enemy working party out. That night also, Company Hqrs, moved to my shelter, much to my joy, for I got properly cooked food.

<u>24th</u>. The third day passed pretty quietly, with the exception of an hour or two in which both German and British artillery steadily shelled our trenches; this was eventually rectified so far as concerned our own artillery, when we had managed to establish communication, but it was decidedly unpleasant while it lasted.

That night we "sideslipped" to the extreme left and relieved B Coy. who had moved there the night before, and had spent a most unholy day under continuous German shelling, attended by a number of casualties.

The prospect was npt pleasant, the trench was very wide and all chalk, and the traverses had not been touched.

However, during the remainder of the night, which was quiet, my men got through a fair amount of work in deepening the trench itself to provide shelter from shell-fire.

25th. The fourth morning, I had hardly had breakfast when - ssss - Bang - a whizz-bang burst just over the parados. After that, throughout the whole day until evening stand-to, with about two intervals of a couple of hours duration, shells of all sorts and sizes fell round our trenches.

The fire was never exactly heavy, but it was so absolutely, inevitably continuous.

My men hugged the bottom of the trench and luckily in my platoon there were no casualties. One whizz-bang burst at Company Headquarters, though, and Harvey got a small bit in the nose, nothing vey serious. He spent that night and the next day at Battalion Hqrs., and turned up again the following evening in quite good form.

That night passed pretty quietly and uneventfully except for the bitter cold in the early morning, in fact it snowed for a few minutes at about 4 a.m. As one was unable to sleep during the day (owing to whizz-bangs) one found that through the night, when one was supposed to keep awake, it was the hardest thing in the world to keep one's eyes open. That night, I tried digging and found that that was the only way to keep awake: but one felt extremely tired after the last few days, and could not go on digging ad infinitum, so after going up and down the line a bit, visiting the sentries and waking up slumberers, I finally sat down and lit a cigarette. The next thing I knew was waking up with a start, with someone hoarsely whispering "The C.O.'s here, Sir"! I leapt to my feet and giving my best salute, said "Good evening,Sir",in a wide awake voice, as if I had just come round the traverse. He was standing on the firestep looking over the parapet, so he may not have noticed my stolen slumber,but he asked me as we were going round the Company how much sleep I was getting.

When I said I'd had 4 hours in 4 days, he said that was not enough.

<u>25th.</u> The fifth day passed much in the same way as the preceding one, except that there were half a dozen casualties or so in my platoons. They were all wounded, except in one very sad instance.

I was sitting in my customary place just by the traverse, when suddenly there was an explosion that seemed to come from just overhead (I think it was really on the traverse but on the other side), and a shower of chalk fell on my head leaving me quite dazed for a few seconds. Then I heard a shout of "Stretcher Bearer"! coming from the next bay, and then "The Sergeant's got a Blighty one". Then a man came round the corner, seeking the stretcher bearers and informed me that "Sergeant B..had got a Blighty one".

A minute or two had elapsed since the shell burst, and then something made me go round at once, in case-----. The sight that met my eyes on rounding the corner was bad enough; one man was leaning against the fire step bleeding profusely from a severe wound in the leg, while Sergeant Barber was on all fours on the bottom of the trench, his face like wax, a string of saliva from his mouth and a pool of blood beneath him. With the aid of my servant we turned him over. His femoral artery was severed, but the blood was no longer spouting from the wound, but just oozing. We applied pressure above the wound at once; the stretcher bearers arrived and put on a tourniquet; at first we thought he was reviving, but he died a munite or two later without having made a sound. A"Blighty one" !!

At dusk that evening H..sent for me and told me that I was to report at Battalion Headquarters at "Stand-to" next morning with my servant for a sleep.

Accordingly at 4.30 a.m. (the 27th) we set out, and arrived at Hqrs.at 4.45. I found Hutchins on duty and after a glass of whisky and a couple of biscuits, I threw myself down on a kind of sofa by the fire and did not wake up till breakfast time; then I slept again till lunch (this time on G's bed in a dugout), and then again till tea.

After tea I was kept busy for a time running messages for the C.O. to the Trench Mortar Officer and back, as apparently a party of Boches had come bombing down "Southern Avenue" (from Guémappe) in the direction of C.Coy., and a barrage was required (the Boche, by the way, had done the same thing the afternoon before, coming to within 30 yards of the trench before being discovered and driven away; they were apparently the 62nd Bavarians).

We dined at 7, as we were to be relieved that night by the Suffolks and were going back into reserve at Neuville Vitasse. After dinner we started back. During my stay at Headquarters I heard two very encouraging reports.

(1) The French had done an attack in the South, advancing 15 kilometres and capturing Metz.

(2) We had captured the whole of the Belgian coast including, of course, Ostend and Antwerp. The first report I believed implicitly as the doctor had it from the Staff Captain, who had it from someone at Corps Hqrs. The second we were not so sure about.

I had just arrived at Company H.Q. and reported to H..when a Battalion Orderly turned up with a chit ordering one officer and 4 N.C.Os.per company to stay on for 24 hours in order to show the relieving Suffolk Company round the trenches. Of course, then, I had to stay from A Coy.as I had had some rest during the day.

Accordingly, on the arrival of the Suffolk Coy.,I transferred self and servant to Company H.Q. and having told the company commander all I knew about the trenches there, I settled myself for sleep in the bottom of the trench, but time passed and it got colder and colder and the chalk got harder and harder and finally about 2 a.m. I asked the Coy. Commander of the Suffolks whether I could go and get my sleep at the Coy.H.Q. on the right as I had already told him all there was to know about the trench. He agreed willingly and we were just starting when all the Boche guns on our front and the ones to our left suddenly opened a barrage. It did not come anywhere near us though, but was far to the left, so predicting an attack on the XVth Division (to our left) we went on our way. This day was the 28th March, the seventh day.

We arrived at the other Company H.Q. - a dug out just in rear of the front line, but there were no vacant beds there, so they gave me a drink and directed me to my old shelter in the front line. When I arrived there, I got down on a bed, and was soon asleep. I was wakened at 5 by the noise of shells bursting all round. I sat up and realized that a furious barrage was being put on us, and, moreover on our front line, too. I decided to stay in the hut until the Boche was actually about to come over, and then go out and help, if I could; after all the hut was proof against all splinters and, better still, against whizz-bangs and very light shells. So I sat there for quite a time - I believe till about 8 o'clock while the barrage went on. Three times a light shell seemed to have burst right on top, but did no harm beyond putting out the candles. The stretcher-bearers took up their stand there, and wounded began to drift in, to be dressed. The bad cases were laid on the beds, of which there were seven, while the lighter ones sat about. Going back was out of the question for them, owing to the shelling, and I am afraid that the badly wounded ones at any rate, must have all become prisoners.

At about 8, the barrage seemed to slacken a bit, and I went out into the trench and took up my position in one of the fire-bays. There seemed to be plenty of men still left, but I was told that most of the casualties were men from the Company on the left, who had received a terrific smashing from the barrage.

The other occupants of my fire-bay were a Lewis Gun Corporal with his Lewis Gun, the No.2 of the team and a man who was crouched on the ground, shaking, obviously suffering a bit from shell-shock. He was employed in filling empty magazines. The Corporal told us that his gun did'nt belong to the platoon (in fact there was another gun in the bay to the left) but it had been buried and he had got it out and put it in working order again.

The barrage was still going on, meanwhile, and shells of all sorts and kinds were bursting near, but none fell actually in the bit of trench just there, although there was a good deal of metal flying about, and the smell of the fumes was very unpleasant.

After a time, the barrage seemed to lift, and then soon a man arrived who said he believed the Boche had broken through on the left. Thompson a G.H. who was attached to this company for 24 hours volunteered to run back with a message to Battalion H.Q. to ask what they were to do.

He started off and got fired at promptly by the Boche, so dropped into a shell hole. He lay there so long, that I thought he must be hit, but suddenly he was off again, and disappeared out of sight round the turn in the road.

I then said I would go along to the left, and see whether I could see any signs of the Boche. I went some way and saw nothing but a few of our men, so as it was useless to go without a bombing party, I came back and collected one. We then broached a box of bombs, only to find them undetonated; we tried another with the same result.

While the men were detonating them the platoon commander of that platoon came back again with a couple more officers; altogether there were the four of us officers and about 30 men in that bit of trench. I had a vague feeling as if we were all quite deserted and on a desert island! They began discussing about getting a message back to H.Q. but there were no runners about there, and no one seemed to know the exact whereabouts of the place. Of course I knew it well, so I offered to go. They agreed gladly, and gave me two men to take with me; the message was that "The Boche were believed to have broken through, away on the left, and, in that event, what were they to do - stay on or retire?" I told my two men to follow after me as best they could, and then got out of the trench and ran back by the side of the road as fast as I could. After a moment - Crack - Crack - two bullets went past me and I dropped in a shell hole. I was much impeded by my trench coat and fur lining, which put me very much out of breath. After waiting a minute, I got up and ran on again and the performance was repeated, the Boche were a good way off, and so long as I got to cover as soon as they started firing, and stayed there until thay had forgotten about me, the odds were heavily in my favour. I think one of the men following after me was hit.

I soon got out of effective range, and at length arrived at the Battalion Headquarters, very hot and very out of breath. I met the Adjutant quite soon, and gave him the message, As soon as I had got my breath back, I reported to the Colonel, I saw near, and asked what I was to do. Everybody seemed in a great flurry, and even Colonels and Majors walked about armed with rifles and bayonets.

The Colonel told me to take some of the men standing round, and man a trench he pointed to. I collected some with great difficulty, since they seemed dazed and bewildered, and would not do what one told them, only to find the trench already chock-full of men. Then I saw Major M..of the King's Own, whom I knew, and he told me to take my men to the point on Map 11 marked X. He came too, and we all ran across the open to the place, where we found some kind of roughly improvised breastworks. The position did'nt seem much use as it ran at right angles to our original line and was behind the trench which I had been to before (marked No.2). However, I dispersed my men amongst the fire-bays and presently one or two officers in the Suffolks came along and gave out a little ammunition; this seemed to be scarce, as of course most of it was in the front line; in fact, there were no bombs at all. Suddenly we saw a black mass of men coming running in our direction over the rising ground to the left. At first we thought they must be Boches and some of the men loosed off their rifles at them until a fellow shouted that they were our own men, and so they were - refugees from the front line. Luckily there were no casualties amongst them - so far as I could see - from our fire; but they certainly did look amazingly like advancing Germans!

At this point M.. came along again and told me to take my men across to the point where, on Map 11, No.2. line crosses the Wancourt - Tilloy road, and to man the trench there. I had only a few men - cooks and H.Q. people they seemed to be - and they certainly needed a lot of driving. Accordingly, we ran across, and Major M.. came too with the rest. We disposed them over a bit of trench, if trench it could be called, and men were sent along to the left a bit to keep an eye on the Boche and see that he was'nt getting between us and the XVth Division. I managed to get a little bread at this juncture which a Suffolk subaltern and I shared together, it was the first food we had had that day, although it was getting on for 10 o'clock, and it was very welcome. We now sighted some Boches about 300 yards away and we exchanged shots with them. A machine gunner to the right caught some Boche Horse Artillery splendidly, as it was coming over the hill. The Boche artillery also had now got its range and began shelling the whole extent of No.2 line, making things rather unpleasant.

At this point, I went along to the left to find out whether we were in touch with the XVth Division. None of the men I found in that direction seemed to know anything about it, and so, to get information about that and also to find out what was happening, I went along to the right, to seek out some senior officer. On the way, to my amazement, I found five or six men quite drunk; they had apparently got hold of the rum issue, which had never been given out. When I got to the corner of No.2 line and the sunken road of Battalion H.Q., I met a Gordon sergeant. Where he had come from I dont know, unless he was one of the four N.C.Os. per Company who had been left behind. He said he had just been along to report about the whereabouts of the XVth Division, that he had been along and found them all right but had missed the way back and ran into a German post and been wounded. I then saw he had been hit in the leg.

His story did'nt sound very hopeful, so I decided to go back at once and see for myself how the land lay. On

On the way back I found two men lying in the bottom of the trench. A shell had just burst and knocked their brains out, and there were pools of blood about, it was a nice sight.

When I got back later, I told my friend, the Suffolk subaltern, and we took a sergeant with us and set off. The trench turned right to the rear here, as can be seen on the map, and ran past old gun positions and artillery shelters.

After we had gone some way, and seen no signs of any XVth Division we sent the sergeant back to fetch along some men to man this part at any rate, as a beginning. We then went on and after a bit we suddenly saw some men in a Scottish Regiment in the trench I have marked Neuville Vitasse Switch but away to the left, off Map 11. We made our way to them and found them to be the 8/10th Gordons. I found the platoon officer and asked him how the land lay. He pointed out the Boches some 300 yards in front. The position then seemed roughly as per map opposite.

Thus there was a large gap to be filled up. He offered to move his men along the trench as far as the railway and I agreed to provide men for the rest. After giving us a drink of whisky from his flask we hurried back and met our sergeant in the company of the Suffolk Adjutant. We pointed out the big gap in the lines, and he asked how many men would be needed to fill it. I said at least 30, to form 6 posts of 5. He said he could not spare them, but I pointed out how far we were from the XVth Division and he finally said he would see. Very soon about 24 men came along and I arranged them in posts along the gap under an N.C.O. per post. They seemed very stupified and unwilling to move and had to be driven. They were a motley crowd, one man being even from the next Brigade! After we had got them in their places, the sergeant and I went to a shelter and I sent off a report to the Adjutant.

Five minutes later, a Colonel and a Major came along. They questioned me about the trench ahead and, on learning that it led to the Neuville Vitasse Switch, informed me that the Boche had broken through the Brigade on the right and we would have to retire down my trench, and take up a new position in the Neuville Vitasse Switch; the rest of the men were to go down first, then my men, and finally a rearguard was coming on behind. The Colonel also gave me permission to rejoin my Battalion upon reaching the Neuville Vitasse Switch.

Some of the men soon arrived down the trench and passed to the rear. Then I saw most of the rest running back over the open, so I told my men to go. The trench back was not continuous, but though fired at we had no casualties. The Boche, all along, seemed a poor shot.

We had no sooner got into the switch, then the 8/10th, just to our left, began retiring back from it. (I have since learnt that the Boche had broken through the other side of the Cambrai Road, and that that was the reason for the retirement of the XVth Division). I shouted to Major M.. who was near by asking him what we were to do. He shrugged his shoulders in despair, so I gave the order to retire to the next line (No.4) which was not much of a trench. I ran back along the road with one or two others pursued by the wild shots of the Boche, and when I got to No.4, I found we were amongst 8/10th people. There was an officer there. So finding that several of the men I had collected had rejoined the Suffolks on retiring to No.4 line, I left the remainder under his charge and set off to rejoin my own regiment. I went some way along among 8/10th men and suddenly came abruptly to the end of the trench. I learnt from an N.C.O. near by that my Battalion were in the Army line some way back, and so I set off for the rear, thankful to have a prospect of seeing my company again. I had not gone far when, looking back, I saw the 8/10th retiring again.

At length I reached the Army line - a very well-made trench - after threading my way through an enormous belt of wire.

After going some way along to the right (as one faces one's front) I came upon the Suffolks again. They had just reached there and seemed thoroughly re-organized under their respective officers.

I found the officer I had been with earlier in the day (the time was now about 2.30 p.m.) and he told me that the Gordons were just coming back into the Army Line, a bit to the right, from a trench they had been occupying some way in front. (See Map.lll-Trench marked "Objective of Counter-attack").

I went along a bit, and there sure enough were Harvey and the rest of the Company just coming down the railway. They greeted me as one risen from the dead, and we exchanged questions as to what had befallen each other.

We now had to get the men sorted along the trench, and this took a little time; but at last we were all arranged properly, and I was just contemplating an inroad on the officers ration bag, for I was feeling ravenous, and very tired, whenthere came the order "1st Gordons, fix bayonets. over the top, and take back the trench you have just evacuated"

We were amazed; it seemed madness to launch a mere battalion, depleted in numbers, without bombs, and unprovided with artillery support even, against the countless Germansin front, and when we got there what were we to do? We should have both flanks in the air, then.

The only conclusion I have been able to come to since is that it was a mere sacrifice, intended possibly to puzzle the Boche and check him momentarily, while the troops in the army line were getting time to reorganize.

It was certainly successful, in that respect, as the army line is still the front line, so perhaps our counter-attack was some use after all.

However there was no doubt about the order so we set out, walking. The men were dead tired after 64 days in the line and could only go slowly. We were in dead ground and consequently met with no fire.

Finally we came to a trench quite unoccupied and I asked C..who was with me if this could be our objective by any chance.

He replied wearily that he thought it was, but had forgotten. I was delighted, of course, if it really was, since we had had no casualties, so we stopped there; but just then Harvey came up on the right and said it was further ahead, so we continued our progress.

Everyone was dreadfully tired and it was more like a funeral march, so slowly did we go. A few paces further and we caught sight of a black swarm of men lined up in front like ants, firing at us, and still the funeral march went on. Spurts of dust knocked up by bullets, and the sharp crack of their passing by in the air, were everywhere. We were very near the German trench, when suddenly I felt as if a cart horse had kicked me on the knee, and collapsed, and at the same moment I felt another kick in the back and I subsided in the bottom of a shell-hole, and for a space gave myself up to the most atrocious language, and the hugging of my wounds. My knee bled copiously, and after a bit I got out my field dressing and dressed the wound roughly. The bullet had gone right through. I could not reach my back, and anyway I had only the one dressing, and so, for a time, I occupied myself solely with trying to get the best cover I could from a ridiculously shallow shell-hole.

All at once I heard my name called from just behind. I looked over and saw two of my men in a shell-hole about 3 yards back a much bigger one than mine. They suggested that I should try and crawl to their hole; I made an attempt, but my back was very painful, and my body felt half paralysed. Then one of them crawled out and dragged me across by the hands and I rolled down into their shell-hole. They gave me a drink of water, and then proposed that I should run back with their assistance. I told them that it was quite impossible, that I could not move, and that the best thing would be for me to stay there until darkness came, and perhaps the stretcher bearer would be able to come up. They told me that the advance was held up, that the men were lying in shell holes everywhere and that soon they would be ordered to get back again and then I would be taken prisoner. We argued for some time but I was unable to move and soon they saw it was useless.

Presently the Sergeant Major came along crawling, and dropped into our hole. He told us that Harvey had been killed. (He really died of wounds the following evening [March 29th] at a C.C.S), then he went on again; presently word came that everyone was to get back. My two men made a last vain appeal to me to come back with them and then disappeared and I was left alone.

First, I took my equipment off and settled myself as comfortably as was possible under the circumstances. After that I must have become unconscious for later I came to with a start and looking at my watch, saw that an hour had passed. I thought how nice it would be to get to a comfertable hospital in London and see everybody again. That decided me t that I really must try to get back; the truth was that I was feeling better.

I just put my head cautiously over the edge and looked about; the Germans had not advanced at all further; I could not see them, but they were still firing occasional shots. Then a movement caught my eye some 40 yards back, and suddenly about half a dozen men rose from shell-holes there, and ran back to the trench just behind; they were fired at but without effect. I was delighted, having thought that they must all have got back to the army line; if only I could reach them now! I set out crawling flat on my stomach, propelling myself along with my hands and right foot. I chose my way through where the weeds were thickest, which cover the ground in that part. I flopped into shell-hole after shell-hole, taking a short rest in each, and then making a beeline for the next one. It was very exhausting, but at last I scrambled into a kind of trench about 10 yards long and found to my joy two other men there, one of them wounded in the arm. I nearly embraced them on the spot - there is nothing so awful as being wounded and alone.

They told me that the others were in the trench away to the right, but our trench was not connected with it, so it would be best to work round by deep shell-holes to the rear.

The unwounded man went on ahead to choose the best way, and the wounded man and I (he helping me) followed to the best of our power. We worked round to the rear, and after we had gone some way, we saw and waved to them where they stood in the trench (they manned this trench for some time, firing at the Boche) soon we came near, and a Sergeant came out, lifted me on his back and carried me in. I was overjoyed at being back amongst our own fellows. Graves, the Mess waiter, now took charge of me, and leaning on him I walked slowly back down the Communication Trench, and then down the railway when the way down the former became difficult. I reached the Army Line and went on to the Aid post, where I found my servant.

The Doctor dressed my wounds and then I had a good drink. The C.O. came up and talked to me, and then the Doctor informed me that there were no stretcher-bearers available as all had become casualties, and that I had better walk if I could. So I started off with my servant, walking. The Boche was shelling the back areas quite heavily, but none came too near us. We walked and walked, and part of the way my servant pushed me down the railway on a trolley.

We got to the Arras - Bapaume road at last. The Detail Camp was quite deserted and smashed to pieces as were the Carlisle and York lines. Crossing the road we met, to my surprise Captain Lawrence, whom I had not seen since June 1917 and another man. They directed us to the Advanced Dressing Station and we plodded on; it began to rain and I soon got soaked and cold, and had to put on my trench coat again, which my servant had been carrying. We had to cross innumerable trenches which always proved the most difficult obstacles for me. It was getting dark now and just as we were getting near the Station Yard to which L.. had directed me, I felt faint and had to sit down for I had already walked nearly 4 miles. I sent my servant on to find something to carry me, if it was only a couple of men. But after what seemed an interminable time of waiting, I began to think that he must have got lost, [illegible] started off walking by myself. I managed to get to a steep ridge overlooking the station yard, and feeling helpless to climb down it, I called to a man walking along the road below, to come up and help me down,He took no notice, but went on up the road mumbling, I could have slain him.

So I had to get down myself, and in the yard I met my servant who said that the Advanced Dressing Statinn had just been moved further back, but that he had managed to get hold of an ambulance. We went to it and the man said he was just going back to the line for more cases. However I got in and we drove back again to near the Detail Camp. Then we all got out and went into a narrow trench with overhead cover (they were shelling) and waited there a weary twenty minutes. At last, two or three more cases arrived, and we all packed in, and the car moved off, so we arrived at last safely at the Advanced Dressing Station.

1ST BATTALION, THE GORDON HIGHLANDERS.

1918. APPENDIX.

March.	WANCOURT SECTOR RIGHT.
1st.	Slight shelling, quiet day. Bright in the morning but began snowing hard in the afternoon. Work digging new trench both sides of Kestrel Avenue & Wiring. Casualties nil.
2nd.	Quiet day, dull & cold, began snowing about 1.30 p.m. Work cleaning up trenches. Relieved by 8th Battn. K.S.L.I. & 2 Platoons W Company 2nd Suffolk Regt. Relief complete 9.5 p.m. Battn. moved back to support dugouts. Casualties 1 wounded.
	SUPPORT DUGOUTS.
3rd.	Quiet day, cold & sky cloudy. Casualties nil.
4th.	Quiet day, cold wind blowing sky over cast, A Coy. worked on new trench in front of Buzzard. Work had to be discontinued on account of darkness, work resumed at 5 a.m. morning of 5th. Casualties nil.
5th.	Quiet day. Fairly bright sunshine. Work on signals cable & new trench in front of Buzzard. C Coy. relieved W Coy. 2nd Suffolks in RAKE TRENCH. Relief complete 9.15 p.m. Battn. H.Q. moved into new headquarters. A & D Coys Bathed. Casualties nil.
6th.	Quiet day, sun shining brightly. Work on new Battn. H.Q. Sub Lieut. J. Clarke reported from R.N.V.R. and was posted to A Coy. Casualties Nil.
	LEFT SECTOR WANCOURT.
7th.	Quiet day, sun shining brightly. Work on support dugouts. Relieved 2nd Suffolk Regt. in Left WANCOURT SECTOR. Relief complete 6.30 p.m. Casualties Nil. Relieved by 8th K.O.R.L.R. in support dugouts.
8th.	Quiet day. Sun shining brightly. Work digging of new trench and bays in RAKE Trench. Casualties - 1 killed 1 wounded.

1918. APPENDIX.

March.

9th. Quiet sunny day. Few shells fell near Battn. H.Q. from 7 to 9 p.m. Work on RAKE Trench. Casualties - Capt. C.H. HORSWELL & 5 O.R. wounded.

10th. Sunny quiet day. Work on RAKE still continues also work on SHOVEL. C Coy. H.Q. moved from RAKE to KEY Support. D Coy. from CAVALRY trench to NEW BISON. Casualties 1 O.R. wounded.

11th. Very quiet day. Sun shining brightly. Usual work on RAKE & SHOVEL trenches. Casualties - Nil.

12th. Sun shining brightly, quiet day. Battn. relieved by 8th King Own R.L. Regt. After relief dispositions were as follows - A Coy. RAKE, D Coy. SHOVEL & NORTHERN Trench. B, C & Battn. H.Q. Support dugouts. Relief complete 9.15 p.m. Casualties - Nil.

WANCOURT SECTOR SUPPORT DUGOUTS.

13th. Quiet day. Our artillery commence Harassing fire on enemy's positions. Casualties nil.

14th. Fairly dull day but brightened towards noon. 7.30 p.m. C Coy. relieved D in SHOVEL & NORTHERN TRENCH. Nightly harassing fire of our artillery on enemy's lines still continues. Casualties Nil.

15th. Quiet day, sunny but chilly north Easterly wind blowing. Harrassing fire still continues, Casualties - 1 O.R. wounded.

16th. Quiet day. Enemy shell front slightly in retaliation to our harrassing bombardment. B Coy. relieved C Coy. in SHOVEL & NORTHERN trenches. Casualties - 1 O.R. wounded.

17th. Quiet day. Weather threatening. Casualties 1 O.R. wounded.

18th. Weather fine, slightly cloudy. Quiet day. C Coy. relieved B in SHOVEL & NORTHERN trenches. D Coy. Relieved A in RAKE. Relief complete 9.30 p.m., 2 O.R. wounded.

19th. Quiet day. Raining. Casualties - Nil.

1918. APPENDIX.

March.

20th. Quiet & misty day, cloudy in the morning but brightened in the afternoon. B Coy. relieved C in SHOVEL & NORTHERN trenches, relief complete 9.45 p.m. Casualties Nil.

21st. Misty day till 10 a.m. afterwards weather fine & sunny. Great enemy offensive begins on our right. Our front quiet except for Heavy Enemy barrage.
21st to 29th already recorded.

30th. Battalion after being relieved from NEUVILLEVITASSE by 21st Battn. Canadian Inf. marched to RIVIERE. Every one was in their billets by 8.30 a.m. After a hot breakfast all ranks slept till 12.30 p.m., then had dinners. At 2.30 p.m. Battn. march off for WARLUZEL. Route BEAMETZ les LOGES Gouy en ARTOIS SOMBRIN. Although it rained all the time and the roads were heavy the distance about 15 kilometres. The men marched well and were in good spirits. Only 5 men fell out. Battn. reached WARLUZEL at 7.30 p.m. A draft of 63 O.R. joined here. The total distance that day was about 29 kilometres and this after 7 days continuous fighting & 52 days in the trenches.

31st. Day of Resting & getting cleaned up.

H.S. GAMMELL, Capt.,
A/Adjt. 1st Bn. The Gordon Highlanders.

1ST BATTALION, THE GORDON HIGHLANDERS.

1918. **APPENDIX.**

March. **WANCOURT SECTOR RIGHT.**

1st. Slight shelling, quiet day. Bright in the morning but began snowing hard in the afternoon. Work digging new trench both sides of Kestrel Avenue & Wiring. Casualties nil.

2nd. Quiet day, dull & cold, began snowing about 1.30 p.m. Work cleaning up trenches. Relieved by 8th Battn. K.S.L.I. & 2 Platoons W Company 2nd Suffolk Regt. Relief complete 9.5 p.m. Battn. moved back to support dugouts. Casualties 1 wounded.

SUPPORT DUGOUTS.

3rd. Quiet day, cold & sky cloudy. Casualties nil.

4th. Quiet day, cold wind blowing sky over cast, A Coy. worked on new trench in front of Buzzard. Work had to be discontinued on account of darkness, work resumed at 5 a.m. morning of 5th. Casualties nil.

5th. Quiet day. Fairly bright sunshine. Work on signals cable & new trench in front of Buzzard. C Coy. relieved W Coy. 2nd Suffolks in RAKE TRENCH. Relief complete 9.15 p.m. Battn. H.Q. moved into new headquarters. A & D Coys Bathed. Casualties nil.

6th. Quiet day, sun shining brightly. Work on new Battn. H.Q. Sub Lieut. J. Clarke reported from R.N.V.R. and was posted to A Coy. Casualties Nil.

LEFT SECTOR WANCOURT.

7th. Quiet day, sun shining brightly. Work on support dugouts. Relieved 2nd Suffolk Regt. in Left WANCOURT SECTOR. Relief complete 6.30 p.m. Casualties Nil. Relieved by 8th K.O.R.L.R. in support dugouts.

8th. Quiet day. Sun shining brightly. Work digging of new trench and bays in RAKE Trench. Casualties - 1 killed 1 wounded.

1918. APPENDIX.

March.

9th.	Quiet sunny day. Few shells fell near Battn. H.Q. from 7 to 9 p.m. Work on RAKE Trench. Casualties - Capt. C.H. HORSWELL & 5 O.R. wounded.
10th.	Sunny quiet day. Work on RAKE still continues also work on SHOVEL. C Coy. H.Q. moved from RAKE to KEY Support. D Coy. from CAVALRY trench to NEW BISON. Casualties 1 O.R. wounded.
11th.	Very quiet day. Sun shining brightly. Usual work on RAKE & SHOVEL trenches. Casualties - Nil.
12th.	Sun shining brightly, quiet day. Battn. relieved by 8th King Own R.L. Regt. After relief dispositions were as follows - A Coy. RAKE, D Coy. SHOVEL & NORTHERN Trench. B, C & Battn. H.Q. Support dugouts. Relief complete 9.15 p.m. Casualties - Nil.
	WANCOURT SECTOR SUPPORT DUGOUTS.
13th.	Quiet day. Our artillery commence Harassing fire on enemy's positions. Casualties nil.
14th.	Fairly dull day but brightened towards noon. 7.30 p.m. C Coy. relieved D in SHOVEL & NORTHERN TRENCH. Nightly harassing fire of our artillery on enemy's lines still continues. Casualties Nil.
15th.	Quiet day, sunny but chilly north Easterly wind blowing. Harrassing fire still continues, Casualties - 1 O.R. wounded.
16th.	Quiet day. Enemy shell front slightly in retaliation to our harrassing bombardment. B Coy. relieved C Coy. in SHOVEL & NORTHERN trenches. Casualties - 1 O.R. wounded.
17th.	Quiet day. Weather threatening. Casualties 1 O.R. wounded.
18th.	Weather fine, slightly cloudy. Quiet day. C Coy. relieved B in SHOVEL & NORTHERN trenches. D Coy. Relieved A in RAKE. Relief complete 9.30 p.m., 2 O.R. wounded.
19th.	Quiet day. Raining. Casualties - Nil.

1918. APPENDIX.

March.

20th. Quiet & misty day, cloudy in the morning but brightened in the afternoon. B Coy. relieved C in SHOVEL & NORTHERN trenches, relief complete 9.45 p.m. Casualties Nil.

21st. Misty day till 10 a.m. afterwards weather fine & sunny. Great enemy offensive begins on our right. Our front quiet except for Heavy Enemy barrage.
21st to 29th already recorded.

30th. Battalion after being relieved from NEUVILLEVITASSE by 21st Battn. Canadian Inf. marched to RIVIERE. Every one was in their billets by 8.30 a.m. After a hot breakfast all ranks slept till 12.30 p.m., then had dinners. At 2.30 p.m. Battn. march off for WARLUZEL. Route BEAMETZ les LOGES Gouy en ARTOIS SOMBRIN. Although it rained all the time and the roads were heavy the distance about 15 kilometres. The men marched well and were in good spirits. Only 5 men fell out. Battn. reached WARLUZEL at 7.30 p.m. A draft of 63 O.R. joined here. The total distance that day was about 29 kilometres and this after 7 days continuous fighting & 52 days in the trenches.

31st. Day of Resting & getting cleaned up.

H.S. GAMMELL, Capt.,
A/Adjt. 1st Bn. The Gordon Highlanders.

1ST BATTALION, THE GORDON HIGHLANDERS.

1918. | APPENDIX.

March. WANCOURT SECTOR RIGHT.

1st. Slight shelling, quiet day. Bright in the morning but began snowing hard in the afternoon. Work digging new trench both sides of Kestrel Avenue & Wiring. Casualties nil.

2nd. Quiet day, dull & cold, began snowing about 1.30 p.m. Work cleaning up trenches. Relieved by 8th Battn. K.S.L.I. & 2 Platoons W Company 2nd Suffolk Regt. Relief complete 9.5 p.m. Battn. moved back to support dugouts. Casualties 1 wounded.

SUPPORT DUGOUTS.

3rd. Quiet day, cold & sky cloudy. Casualties nil.

4th. Quiet day, cold wind blowing sky over cast, A Coy. worked on new trench in front of Buzzard. Work had to be discontinued on account of darkness, work resumed at 5 a.m. morning of 5th. Casualties nil.

5th. Quiet day. Fairly bright sunshine. Work on signals cable & new trench in front of Buzzard. C Coy. relieved W Coy. 2nd Suffolks in RAKE TRENCH. Relief complete 9.15 p.m. Battn. H.Q. moved into new headquarters. A & D Coys Bathed. Casualties nil.

6th. Quiet day, sun shining brightly. Work on new Battn. H.Q. Sub Lieut. J. Clarke reported from R.N.V.R. and was posted to A Coy. Casualties Nil.

LEFT SECTOR WANCOURT.

7th. Quiet day, sun shining brightly. Work on support dugouts. Relieved 2nd Suffolk Regt. in Left WANCOURT SECTOR. Relief complete 6.30 p.m. Casualties Nil. Relieved by 8th K.O.R.L.R. in support dugouts.

8th. Quiet day. Sun shining brightly. Work digging of new trench and bays in RAKE Trench. Casualties - 1 killed 1 wounded.

1918. APPENDIX.

March.

9th. Quiet sunny day. Few shells fell near Battn. H.Q. from 7 to 9 p.m. Work on RAKE Trench. Casualties - Capt. C.H. HORSWELL & 5 O.R. wounded.

10th. Sunny quiet day. Work on RAKE still continues also work on SHOVEL. C Coy. H.Q. moved from RAKE to KEY Support. D Coy. from CAVALRY trench to NEW BISON. Casualties 1 O.R. wounded.

11th. Very quiet day. Sun shining brightly. Usual work on RAKE & SHOVEL trenches. Casualties - Nil.

12th. Sun shining brightly, quiet day. Battn. relieved by 8th King Own R.L. Regt. After relief dispositions were as follows - A Coy. RAKE, D Coy. SHOVEL & NORTHERN Trench. B, C & Battn. H.Q. Support dugouts. Relief complete 9.15 p.m. Casualties - Nil.

WANCOURT SECTOR SUPPORT DUGOUTS.

13th. Quiet day. Our artillery commence Harassing fire on enemy's positions. Casualties nil.

14th. Fairly dull day but brightened towards noon. 7.30 p.m. C Coy. relieved D in SHOVEL & NORTHERN TRENCH. Nightly harassing fire of our artillery on enemy's lines still continues.. Casualties Nil.

15th. Quiet day, sunny but chilly north Easterly wind blowing. Harrassing fire still continues, Casualties - 1 O.R. wounded.

16th. Quiet day. Enemy shell front slightly in retaliation to our harrassing bombardment. B Coy. relieved C Coy. in SHOVEL & NORTHERN trenches. Casualties - 1 O.R. wounded.

17th. Quiet day. Weather threatening. Casualties 1 O.R. wounded.

18th. Weather fine, slightly cloudy. Quiet day. C Coy. relieved B in SHOVEL & NORTHERN trenches. D Coy. Relieved A in RAKE. Relief complete 9.30 p.m., 2 O.R. wounded.

19th. Quiet day. Raining. Casualties - Nil.

1918. APPENDIX.

March.

20th. Quiet & misty day, cloudy in the morning but brightened in the afternoon. B Coy. relieved C in SHOVEL & NORTHERN trenches, relief complete 9.45 p.m. Casualties Nil.

21st. Misty day till 10 a.m. afterwards weather fine & sunny. Great enemy offensive begins on our right. Our front quiet except for Heavy Enemy barrage. 21st to 29th already recorded.

30th. Battalion after being relieved from NEUVILLEVITASSE by 21st Battn. Canadian Inf. marched to RIVIERE. Every one was in their billets by 8.30 a.m. After a hot breakfast all ranks slept till 12.30 p.m., then had dinners. At 2.30 p.m. Battn. march off for WARLUZEL. Route BEAMETZ les LOGES Gouy en ARTOIS SOMBRIN. Although it rained all the time and the roads were heavy the distance about 15 kilometres. The men marched well and were in good spirits. Only 5 men fell out. Battn. reached WARLUZEL at 7.30 p.m. A draft of 63 O.R. joined here. The total distance that day was about 29 kilometres and this after 7 days continuous fighting & 52 days in the trenches.

31st. Day of Resting & getting cleaned up.

H.S. GAMMELL, Capt.,
A/Adjt. 1st Bn. The Gordon
Highlanders.

1ST BATTALION, THE GORDON HIGHLANDERS.

1918.		APPENDIX.
March.	WANCOURT SECTOR RIGHT.	
1st.	Slight shelling, quiet day. Bright in the morning but began snowing hard in the afternoon. Work digging new trench both sides of Kestrel Avenue & Wiring. Casualties nil.	
2nd.	Quiet day, dull & cold, began snowing about 1.30 p.m. Work cleaning up trenches. Relieved by 8th Battn. K.S.L.I. & 2 Platoons W Company 2nd Suffolk Regt. Relief complete 9.5 p.m. Battn. moved back to support dugouts. Casualties 1 wounded.	
	SUPPORT DUGOUTS.	
3rd.	Quiet day, cold & sky cloudy. Casualties nil.	
4th.	Quiet day, cold wind blowing sky over cast, A Coy. worked on new trench in front of Buzzard. Work had to be discontinued on account of darkness, work resumed at 5 a.m. morning of 5th. Casualties nil.	
5th.	Quiet day. Fairly bright sunshine. Work on signals cable & new trench in front of Buzzard. C Coy. relieved W Coy. 2nd Suffolks in RAKE TRENCH. Relief complete 9.15 p.m. Battn. H.Q. moved into new headquarters. A & D Coys Bathed. Casualties nil.	
6th.	Quiet day, sun shining brightly. Work on new Battn. H.Q. Sub Lieut. J. Clarke reported from R.N.V.R. and was posted to A Coy. Casualties Nil.	
	LEFT SECTOR WANCOURT.	
7th.	Quiet day, sun shining brightly. Work on support dugouts. Relieved 2nd Suffolk Regt. in Left WANCOURT SECTOR. Relief complete 6.30 p.m. Casualties Nil. Relieved by 8th K.O.R.L.R. in support dugouts.	
8th.	Quiet day. Sun shining brightly. Work digging of new trench and bays in RAKE Trench. Casualties - 1 killed 1 wounded.	

1918. APPENDIX.

March.

9th. Quiet sunny day. Few shells fell near Battn. H.Q. from 7 to 9 p.m. Work on RAKE Trench. Casualties - Capt. C.H. HORSWELL & 5 O.R. wounded.

10th. Sunny quiet day. Work on RAKE still continues also work on SHOVEL. C Coy. H.Q. moved from RAKE to KEY Support. D Coy. from CAVALRY trench to NEW BISON. Casualties 1 O.R. wounded.

11th. Very quiet day. Sun shining brightly. Usual work on RAKE & SHOVEL trenches. Casualties - Nil.

12th. Sun shining brightly, quiet day. Battn. relieved by 8th King Own R.L. Regt. After relief dispositions were as follows - A Coy. RAKE, D Coy. SHOVEL & NORTHERN Trench. B, C & Battn. H.Q. Support dugouts. Relief complete 9.15 p.m. Casualties - Nil.

WANCOURT SECTOR SUPPORT DUGOUTS.

13th. Quiet day. Our artillery commence Harassing fire on enemy's positions. Casualties nil.

14th. Fairly dull day but brightened towards noon. 7.30 p.m. C Coy. relieved D in SHOVEL & NORTHERN TRENCH. Nightly harassing fire of our artillery on enemy's lines still continues.. Casualties Nil.

15th. Quiet day, sunny but chilly north Easterly wind blowing. Harrassing fire still continues, Casualties - 1 O.R. wounded.

16th. Quiet day. Enemy shell front slightly in retaliation to our harrassing bombardment. B Coy. relieved C Coy. in SHOVEL & NORTHERN trenches. Casualties - 1 O.R. wounded.

17th. Quiet day. Weather threatening. Casualties 1 O.R. wounded.

18th. Weather fine, slightly cloudy. Quiet day. C Coy. relieved B in SHOVEL & NORTHERN trenches. D Coy. Relieved A in RAKE. Relief complete 9.30 p.m., 2 O.R. wounded.

19th. Quiet day. Raining. Casualties - Nil.

1918. **APPENDIX.**

March.

20th. Quiet & misty day, cloudy in the morning but brightened in the afternoon. B Coy. relieved C in SHOVEL & NORTHERN trenches, relief complete 9.45 p.m. Casualties Nil.

21st. Misty day till 10 a.m. afterwards weather fine & sunny. Great enemy offensive begins on our right. Our front quiet except for Heavy Enemy barrage.
21st to 29th already recorded.

30th. Battalion after being relieved from NEUVILLEVITASSE by 21st Battn. Canadian Inf. marched to RIVIERE. Every one was in their billets by 8.30 a.m. After a hot breakfast all ranks slept till 12.30 p.m., then had dinners. At 2.30 p.m. Battn. march off for WARLUZEL. Route BEAMETZ les LOGES Gouy en ARTOIS SOMBRIN. Although it rained all the time and the roads were heavy the distance about 15 kilometres. The men marched well and were in good spirits. Only 5 men fell out. Battn. reached WARLUZEL at 7.30 p.m. A draft of 63 O.R. joined here. The total distance that day was about 29 kilometres and this after 7 days continuous fighting & 52 days in the trenches.

31st. Day of Resting & getting cleaned up.

H.S. GAMMELL, Capt.,
A/Adjt. 1st Bn. The Gordon Highlanders.

76th Bde.
3rd Div.

WAR DIARY

1st BATTALION

THE GORDON HIGHLANDERS

APRIL 1 9 1 8

Instructions regarding War Diaries and Intelligence Summaries are contained in F. S. Regs., Part II. and the Staff Manual respectively. Title pages will be prepared in manuscript.

WAR DIARY
or
~~INTELLIGENCE SUMMARY.~~
(Erase heading not required.)

Army Form C. 2118.

Vol 43

Place	Date	Hour	Summary of Events and Information	Remarks and references to Appendices
En Route In the Field	1.4.18		Battalion marched from WARLUZEL to LIENCOURT leaving at 8.30 AM and embussed at 11 A.M and proceeded to the BRUAY AREA. Route FREVENT S^t POL OURTON. Battalion arrived OURTON at 3 pm & was billeted there. billets very good & men able to rest thoroughly.	
OURTON	2.4.18		Battalion cleaned up and reorganised. Weather fine and all ranks began to lose look of tiredness after the heavy work on the previous days.	
"	3.4.18		Work of reorganisation still continues. Battalion already looking smart. Companies train under their own arrangement attention being paid to Lewis guns & other specialist work.	
En Route	4.4.18		Battalion marched from OURTON to FOSSE 10 (SAINS en GOHELLE) arriving 2 pm. Battalion was billeted in miners houses and very comfortably billeted.	
FOSSE 10	5.4.18		Battalion carried Training under Company arrangements in billets on account of rain.	
"	6.4.18		Training under Company arrangements in specialist subjects. Draft of 57 arrived mostly boys of 19 who are keen and should make good soldiers.	
"	7.4.18		Church parade in Church Army hut. B & D Coys work in Afternoon on the MAISTRE LINE	
"	8.4.18		Rainy day A & C Coy work on MAISTRE LINE D Coy firing on Range B Coy Company training	
"	9.4.18		Foggy day A Coy on Range but impossible to shoot on account of fog. C Coy Company training	
"	10.4.18		B & D Coy work on MAISTRE LINE	
	10.4.18		Battalion in morning received orders to get ready to go into action inspection of Lewis guns etc. carried out. Afternoon Companies out working on MAISTRE LINE	
	11.4.18		Battalion got ready to move to BARLIN HERSIN Area but the order was cancelled just as Batt was falling in to move off. At 1 pm Battalion embussed and proceeded to battle Area in neighbourhood of HINGES. debussed on Road LE CAUREY nr BERNENCHON and deployed and moved forward in artillery formation on line of Canal between BOIS de PACAUT & Bridge near LES CAUDRONS. The enemy encountered Remnants of 51st Division far side of Canal. Quiet night	

D. D. & L., London, E.C.
(A8004) Wt. W1771/M2-31 750,000 5/17 Sch. 52 Forms/C2118/14

Instructions regarding War Diaries and Intelligence Summaries are contained in F. S. Regs., Part II. and the Staff Manual respectively. Title pages will be prepared in manuscript.

WAR DIARY
or
~~INTELLIGENCE~~ SUMMARY.

(Erase heading not required.)

Army Form C. 2118.

Place	Date	Hour	Summary of Events and Information	Remarks and references to Appendices
Hinges Locton	12.4.18		Battn Head quarters in front of HINGES D Coy on the left in Pacaut Wood to La PANNERIE FARM C Coy from La PANNERIE FARM to Bridge heads. B Coy along canal bank [illegible] drawbridge [illegible] A staff car ran into ditch close to Battn H Q, consequently [illegible]. Battn H Q shifted to adjoining orchard, and later into the village of HINGES. [illegible] ordered to withdraw to [illegible] along canal bank [illegible] killed. C & D Coy hold bridge heads. [illegible] the canal bank on the rising ground.	
	13.4.18		Quiet day slight shelling, [illegible] during the day but enemy [illegible] Post established on enemy side of canal [illegible] opposition. Evening Battn relieved by 1st Battn Royal Welsh Fus. [illegible] AM Battalion then moved to OBLINGHEM	
OBLINGHEM	14.4.18		Battn rested and reequipped with [illegible] at 8 pm to take over line from 9th Inf Bde. [illegible] front occupied. AVELETTE to S.E. of LOCON no continuous trench [illegible] or shell holes. Battn H Q in [illegible] on canal bank [illegible] Quiet night	
	15.4.18		Slight shelling on front two companies but scarcely any casualties [illegible] in the open. Precautions taken to hide Battn H Q [illegible] to Bde H Q only. Power Buzzer [illegible] left post at night	
	16.4.18		Quiet day 4th Division on our left made a successful [illegible]	
	17.4.18		Very quiet day warned to expect enemy attack, but it did not come off. [illegible]	
	18th		Shelled intermittently still expect attack [illegible] B Coy capture a prisoner of 467 RIR [illegible]	

D. D. & L., London, E.C.
(A8004) Wt. W1771/M2731 750,000 5/17 Sch. 52 Forms/C2118/14

Instructions regarding War Diaries and Intelligence Summaries are contained in F. S. Regs., Part II. and the Staff Manual respectively. Title pages will be prepared in manuscript.

WAR DIARY
or
INTELLIGENCE SUMMARY.
(Erase heading not required.)

Army Form C. 2118.

Place	Date	Hour	Summary of Events and Information	Remarks and references to Appendices
Le Hougomont Sector	19.4.18		Slight shelling but no attack on the part of the enemy. Casualties Nil	
	20.4.18		Quiet day. CQMS JACKSON killed when taking up rations, 1 other rank killed & two wounded. C Coy moved over to the left and took over 500 yds of line along the Canal bank from AVELETTE draw bridge.	
	21.4.18		Very bright day, enemy shell AVELETTE bridge and try for Battn H.Q. but dont obtain a hit.	
	22.4.18		Quiet day. Our artillery put a creeping barrage on enemy's line 4 a.m., only slight retaliation.	
In Support VENDIN & BETHUNE	23.4.18		Quiet day relieved by 1st Battn Royal Fusiliers (9th Inf Bde) in the evening. Battn moved back to billets in VENDIN LES BETHUNE	
	24.4.18		Spent in cleaning up and refitting	
	25.4.18		Quiet day no parades as no movement was allowed but companies given specialist training in billets	
	26.4.18		Brigade relieve 8th Bde in the line. Battalion in Brigade reserve. Coys billeted in Hangars near LANNOY. Battn H.Q. on CHOCQUES–BETHUNE Road in relief of 1st HAMPSHIRE Regt.	
	27.4.18		Quiet day no movement being allowed outside hangars. Evening C Coy carry wire D Coy wiring in front of Hangars	
	28.4.18		Quiet day. Evening work continued	
	29.4.18		Quiet day. Same work	
	30.4.18		Quiet day weather inclined to be wet. B & D Coys shelled out of hangars. 21 Casualties. Usual work	

[signature]
Lieut. Col.
Commanding
1st Gordon Highlanders.

76th Brigade.

3rd Division.

1st BATTALION GORDON HIGHLANDERS ::: M A Y 1918.

1st Gordon Hrs

WAR DIARY
or
~~INTELLIGENCE SUMMARY.~~
(Erase heading not required.)

Army Form C. 2118.

Instructions regarding War Diaries and Intelligence Summaries are contained in F. S. Regs., Part II. and the Staff Manual respectively. Title pages will be prepared in manuscript.

VR 44

Place	Date	Hour	Summary of Events and Information	Remarks and references to Appendices
CHOCQUES	1/5/18		Quiet day.	
	2/5/18		A and C coys moved to SHROPSHIRE LINE, W. of HINGES in view of occasional shelling of ABBAYE, LANNOY and CLARENCE RIVER areas.	
	3/5/18		Some shelling of ABBAYE grounds in morning. B and D coys confined to the shelter trenches and B coys preparations for attack on orchard in W11 A+B [Sheet 36a S.E.] hindered in consequence.	2/Lt C. Dickie & 7 OR wounded
	3/4/5/18		B coy paraded shortly before midnight and reached their assembly positions in time for zero hour (2.30 am). Parties of D coy carried up wire ammunition, haversacks and water bottles for the assaulting platoons and dumped them in a breastwork which formed the coy battle H.Q. just across the canal. The attack was made by 5 platoons, 1 platoon of D coy being attached to B coy. Hostile reply to our barrage was negligible. The scheme of assault worked exactly according to programme, the enemy was completely surprised, and ~~the~~ the ~~line consolidated~~ objective was reached and consolidation started by 3 am. 3 light m.gs. and 42 prisoners were taken and a number of the enemy killed. Lt J.W. Orr, Sgts J. Scott and J. Thomson were wounded (the latter remaining at duty) 3 men were killed and 8 wounded. The day passed quietly and B coy was relieved together with 8th Kings Own by 1st Northumberland Fusiliers that night, the coy getting away without casualties in spite of some shelling during the relief.	

D. D. & L., London, E.C. (A8004) Wt. W1771/M2-31 750,000 5/17 Sch. 52 Forms/C2118/14

Army Form C. 2118.

Instructions regarding War Diaries and Intelligence Summaries are contained in F. S. Regs., Part II. and the Staff Manual respectively. Title pages will be prepared in manuscript.

WAR DIARY
or
INTELLIGENCE SUMMARY.
(Erase heading not required.)

Place	Date	Hour	Summary of Events and Information	Remarks and references to Appendices
CHOCQUES	4/5/18		The Bn was relieved in Bde Reserve that night by 13 King's (Liverpool) Regt. Bn HQ remained where it was, and the coys came back to shelters on the bank of the [illegible] except D coy which remained in the ASSAYE [illegible].	
	5/5/18		D coy moved to open trench on S. side of CHOCQUES-[illegible] road. Quiet day.	
	6/5/18		Baths at LAPUGNOY. The Corps Commander came to congratulate the Bn on B coy's successful attack. C coy moved into billets in CHOCQUES.	
	7/5/18		Quiet day. Lt & QM S. T. JENNINGS [illegible].	
[illegible] LOCON	8/5/18		Relief of 1st R.S.F. in Left subsection of Right Bde [illegible] of the line was familiar. D coy [illegible] 3 [illegible] and 6 wounded on the way up.	
	9/5/18		Some hostile shelling (apparently registration and [illegible] of expected attack) [illegible] morning.	
	10/5/18		Left front coy (A) shelled rather [illegible] all morning. 2/Lt R. Wood badly wounded. Major [illegible] wounded slightly when going round the line at night.	
	11/5/18		Quiet in front line. Some shelling of back areas.	
	12/5/18		Left coy again shelled. 2/Lt [illegible] wounded.	
	13/5/18		Quiet	
	14/5/18		Aeroplane activity owing to fine weather and good visibility.	
	15/5/18		Quiet.	
	16/5/18		Relief by 4th Royal Fusiliers and back to CHOCQUES. No casualties. All coys now in billets.	

D. D. & L., London, E.C.
(A8004) Wt. W1771/M2 31 750,000 5/17 Sch. 52 Forms/C2118/14

Instructions regarding War Diaries and Intelligence Summaries are contained in F. S. Regs., Part II. and the Staff Manual respectively. Title pages will be prepared in manuscript.

WAR DIARY
or
INTELLIGENCE SUMMARY.
(Erase heading not required.)

Army Form C. 2118.

Place	Date	Hour	Summary of Events and Information	Remarks and references to Appendices
CHOCQUES	17/5/18		Cleaning up, inspections, pay out.	
	18/5/18		Baths. 2/Lts J.W. Henderson & L.W. Moran joined.	
	19/5/18		Service in orchard beside H.Q. details billet taken by Major Pryde from Division. Two working parties of 250 each worked on cable burying in HINGES CHATEAU grounds. One party lost Lt A. McL. BELL killed and 7 other casualties.	
	19/20th		The other came in for a gas bombardment of HINGES including the chateau and grounds. They had about 7 men wounded and Lt R.J. ABERDEIN and 11 others gassed before getting back to billet. The effects of the gas made themselves felt about 8 am and by nightfall about 120 cases had been reported, including Capt W.A. Dyke, 2/Lt J.W. Henderson, 2/Lt W.H. Gunn. Relief of 2nd Royal Scots in Bde Reserve that evening. They had suffered much more heavily than the Battalion, and were much reduced. They had withdrawn to the SHROPSHIRE LINE from the SUFFOLK LINE in HINGES.	
	21/5/18		Quiet.	
	22/5/18		One coy worked for front line Battalion on the canal bank.	
	23/5/18		Usual work.	
	24/5/18		Heavy rain during morning. Relief of 2/Suffolk Regt in left subsection. No casualties.	

D. D. & L., London, E.C.
(A8004) Wt. W1771/M2-31 750,000 5/17 Sch. 52 Forms/C2118/14

Instructions regarding War Diaries and Intelligence Summaries are contained in F. S. Regs., Part II. and the Staff Manual respectively. Title pages will be prepared in manuscript.

WAR DIARY
or
INTELLIGENCE SUMMARY.
(Erase heading not required.)

Army Form C. 2118.

Place	Date	Hour	Summary of Events and Information	Remarks and references to Appendices
HINGES	25/5/18		Quiet. Garrisons of posts worked at connecting up posts at night. B coy's reserve platoon on canal bank & Bn HQ made concertinas every day (about 50) and they were put out in front of the front line.	
	26/5/18		Some shelling during night round Bn HQ chiefly gas. Usual work and wiring. Casualties 1 OR wounded	
	27/5/18		Quiet. 5 new officers joined — 2/Lts Harper, Mellis, Brown, Dickie and Philip.	
	28/5/18		Quiet. Casualties nil	
	29/5/18		Some shelling of canal bank round PONT HINGES during day, & gas shelling near of Bn HQ by night. 2 horses wounded.	
	30/5/18		Quiet day. Usual work.	
	31/5/18		Quiet. Casualties nil.	

R. A. Wolfe-Murray Lt Colonel
Cmdg 1st Bn The Gordon Highlanders

D. D. & L., London, E.C.
(A8004) Wt. W1771/M2731 750,000 5/17 Sch. 52 Forms/C2118/14

76th Brigade.

3rd Division.

1st BATTALION GORDON HIGHLANDERS ::: JUNE 1918.

Instructions regarding War Diaries and Intelligence Summaries are contained in F. S. Regs., Part II. and the Staff Manual respectively. Title pages will be prepared in manuscript.

WAR DIARY

~~or~~

~~INTELLIGENCE SUMMARY.~~

(*Erase heading not required.*)

Army Form C. 2118.

Z6
3

1st Gordon H[illegible]

Vol 45

Place	Date	Hour	Summary of Events and Information	Remarks and references to Appendices
HINGES	1-6-18		Quiet day. HINGES shelled gas and HE evening and early morning	
	2-6-18		Quiet. Battn HQs gas shelled morning "Stand To"	
	3-6-18		Quiet. Lieut E.F. Harvie MC joined the Bn	
	4-6-18		Battn was relieved in the line by the 2nd Suffolk Regt and went into Brigade Reserve (Trenches side of CHOCQUES HILL)	
CHOCQUES	5-6-18		Cleaning up and routine inspections Lt E F HARVIE MC took over command of A Coy	
	6-6-18		Inspections – 1 Coy on Range.	
	7-6-18		2 Coys on range – 2 Coys practising attack in open warfare by platoons Sports in afternoon and evening	
	8-6-18		1 Coy on Range – 3 Coys practising attack – Sports in evening	
	9-6-18		Coys practised attack over flagged course – Inter Coy Football and Tug of War afternoon and evening	
	10-6-18		Battn practised attack over flagged course – Sports in the evening	
	11-6-18		Battn practised attack under Brigade arrangements – Lt R N Preston MC joined Bn from Base – Sports afternoon and evening	
	12-6-18 (cont.)		Battn practised attack under Brigade arrangements – G.O.C Divn present	

A6945 Wt. W11422/M1160 350,000 12/16 D. D. & L. Forms/C./2118/14.

Army Form C. 2118.

Instructions regarding War Diaries and Intelligence Summaries are contained in F. S. Regs., Part II. and the Staff Manual respectively. Title pages will be prepared in manuscript.

WAR DIARY
or
INTELLIGENCE SUMMARY.
(*Erase heading not required.*)

Place	Date	Hour	Summary of Events and Information	Remarks and references to Appendices
	12-6-18	11-45PM	Night operation – attack over course practised – 2/Lt D.H. MacGregor reported back to Battn from III Div. Wing.	
HINGES	13-6-18		Moved into the line for the attack – Relieved the 1st Bn North'd Fus. in the left subsection – Battn HQs and 2nd Suffolk Bn HQs shared HQs in Surplus House – relief quiet but very late. – all carrying for the attack finished, the dump on CANAL BANK being completed on 12/13th. The men had taken up all they would require for the attack.	
	14-6-18		Anniversary of Infantry Hill – Quiet day – some registration by our artillery. Enemy artillery was normal. – C.O. Adjt + Sigs Officer and the C.O. and Adjt of the 2nd Suffolk Regt moved to forward Battle HQ (a fortified house on eastern slope of HINGES HILL), about 10 P.M.	
			A and D Coys advanced under barrage at Zero hour (11-45 PM) B + C Coys (in support to them respectively) advancing from behind CANAL BANK and occupying our old front line.	
	15-6-18 cont		No reports came through till 2 AM except from walking wounded and a few prisoners which were of course not very reliable.	

A6945 Wt. W11422/M1160 350,000 12/16 D. D. & L. Forms/C./2118/14.

Instructions regarding War Diaries and Intelligence Summaries are contained in F. S. Regs., Part II. and the Staff Manual respectively. Title pages will be prepared in manuscript.

WAR DIARY
or
INTELLIGENCE SUMMARY.
(Erase heading not required.)

Army Form C. 2118.

Place	Date	Hour	Summary of Events and Information	Remarks and references to Appendices
	15-6-18 cont		About 2 AM the Support Coy reported the situation in front obscure	
			About 4-AM definite word was received that both assault Coy Comdrs	
			(Capt J. Wilson and Lieut E.F. Harrie MC) had been killed and their CSMs	
			wounded shortly after ZERO and that both flanks were on their objective	
			and in touch with 2nd Suffolk Regt on the Right and 1st Rifle Brigade	
			(4th Div) on the Left. 2/Lieuts J. Mellis and W.F. Wishart had also been	
			killed and Lieut W. Murray 2/Lts W.J. Mackenzie and W.R. Morren wounded.	
			About 5·30 AM, it now being broad daylight, platoons of the Support Coy	
			rushed the machine guns which had held up the centre platoons.	
			and captured several light machine guns and about 35 prisoners. This	
			allowed our whole objective to be consolidated by means of Posts from	
			Y on Left to X on Right including STRAFED HOUSE and LONE-TREE cross	
			roads. — The enemy put down short but heavy barrages on the CANAL	
			BANK about every hour during the afternoon and throughout the night but	
			we suffered no casualties none of our men being there	
			Wires of congratulations were received from Gen. Deverell cmdg III Div	

A6945 Wt. W11422/M1160 350,000 12/16 D. D. & L. Forms/C./2118/14.

Army Form C. 2118.

Instructions regarding War Diaries and Intelligence Summaries are contained in F. S. Regs., Part II. and the Staff Manual respectively. Title pages will be prepared in manuscript.

WAR DIARY
or
~~INTELLIGENCE SUMMARY.~~
(Erase heading not required.)

Place	Date	Hour	Summary of Events and Information	Remarks and references to Appendices
			and Gen Moreland the Corps commander	
	16-6-18		A certain amount of shelling on our old Front line (Blue Line) and short bursts on CANAL BANK during the day, but the enemy made no attempt to counter attack.	
			Dispositions were altered during the night - 3 Coys of the 2nd Suffolk Regt taking over the Battn front in addition to their own. -	
			The Battn moved back into Brigade Reserve in CHOCQUES	
			Relief was complete just before daylight with no casualties - 12 hostile Light machine Guns which had been captured by the Battn on the 15th were brought out. - Coys in bivouacs in and around BRASSERIE - Battn HQs at SAN SAVEUR	
	17-6-18		Usual quiet day and cleaning up - Corps and Div General called at Battn HQ during the day. - 2/Lt J. Clark MC and 2/Lt S.E. Clark rejoined Battn from L.G. School - 2/Lt G. Henderson MM joined the Battn	
	18-6-18		Baths and the range during the day. - In the evening Battn marched by Coys to the Sandpit cemetery for the funeral of the 4 Officers	

A6945 Wt. W11422/M1160 350,000 12/16 D. D. & L. Forms/C./2118/14.

Instructions regarding War Diaries and Intelligence Summaries are contained in F. S. Regs., Part II. and the Staff Manual respectively. Title pages will be prepared in manuscript.

WAR DIARY
or
INTELLIGENCE SUMMARY.
(*Erase heading not required.*)

Army Form C. 2118.

Place	Date	Hour	Summary of Events and Information	Remarks and references to Appendices
	18-6-18		who had been killed in action.	
	19-6-18		Section and platoon training under Coy arrangements during	
			the morning – Battⁿ relieved 8th K.O.R.L. Regt in the BATTLE ZONE (Trench	
			running in front of and through HINGES). Coys paraded about 10 PM.	
	20-6-18		Quiet day – no casualties	
	21-6-18		Quiet day – usual working and carrying parties during the night	
	22-6-18		Quiet day – CANAL BANK and GORDON LINE lightly shelled during the night.	
			Lieut R.W. Preston M.C. joined off course.	
	23-6-18		Quiet day – SHROPSHIRE LINE and Battery positions in rear shelled during	
			the evening – Battⁿ relieved 8th K.O.R.L. Regt in front line – enemy	
			machine guns and snipers very active – 2/Lt D. Rangelands	
			wounded – 2 o.Ranks killed and 4 o.Ranks wounded.	
	24-6-18		Battⁿ H.Qrs. GORDON HOUSE STINK LANE came in for a [illegible] of shelling	
			and M.G. fire – Coys in front line subjected to large amount	
			of M.G. and rifle fire – 1 OR killed and 7 o.Ranks wounded.	
			7 new Officers joined Lieut Goodall 2/Lts Hitchins, Wood	

A6945 Wt. W11422/M1160 350,000 12/16 D. D. & L. Forms/C./2118/14.

Army Form C. 2118.

Instructions regarding War Diaries and Intelligence Summaries are contained in F. S. Regs., Part II. and the Staff Manual respectively. Title pages will be prepared in manuscript.

WAR DIARY
or
INTELLIGENCE SUMMARY.
(*Erase heading not required.*)

Place	Date	Hour	Summary of Events and Information	Remarks and references to Appendices
			Johnston, Stephen, McIndoe & Davidson. also 71 O.Ranks	
	25.6.18		Quiet day – enemy artillery below normal.	
	26.6.18		Quiet day – Inter Coy relief. D Coy relieved B Coy in front line posts – A Coy relieved C Coy in front line posts – HINGES and back areas shelled – considerable amount of MG fire.	
	27.6.18		Noisy day – HINGES, HINGETTE and CANAL BANK shelled intermittently for about 24 hours – 2/Lt D. McLean joined the Battn.	
	28.6.18		Quiet day – Slight MG fire round Battn HQs (GORDON HOUSE area)	
	29.6.18		Quiet day – Battn relieved in front line by 2nd Suffolk Regt – moved back into Brigade Reserve in CHOCQUES (good relief).	
	30.6.18		Quiet day – usual cleaning up and baths for the Battn.	

R. A. Wolfe Murray Lt Colonel
Cmdg 1st Bn The Gordon Highrs

A6945 Wt. W11422/M1160 350,000 12/16 D. D. & L. Forms/C./2118/14.

Letter written By.Lt.D.D.A.Lockhart, dated 29th June 1917

1st Gordon Highlanders,
No.8 Red Cross Hospital, ROUEN.

My last letter I wrote to you was, I think, from Le Touquet, where I was going through a Lewis Gun Course. A great deal has happened since then.

After my course was ended, I went up the line to Arras, where I found the Battalion in billets.

I went back to my old company - C -, where I found pretty well the same officers as before - Davidson, a cousin of the Eliott-Lockharts (incidentally) in command of it, and besides him Sanderson a D.S.O., Dove and myself - just the four of us. Just when I arrived, the whole Battalion started practicising a stunt, which was to take place in about 10 days time. The first wave were to go over without a barrage, running and taking the German first line trench, that was to be C & D Coys. The second wave were to follow (A & B Coys) and passing over us they were to walk on whilst a barrage was to be put on the German second line for a couple of minutes. Then they were to take the German second line.

Well I had quite a jolly time during the 10 days I spent in Arras. Every morning we practised the assault, and then came back into the town about 11 o'clock and were free for the rest of the day.

On Tuesday night, June 12th we moved up into our front line trench in front of Monchy - le - Preux. On Thursday morning the 14th at 7.20 a.m. we went over, getting the German front line easily. The part of it I arrived at there were three Bosches who upon being playfully threatened in the ribs with bayonets by a corresponding number of Gordon Highlanders put their hands up wisely and screamed "Kamerad". There was a very stout one who began running away along the trench; I fired at him with my revolver but am not quite certain whether I hit him.

As soon as I got in, I made sure I was in touch with D Coy.on my left, sent a message along to Company Headquarters to the effect that I was, and started my platoon to dig themselves in (the Boche trench was only about 3 feet deep and not that in parts). We took the Germans in the trench entirely by surprise; some of my men told me that when they came to the trench they found Germans asleep and had to prod them with the bayonet and wake them up to take them prisoner. A and B. Companies also got their objective.

By three o'clock in the afternoon we got the trench good and deep, and it was lucky, because at about 5.30 p.m. the Germans put up a terrific barrage on our trench for about half an hour. It was absolute hell, but extraordinarily enough we had not one casualty in my platoon. Unfortunately, the other platoon in the Company had about 20 or 30 casualties including 2 sergeants, and poor Davidson and Dove were killed. That left just Sanderson (the D.S.O) and me in the Company. Sanderson took command.

A and B Companies after resisting counter-attacks successfully suffered so many casualties that they finally had to form themselves into two posts and eventually one of the posts had to come back 70 yards and the other almost entirely. The difficulty of course was that our left flank was entirely in the air.

On the Friday night the Bosches got round and attacked D.Coy., but after a sharp fight they were entirely repulsed with many casualties. I spoke to a wounded German who was brought in prisoner. He told me that we'd given them a bad beating and that they were at their wits ends, that they had suffered many casualties. Also that everyone in Germany now knew that Germany would be defeated.

Saturday morning I amused myself sniping at a bombing post the Germans had shoved forward. I hit two Germans to the best of my belief.

In the evening Sanderson who had been back to Battalion Hqrs. returned with news that we would have to attack at 1.45 a.m. on the next day, Sunday and recapture the top of the hill. Infantry Hill that is. The orders, from Brigade or wherever it was, seemed very vague, the distance to our objective was 250 yards or so, there was no word of any barrage, and finally the men who had hardly closed their eyes since the Wednesday, except in snatches, and had had a lot of hard work were dead beat. However we had to go, so at 1.45 a.m. we got over the parapet and began silently walking forward. As soon as the Bosches got wind of it we were to double forward. We had gone some 50 yards I suppose when the Germans opened a perfect storm of fire on us. We began to double but I was hit through the thigh almost at once and fell. My platoon sergeant who tried to rally those who were left was hit in the head and killed. The remainder dropped in shell-holes and opened fire. I tried to get them to go on but they took no notice and one does'nt blame them, as it would have been no use if they had. So when I had got over my first surprise at being hit, I crawled back to them and lay there for a bit. By now it was getting light, the German machine-gun and rifle fire was still sweeping over us and so the order came along from Sanderson that the men were to get back to the trench as best they could. So they went and after a bit I managed to drag myself a bit further back to another shell-hole where I settled myself, took the haversack off my back, also the waterproof sheet, and with those and a pack a man had left behind I built up a rough additional cover from fire and awaited events.

It was now getting quite light and I fully contemplated the possibility of having to spend Sunday in my shell-hole until dark came again and I might manage to drag myself in. However, my water bottle was full, I had some concentrated meat on me Mother had given me, and also hoped to find some food in the pack I had used for a fortification.

However, to my surprise, stretcher-bearers came out and one of them, quite a little fellow, took me on his back and ran with me to our trenches. He fell down about twice, but finally deposited me safely in the trench and ran off for some one else. Sanderson came up and wished me good luck and said "good-bye" to me. He was killed later. I remained a little while in a sheltered bit of trench, as the Germans were putting a barrage on the trench again. As soon as it stopped I made my way down the Communication Trench to the Dressing Station, where I was dressed and taken back on a stretcher. I was carried back about a mile or so and then put in an ambulance and driven back to Arras where I was more fully dressed. Then I was driven to the Casualty Clearing Station at Duisans, where I was put to bed and had my wound properly attended to. I spent about three days there and then was moved down here, where I have been about a week.

76th Brigade.

3rd Division.

1st BATTALION GORDON HIGHLANDERS ::: JULY 1918.

76/3

Army Form C. 2118.

1 Gordon Hrs

Vol 46

Instructions regarding War Diaries and Intelligence Summaries are contained in F. S. Regs., Part II, and the Staff Manual respectively. Title pages will be prepared in manuscript.

WAR DIARY
or
~~INTELLIGENCE SUMMARY.~~
(Erase heading not required.)

Place	Date	Hour	Summary of Events and Information	Remarks and references to Appendices
CHOCQUES	1-7-18		2 Coys on Range – 2 Coys Baths – A few E H.V. shells on Coy areas during the night. Sgts mess and mens reading room arranged for in the Brasserie.	
	2-7-18		1 Coy on Range – 3 Coys training – Cable burying fatigue near HINGES (400 men) by night, back 6 AM 3/7/18.	
	3-7-18		No training in consequence of fatigue – H Q details on range. Platoon football competition on 'C' coys field	
	4-7-18		1 Coy on range – 1 coy on training area near Station. Platoon football competition continued. Lt Col R.A. Wolfe Murray DSO MC on leave.	
HINGES	5-7-18		Battn ceremonial parade on football ground in the morning, 11.30 AM to 12.30 PM. Relief of 8th K.O.R.L. Rgt in the Battle Zone. Relief complete 1-5 AM – very quiet.	
	6-7-18		1½ Coys CANAL BANK. 7 platoons GORDON LINE. 3 platoons SUFFOLK LINE. Very hot. flies very bad. Work on improving CANAL BANK and GORDON LINE	
	7-7-18		Very quiet – work as usual – 1 O.R. wounded.	

Army Form C. 2118.

Instructions regarding War Diaries and Intelligence Summaries are contained in F. S. Regs., Part II. and the Staff Manual respectively. Title pages will be prepared in manuscript.

WAR DIARY
or
~~INTELLIGENCE SUMMARY.~~

(*Erase heading not required.*)

Place	Date	Hour	Summary of Events and Information	Remarks and references to Appendices
HINGES	8/9-7-18		Very quiet	
	10-7-18		The Divisional Commander visited the line.	
	11-7-18		Very quiet. Relief of 8th K O R L Regt in Forward Zone Relief complete 12 Midnight	
	12-7-18		Rain for first time for weeks not enough however to make front Posts	
			bad. Work by night improving fire positions laying duckboards	
			putting out wire.	
	13-7-18		Usual work. casualties 1 O.R wounded. Heavy rain in afternoon	
	14-7-18		Hostile artillery more active than usual both day and night; also	
			enemy machine Guns. 2/Lt D McLean killed by M.G. bullet when	
			out on patrol. - 7 O.R wounded chiefly amongst carrying parties	
			from Support to Front Line.	
	15/16-7-18		Usual work - quiet.	
	17-7-18		Quiet day - Relief by 2nd Suffolk Regt	
CHOCQUES	18-7-18		Usual cleaning up after coming out of the Line. Bn Paid out. 2 Coys baths	
	19-7-18		2 Coys (C + D) on range - 2 Coys baths.	
	20-7-18		2 Coys (A + B) on range - 2 Coys training. Sports - C Coy	

A6945 Wt. W11422/M1160 350,000 12/16 D. D. & L. Forms/C./2118/14.

Instructions regarding War Diaries and Intelligence Summaries are contained in F. S. Regs., Part II. and the Staff Manual respectively. Title pages will be prepared in manuscript.

WAR DIARY
or
~~INTELLIGENCE SUMMARY.~~
(Erase heading not required.)

Army Form C. 2118.

Place	Date	Hour	Summary of Events and Information	Remarks and references to Appendices
CHOCQUES			played 20th KRRC at Soccer - result KRRC 2 goals 'C' Coy 1 goal. - Concert in Brasserie yard in the evening by 20th KRRC. Brig Gen Porter CMG DSO was present.	
	20-7-18		Reveille 4-30 AM - Battn on cable laying fatigue - Officers and NCOs on tactical exercise in manning reserve trenches East of VENDIN and OBLINGHEM - 6 to 9 pm.	
	21-7-18		Church Parade under shell fire from enemy Long Range gun - CHOCQUES and SANSAVOUR shelled. - Opening of War Savings certificate campaign	
	22-7-18		Battn marched to tracer bullet demonstration at Sandpit range in the morning, back for dinners. E. artillery shelled 'A' & 'D' Coy areas Coys were moved to Railway Cutting and trenches behind P. of War cages. 'C' Coy area shelled in the evening. casualties 2 O.R. wounded.	
	23-7-18		Very heavy rain all day. - Ceremonial drill parade cancelled Battn proceeded from Bde Reserve to Battle Zone and relieved 8th K.O.R.L. Regt. - Three days W.S.C. campaign finished. established a record for a unit - 2059 certificates purchased.	
HINGES	24-29 -7-18		Normal tour except for slightly increased shelling on Battn HQs	

A6945 Wt. W11422/M1160 350,000 12/16 D. D. & L. Forms/C./2118/14.

Army Form C. 2118.

Instructions regarding War Diaries and Intelligence Summaries are contained in F. S. Regs., Part II. and the Staff Manual respectively. Title pages will be prepared in manuscript.

WAR DIARY
or
INTELLIGENCE SUMMARY.
(Erase heading not required.)

Place	Date	Hour	Summary of Events and Information	Remarks and references to Appendices
HINGES			Work on GORDON LINE and CANAL BANK - Two platoons carrying each night for front line Battn.	
	29-7-18		Relief of 8th KORL Regt in Forward Zone - Quiet relief - casualties nil.	
	30-7-18		The front line much as before but very dirty - cleaning up.	
	31-7-18		Slight shelling of PARK LANE and Battn H.Qs during night and morning stand to - casualties 1. OR wounded.	

R. Hope Murray ? Colonel
Cmdg 1st Gordon Highlanders

A6945 Wt. W11422/M1160 350,000 12/16 D. D. & L. Forms/C./2118/14.

76th Brigade.

3rd Division.

9------------

1st BATTALION GORDON HIGHLANDERS ::: AUGUST 1918.

1st Gordon Hdrs

Instructions regarding War Diaries and Intelligence Summaries are contained in F. S. Regs., Part II. and the Staff Manual respectively. Title pages will be prepared in manuscript.

~~WAR DIARY~~ *or* INTELLIGENCE SUMMARY.

(Erase heading not required.)

Army Form C. 2118.

Place	Date	Hour	Summary of Events and Information	Remarks and references to Appendices
HINGES	1/8/18		Heavy shelling of HINGES by enemy artillery – very heavy rain all day and night.	
	2/8/18		LABEUVRIERE and CHOCQUES shelled by enemy HV gun – very light shelling of front line system – heavy rain all day.	
	3/8/18		Back areas again shelled by HV gun – [illegible] for Brigade relief.	
	4/5/8/18		Quiet days – nothing of importance to report.	
	6/8/18		Battn relieved in front line by the Wiltshires and moved back to embussing point at CHOCQUES – hot meal served to all before embussing at 4 AM	
LIERES	7/8/18		Battn arrived LIERES at 6.10 AM – Billetted in barns – very comfortable – Coys paid out in evening.	
	8/8/18		2 Coys at baths – 2 Coys training and at range.	
	9/8/18		2 Coys at baths – 2 Coys training – The Army Commander Gen Sir W Birdwood visited the Battn during dinners. Sports were held in the afternoon.	

A6945 Wt. W11422/M1160 350,000 12/16 D. D. & L. Forms/C./2118/14.

Instructions regarding War Diaries and Intelligence Summaries are contained in F. S. Regs., Part II. and the Staff Manual respectively. Title pages will be prepared in manuscript.

WAR DIARY
or
INTELLIGENCE SUMMARY.
(*Erase heading not required.*)

Army Form C. 2118.

Place	Date	Hour	Summary of Events and Information	Remarks and references to Appendices
LIERES	10/8/18		All Coys at Training till 11-AM - 1 PM Batt^{n} paraded and marched to main road between FERFAY and BELLERY - His Majesty The King passed along the road in his motor car - The men of the Batt^{n} recognised His Majesty and cheered lustily.	
	11/8/18		Church Parade - The Divisional Commander (Maj Gen Deverell) was present - Afternoon - Batt^{n} Boxing Competition was held in the grounds near Transport Lines - very interesting - some good bouts	
	12/8/18		Batt^{n} paraded for training during the morning - Batt^{n} route marched to Ranges and FERFAY where XIII Corps Sports were held. - Batt^{n} Tug of War team ran into 2nd place Transport Turn-out obtained 4th place.	
	13/8/18		4 Coys at Training - Batt^{n} visited by Corps Commander and Brig. General - Commanding Officer inspected Mob. Reserve and Transport loaded up ready to move to SUS-ST-LEGER	
	14/8/18		Batt^{n} marched to PERNES and entrained for SUS-ST-LEGER "B" Coy detailed for loading and unloading - (cont)	

A6945 Wt. W11422/M1160 350,000 12/16 D. D. & L. Forms/C./2118/14.

Instructions regarding War Diaries and Intelligence Summaries are contained in F. S. Regs., Part II. and the Staff Manual respectively. Title pages will be prepared in manuscript.

WAR DIARY
or
INTELLIGENCE SUMMARY.
(Erase heading not required.)

Army Form C. 2118.

Place	Date	Hour	Summary of Events and Information	Remarks and references to Appendices
	14/8/18	(Cont)		
SUS-ST-LEGER			Great search for Billets – Battn in G H Q Reserve under 24 hours notice. –	
	15/8/18		Coy parades – Platoon training. – Sports – inter platoon football.	
	16/8/18		Coy parades – platoon training – Sports – inter Coy football matches. – Battn was paid out. – Divisional General visited Coys during training.	
	17/8/18		2 Coys at baths – 2 Coys training – Rounders match between Officers of Battn and 2nd Suffolk Regt.	
	18/8/18		Church parade – Divisional Commander was present and presented Medal Ribbons – Sports in the afternoon and Divisional Band played in the area.	
	19/8/18		Battn under orders to move – Coy commanders present at Conference held at Bde H.Qrs. – Battn paraded at 8.30 PM to march to BERLES-AU-BOIS. – arrived just after midnight.	
BERLES-AU-BOIS	20/8/18		Battn lay out in orchards all day – paraded ready to move off at 10 PM and proceeded to assembly position behind AYETTE	

A6945 Wt. W11422/M1160 350,000 12/16 D. D. & L. Forms/C./2118/14.

Instructions regarding War Diaries and Intelligence Summaries are contained in F. S. Regs., Part II. and the Staff Manual respectively. Title pages will be prepared in manuscript.

WAR DIARY
or
~~INTELLIGENCE SUMMARY.~~
(*Erase heading not required.*)

Army Form C. [illegible]18.

Place	Date	Hour	Summary of Events and Information	Remarks and references to Appendices
	(cont)			
AYETTE	20/8/18		as Reserve Battn to the Reserve Brigade – All in position by 12-30 AM.	
	21/8/18		At ZERO hour (4-50 AM) the Battn moved forward in column of route	
			through a dense mist for about a mile and on breasting	
			the ridge West QUESNOY FARM split up into artillery formation.	
			The advance was made in previously arranged bounds and	
			came into action between Battn and Bde HQrs and maintained	
			that front. – Owing to the mist it was not possible to see further	
			than about 100x – about 11 AM the mist lifted – by this time the	
			Battn had reached the Valley West of COURCELLES but the RAILWAY	
			EMBANKMENT had not been taken and the forward Coys therefore	
			took up their position in a ~~[illegible]~~ SUNKEN ROAD about 300x West of where	
			they were supposed to occupy. – Some M.G. and shell fire during	
			the day – In the evening A & D Coys went to cooperate in an	
			attack on the RAILWAY EMBANKMENT just North of ACHIET LE GRAND	
			with 63rd Division on the Right – about 7 PM it was discovered	
			that the attack on the Right had taken place and was unsuccessful	

Instructions regarding War Diaries and Intelligence Summaries are contained in F. S. Regs., Part II. and the Staff Manual respectively. Title pages will be prepared in manuscript.

Army Form C. 2118.

WAR DIARY
~~or~~
~~INTELLIGENCE SUMMARY.~~
(Erase heading not required.)

Place	Date	Hour	Summary of Events and Information	Remarks and references to Appendices
	(cont) 21/8/18		at the request however of the O.C. ANSON Battn 63rd Div (the next Bn on the Right) the attack was undertaken and launched over the ridge about 1500x short of the embankment about 7-30 PM. - there was no artillery support - hostile Machine Gun, Rifle and artillery fire was very intense and the attack was held up half way down the forward slope, about 50% casualties being sustained and the Commanding Officer (Lt Col R.A. Wolfe Murray DSO MC) was wounded while personally leading the charge. The Battn was withdrawn after dark to the Blue Line.	RP.
	22/8/18		Battn rested all day - Major Pearson came up and took over command. The Battn moved up after dark with the remainder of the Bde to assembly positions for attack on GOMIECOURT the following morning. The Battn was to guard the Right flank of the attack to be delivered by the two other Battns of the Bde as the taking of GOMIECOURT alone would make a pronounced salient in our line - enemy was found to have a MG in the assembly position for the two flanking Coys and this had to be dislodged before	

A6945 Wt. W11422/M1160 350,000 12/16 D. D. & L. Forms/C./2118/14.

Instructions regarding War Diaries and Intelligence Summaries are contained in F. S. Regs., Part II, and the Staff Manual respectively. Title pages will be prepared in manuscript.

WAR DIARY
or
~~INTELLIGENCE SUMMARY~~.
(*Erase heading not required.*)

Army Form C. 2118.

Place	Date	Hour	Summary of Events and Information	Remarks and references to Appendices
	(cont) 22/8/18		the assembly.	
	23/8/18		When the attack started the two Right flank Coys met some opposition on the RAILWAY EMBANKMENT halfway to their objective, and were exposed to considerable MG fire from their Right and Right rear - They dug in however well on the flank and undoubtedly saved a large number of casualties in the assaulting Battns. The 2nd Division went through at 11 AM and this relieved the pressure - about 4 PM the Battn moved forward to a position just S.E. of GOMIECOURT and dug themselves in - the night passed quietly on the front except for some Gas shelling between the village and the RAILWAY EMBANKMENT.	
	24/8/18		Battn rested all day - movement being kept down to the minimum owing to being in view from BAHAGNIES and SAPIGNIES about one mile in front. - The Battn was withdrawn about 8.30 PM to the PURPLE LINE West of DOUCHY where they rested in Open trenches	

A6945 Wt. W11422/M1160 350,000 12/16 D. D. & L. Forms/C./2118/14.

WAR DIARY

or

INTELLIGENCE SUMMARY.

(Erase heading not required.)

Army Form C. 2118.

Instructions regarding War Diaries and Intelligence Summaries are contained in F. S. Regs., Part II. and the Staff Manual respectively. Title pages will be prepared in manuscript.

Place	Date	Hour	Summary of Events and Information	Remarks and references to Appendices
DOUCHY	25/8/18		The Batt^n rested all day - heavy rain fell -	
	26/8/18		Fine day - Batt^n moved in the evening to trenches situated in front of HAMLINCOURT	
	27/8/18		During the day the enemy shelled intermittently round about the Batt^n area and HAMLINCOURT	
	28/8/18		On the night of the 28th inst the Batt^n moved forward from the trenches in front of HAMLINCOURT and relieved the 2nd Grenadiers in the front line S W of ECOUST.	
	29/8/18		Batt^n pushed out patrols to keep in touch with the enemy - one platoon of the left Coy advanced too far and was practically wiped out by M G fire from the flank. The Batt^n was to cooperate with the 8th West Yorks (62 Div) in a small operation but owing to the very limited time for assembly purposes the venture did not take place.	
	30/8/18		The Batt^n advanced in conjunction with the 2nd Suffolk Regt who took ECOUST on our left but owing to the troops on the	

A6945 Wt. W11422/M1160 350,000 12/16 D. D. & L. Forms/C./2118/14.

Instructions regarding War Diaries and Intelligence Summaries are contained in F. S. Regs., Part II. and the Staff Manual respectively. Title pages will be prepared in manuscript.

WAR DIARY
or
INTELLIGENCE SUMMARY.
(Erase heading not required.)

Army Form C. 2118.

Place	Date	Hour	Summary of Events and Information	Remarks and references to Appendices
MORY + ECOUST	30/8/18		left having to fall back under a heavy counter attack our left Coy was left in the air and they suffered heavy casualties – on the Right the Battn reached its objective with very few casualties. The Battn dug in and consolidated the position. The Brigade were relieved at night with the exception of the Battn and 1 Coy of the 8th K.O.R.L. Regt. who came under the orders of the G.O.C. 9th Brigade.	
	31/8/18		The 9th Bde attacked on a 3 Battalion front in the morning – ECOUST was retaken – The Battn gained its objectives + dug in – The Adjutant (Capt H.S. Sammell MC) was killed while reconnoitring with a view to moving some other troops into position preparatory to the attack	
In the Field 5/9/18			M. E. Pearson Major Comdg 1st Bn The Gordon Highrs.	

A6945 Wt. W11422/M1160 350,000 12/16 D. D. & L. Forms/C./2118/14.

1st Batt. The Gordon Higrs.

[illegible] doing duty with battalion [illegible]

[illegible] [illegible]

Capt. [illegible] M.C. — Capt. [illegible] (Transport Officer)

J. [illegible]

B. [illegible]

[illegible] Gordon

Lieut. [illegible] M.C. — Lieut. W.R. Broadhurst

[illegible] Gillespie — " W.R. Berridge

W. Webster — " H. [illegible]

[illegible] (Sig. Officer)

2/Lieut. R. Stephen — 2/Lt. [illegible] Fraser

J. Watson — " W.J. Henderson

J. Clark M.C. (Intell. Officer)

[illegible] Howard

Lieut. D. Hutton – Asst. Adjutant.

" [illegible] Jennings – Quartermaster.

Attached

Captain J. Stewart D.S.O. M.C. – R.A.M.C.

Revd. [illegible] Cracker – Chaplain.

4 Offrs – Killed.

13 " – Wounded.

D Hutton Lieut

A/Adjt. 1st Bn. The Gordon Highrs.

76th Brigade.

3rd Division.

<u>1st BATTALION GORDON HIGHLANDERS :: SEPTEMBER 1918.</u>

WAR DIARY

or

~~INTELLIGENCE SUMMARY.~~

(Erase heading not required.)

1st Gordon Hrs 8th

Army Form C. 2118.

76/3

Instructions regarding War Diaries and Intelligence Summaries are contained in F. S. Regs., Part II. and the Staff Manual respectively. Title pages will be prepared in manuscript.

Place	Date	Hour	Summary of Events and Information	Remarks and references to Appendices
	Sept.	1918.		
VRAUXOURT	1st		9th & 76th Inf. Bde took objective intended for the centre battn the previous day. 8th R O R L did this without a barrage before daylight. Patrols pushed out and NOREUIL found to be strongly held with sniping and shelling. Battn H.Q. moved forward to ECOUST-MORY road.	
	2nd		8th Bde passed thro' battn at 5.30 AM. Quiet and no shelling. 1st Scots Guards moved in behind battn at dusk. Capt H.S. GAMMELL M.C. buried in cemetery DOUCHY-LES-AYETTE	
	3rd		Battn withdrawn at 1 AM and marched back to rest trenches between MOYENVILLE and AYETTE arriving 5 AM. Battn rested and paid during the afternoon. Fine and warm.	

A6945 Wt. W11422/M1160 350,000 12/16 D. D. & L. Forms/C./2118/14.

Instructions regarding War Diaries and Intelligence Summaries are contained in F. S. Regs., Part II. and the Staff Manual respectively. Title pages will be prepared in manuscript.

WAR DIARY
or
~~INTELLIGENCE SUMMARY.~~
(Erase heading not required.)

Army Form C. 2118.

Place	Date	Hour	Summary of Events and Information	Remarks and references to Appendices
AYETTE	Sept 4th		2 coys and HQ had baths at BOIRY ST MARTIN. Other 2 coys inspections and platoon training. 2nd Lt D. KENNEDY buried at DOUCHY LES AYETTE in forenoon. Battn rested in afternoon. Fine and warm. Camp improved	
	5th		Coys practised extended order and compass marching during forenoon. Bn parade at 2.15 P.M. for distribution of gallantry cards by Major W. G. Pearson. Lt Col The Hon W. Fraser D.S.O. M.C took over command of the battn in the evening.	
	6th		Bn moved to GAUDIEMPRE at 10.55 AM. Halt from 2-4 PM for dinners. Arrived in billets 6.45 P.M. Billets fair. Good weather	
GAUDIEMPRE	7th		Battn cleaned up and improved billets. Brig Gen Burnett D.S.O. visited the battn in the evening. Showery	
	8th		Church parade. N.C.Os and L.G. classes formed and training programme arranged. LT R.T. PRIE took over Adjutant vice LT D HUTTON. Heavy rain all day.	
	9th		7.30 AM Inspection. 9 AM Coy inspection. 9.30-12.30 R.S.M.s parade rapid loading artillery formation sentry drill. Specialists under own instruction. Lecture on "Formations" by C.O to all officers and N.C.Os at 2.30 PM. Showery.	

A6945 Wt. W11422/M1160 350,000 12/16 D. D. & L. Forms/C./2118/14.

Instructions regarding War Diaries and Intelligence Summaries are contained in F. S. Regs., Part II. and the Staff Manual respectively. Title pages will be prepared in manuscript.

WAR DIARY
or
~~INTELLIGENCE SUMMARY.~~
(Erase heading not required.)

Army Form C. 2118.

Place	Date	Hour	Summary of Events and Information	Remarks and references to Appendices
	Sept.			
GAUDIEMPRE	10th		7.30 AM Morning inspection 9–12.30 P.M. Coy. inspection. C.Os parade march discipline	
"			sentry drill handling of arms. 2.30 P.M. Lecture by C.O. to all officers and platoon sgts.	
"			Musketry at 2.30 P.M. Heavy rain all day which interfered with training	
GAUDIEMPRE	11th		7.30 A.M. Parade only. Bn. marched to ADINFER WOOD starting 1.55 P.M.	
ADINFER			Reached trenches about 5 P.M. Only a few shelters available in trenches. Showery	
WOOD			in forenoon but cleared up in afternoon Draft 1 Cpl. + 50 O.R. all out for first time	
			joined batt. and posted to coys.	
SAPIGNIES	12th		Batt. moved to SAPIGNIES area at 10.15 A.M. Rain at intervals. Batt. arrived	
			about 1 P.M. Billets comfortable chiefly old German huts. Batt. paid out.	
"	13th		7.30 A.M. Inspection 9–12. Coy inspection fire and movement exercise 1.45 Batt. attended	
			demonstration of cooperation with tanks and returned to camp about 5.30 P.M. Good weather	
"	14th		7.30 AM Inspections 9–12.30. Coy inspections, artillery formations platoon and companies in	
			the attack arm drill. Draft 114 O.R. all under 19 years of age joined batt. from 52nd Grad. Batt.	
"	15th		Church parade 10.30 A.M. under Major PRYDE. Batt. moved to FREMICOURT at	
FREMICOURT			2.20 P.M. Billets indifferent. Slight hostile bombing at night and one E.A. brought	
			down in flames. Fine day.	

A6945 Wt. W11422/M1160 350,000 12/16 D. D. & L. Forms/C./2118/14.

Instructions regarding War Diaries and Intelligence Summaries are contained in F. S. Regs., Part II, and the Staff Manual respectively. Title pages will be prepared in manuscript.

WAR DIARY
or
~~INTELLIGENCE SUMMARY.~~

(*Erase heading not required.*)

Army Form C. 2118.

Place	Date	Hour	Summary of Events and Information	Remarks and references to Appendices
FREMICOURT	Sept 16th		Battn moved to sunken road between MORCHIES and BEUMETZ-LES-CAMBRAI at 8.30 AM. Shelters few and indifferent. Timber and iron obtained and shelters improved during afternoon. Lt A.B. TERRIS joined and posted to A Coy. Fine day. V heavy thunderstorm at night and battn nearly all got soaked owing to poor shelters.	
BEUMETZ-LES-CAMBRAI	17th		9-12.30 Coy. inspections. Platoon in attack. Handling of arms. 2.30-4.15 Demonstration of platoon in attack by C.O. to all officers and N.C.Os. Owing to observation from BOURLON WOOD ground for training limited. Shelters improved. Fine and warm during day but rain at night.	
	18th		9-12.30 Coy. inspection, consolidation, coys in attack in open warfare, handling of arms 2.30-4 P.M. Practice wire cutting Nos 1 & 2 of L.Gs on range. Lecture by C.O. to O.C. Coys and Platoon commanders. Lt Gillespie took over command of A Coy vice Capt. D. Macfarlane on leave to U.K.	
	19th		9-12.30 Coy. inspection. Coy in attack under barrage. Shell hole consolidation. Handling of arms. 2-4 Company, platoon and section commanders under C.O. for tactical exercise in MORCHIES-LOUVERVAL valley. Following officers joined and posted to coys. A Coy 2nd Lt R COLE, B Coy 2nd Lt J.K DONALD, J CROMBIE, G COTTRELL, C Coy 2nd Lt J. LESLIE, D Coy 2nd Lt B. DUTHIE. D.S. SERVICE 20 M Ms & 3 bars to M.M. awarded to N.C.Os & men of the battn for August 21st	

Instructions regarding War Diaries and Intelligence Summaries are contained in F. S. Regs., Part II. and the Staff Manual respectively. Title pages will be prepared in manuscript.

WAR DIARY
or
~~INTELLIGENCE~~ SUMMARY.
(Erase heading not required.)

Army Form C. 2118.

Place	Date	Hour	Summary of Events and Information	Remarks and references to Appendices
	Sept			
BEUMETZ -LES- CAMBRAI	20th		9AM–12.30PM. Bn practised attack under a barrage along MORCHIES–LOUVERVAL valley. Dull but no rain	
	21		9AM–12.30PM. Bn practised attack under barrage on MORCHIES village. Coys practised in rapid loading and unloading of L.G.s etc from limbers. Battn paid out. C.O. visited the line and assembly trenches. Fine	
"	22		9-30–10.30AM Coy inspections and arm drill. Divine service in afternoon. 2 officers per coy went round the line in early morning to visit assembly trenches. Fine	
"	23		9–12.30. Coys at disposal of O.C. Coys. 2nd LT MANSON joined and posted to 'C' Coy. Fine day	
"	24		9–12.30 Coys at disposal of O.C. Coys. All steel helmets painted. Fighting equipment issued. Dull occasional showers	
"	25		Battn bathed at BEAUMETZ-LES-CAMBRAI and issued with clean clothing. Model of ground to be attacked inspected by companies during the day. Dull, a little rain. Capt D.R.G. [illegible] to England for 6 months tour of duty. Lieut FYVIE takes over duties of TO	

A6945 Wt. W11422/M1160 350,000 12/16 D. D. & L. Forms/C./2118/14.

Army Form C. 2118.

Instructions regarding War Diaries and Intelligence Summaries are contained in F. S. Regs., Part II. and the Staff Manual respectively. Title pages **will be prepared in manuscript.**

WAR DIARY
or
~~INTELLIGENCE SUMMARY.~~
(Erase heading not required.)

Place	Date	Hour	Summary of Events and Information	Remarks and references to Appendices
BEAUMETZ -LES- CAMBRAI	Sept 26th		Reveille 7.30 AM C.O. inspected and addressed each coy. Men rested 2-5 P.M. Battn. moved off to assembly positions at 7.30 P.M. Fair rain during the night.	
	27th.		See attached report on operations Sept 27th. Fine day.	
	28th		Battn. remained in STATION AVENUE and SHERWOOD SWITCH till 3 P.M. when coys. marched back to HAVRINCOURT and occupied trenches and shelters near CHATEAU. Accommodation very bad. Slight rain during morning but cleared up after 12 noon. Very cold night.	
	29th		Battn. rested cleaned up and reorganised. Shelters improved. Dull and cold.	
	30th		Battn reorganised during forenoon. C.S.M. ROLLO D.C.M. M.M. buried in cemetery N. of HAVRINCOURT. Bn moved to trenches in front of RIBECOURT at 5.30 P.M. No shelter. At 11 P.M. orders received to attack RUMILLY. O.C. Coys came to HQ and arrangements were made for attack. Bn marched off at 1.30 AM.	

[signature] Lt. Col.
Commanding
1st Gordon Highlanders

A6945 Wt. W11422/M1160 350,000 12/16 D. D. & L. Forms/C./2118/14.

76th Infy Brigade

Report on Operations carried out 1st Bn The Gordon Highlanders September 27th 1918

Assembly I. On the night of Sept. 26th the Bn moved up to assembly positions in CANAL TRENCH, SLOANE AVENUE & KNIGHTSBRIDGE. The night was extremely dark which made the assembly difficult, but there was very little hostile shelling and it was completed without casualty.

It was understood that gaps had been cut through the wire in rear of LONDON SUPPORT & LONDON TRENCH, but a reconnaissance failed to discover these. There was a considerable quantity of wire which formed a very serious obstacle to an advance, more especially in bad light through enemy shell-fire.

Under these circumstances it was at first decided to move forward at ZERO hour by trenches (JERMYN STREET & KNIGHTSBRIDGE) as far as our front, but this plan had to be discarded later owing to condition of the trenches - the result of some rain during the night.

It was therefore decided to cut one efficient gap in the wire and to pass the whole Battalion through this gap by platoons.

Advance II. The Battalion move off from its assembly position at ZERO + 25 minutes, by which time it was becoming light, & passed through the gap in the wire according to plan. Some difficulty was experienced in crossing LONDON SUPPORT & LONDON TRENCH, which caused a certain amount of confusion, which was more difficult to deal with on account of the inexperience of platoon commanders and the shortage of N.COs.

In No Mans Land, companies opened out into artillery formation and advanced towards the RED LINE. Few casualties were sustained during this part of the advance in spite of considerable machine gun fire from the front and the left flank.

The Attack III As the leading Coys (C & D) pass the crest of the ridge M.G. fire became hostile & it became evident that SNAKE & SEAL TRENCHES were still in the hands of the enemy, although the barrage had passed over them. The advance was therefore continued by rushes, sections supporting each other with fire and both SNAKE & SEAL TRENCHES were captured.

During this part of the advance the casualties to the two leading companies were considerable, especially in N.COs & they were much disorganised.

The left support company also, which had kept too close to the leading company had become involved.

The commanders of A + C Companies collected as many men as they could from their companies and led them forward under the barrage, which had paused in advance of the RED LINE + captured the SUNKEN ROAD + LINCOLN TRENCH. A large number of prisoners + some machine guns were taken in the SUNKEN ROAD.

The two SUPPORTING COMPANIES, continued the advance towards FLESQUIERES + entered the village. Here they became very much mixed, the greater portion moving through the south part of the village.

Captain Lee (commanding "B" Coy) realising this, attacked the northern part of the village with as many men as he could collect (about 60) and succeeded in getting through it + reaching SHERWOOD SWITCH, east of the village, in touch with the Irish Guards on his left.

This further advance was held up by very heavy M.G. fire from the left flank + the BEETROOT factory, and by Field Guns firing over open sights from the E. + N.E.

The remainder of the Battalion - the supporting companies had continued to advance after capturing their first objective - had meanwhile reached the SUNKEN ROAD in K.24 a. Owing to very heavy losses in NCOs disorganisation was extreme, + the advance was further held up by two or three enemy machine guns in action in SCORN TRENCH.

Re-organisation was undertaken as quickly as possible, + parties were pushed up SHERWOOD AVENUE from the SOUTH.

A small party moving down SCORN TRENCH under Sgt Christie succeeded in silencing the machine gun which had been causing most of the trouble.

Consolidation IV At this point the 62nd Division (185th Infy Bde) which had been moving up close behind the Battalion passed through + occupied STATION AVENUE on the front of this battalion without much opposition.

The Battalion remained in occupation of SHERWOOD SWITCH, which was consolidated until night, when two companies were moved forward into STATION AVENUE by order of 76th Infy Bde.

Remarks on the Operations

The battalion went into action very much under strength in NCOs and very heavy casualties were sustained in NCOs during the early part of the advance.

The men were very untrained, a large percentage were boys of 18½ years who had no fighting experience & insufficient discipline, and they did not understand the necessity for sticking to their section commanders (all Lance Corporals or Privates) was very low on the whole, before the operation.

The NCOs did magnificent work and there are many instances of the Cadres doing almost alone the work of their Commands. Companies became mixed as must happen, & owing to lack of Cadres disorganisation was very great.

Casualties were greatly increased by the lack of training & lack of NCOs.

Most of the platoon commanders were entirely lacking in experience, but in spite of this some of them did good work.

In order to realise how the battalion suffered in NCOs - two companies came out of action with one Corporal each, one company came out with one Sergeant, one with two Sergeants.

P. T. Pirie Capt for
Lt Colonel
Commanding 1st Bn The Gordon Highlanders

3/10/18.

1st Battalion The Gordon Highlanders

Nominal Roll of Officers on strength of Bn on 30-9-18.

Lt Col The Hon W. Fraser DSO MC Commanding.
Major N. G. Pearson MC 2nd in Command
Captain P. T. Pirie Acting Adjutant
Lieut D. Hutton Asst. Adjutant
" S. T. Jennings Quartermaster
" H. Fyvie Transport Officer
" C. D. McHutchins Signalling Officer
2/Lt W. G. Henderson Intelligence Officer (Leave to UK)

"A" Company

Capt S P Gillespie MC Commanding
Lt W. R. Broadhurst
" A B Torrie
" J. P. Logie
Capt D Macfarlane (Leave to UK)

"B" Company

Capt C. H. Lee DSO MC Commanding
2/Lt R Stephen
" J Crombie
" J. K. Donald
" G Cottrell

"C" Company

Capt R. W. Preston MC Commanding
Lieut W. Webster
2/Lt J. Leslie
" R Manson

Capt R. K. Gordon MC Commanding
Lt W. P. Beveridge (Leave to UK)
" S. O. Goodall
2/Lt D M Fraser
" B Duthie
" D. S. Service

Attached.

Captain J. L. Stewart DSO MC - RAMC
Revd D Conacher CF

Detached.

Capt A M Richardson, Educational Officer XIII Corps School
" I. M. Frame Hospital
2/Lt J W K Smith Base for Dentures

W. Fraser

Lieut. Col.
Commanding
1st Gordon Highlanders

76th Brigade.

3rd Division.

1st BATTALION GORDON HIGHLANDERS ł:: OCTOBER 1918.

REPORTS ON OPERATIONS ATTACHED.

Instructions regarding War Diaries and Intelligence Summaries are contained in F. S. Regs., Part II. and the Staff Manual respectively. Title pages will be prepared in manuscript.

WAR DIARY
or
~~INTELLIGENCE~~ SUMMARY.
(*Erase heading not required.*)

1st Gordons Hrs 76/3 Vol. 49

Army Form C. 2118.

Place	Date	Hour	Summary of Events and Information	Remarks and references to Appendices
RUMILLY	1 10/18		See report on operations.	
	2 10/18		"A" & "C" Companies occupied posts N. and N.E. of RUMILLY and "B" and "D" Companies were withdrawn to trenches near MASNIERES and no longer under command of O.C. 2nd Suffolk Regiment. "A" and "C" Companies were relieved at 17.00 by 8th K.O.R.L. Regiment and returned to MASNIERES where they were accomodated in cellars together with Battalion H.Qrs.	
MASNIERES	3 10/18		The Battalion were rested and time spent in re-organization as far as possible. There were no casualties and situation normal, the weather all day was very favourable	
"	4 10/18		A draft of 20 other ranks were sent from details to each Company. The Battalion relieved the 2nd Suffolks in posts E. of RUMILLY and the relief completed by 02.00 on the 5 10/18. The Battalion carried on with the consolidation of posts. There was practically no activity by enemy and consequently no casualties. Battalion H.Qrs. G 15c. 9.2 in centre of village. "B" "C" & "D" Companies in posts on N.E. of RUMILLY and "A" Company in reserve in trench 100x S. of village.	

A6945 Wt. W11422/M1160 350,000 12/16 D. D. & L. Forms/C./2118/14.

Instructions regarding War Diaries and Intelligence Summaries are contained in F. S. Regs., Part II. and the Staff Manual respectively. Title pages will be prepared in manuscript.

WAR DIARY

or

INTELLIGENCE SUMMARY.

(Erase heading not required.)

Army Form C. 2118.

Place	Date	Hour	Summary of Events and Information	Remarks and references to Appendices
	5/10/18		During the day the situation was quiet and 1 other rank only casualty the work of consolidation was proceeded with by night	
	6/10/18		The Battalion occupying posts E. of RUMILLY - the day was very quiet and casualties 1 or. killed but hand 3 wounded.	
	7/10/18		At 17.00 the Battalion returned to cellars at MASNIERES and came under orders of G.O.C. 9th Brigade as reserve Battalion. The weather inclined to be wet during the evening and casualties were nil	
	8th/10/18		See report on Operations.	
	9/10/18		Guards Brigade passed through 9th Brigade at 03.45 and Battalion returned	
	9/10/18		to MASNIERES and were accomodated in RUMILLY TRENCH. The Battn. now under orders of 76th Brigade. The Battalion moved to HAVRINCOURT at 12.15, arriving there about 15.00. There was no billets and Battalion accomodated in disused trenches. A hot meal issued shortly after arrival. A draft of 111 other ranks joined Battalion.	
	10/10/18		Battalion resting time spent in cleaning up and making of shelters in the trenches.	

A6945 Wt. W11422/M1160 350,000 12/16 D. D. & L. Forms/C./2118/14.

Instructions regarding War Diaries and Intelligence Summaries are contained in F. S. Regs., Part II. and the Staff Manual respectively. Title pages will be prepared in manuscript.

WAR DIARY
or
~~INTELLIGENCE SUMMARY.~~
(Erase heading not required.)

Army Form C. 2118.

Place	Date	Hour	Summary of Events and Information	Remarks and references to Appendices
HAVRINCOURT	11/10/18.		Early morning inspection 07.30. – Wash Ins. Breakfasts 08.00. Companies were at disposal of Company Commanders for re-organization. All rifles were inspected by Armourer Sergt. and Box Respirators inspected by Bde. Gas N.C.O. A. Coy. and Transport had Baths and received a clean change in HAVRINCOURT. The following honours were awarded:- The D.S.O. – Capt. Lee MC; Bar to MC. – 2nd Lt. J Clark MC; – The MC. – Capt. J. McGreane, Capt S.P. Gillespie, Lieut. J. Mounder, 2Lt. W.G. Henderson. The D.C.M. – No. 17484 L/Cpl. A.S. Anderson. A Lewis Gun class in each Company consisting of 8 men each under Coy. L.G. Instructors started. A draft of 3 Officers and 39 O.R. arrived and Officers were posted – 'A' Coy. Lieut. D.G. MILNE; 'B' Coy – 2nd Lt. C.A.S. SINCLAIR; 'D' Coy 2nd Lieut. H.E. ROBERTSON.	
"	12/10/18.		Routine as usual. B C D and H.Q. Companies had baths at HAVRINCOURT and received a clean change of clothing. All the Lewis Guns were inspected by the Armourer Sergt. Companies on return from Baths carried on with close order drill and handling of arms. Companies were issued with leather jerkins.	

A6945 Wt. W11422/M1160 350,000 12/16 D. D. & L. Forms/C./2118/14.

Army Form C. 2118.

Instructions regarding War Diaries and Intelligence Summaries are contained in F. S. Regs., Part II. and the Staff Manual respectively. Title pages will be prepared in manuscript.

WAR DIARY
or
~~INTELLIGENCE SUMMARY~~.
(Erase heading not required.)

Place	Date	Hour	Summary of Events and Information	Remarks and references to Appendices
HAVRINCOURT	13/10/18		Major Pearson took over temporary command of 8th Kings Own. Lieut [illegible] returned from leave. Reveille 06.00, Breakfasts 07.00. The Battalion moved to MARCOING - Bde O.O. No. dated . The Battalion marched off at 10.30 and reached destination at 12.30. The billets were not very good principally consisting of partly destroyed houses. The weather was fine but the roads a bit muddy owing to rain overnight. The afternoon was utilized to improving the billets.	
MARCOING	14/10/18		Lieut. Berridge took over command of D. Company from 2nd Lt. D.M. FRASER.	
			Routine as usual. 09.45 The Battalion paraded for inspection by Commanding Officer. 10-30 to 11-45 Platoon training. 12 noon Battalion parade for presentation of Gallantry Cards to Officers NCO's & men. 14.30 Lecture by C.O. to all Officers & NCO's on Discipline and drill. All Companies were issued with clothing from Q.M. Stores.	
	15/10/18		Routine as usual. 09.00 Company inspections 09.30 to 10.30 Saluting drill and handling of arms. 10.30 to 11.45 [illegible] and [illegible] 12 noon [illegible] parade under Adjutant practising falling in to pipes. [illegible] from each Company was on salvage work in village all day. A draft of 4 Officers and	

A6945 Wt. W11422/M1160 350,000 12/16 D. D. & L. Forms/C./2118/14.

Instructions regarding War Diaries and Intelligence Summaries are contained in F. S. Regs., Part II, and the Staff Manual respectively. Title pages will be prepared in manuscript.

WAR DIARY

or

~~INTELLIGENCE SUMMARY~~.

(*Erase heading not required.*)

Army Form C. 2118.

Place	Date	Hour	Summary of Events and Information	Remarks and references to Appendices
MARCOING	15/10/18		149 OR. arrived. Quite a good draft which consisted of casuals from the 51st Division. The Officers were posted 2nd Lt. J. Cranford to "A" Coy, 2nd Lt. A. Bonner to "B" Coy, 2nd Lt. I. Grant to "C" Coy, 2nd Lt. H. Arnold to "D" Coy.	
"	16/10/18		Routine as usual. 09.00 Coy. Inspections. Owing to wet weather Companies were at the disposal of Company Commanders & they carried on indoors with Musketry, Lewis Gun Classes and Lectures. The usual Salvage parties were at work in the village. Inter-platoon football matches were played during the afternoon.	
"	17/10/18		Routine as usual 09.00 Company Inspections; 09.30 to 10.00 Saluting drill and handling of arms. 10.00 to 12.00 platoon in attack; 12.00 to 12.30 March discipline - lecture and practise. The usual Lewis Gun Classes were on from 10.00 to 12.30. Capt. J. McGeane MC rejoined from Hospital.	
	18/10/18		Routine as usual. 09.00 Company Inspections. 09.30 to 10.00 Saluting drill. 10.00 to 11.30 Platoon in the Attack. 11.45 to 12.30 Rapid aiming loading & firing. Capt. J. McGeane, MC, took over command of "C" Coy vice Capt. D. McFarlane.	

A6945 Wt. W11422/M1160 350,000 12/16 D. D. & L. Forms/C./2118/14.

Army Form C. 2118.

WAR DIARY
or
~~INTELLIGENCE SUMMARY.~~
(*Erase heading not required.*)

Instructions regarding War Diaries and Intelligence Summaries are contained in F. S. Regs., Part II. and the Staff Manual respectively. Title pages will be prepared in manuscript.

Place	Date	Hour	Summary of Events and Information	Remarks and references to Appendices
MARCONG CATTENIERES	19/10/18	-	Routine as usual. The Battn moved to CATTENIERES at 14.00. The weather was good and the billets were an improvement on the previous ones, only they were not clean. The Battalion arrived about 17.30 & were fortunate in arriving before the rain came. There was a Company Commanders Conference at 21.00.	
" QUIÉVY.	20/10/18		Reveille 07.00 - Breakfasts 07.45. The Battalion moved to QUIÉVY at 11-20. The weather was very unsettled and it rained throughout the march. The Battalion arrived about 14.00 and had quite good billets. A rum ration was issued to the Battn. The Battn was complimented by the C.O. on its good marching in spite of bad conditions, also the Transport on turnout of horses, wagons and harness on the 19th inst.	
QUIÉVY	21/10/18		Reveille 07.00 - Breakfast 07.45 - sick parade 08.30. O. Room 12.00. The Battn is on 2 hours notice to move. Companies were at disposal of O.C. Coys for cleaning of billets &c. Lecture at 14.00 by C.O. to all Officers on open warfare. 1 Officer per Company reconnoitred road to SOLESMES. Lieut W.R. Broadhurst took over command of HQ Company. CSM J Ritchie MC taken on strength & posted to HQ Coy.	

Instructions regarding War Diaries and Intelligence Summaries are contained in F. S. Regs., Part II. and the Staff Manual respectively. Title pages will be prepared in manuscript.

WAR DIARY

~~or~~

~~INTELLIGENCE~~ SUMMARY.

(*Erase heading not required.*)

Army Form C. 2118.

Place	Date	Hour	Summary of Events and Information	Remarks and references to Appendices
QUIÉVY	22/10/18		Routine as usual. Companies were at disposal of O's C. Coys. & all ammunition &c. preparatory to going into action were carefully checked & made up. The Battn moved to SOLESMES after dinners arriving there about 17.00 and found good billets awaiting them. 1 Officer per Company & 1 NCO per platoon accompanied Intelligence Officer and were shown positions of assembly for following morning - about 400x W. of the village of ROMERIES. 2nd Lt E.A.H. Goldfinch reported & was posted to "A" Company.	
ROMERIES	23/10/18		The Battalion attacked & took ROMERIES (~~See OO No~~ see report on operations.	
"	24/10/18		The Battn were in front of Romeries during the night of the 23rd-24th & returned to Billets in Romeries about 09.00. Capt Preston MC rejoined from Hospital and took command of "D" Company. 2nd Lt. J.L. Ewing reported and posted to "D" Company.	
"	25/10/18		The Battn remained in Romeries & time spent in re organisation & salvage of captured material. CSM G Stewart taken on strength.	
"	26/10/18		The Battn moved to ESCARMAIN in the forenoon & took over billets from 2nd RSF. 8th Bde. 1 Officer per Company accompanied the I.O &	

A6945 Wt. W11422/M1160 350,000 12/16 D. D. & L. Forms/C./2118/14.

Instructions regarding War Diaries and Intelligence Summaries are contained in F. S. Regs., Part II. and the Staff Manual respectively. Title pages will be prepared in manuscript.

WAR DIARY

or

~~INTELLIGENCE SUMMARY.~~

(*Erase heading not required.*)

Army Form C. 2118.

Place	Date	Hour	Summary of Events and Information	Remarks and references to Appendices
ESCARMAIN	26/10/18		and reconnoitred roads to RUESNES.	
	27/10/18.		Routine as usual. The Battalion moved to RUESNES during the evening and relieved units of 2nd Division in main line of resistance N.E. of RUESNES A+B. Companies in main line of resistance and C+D. Coys. in support in houses in outskirts of BERMERAIN. Before leaving Escarmain the Battn. had two casualties (wounded) from an H.E. shell.	
RUESNES	28/10/18.		The Battalion in posts in main line of resistance reserve companies as before - the dispositions of two front companies were slightly changed & new posts dug & strengthened. No casualties but heavy gas shelling during the night. C.S.M. A. Anderson taken on strength also [illegible]	
	29/10/18		The enemy artillery quiet all day. The Battalion were relieved by the 52nd Light Infantry about 18.00 and moved to St. PYTHON arriving there about 21.00. The billets were good and a hot meal ready for the men on their arrival. Capt. Lee, D.S.O. M.C. was wounded during the relief.	

A6945 Wt. W11422/M1160 350,000 12/16 D. D. & L. Forms/C./2118/14.

Army Form C. 2118.

Instructions regarding War Diaries and Intelligence Summaries are contained in F. S. Regs., Part II. and the Staff Manual respectively. Title pages will be prepared in manuscript.

WAR DIARY
or
~~INTELLIGENCE SUMMARY.~~
(Erase heading not required.)

Place	Date	Hour	Summary of Events and Information	Remarks and references to Appendices
St. PYTHON	30/10/18		Reveille 07·30, Breakfasts 08·00 Sick parade 09·00 Companies were at disposal of O.C. Companies for cleaning up, kit inspections &c. The Battalion were paid out.	
"	31/10/18.		Reveille 07·00, Breakfasts 08·00, sick parade 09·00. H.Q. Coy. and 'A' Coy had baths and clean clothing issued. The Battalion moved to CARNIERES and took over billets from 1st Irish Guards, arriving at destination about 14·00. The billets were exceptionally good & clean. A draft of 217 O.R. joined the Battalion - quite a good draft. A draft of four Officers joined & were posted:- Capt. J.R.E. Guild to 'A' Company, 2nd Lt. Scott to 'B' Coy 2nd Lt. W.J. Jamieson to 'C' Company and 2nd Lieut. G.G.O. Fraser to 'D' Company. Regtl. S/M K. Mathieson reported from Depot in Aberdeen.	

[signature]
Lieut. Col.
Commanding
1st Gordon Highlanders.

A6945 Wt. W11422/M1160 350,000 12/16 D. D. & L. Forms/C./2118/14.

Report on the Capture of RUMILLY by 1st Bn. The Gordon Highlanders assisted by the 2nd Bn The Suffolk Regt

On receipt of orders yesterday afternoon to arrange for the capture of RUMILLY, "A" & "C" Coys 1st Bn The Gordon Highrs were withdrawn from their positions in support of the 8th Bn K O R L to PLAISIR TRENCH. Here the two coys being very weak were organised into 5 bombing squads & coy HQ & placed under command of CAPT. PRESTON M.C.

The operation was to be undertaken by "A" & "C" Coys supported by as many men of the Suffolk as could be collected & the adjutant of the Suffolks reported to me at 5 pm & arranged to collect as many men as possible of his battalion at the assembly position.

A runner from the 76th Bde T M Battery reported to me at 5·30 pm & was ordered to bring the two sections of the battery which were to support the operation to the assembly position at 6·20 pm.

"A" & "C" Coys reached the assembly position.

Two sections of the T M. battery reported to me there and were attached to Coy. HQ.

The adjutant of the Suffolks reported to me at the same time & reported that he had been unable to find any men of his battalion to support the operation.

The operation had been as carefully prepared as time permitted. The village had been divided into sections & a squad detailed to deal with each section.

The village had been shelled with heavy guns between 6. & 6·30 pm. At 6·30 pm the barrage of field guns opened. It was very ragged & many shells were falling as much as 300 yards behind the barrage line. At Zero + 5 minutes "A" & "C" Coys advanced from their assembly positions & closed up under the barrage. At Zero + 10 minutes they commenced the advance. Each squad proceeded to mop up the section of the village allotted to it. As soon as the coys had started I returned to my HQ. & discovered about 100 men of the Suffolks in their vicinity. These were sent on to the village under guidance of SGT CHRISTIE MM 1st Bn The Gordon Hrs. They presently caught up the barrage & assisted in mopping up.

Trench Mortars were not used in the operations.

The attack was completely successful & about 80 prisoners were captured including a battalion commander. A large number of machine guns have since been found in the village. Elements of the enemy still remained, but they were captured or escaped during the night. A position was consolidated north of the village & placed under command of CAPT GILLESPIE M.C as CAPT PRESTON MC had been wounded. Casualties were suffered as follows:– One officer killed, one wounded One Sgt killed, two wounded one of whom is dying of wounds. SGT CHRISTIE MM was slightly wounded. These casualties were all inflicted by our own shells falling short

2/10/18.

[illegible] Lt Col
Comdg 1st Bn The Gordon Hrs

Report on Operations by 1st Bn The Gordon Highlanders.

At about 11 pm on Sept 30th orders were received that the 76th Inf Bde. would attack RUMILLY and the enemy positions south & east of it at 6am on the 1st Oct. A Brigade conference was held at HQ 4th Y & L. 62nd Division where details were settled about guides to assembly positions. The plan of attack was explained. This conference ended about 12.30 am Oct 1st.

Coy. Commanders were assembled at HQ. 1st Bn The Gordon Highrs at 12.45 am & companies moved off at 1.30 am.

Plan of Attack. – The 76th Inf Bde. was to attack & capture a line from G 11 b 1.0 to G 23 d 1.3 including the village of RUMILLY.

The 2nd Bn The Suffolk Regt. was to attack on the left & capturing the village to advance beyond it to the line aforesaid. The 8th K.O.R.L. were to attack on the left in N.E. direction as far as the grid line joining G 16 central & G 22 central – thence in an easterly direction to the line aforesaid. The 1st Bn The Gordon Highrs were to be in support, – two companies supporting the left of the Suffolk with orders to advance round the west side of the village should the former be held up – two companies supporting the right of the Kings Own with orders to fill a gap which was liable, on account of the direction of the advance, to occur between them & a New Zealand battalion which was to attack on the right. The Commanding Officer was ordered to go with the right two companies & to make his HQ with the OC 8th K.O.R.L.

The two left coys were placed under command of Capt C.H. Lee MC who was to make his HQ. with the OC 2nd Suffolks

The Assembly – The arrangements for guides were as follows:–

Right Companies. – Two guides were provided by 4th Y & L. (62nd Div) to guide them as far as the Lock Bridge (K 24 b) where 4 guides per coy were to meet them & lead them into their assembly positions in G 27 a.

The guides of the 4th Y & L. led coys by a very difficult route & Lewis Guns had to be carried on the men from the bn. area to the assembly positions. The coys moved off at 1.30 am – they did not arrive at the Lock Bridge until 4.35 am & eventually reached the assembly position at 5.40 am.

Left Companies. – Guides were provided from Bde. HQ. to lead these coys to HQ 185 Bde (K 22 a 9.7) where guides from the 5th Duke of Wellington's Regt. were to meet them & take them to their assembly positions, in G 19 b & G 20 a. These latter guides were uncertain of position & the coys were eventually formed up immediately behind the wire west of RUMILLY TRENCH, in G 20 a. They reached this position at about 5 am.

The Barrage – The barrage opened at 6 am. Throughout the operation it was extremely ragged & many casualties were thus caused to our own men.

The Attack. The right companies ("A" & "C") These coys advanced in rear of the Kings Own, who had only arrived on the scene of battle in sufficient time to get into artillery formation & go forward under the barrage. The right company of the Kings Own maintained touch with the New Zealanders throughout the advance with the result that a gap appeared between this coy & that on its left. This was filled by the two coys of the 1st Bn The Gordon Hrs.

Heavy machine gun fire from the left flank hampered the operation, as well as fire from posts in G 22 a., b, & c & G. 23 a & b.

The objective was eventually gained about am with light casualties & about 800 prisoners were taken by the battalion.

Left companies – The 2nd Bn The Suffolk Regt. assembled in RUMILLY TRENCH. As soon as the assembly was complete about 5 am units of the 62nd Division proceeded to withdraw & thus portions of the trench were left unoccupied. Apparently these were not patrolled before Zero & the enemy was able to infiltrate machine guns into them. These guns were naturally unaffected by the barrage & opened immediately the advance commenced. The two left companies of the Suffolks were thus held up not far from their assembly position in G. 14 c & d. The two coys of the 1st Bn The Gordon Hrs also suffered casualties from this fire (the commander of "B" Coy being severely wounded) They succeeded, however in pushing forward in spite of very intense machine gun fire & eventually reached a line facing NE. in G. 14 b with their left on the railway about G. 8 d 5.0 Here they were held up by very intense M.G fire from a quarry close in front of them & from the railway sidings in G. 9 c.

Subsequent Events – Right companies – About two hours after the objective had been gained the enemy commenced to advance from the direction of SERANVILLERS, apparently intending to counter attack. He was engaged at long range with rifle & artillery fire & retired back to the village. About the same time very heavy shell-fire was directed on our positions from the right flank. Machine gun fire from the left was very accurate. As men were very crushed in these positions it was decided to withdraw the two Coys of this battalion some 500 yds in order to introduce the principle of depth into the consolidation and to save casualties. At the same time it became certain that much of RUMILLY was still in the hands of the enemy. One coy was therefore withdrawn behind ridge G 22 d, the other was ordered to form a defensive flank towards RUMILLY in G 22 a. Very heavy casualties were incurred in these positions from hostile artillery especially by the right coy. which was then brought still further back. (This coy numbered at this time about 20 rifles)

Left companies. – No touch was gained with these coys during the whole day. Capt Lee M.C. made repeated efforts to get forward to the position which they had reached but was as often driven back by machine gun fire. They were eventually withdrawn after dark.

The Attack on RUMILLY. At about 4 pm it became almost certain that the whole of RUMILLY was held by the enemy, & a personal reconnaissance disclosed German

German machine gunners at G. 21 a 8 4. They were very alert & ready to take advantage of any target offered to them. This fact was reported to 76 Bde. HQ.

About 4.30 pm orders were received to attack RUMILLY from the south at 6.30 pm with "A" & "C" Coy of this battalion. They were to be supported by a body of the 2nd Suffolks & two sections of the 76th T.M. Battery.

The account of this operation has been forwarded separatily.

Remarks.

1. The night of the assembly was very dark & wet which greatly enhanced the difficulty of the operation.
2. The men had marched from HAVRINCOURT that evening & owing to lack of accomodation they had not settled into the new area until nearly 11 pm. As it was not known that a further move was contemplated that night they had been hard at work improving the accomodation.
3. The route selected by the battalion of the 62nd Div. which was responsible was not suitable for coy at night. Lewis Guns had to be carried, much of the route was very bad going, part of it was through trenches & this in spite of the fact that the whole journey could have been done by road. In result 3 hours were occupied in traversing a distance of 4,000 yards.
4. The Bn was extremely weak when the operation was undertaken & almost entirely devoid of senior NCOs. Few officers had any experience. In these circumstances the young soldiers (boys of 18½) of which it was largely composed, acquitted themselves in a very satisfactory manner.

[signature]
Lt Col

2/10/18

Commdg 1st Bn The Gordon Highlanders

1

Report on Operations of 1st Bn The Gordon Highrs Oct 8th 1918.

Preliminary Events. The battalion had been standing by since ZERO hour 4·30 am ready to move at ¼ hour notice. It came under direct orders of the 9th Inf Bde about 2·pm.

At 3·45 pm an order was received to the effect that the King's Own would carry out an attack on the green line in conjunction with the 2nd Div. who were to attack FORENVILLE. The Bn was to replace the King's Own in the old British front line with two companies – one company was to be disposed behind this line. (The Bn consisted of only three companies at the time).

Orders were issued and the Bn. moved off at 4·pm.

Orders for Attack. At 4 pm an order was received for the O.C. 1st G.H. to report to the G.O.C. 9th Inf. Bde. He did so at 4·5 pm & was informed that the battalion would probably have to attack LA TARGETTE & the CAMBRAI – ESNES ROAD north of it at 6·30 pm.

The attack was to depend on whether the attack of the 2nd Div. on FORENVILLE was successful. The King's Own were to attack on the left of the Bn. and the boundary between battalions was pointed out on the map.

Orders were immediately sent out to the Bn which was proceeding to the positions originally ordered, to concentrate on either side of the Crucifix G.29 b. & the Comdg. Officer proceeded to H.Q. the King's Own, in order to learn their plan of attack.

He reached his own battalion in G29 b at 5·15 pm.

Orders for the attack were issued verbally and the battalion moved off at 5·30 pm.

The Advance. As SERANVILLERS & the ground to the South of it was definitely reported to be in our hands & the situation to the north of it was uncertain, it was decided to advance south of the village & to attack the objective from the right and not frontally.

Two companies (B & D) were to carry out the attack – one was retained in reserve. Bn. H.Q. moved forward with the battalion, a rear report centre being left at the Crucifix in touch with Brigade by a wire which was laid by the battalion.

The Battalion crossed the Red Line at 6·10. No definite orders had been received to carry out the attack; it was therefore carried out without orders at 6·30 pm.

The Attack. These orders eventually reached Rear Battalion H.Q. at 6·35 pm. The attack was carried out by B & D Companies and LE TARGETTE was captured without difficulty. The situation on the left was still somewhat obscure as the enemy had a machine-gun post N of the buildings in the ESNES – CAMBRAI road.

This was dealt with about an hour later, but touch was not obtained with the King's Own for some considerable time.

The whole advance & the attack was carried out in pitch darkness which made it very difficult for all ranks to locate themselves.

SERANVILLERS. Shortly after the attack started it became evident that SERANVILLERS was still occupied by the enemy. Machine Gun & rifle fire was still coming from the western end of the village. This fact was reported to Bde. H.Q. with the request that orders might be given for it to be mopped up.

The Reserve Coy. The reserve company of this battalion which had been ordered forward to H. 20 central could not be immediately found in the darkness.

Later touch was obtained with this coy & it was sent forward with exception of 1 platoon which was retained in battalion reserve.

Its orders were to assist the left forward company in clearing the road with 1 platoon, which was then to dig in, echeloned in rear of the left flank of the battalion.

The second platoon was to dig in in the same way in rear of the right flank. These orders were carried out & the line was consolidated as shown in disposition map already forwarded to 9th Inf Bde.

SERANVILLERS. As soon as the position at LA TARGETTE was satisfactory it was intended to mop up SERANVILLERS with the reserve platoon of the battalion starting from the eastern end of the village and driving the enemy in a westerly direction, but this operation was rendered impossible by the enemy artillery, which commenced to bombard the village very heavily with H.E. & Gas, especially at the Eastern end. It was considered that this bombardment would sufficiently demoralise the enemy in the village who had given no sign of life for some time, and that they could be collected in the morning. The operation was therefore abandoned.

Remarks. The operation was rendered difficult by the very hasty nature of the preparations & the absence of definite orders. The difficulties were increased by the darkness of the night & the large amount of gas employed by the enemy round the village of SERANVILLERS and in parts of the valley between it & CREVECOEUR.

The withdrawal. Orders were received about 2 am that the battalion would withdraw from the positions gained by 4.30 am in order that the barrage to cover ~~the~~ a further advance might be put down on them. This operation was carried out without difficulty.

[signature]
Lieut. Col.
Commanding
1st Gordon Highlanders.

Report on operations by 1st Bn. The Gordon Highlanders
October 23rd & 24th 1918.

Assembly. 1. At 4 pm. Oct 22nd the battalion marched from QUIEVY to SOLESMES. The march was rendered somewhat tiring by the enormous amount of traffic on the road which made progress very slow.

In SOLESMES the battalion was billeted in houses. In view of the size of the town & the large number of civilians in it special orders were issued to prevent men straying.

At 12.30 hot tea & sausages were issued to the men, and at 1am the coys moved off at intervals of 10 minutes.

About 12.30 am a S.O.S signal was put up from the front line in response to which our artillery put down a very heavy barrage in front of ROMERIES. The enemy reply was very heavy especially on the exits from SOLESMES, & a considerable number of casualties were caused (the O.C. "A" Coy was wounded) & a great deal of disorganisation. Companies were reformed outside the town & the advance to assembly positions continued. Re-organisation was facilitated by the lightness of the night. A few casualties were suffered in the assembly positions from enemy (G) shell fire. The positions had been carefully reconnoitred by companies earlier in the evening and no difficulty was experienced in finding them.

Plan of Attack. 2. The task of the battalion was to capture & mop up the village of ROMERIES and to consolidate the line of the light railway beyond it. In view of difficulties recently experienced owing to inefficient mopping up, it was decided to detail certain platoons to go to definite points in the village where they were to make posts and from these posts to carry out the mopping up in their vicinity. The general plan was as follows:- "B" & "D" Coys were to make good the N.E. bank of the river HASPRES, on which line "A" & "C" Coys were to pass through them & advance to the final objective. In addition "B" Coy was to detail one platoon to deal with wood in W 27 d & one platoon to deal with the main railway. These platoons were then to make posts in W 28 a as shown on attached map. Details of objectives of coys & platoons were as shown on attached map.

The Attack. 3 At 3.20 am "B" & "D" Coys ("B" on the right) advanced under the barrage. A considerable number of machine guns were encountered in the orchards and on the railway in front of the village. The opposition on the right was not so determined as on the left & "B" Coy captured several guns & reached its objective under the barrage. "A" Coy then passed through and consolidated the final objective. On the left "D" Coy was held up almost immediately by intense fire from the cemetery & the orchard behind it, & lost the barrage. The advance was continued by rushes, but at considerable cost. The HASPRES was found to be a considerable obstacle & the bridges had been blown up. Eventually the objective on the N.E. bank was gained & 3 platoons

of "C" Coy passed through + continued the advance.
Heavy machine gun fire was still coming from a house 100 yds. south of the church, and Capt. BEVERIDGE Cmdg "D" Coy was killed in a most gallant attack on these guns. Sgt. LAWSON then in command of the platoon concerned formed up some prisoner already captured + screened by them again advanced against the house, and succeeded in silencing the opposition by shooting the gunners. One platoon of "C" Coy finding the advance on the left held up by machine gun fire advanced round the right of the village + reached its objective.

4\. Resistance was very determined at certain points both in front of the village + in the village itself, but on the whole the enemy surrendered easily. A large number of prisoners were captured including a battalion commander.

Remarks 5. (a) A field gun barrage has little effect on machine guns in houses, + such guns do great damage when manned with determination.

(b) The system of establishing posts at certain selected points in villages and mopping up from these posts is a good one. It prevents the enemy re-appearing after our troops have passed through. In this case the whole village was mopped up very quickly after the leading coys had reached their objectives.

(c) An S.O.S signal sent up without due cause during assembly may do great harm.

(d) In cases where there is no cover in the assembly positions, a long wait in those positions should be avoided. The men get cold + much of the enthusiasm evaporates. Where the assembly presents no great difficulty a margin of a quarter to half an hour should be ample.

(e) It is strongly recommended that boys of 18½ years should not be sent to fighting battalions. Although perhaps 10% of these boys may do quite well the remainder are quite useless. They do not possess the necessary stamina + a battalion however weak is better off without them.

[signature]

24-10-18.

Lieut. Col

Cmmdg. 1st Bn. The Gordon Highlanders.

1st Battalion The Gordon Highlanders
Nominal Roll of Officers serving in Battalion [illegible]

Lt Col The Hon R Fraser DSO MC - Commanding Officer
Major [illegible] G [illegible] - 2nd in Command
Captain [illegible] - A/Adjutant
Lieut [illegible] Hutton - Transport Officer
" S T Jennings - Quartermaster
" C R W Hutchins - Signalling Officer
2/Lt W G Henderson MC - Intelligence "

"A" Company
Capt S K Gillespie MC Comdg
" J S E Guild
2/Lt J M Robb
" R A H Goldfinch
" A Mowat

"B" Company
Lieut R G Miles Comdg
2/Lt R Stephen
" J Crombie
" H Burns
" A S Sinclair
" A Benner
" A Scott

C Company
Captain J M Frame MC Comdg
" D Macfarlane
2/Lt R Davidson
" J Grant
" J Leslie
" W G Jamieson

D Company
Captain R W Preston MC Comdg
2/Lt H E Robertson
" T Ewing
" A Arnold
" D M Fraser
" G C O Forbes

Attached
Captain J L Stewart DSO MC - RAMC
Revd D Conacher - CF

Detached
Captain A M Richardson XIII Corps HQ
Lieut W Webster Hospital
2/Lt J W K Smith do
" G Cottrell do
" W S McColm do

Strength of Battalion
Officers = 36
O.R. = 984

[signature]
Lieut. Col.
Commanding
1st Gordon Highlanders

76th Brigade

3rd Division.

1st BATTALION GORDON HIGHLANDERS ::: NOVEMBER 1918.

Instructions regarding War Diaries and Intelligence Summaries are contained in F. S. Regs., Part II. and the Staff Manual respectively. Title pages will be prepared in manuscript.

WAR DIARY
~~or~~
~~INTELLIGENCE SUMMARY.~~
(Erase heading not required.)

Army Form C. 2118.

1 Gordon Hrs
N8 50

Place	Date	Hour	Summary of Events and Information	Remarks and references to Appendices
CARNIERES	1/11/14.		Reville 07.00; Morning Inspection - iron rations 07.45, Breakfasts 08.00. Sick parade 08.30. Orderly room 14.00. 09.00 to 10.30 Company inspections and organization on parade; 10-45 to 11-30 Handling of arms. 'D' Company had bath and change of clothing. 11-30 to 12.00 Musketry exercises - rapid loading, aiming & firing. 12.00 to 12.30 Saluting - lecture and drill.	
"	2/11/14.		Reville 07.00 Breakfasts 08.00; 09.00 to 09-30 Company inspections. 09-40 to 10-30 RSM's parade - Battalion falling in to fifes. 10-40 to 11-30 Handling of arms. 11-30 to 12-30 Sentry and saluting drill. 12.00 to 12.45 all [illegible] ranks, NCOs under RSM.	
"	3/11/18		Reville 07.30; Breakfasts 08.30. The companies were at the disposal of Coy. Commanders. The Battalion moved to QUIEVY at 17.00 and marched to destination under very wet conditions arriving about 11.00. The billets were good and the men received a hot meal at 19.30 and a rum ration at 20-30. Lieut C.B.W. Hutchison went on special leave. A draft of 4 Officers and 6 Casuals (O.R.) joined and Officers were posted to Companies as follows:- Lieut J Paxton to HQ & takes over command of HQ Company	

A6945 Wt. W11422/M1160 350,000 12/16 D. D. & L. Forms/C./2118/14.

Army Form C. 2118.

Instructions regarding War Diaries and Intelligence Summaries are contained in F. S. Regs., Part II. and the Staff Manual respectively. Title pages will be prepared in manuscript.

WAR DIARY
or
~~INTELLIGENCE SUMMARY.~~
(*Erase heading not required.*)

Place	Date	Hour	Summary of Events and Information	Remarks and references to Appendices
QUIEVY	3/11/18		Lieut. G H Strachan to "C" Company, 2nd Lieut. R. Miller to "D" Company, 2nd Lieut. W. Mearns to "A" Company. 2nd Lieut. J. Leslie appointed temporary Assistant Adjutant.	
	4/11/18		Reville 05·00, Breakfasts 06·00. Blankets & packs were dumped & Battalion moved "in fighting order" at 07·20 to ROMERIES and arrived at destination about 10·00. The Billets were none too good as most of the houses were roofless – the Battalion is under short notice to move forward. A draft of 33 joined Battalion.	
ROMERIES	5/11/18		Reveille 05·00 Breakfasts 06·00 The Battalion under an hours notice and likely to move to ORSINVAL. Dinners 12·00. The weather has been very wet all day. Lieut. A. Bourne and 2nd Lieut. D.M. Fraser took over command temporary of "D" Company vice Capt. R. Preston, MC who goes on leave to UK.	
	6/11/18		Reville 07·30, Morning Inspection 08·15; Breakfasts 08·30; 09·30 to 10·00 Company Inspections. Owing to wet weather all parades were restricted to lectures by platoon commanders in billets to their platoons. Six Lewis gun classes	

Army Form C. 2118.

Instructions regarding War Diaries and Intelligence Summaries are contained in F. S. Regs., Part II. and the Staff Manual respectively. Title pages will be prepared in manuscript.

WAR DIARY
~~or~~
~~INTELLIGENCE SUMMARY.~~
(Erase heading not required.)

Place	Date	Hour	Summary of Events and Information	Remarks and references to Appendices
ROMERIES	6/11/18		each of eight other ranks were started under Lewis Gun Instructors and also ~~a~~ R.S.M's class of 32 N.C.O's. The weather continues to be [illegible].	
	7/11/18.		Reveille 07.00; Morning Inspections 07.45; Breakfasts 08.00. Company [illegible] 09.00 to 09.30; 09.30 to 12.00 Battalion parade practising [illegible] and open warfare. 12.00 Warning order received from Brigade to be prepared to move. 14.15 Lecture by Commanding Officer to all Officers on "Open Warfare". The weather still bad [illegible] all day.	
	8/11/18		Reveille 07.00, Breakfast 08.00. 09.45 The Battalion moved to FRASNOY [illegible] to the scarcity of accomodation went on to GOMMEGNIES [illegible] [illegible] of part of houses occupied by civilians.	
GOMMEGNIES	9/11/18.		Reveille 07.00; Morning Inspection - Iron Rations 07.45; Breakfasts 08.00. Battalion paraded at 09.00 & marched to Le Grand Sart as billets in Gommegnies were required for Corps. Arrived at Le Grand Sart about 10.00 and men were billeted mostly in houses. 11-30 to 12-45 Companies under O.C. Coys for drill and handling of arms. A fatigue party of 100 OR were working cleaning roads. 1 Sergt & 3 OR [illegible].	

A6945 Wt. W11422/M1160 350,000 12/16 D. D. & L. Forms/C./2118/14.

Army Form C. 2118.

Instructions regarding War Diaries and Intelligence Summaries are contained in F. S. Regs., Part II. and the Staff Manual respectively. Title pages will be prepared in manuscript.

WAR DIARY
or
~~INTELLIGENCE SUMMARY.~~

(*Erase heading not required.*)

Place	Date	Hour	Summary of Events and Information	Remarks and references to Appendices
LE GRAND SART	10/11/18		Reveille 06.00; Breakfasts 07.00; The Battalion moved to LONGUEVILLE, passing starting point at 09.30. Billets were taken over from 2nd Scots Guards and were composed for most part of barns. The Battalion arrived about 14.00 and men received dinners at 15.00. The Battalion under orders to move eastwards tomorrow.	
LONGUEVILLE	11/11/18.		Reveille 06.00. Breakfasts 06.45; 09.00 the Battalion ready to move off when word received from Brigade that Armistice had been signed and Battalion to remain in billets here. 12.00 Battalion parade & C.O intimated to men that armistice had been signed. A draft of 5 Officers joined and were posted to Companies: Lieut. G. McDonald M.C. to "D" Coy. Lieut. H. A. Hewatt, M.C. to "A" Coy. Lieut. E. L. Mitchell to "B" Coy. Lieut. R.C. Davidson, M.C. to "C" Coy & 2nd Lieut. A. W. Esson to "B" Coy.	
"	12/11/18		Reveille 07.00; Morning Inspection 07.45; Breakfasts 08.00. 09.00 to 12.00 A. B. D & HQ Companies were working on roads. "C" Coy at disposal of QM for clothing &c.	
	13/11/18		Routine as usual. 09.00 to 12.00 Coys. were on fatigue cleaning roads.	

A6945 Wt. W11422/M1160 350,000 12/16 D. D. & L. Forms/C./2118/14.

Instructions regarding War Diaries and Intelligence Summaries are contained in F. S. Regs., Part II. and the Staff Manual respectively. Title pages will be prepared in manuscript.

WAR DIARY
or
INTELLIGENCE SUMMARY.
(Erase heading not required.)

Army Form C. 2118.

Place	Date	Hour	Summary of Events and Information	Remarks and references to Appendices

Wt. W1422/M1160 350,000 12/16 D. D. & L. Forms/C2118/14.

Instructions regarding War Diaries and Intelligence Summaries are contained in F. S. Regs., Part II. and the Staff Manual respectively. Title pages will be prepared in manuscript.

WAR DIARY

~~or~~

~~INTELLIGENCE SUMMARY.~~

(Erase heading not required.)

Army Form C. 2118.

Place	Date	Hour	Summary of Events and Information	Remarks and references to Appendices
LONGUEVILLE	13/11/18.		All subaltern Officers paraded under R.S.M. for drill &c. The N.C.O.s class were under the drill Sergeant. A draft of 2 Officers joined & were posted 2nd Lieut. J. J. Oaston to B Coy 2nd Lieut. H. D. Thomson to C. Coy. Lieut D. J. Milne transferred to A. Company, Lieut J. A. Hewitt MC to D. Coy. Lieut C. McDonald, MC takes over command of B Coy vice Lieut. D. J. Milne	
	14/11/18.		Routine as usual. 09.00 to 12.30 B. C. D. & HQ. Coy inspections and 1 hour's ceremonial drill and remainder of forenoon spent scrubbing equipment. A. Company were on road fatigue. Officers & N.C.O.s classes were on parade as usual from 09.30 to 12.30.	
	15/11/18		Routine as usual. Starting from 07.00 A.B.C.D. HQ had baths in the village but there was no clean change of clothes. Ten casuals joined Battalion. Capt J. W. Taylor reported and posted to C Coy. A full rum ration was issued to Battalion at 20 30.	
	16th		Routine as usual. The Battalion moved to MONPLAISIR passing starting point at 11-15 hours and arrived at destination at 12.20 The Billets were good and dinners issued ½ hour after arrival.	

D. D. & L., London, E.C. (A8004) Wt. W1771/M2-31 750,000 5/17 Sch. 52 Forms/C2118/14

Instructions regarding War Diaries and Intelligence Summaries are contained in F. S. Regs., Part II. and the Staff Manual respectively. Title pages will be prepared in manuscript.

WAR DIARY
or
~~INTELLIGENCE SUMMARY.~~

(*Erase heading not required.*)

Army Form C. 2118.

Place	Date	Hour	Summary of Events and Information	Remarks and references to Appendices
MONPLAISIR.	17/11/18		Routine as usual. 11.00 hours [illegible] Church Parade. [illegible] D. Cutton returned off leave and took over duties of Battalion Transport Officer. The Battn received a clean change of clothing. The following decorations were awarded: Capt. [illegible] Bar to M.C., Lieut. Irviss the M.C. + 2nd Lieut [illegible] the M.C. C.S.M. Matthews, M.M. the D.C.M. and Sergt. [illegible] M.M. the D.C.M.	
	18/11/18		Routine as usual. The Battalion moved to LOUVROIL passing starting point at 12.09 hours arriving at [illegible] about 13.00 hours. The billets were [illegible]. [illegible] 14 O.R. were sent to [illegible].	
LOUVROIL	19/11/18		Routine as usual. 09.00 to 12.30 Companies were at disposal of O.C. Coys for ½ hour ceremonial drill and remainder of forenoon [illegible] for cleaning.	
	20/11/18		Routine as usual. The Battalion moved to ROUSIGNIES passing starting point at 08.50 hours, arriving at destination about 12.30. The billets were good.	

D. D. & L., London, E.C.
(A8004) Wt. W1771/M2731 750,000 5/17 Sch. 52 Forms/C2118/14

Instructions regarding War Diaries and Intelligence Summaries are contained in F. S. Regs., Part II. and the Staff Manual respectively. Title pages will be prepared in manuscript.

WAR DIARY
or
~~INTELLIGENCE~~ SUMMARY.
(Erase heading not required.)

Army Form C. 2118.

Place	Date	Hour	Summary of Events and Information	Remarks and references to Appendices
BOUSIGNIES	21/11/18		Routine as usual. 'B' 'C' & HQ Coys. on road fatigue both morning and afternoon. 'A' and 'D' Companies 09.00 to 10.30 at disposal of Coy. Commanders for drill &c. the remainder of forenoon being spent in cleaning up &c. Lieut. Hitchins returned from leave and posted to 'C' Coy.	
	22/11/18		Routine as usual. 'B' 'C' & HQ Companies on fatigue on roads from 09.00 but owing to frost ~~the~~ fatigue was cancelled. Companies were at disposal of O's C. for ceremonial drill & cleaning. Inter-Company football matches were played from 11-30 to 12-30 and in the afternoon	
	23/11/18		Routine as usual. The usual road fatigue was again cancelled owing to frost. 09.00 to 11-30 Companies at disposal of O's C. for ceremonial drill and handling of arms &c. 11-30 to 12-30 was utilized for recreation and in the afternoon football matches were also played. The Battalion were paid out.	
	24/11/18		Reveille 07-30 Breakfasts 08.15. The Battalion moved to LOBBES at 10.9 arriving at destination about 13.30. Billets were good.	
LOBBES	25/11/18		Lieut K.C. Davidson M.C. & 3 NCO's left Battalion to proceed to Aberdeen	

A6945 Wt. W11422/M1160 350,000 12/16 D. D. & L. Forms/C./2118/14.

Instructions regarding War Diaries and Intelligence Summaries are contained in F. S. Regs., Part II. and the Staff Manual respectively. Title pages will be prepared in manuscript.

WAR DIARY
or
~~INTELLIGENCE SUMMARY.~~
(Erase heading not required.)

Army Form C. 2118.

Place	Date	Hour	Summary of Events and Information	Remarks and references to Appendices
LOBBES	25/11/18		to bring out Regimental Colours. Reveille 07.30 hours Breakfasts 08.15 the Battalion moved to THY-LE-CHATEAU passing starting point at ~~09~~ 10.50 arriving at destination about 15.30 hours. The rations were not received until almost time for marching off & Battalion marched without breakfasts. The Billets were good & Battalion received a hot meal about an hour after arrival. Major Rose MC proceeded to Aberdeen to supervise the bringing out of the Colours. Capt. Preston MC reported from leave and took over command of "D" Coy vice Lieut. Hewatt, MC.	
THY LE CHATEAU	26/11/18		Reveille 06.00 Breakfasts 06.45. The Battn. moved to METTET passing starting point at 8.50 and arrived at destination at 12.45 hrs. The billets were good. 6 ors. proceeded to F.A. to accompany motor ambulances proceeding to frontier to bring back released prisoners as escorts.	
METTET	27/11/18		Reveille 07.00 Morning Inspection 07.45 Breakfasts 08.00. The weather today very wet and Coys. at disposal of O.C. for cleaning.	

A6945 Wt. W11422/M1160 350,000 12/16 D. D. & L. Forms/C./2118/14.

Instructions regarding War Diaries and Intelligence Summaries are contained in F. S. Regs., Part II. and the Staff Manual respectively. Title pages will be prepared in manuscript.

WAR DIARY
~~or~~
~~INTELLIGENCE SUMMARY.~~
(*Erase heading not required.*)

Army Form C. 2118.

Place	Date	Hour	Summary of Events and Information	Remarks and references to Appendices
METTET	27/11/18		Lieut. Paxton delivered a short lecture to each Company on Education.	
	28/11/18		Reveille 07.00, Breakfast 07.45. The Battalion moved to ANHÉE arriving at destination about 13.30 hours. The weather was very wet and consequently roads were bad for marching.	
ANHÉE	29/11/18		Reveille 07.00 Breakfast 07.45. The Battalion moved to BRAIBANT passing starting point at 08.56 and arriving at destination about 12.45. Billets were good.	
BRAIBANT.	30/11/18		Routine as usual. The Battalion moved to CINEY arriving about 10.00 hours and whole Battalion were billeted in Chateau.	

[signature]
Lieut. Col.
Commanding
1st Gordon Highlanders

A6945. Wt. W11422/M1160 350,000 12/16 D. D. & L. Forms/C./2118/14.

Reinforcements (Officers) November 1918.

Lieut C.H. Strachan, Lieut J. Paxton joined Bn 3/11/18.
2/Lieut W. Mearns 2/Lieut R. Millar. " " 3/11/18.
Capt J. McDonald M.C. Lieut E. P. Mitchell " " 4/11/18.
Lieut F. A. Hewitt M.C. Lieut R. Dandon M.C. " " 4/11/18.
2/Lieut R.W. Evans " " 4/11/18.
2/Lieut J. Ogston 2/Lieut G. L. Thomson " " 13/11/18.
Capt J.W. Taylor. " " 13/11/18.

<u>Officers sent to D. R. C. 15/11/18.</u>

Capt D. Macfarlane, Capt J.W. Taylor. 2/Lieut W. Mearns
2/Lieut R. Stephen. 2/Lieut A. Arnold 2/Lieut A. Scott
" W.G. Jamieson.

Roll of Officers serving with Battalion on 15/11/18.

Lieut. Col. The Hon W. Fraser. D.S.O, M.C. – Commdg.
Major H. G. Pearson, M.C. – 2nd in Command.
Capt. P. S. Pirie. – a/Adjutant.
Lieut S. S. Jennings – Quartermaster.
" D. Hutton – Transport Officer. (Leave)
" J. Paxton – Batt. Intelligence Officer.
2/Lieut. W.G. Henderson M.C. – Asst/Adjutant.
" J. Leslie M.C. – Bde Intelligence Officer.
Lieut. C.D.M Hutchins – Signalling Officer. (Leave)

"A" Coy.

Capt. S. P. Gillespie M.C.
Lieut D. J. Milne.
Lieut. J.R.C. Guild
2/Lieut J.M. Robb.
" C.A.H. Goldfinch
" W.H. Mowat

"B" Coy.

Lieut. J. McDonald M.C. ×
Lieut C. C. Mitchell ×
2/Lieut H. Burns
" A.S. Sinclair
" A.W. Esson. ×
" J. J. Ogston ××

"C" Coy

Capt. J.M. Frame M.C.
Lieut. K.C. Davidson M.C. ×
2/Lieut. R. Davidson
" J. Grant
" G.D. Thomson ××

"D" Coy

Capt. R.W. Preston M.C. (Leave)
Lieut F. A. Hewatt, M.C. ×
2/Lieut. H.C. Robertson
" S.C. Ewing
" D.M. Fraser
" R. Miller

Attached.

Capt. J.C. Stewart D.S.O, M.C. – R.A.M.C.
Rev. D. Conacher – C.F.

Officers serving with Battalion on 30/11/18 as above with following alterations:–

"HQ" Coy. Major H.G. Pearson M.C. } Colour Party
"C" " Lieut K.C. Davidson M.C. } to Aberdeen.
"HQ" " " C.D.M Hutchins Off Leave. Transferred to "C" Coy
" " " D. Hutton Off Leave
"D" " Capt R.W. Preston M.C. Off Leave.
"C" 2/Lieut R. Davidson to Field Ambulance.

W. Fraser

Lieut. Col.
Commanding
1st Gordon Highlanders.

76th Brigade.

3rd Division.

1st BATTALION GORDON HIGHLANDERS ::: DECEMBER 1918.

Instructions regarding War Diaries and Intelligence Summaries are contained in F. S. Regs., Part II. and the Staff Manual respectively. Title pages will be prepared in manuscript.

WAR DIARY
or
~~INTELLIGENCE SUMMARY.~~
(Erase heading not required.)

Army Form C. 2118.

1 Gordon Hrs

V R 51

Place	Date	Hour	Summary of Events and Information	Remarks and references to Appendices
CINEY	1 12/18.		Reveille 07.30, Breakfasts 08.30. A voluntary church service was held at 10.30hrs. The men of the Battalion were paid during the afternoon.	
	2 12/18		Reveille 07.00, Morning Inspection 07.45, Breakfasts 08.00. The Battn. paraded at 10.00 and was inspected by G.O.C. VI and ribbons presented to Officers, NCOs & men. All Companies had hot baths but no clean change of clothing. Major G.K. McNab reported and taken on strength of Battalion.	
	3 12/18.		Reveille 07.00, Morning Inspection 07.45, Breakfasts 08.00, 09.30 Coy Inspections 10-11.15 Handling of arms & 11.15 to 12.30 Cleaning up. All rifles in the Battalion were inspected by the Armourer Sergt.	
	4 12/18		Reveille 06.00, Breakfast 07.00. The Battn moved to SINSIN passing starting point at 10.45 and arrived there about 12 noon. The billets were bad and the weather very wet all day.	
SINSIN	5 12/18.		Reveille 05.30, Breakfasts 06.30. The Battalion moved to HOTTON and reached destination about 12.30. The billets were good but were slightly crowded.	
	6 12/18.		The Battalion moved to La Fosse and Oster arriving at destination at 13.30 hours. The billets were bad.	

A6945 Wt. W11422/M1160 350,000 12/16 D. D. & L. Forms/C./2118/14.

Army Form C. 2118.

WAR DIARY
or
INTELLIGENCE SUMMARY.
(Erase heading not required.)

Instructions regarding War Diaries and Intelligence Summaries are contained in F. S. Regs., Part II. and the Staff Manual respectively. Title pages will be prepared in manuscript.

Place	Date	Hour	Summary of Events and Information	Remarks and references to Appendices
LA FOSSE to OSTER	7/12/18		The Battalion moved to OTTRE arriving at its destination [illegible]. The billets were a slight improvement on the previous [illegible].	
OTTRE	8/12/18		The Battalion moved to COURTIL about [illegible] hours but owing to billets being occupied by Canadians the Battalion halted and had dinner [illegible] road side and arrived in billets about 14.45 hours. Major [illegible] and [illegible] Davidson and colour party reported back with Colours. The billets [illegible] not very good.	
COURTIL	9/12/18		The Battalion moved to BEHO about 10 hours arriving at [illegible]. The billets were again very poor and the [illegible].	
BEHO	10/12/18		The Coys. were at disposal of O.C. Coys. for [illegible] inspection [illegible] socks and generally cleaning up. marched past Corps Commander with fixed bayonets and unfurled colours.	
	11/12/18		The Battalion crossed the frontier about 11.25 hours and moved to ½ in BREITFELD and ½ in NEIDINGEN arriving about [illegible]. The roads were very bad and continued rain fell all day. The billets were [illegible].	
NEIDINGEN & BREITFELD.	12/12/18		The Battalion moved to MANDERFELD & KREUWINKLE arriving at [illegible]. The roads were very bad and the weather was again very wet. The billets were quite good.	

(A9475) Wt W2358/P360 600,000 12/17 D. D. & L. Sch. 52a. Forms/C2118/15

Instructions regarding War Diaries and Intelligence Summaries are contained in F. S. Regs., Part II. and the Staff Manual respectively. Title pages will be prepared in manuscript.

WAR DIARY
or
INTELLIGENCE SUMMARY.
(Erase heading not required.)

Army Form C. 2118.

Place	Date	Hour	Summary of Events and Information	Remarks and references to Appendices
MANDERFELD KREWINKLE	13/12/18		The Battalion moved to factory near HALLSCHLAG arriving about 12.00 hours. The billets were very good but weather continued to be very wet.	
HALLSCHLAG	14/12/18		The Battalion moved to DAHLEM arriving about 12.00 hrs, the weather still very wet but billets good.	
DAHLEM	15/12/18		The Battn moved to TONDORF arriving about 12.00 hours. Roads were very muddy but weather fair. Lieut Peterkin reported & posted to C Coy & 40 OR reported back from leave.	
TONDORF	16/12/18		The Battalion moved to MUNSTEREIFEL at 08.15 hours, arriving at destination about 12-00 hours. The whole Battalion were billeted in a School exceptionally good billets.	
MUNSTEREIFEL	17/12/18		The Battalion moved to EUSKIRCHEN about 08.30 hours, arriving at destination about 11-30 hours. The billets were very good.	
EUSKIRCHEN	18/12/18		The Battn moved to ERP at 10-30 hours arriving 12.00 hrs. The billets were good. The billeting party proceeded to Kierdorf & Bruggen the final destination of the Battalion to arrange billets.	
ERP Kierdorf BRUGGEN	19/12/18		The Battalion moved to destination arriving about 12.00 hours. Batt. H.Q & C Coy	

Instructions regarding War Diaries and Intelligence Summaries are contained in F. S. Regs., Part II. and the Staff Manual respectively. Title pages will be prepared in manuscript.

WAR DIARY
or
INTELLIGENCE SUMMARY.
(Erase heading not required.)

Army Form C. 2118.

Place	Date	Hour	Summary of Events and Information	Remarks and references to Appendices
	19/12/18.		were billeted in KIERDOFF and the remaining Companies in BRUGGEN. The	
			billets were very good.	
BRUGGEN	20/12/18		The day was spent under Company arrangements for cleaning up and	
" KIERDOFF			arranging of Sergeants Mess and Dining Halls for the men.	
"	21/12/18.		The Companies were again at disposal of O's C. Coys for cleaning up &c.	
"	22/12/18.		A voluntary Church Service was held at BRUGGEN at 11.00 hours.	
"	23/12/18		The Companies were at disposal of O's C. Coys for cleaning &c.	
"	24/12/18.		The Companies were again at disposal of O's C. Coys for handling of arms	
			and physical training. Capt. G. J. Burney MC, 2/Lts McChalmers, A.J. Ogilvie, &	
			J.W. Webster joined Battalion.	
"	25/12/18		Xmas Day and was recognised as a holiday. A Xmas dinner was provided	
			for the Battalion and a free issue of beer.	
	26/12/18		The Coys. carried on with physical training, handling of arms, musketry.	
			Capt. G. J. Burney MC took over command of B Coy vice Lieut J. McDonald MC.	
	27/12/18.		~~A~~ C Company had baths & clean clothing and men were issued with	
			new blanket in exchange for old one. The other Coys carried on with usual Training	

(A9175) Wt W2358/P360 600,000 12/17 D. D. & L. Sch. 52a. Forms/C2118/15

Army Form C. 2118.

Instructions regarding War Diaries and Intelligence Summaries are contained in F. S. Regs., Part II. and the Staff Manual respectively. Title pages will be prepared in manuscript.

WAR DIARY
or
INTELLIGENCE SUMMARY.
(Erase heading not required.)

Place	Date	Hour	Summary of Events and Information	Remarks and references to Appendices
BRUGGEN + KIERDOFF	28/12/18		A & B Coys. had baths & clean change of clothing and were issued with 1 new blanket in exchange for old one. The first party for demobilization (40) mostly coal miners, left Battn. under Capt. W.L. Guild. C & D Coys. carried out usual training.	
	29/12/18		A voluntary Church Service was held at Bruggen. D & HQ Coys. had baths and a clean change of clothing and were also issued with 1 new blanket in exchange for old one. A party of 13 OR. left Battalion for demobilization. 2Lt. A. J. Bradshaw joined Battalion.	
	30/12/18		Coys. carried out the usual training & football was played in the afternoon. A party of 26 O.R. proceeded for demobilization under Capt. S.P. Gillespie MB & 2Lieut. J. Grant.	
	31/12/18		Battalion parade at 09.00 hours for presentation of Gallantry Cards. A party of 5 OR. proceeded for demobilization.	

1st BATTALION No. .... Date 3-1-19 GORDON HIGHLANDERS

[signature] Lieut. Col. Commanding 1st Gordon Highlanders

(A9175) Wt W2354/P360 600,000 12/17 D. D. & L. Sch. 52a. Forms/C2118/15.

1st Battalion The Gordon Highlanders

Roll of Officers on strength of Battalion on 21/[illegible]

Lieut Col The Hon W Fraser DSO MC - Commanding
Major J K McNab
R G Fraser MC - 2nd in Command
Captain P T Vize Acting Adjutant
J W Taylor Bn Educational Officer
Lieut R Mutter Transport Officer
S T Jennings - Quartermaster
J Taylor CO MG Coy
2/Lt W G Henderson MC Assistant Adjutant
A T Ogilvie Bn Demobilization Officer

A Coy
Lieut R J Milne
2/Lt J M Kell
E H H Goldfinch
A W Esson
W Mearns
J W K Smith

B Coy
Captain G T Burney MC
Lieut J McDonald MC
E R Mitchell
2/Lt M Burns
A S Sinclair
H J Bradshaw
J J Coyston
J R Chalmers
R Stephen

C Coy
Captain J McFrance MC
G P Peterkin
R Macfarlane
Lieut K C Davidson MC
2/Lt G R Thomson
W G Jamieson

D Coy
Captain R W Preston MC
Lieut J A Hewitt MC
2/Lt T R Ewing
R M Fraser
R Millar
A Arnold
G C O Fettes
J W Webster

Attached
Capt J L Stewart DSO MC - RAMC (on leave to UK)
Revd R Conacher - CF

Detached
Captain S P Gillespie MC Conducting Duty Demobilization
Lieut J K E Guild do do do
2/Lt J Grant do do do
Lieut C R McHutchins VI Corps Guard
2/Lt W A Mowat do do
J Leslie MC Bde Educational Officer
A E Robertson MC Educational Course (UK)
A Scott Hospital
R Davidson do
W S McColm do
J Coombes do
A Bonner do

3rd Division

War Diaries

1st Gordon Highlanders

August. To 31 December

1918

and

1919 - JAN — 1919 APRIL

Instructions regarding War Diaries and Intelligence Summaries are contained in F. S. Regs., Part II. and the Staff Manual respectively. Title pages will be prepared in manuscript.

WAR DIARY
or
INTELLIGENCE SUMMARY.
(Erase heading not required.)

Army Form C. 2118.

a0f0
1 Gord. Hrs
9852

Place	Date	Hour	Summary of Events and Information	Remarks and references to Appendices
KIERDOFF n. BRUGGEN.	1/1/19	–	Being New Year's Day it was a general holiday. The Battalion received the usual New Year's Dinner and concerts were held in the evening.	
	2/1/19	–	The usual Routine was observed. Lieut. J McDonald MC went to F.A. and Lieut [illegible] MC took over temporary command of A Company	
	3/1/19	–	Routine as usual, and from 10.00 to 12.30 cross country running by Companies.	
	4/1/19		The usual early morning inspection. 09.00 to 12.30 Route March. The Commanding Officer proceeded on leave and Major [illegible] took over temporary command of the Battalion. Major McNab proceeded to base and was struck off the strength of the Battalion.	
	5/1/19.		A voluntary church service was held in BRUGGEN.	
	6/1/19.		The Battalion was photographed by an Official photographer.	
	7/1/19.		Routine as usual. A draft of 3 Officers and 50 other ranks [illegible] 2Lieut R. Davidson to "C" Coy. 2Lt W. McColm to "D" Coy. all [illegible]	
	8/1/19		Morning inspection, 09.00 to 10.00 Battalion parade & from 10.00 to 12.30 the usual Education Classes & recreational training were carried out	

(A9175) Wt W2352/P360 600,00, 12/17 D. D. & L. Sch. 52a. Forms/C2118/15

Instructions regarding War Diaries and Intelligence Summaries are contained in F. S. Regs., Part II. and the Staff Manual respectively. Title pages will be prepared in manuscript.

WAR DIARY
or
INTELLIGENCE SUMMARY.
(Erase heading not required.)

Army Form C. 2118.

Place	Date	Hour	Summary of Events and Information	Remarks and references to Appendices
KIERDOFF & BRUGGEN	9/1/19		This was recognized holiday & football &c were played during the day	
	10/1/19		Usual morning inspection 09.00 to 10.00 Battalion parade and usual education & recreational classes.	
	11/1/19		Early morning inspection. 09.00 to 12-30hrs Route march & Lectures.	
	12/1/19		Voluntary Church Services were held in Halls in BRUGGEN.	
	13/1/19		Usual Routine and parades.	
	14/1/19		Routine as usual. 09.00 to 10.00 Battalion Drill. The usual Education & physical training classes were held during the forenoon and inter platoon football during the afternoon.	
	15/1/19		Routine as usual. 09.00 to 10.30 Company Drill & 10.15 to 12.30 usual Education & physical training classes. During the afternoon football and inter company tug o war took place. A draft of 10 O.R. proceeded for dispersal. 2nd Lt. R. Davidson proceeded on leave to U.K.	
	16/1/19		This was observed as a Brigade Holiday and inter company football games were played during the day. 2nd Lt A. Arnold proceeded on leave to U.K.	

Instructions regarding War Diaries and Intelligence Summaries are contained in F. S. Regs., Part II. and the Staff Manual respectively. Title pages will be prepared in manuscript.

WAR DIARY
or
INTELLIGENCE SUMMARY.
(Erase heading not required.)

Army Form C. 2118.

Place	Date	Hour	Summary of Events and Information	Remarks and references to Appendices
KIERDORF + BRUGGEN	17/1/19		Routine as usual. 09.00 to 10.00 hrs Battalion Drill, 10.00 to 12.30 Education +	
			P.T. classes. Inter-platoon football was played in the afternoon.	
	18/1/19		Routine as usual. 09.00 to 11.30 hrs [illegible] 11.30 [illegible]	
			Lecture on "Events of the Week". 11 OR proceeded for dispersal. The Officers	
			played the Officers of 1st R.S.F. in Divisional Football Competition [illegible] 2-0.	
	19/1/19		Routine as usual. A voluntary Church Service was held at 11.00 hours	
			at BRUGGEN. Capt. G.T. Harvey MC proceeded on leave to U.K. [illegible]	
			Lieut McDonald MC took over command of B. Coy vice Capt. Harvey MC on	
			leave. Lieut E.L. Mitchell transferred from B Coy to H.Q. Company.	
	20/1/19		Routine as usual. 09.00 to 10.00 hours Company Drill, 10.15 to 12.30 usual	
			education + P.T. classes were held + football was played in the afternoon.	
	21/1/19		Routine as usual 09.00 to 10.00 hours Battalion Drill, 10.15 to 12.30 usual	
			education + P.T. classes were held + football was played in the afternoon.	
			2nd Lieut. J. Crombie proceeded on leave to U.K.	
	22/1/19		Routine as usual 09.00 to 10.00 Company Drill, 10.15 to 12.30 [illegible]	
			+ P.T. classes. 9 OR proceeded for dispersal.	

(A9175) Wt W2358/P360 600,000 12/17 D. D. & L. Sch. 52a. Forms/C2118/15.

Instructions regarding War Diaries and Intelligence Summaries are contained in F. S. Regs., Part II. and the Staff Manual respectively. Title pages will be prepared in manuscript.

WAR DIARY
or
INTELLIGENCE SUMMARY.
(Erase heading not required.)

Army Form C. 2118.

Place	Date	Hour	Summary of Events and Information	Remarks and references to Appendices
KIERDORF + BRUGGEN	23/1/19.		Being usual Brigade Holiday there were no parades. A + B Coys. had baths at BRUGGEN and clean change of clothing was issued. The Battalion was paid out. Capt. J.R.C. Guild rejoined from conducting duty and 2nd Lieut A.S. McColm proceeded on leave to UK.	
	24/1/19		Routine as usual. HQ + C Companies had baths at BRUGGEN and clean change of clothing was issued. The usual education + P.T. classes were held.	
	25/1/19		Routine as Usual. 09.00 to 11-30 A B C + HQ Coys on Route March. D Coy had baths + clean change of clothing. 2nd Lt. T.J. Lobban joined Battalion and posted to D Company. In the afternoon the Battn. played the 7th K.S.L.I. in 2nd round of Divisional football Competition and won by 4 - 1.	
	26/1/19		Routine as usual. A voluntary church service was held in BRUGGEN at 11-00 hours. 6 O.R. proceeded for dispersal. Capt. S.P. Gillespie, M.C. rejoined from Conducting Duty and took over command of A Coy vice Lieut Hewatt, M.C.	

(A9175) Wt W135/P360 000,000 12/17 D. D. & L. Sch. 52a. Forms/C2118/15.

Instructions regarding War Diaries and Intelligence Summaries are contained in F. S. Regs., Part II. and the Staff Manual respectively. Title pages will be prepared in manuscript.

WAR DIARY
or
INTELLIGENCE SUMMARY.
(Erase heading not required.)

Army Form C. 2118.

Place	Date	Hour	Summary of Events and Information	Remarks and references to Appendices
KIERDORF BRUGGEN	28/1/19.		Routine as usual. 0900 to 10.00 hours Company Drill. 10-15 to 12-30 usual education & P.T. classes were held. Owing to bad weather conditions no sports were held in the afternoon. [illegible] took over command of "D" Coy vice Capt Ruston MC who proceeded on leave. 2nd Lieut C. Robb proceeded on leave to UK.	
	29/1/19.		Routine as usual. 0900 to 10.00 Battalion Drill. 10-15 to 12-30 education & P.T. classes. 2nd Lieut R. Stephen & 13 O.R. [illegible] [illegible]. A Y.M.C.A. was opened in BRUGGEN.	
	30/1/19		Routine as usual. 0900 to 10.00 Company Drill. 10-15 to 12-30 education & P.T. classes. Owing to severe frost no parades [illegible] done.	
	31/1/19		The usual Brigade holiday was [illegible].	

[signature] Lieut. Col.
Commanding
1st Gordon Highlanders

(A9175) Wt W2355/P360 600,000 12/17 D. D. & L. Sch. 52a. Forms/C2118/15.

1st Battalion The Gordon Highlanders

Roll of Officers on Strength of Battalion on 31-1-19

Lt Col The Hon W. Fraser DSO MC Commanding
Major N. G. Pearson MC 2nd in Command
Captain P. T. Piers A/Adjutant
Lieut K. C. Davidson MC - Asst Adjutant
" D. Hutton - Transport Officer
" S. T. Jennings - Quartermaster
" J. Paston - OC "HQ" Coy
" E. G. Mitchell - PT Officer
2/Lt W. G. Henderson MC - Billeting & Sports Officer

"A" Company

Captain S. P. Gillespie MC
Lieut D. J. Milne
2/Lt E. A. H. Goldfinch
" A. W. Esson
" W. Mearns (Education Instr)
" J. W. K. Smith
" A. T. Ogilvie
" W. H. Mowat
Captain J. R. E. Guild

"B" Company

Lieut J. Macdonald MC
2/Lt H. Burns
" A. S. Sinclair
" H. J. Bradshaw
" J. J. Ogston
~~" J. Crombie~~

"C" Company

Captain J. M. Frame MC
" D. Macfarlane
" G. P. Peterkin
Lieut C. D. M. Hutchins
2/Lt G. D. Thomson
" W. G. Jamieson (Education Instr)

"D" Company

Lieut F. A. Hewitt MC
2/Lt T. G. Ewing
" D. M. Fraser
" J. W. Webster
" J. Lobban

Attached

Captain J. G. Stewart DSO MC - RAMC
Revd D. Conacher - C.F.
Captain J. W. Taylor - Bn Education Officer

Detached

Captain G. T. Burney MC Leave to UK
" R. W. Preston MC Leave to UK
2/Lt R. Davidson " " "
" A. Arnold " " "
" J. Crombie " " "
" A. S. McColm " " "
" J. M. Robb " " "
" H. E. Robertson MC Education Course UK
" J. Grant Conducting Dispersal draft to UK
" A. Bonner Hospital
" A. Scott Base
" J. D. Chalmers VI Corps HQ Guard
" R. Miller do do
" G. C. O. Forbes 3rd Div Hotel Cologne

	O	OR	Total
Strength of Bn 31-1-19	48	814	862
Details	14	175	189

1 Gordon Hrs

Vol 53

Army Form C. 2118.

Instructions regarding War Diaries and Intelligence Summaries are contained in F. S. Regs., Part II. and the Staff Manual respectively. Title pages will be prepared in manuscript.

WAR DIARY
or
INTELLIGENCE SUMMARY.
(Erase heading not required.)

Place	Date	Hour	Summary of Events and Information	Remarks and references to Appendices
BRUGGEN KIERDORF	1/2/19		Routine as usual. 09.00 hours to 12.00 hours Route March. 11.00 hours 10 Offrs and 190 O.R. attended Lecture by Earl of Denbigh on "How we won the War". Lieut Sinclair proceeded to U.K. on leave.	
	2/2/19		A voluntary Church Service was held at BRUGGEN at [illegible] hours. Lieut Milne proceeded to U.K. on leave.	
	3/2/19		Routine as usual. 09.00 to 10.00 hours Coy drill, 10.15 to 12.30 Education and P.T. classes.	
	4/2/19		Routine as usual 09.00 to 10.00 hours Battn drill & from 10.15 to 12.30 usual Educational & P.T. classes. Major [illegible] proceeded to U.K. on a month's leave.	
	5/2/19		Routine as usual. Coy drill & usual educational & P.T. classes.	
	6/2/19		Routine as usual. This was observed as a Brigade holiday.	
	7/2/19		Routine as usual 09.00 to 10.00 hours Battalion drill [illegible] education & P.T. classes during forenoon. 2nd Lieut R.D. [illegible] off leave to UK.	
	8/2/19		Routine as usual. 09.00 to 12.00 hours Route March. 2nd Lt R[illegible]	

Instructions regarding War Diaries and Intelligence Summaries are contained in F. S. Regs., Part II. and the Staff Manual respectively. Title pages will be prepared in manuscript.

WAR DIARY
or
INTELLIGENCE SUMMARY.
(Erase heading not required.)

Army Form C. 2118.

Place	Date	Hour	Summary of Events and Information	Remarks and references to Appendices
BRUGGEN KIERDORF	8/2/19		proceeded to UK on leave & 11 OR proceeded to UK for disposal.	
	9/2/19		Routine as usual. A voluntary church service was held at Bruggen at 11.00 hours.	
	10/2/19		Usual routine. 09.00 to 10.00 hours Squad drill without arms & usual education & P.T. classes. Capt D Avey, MC joined Battn & took over command of D Coy.	
	11/2/19		Usual Routine. Company drill & usual P.T. & education classes 2nd Lt W.S. McColm proceeded on leave to UK.	
	12/2/19		Usual Routine 09.00 to 10.00 hours Battn Drill & usual P.T. & education classes. 2nd Lt J Crombie reported off leave to UK & 21 OR proceeded to UK for disposal.	
	13/2/19		Routine as usual, and was observed as Brigade holiday. Capt J McFrame MC proceeded to UK on leave & Capt Peterkin took over temporary command of C Coy.	
	14/2/19		Routine as usual. 09.00 to 10.00 hours Battn Parade & usual P.T. & education classes during forenoon.	

(A9175) Wt W2358/P360 600,000 12/17 D. D. & L. Sch. 52a. Forms/C2118/15.

Army Form C. 2118.

Instructions regarding War Diaries and Intelligence Summaries are contained in F. S. Regs., Part II. and the Staff Manual respectively. Title pages will be prepared in manuscript.

WAR DIARY
or
INTELLIGENCE SUMMARY.
(Erase heading not required.)

Place	Date	Hour	Summary of Events and Information	Remarks and references to Appendices
BRUGGEN & KIERDORF	15/2/19		Routine as usual 09.00 to 11.00 hours. Route march by Companies. 11.30 hours	
			Lecture by Capt. The Master of Saltoun "My experiences in Germany".	
			23 O.R. forwarded to U.K. for dispersal. Lieut. McNeal [illegible] reported	
	15/2/19		to 'B' Coy. The Battn. football team played 3rd Div M T Coy in [illegible]	
			Divisional Cup at DUREN - result 2 goals each.	
	16/2/19		Routine as usual. A voluntary Church service was held at Bruggen	
	17/2/19		at 11.00 hours.	
			Routine as usual. 09.00 to 10.00 Squad drill without arms [illegible]	
			& educational classes during forenoon. Capt. Preston MC Lt. Robb[illegible]	
			and Lt. Arnold reported off leave to UK.	
	18/2/19		Routine as usual 09.00 to 10.00 Battn. Parade [illegible] classes in forenoon	
	19/2/19		Routine as usual. Lecture by J. McDonald MC on Army [illegible]	
			and Lieut. Ewing proceeded on leave to U.K.	
	20/2/19		Routine as usual. 21 O.R. forwarded to U.K. for dispersal. The Battn beat	
			M T Coy in replay of Div. Cup by 4-0.	
	21/2/19		Routine as usual. 09.00 to 10.00 hours. Battn. parade [illegible] classes.	

(A9175) Wt W2358/P360 600,000 12/17 D. D. & L. Sch. 52a. Forms/C2118/15.

Instructions regarding War Diaries and Intelligence Summaries are contained in F. S. Regs., Part II. and the Staff Manual respectively. Title pages will be prepared in manuscript.

WAR DIARY
or
INTELLIGENCE SUMMARY.
(Erase heading not required.)

Army Form C. 2118.

Place	Date	Hour	Summary of Events and Information	Remarks and references to Appendices
	22 2/19		Routine as usual. 09·00 to 12·00 hours Route march. 2nd Lieut J. W. K. Smith & 21 OR to U.K. for dispersal. Battn. beat R.A. in semi final of Div. Cup by 3-2.	
	23 2/19		Usual Routine. A voluntary church service at Bruggue at 11·00 hours	
	24 2/19		" and usual parades. Lieut J. McDonald MC & Lieut Stewart MC & Lt. C. Lalmers proceeded to UK on 2 months leave.	
	25 2/19		Routine & parades as usual. Lieut. Milne reported off leave to UK.	
	26 2/19		Routine as usual. 10·00–11·00 Battn. parade.	
	27 2/19		Routine as usual. G.O.C. 3rd Div. inspected Battalion at 11·00 hours. 2nd Lt. Means proceeded to UK on leave & 2nd Lt Bradshaw on 2 months furlough.	
	28 2/19		Routine as usual & transport reduced to Cadre. Coy drill & L.G. classes.	

R. Ansell, Lieut. Col.
Commanding
1st Gordon Highlanders.

(A9175) Wt W2355/P360 600,00. 12/17 D. D. & L. Sch. 52a. Forms/C2118/15

1st Bn The Gordon Highlanders

Nominal Roll of Officers — 28/12/17?

Lieut-Col	The Hon W Fraser DSO MC	Commanding
Captain	R [illegible]	[illegible]
Lieutenant	G A Davidson MC	Asst Adjt
"	E Sutton	Transport Officer
	A J [illegible]	Quartermaster
	J Paxton	Off. HQ Coy
2/	W G Anderson	[illegible] Officer

A Coy

Capt S P [illegible] MC
" J G C Guild
Lieut H [illegible]
2/Lieut J McGolds?
C A H [illegible]
A W Eason
A T Ogilvie

B Coy

Capt [illegible] MC
Lieut [illegible] Macleod?
2/Lieut [illegible]
J [illegible]
[illegible]

C Coy

Capt [illegible]
Lieut [illegible]
2/Lieut [illegible]
[illegible]
[illegible]

D Coy

Capt [illegible] MC
G W Preston MC
Lieut [illegible] Mitchell
2/Lieut W [illegible]
J [illegible]
A Arnold
J W Webster
W J McLelland?
J Latham
H C Robertson MC

Attached

Capt J W [illegible] — Bn Educ Officer
J [illegible] Stewart — RAMC

Detached

Major [illegible] Pearson MC — Leave to UK
Capt J McFrame? MC — do
2/Lieut J Grant — do
W Morrison — do
W H Mount — do
J L Ewing — do
Lieut E M [illegible] McKinnachie? — do

Capt R Macfarlane — [illegible] Officer
2/Lt H Burns — Conducting duty UK
G C Forbes — 3rd Bn? [illegible] College
A Bowman — Hospital

Army Form C. 2118.

1 Gordon Hrs

Vol 54

WAR DIARY
or
INTELLIGENCE SUMMARY.
(Erase heading not required.)

Instructions regarding War Diaries and Intelligence Summaries are contained in F. S. Regs., Part II. and the Staff Manual respectively. Title pages will be prepared in manuscript.

Place	Date	Hour	Summary of Events and Information	Remarks and references to Appendices
KIERDORF	1/3/19		Route march for 2 Coys. Baths for other 2 Coys. – Final of III Div	
			Football Cup at DÜREN between 1st Bn Gordon Hdrs & 2nd Royal	
			Scots. Result 1st G.H. 2. 2nd R.S. 2. They played 30 minutes extra & both	
			failed to score	
	2/3/19		Voluntary Church Parade – owing to the disbandment of the	
			Battn reorganisation into ½ Coys took place. 2 Coys being	
			composed of men army of occupation & 2 available for release	
			HQ Coy for baths.	
	3/3/19		Battn making ready to move to RIEHL Barracks COLOGNE	
	4/3/19		Reveille 07-00 hrs Breakfast 08.00 – Move postponed till 12-30 hrs	
			Battn arrived at RIEHL Barracks about 17-45 hrs – very bad weather	
COLOGNE	5/3/19		Battn being broken up – 2 Coys going to join 62nd Division	
	6/3/19		Everything ready for move of 2 Coys – Football final between 2nd	
			Royal Scots – 1st Bn The Gordon Hrs. Result 1st G.H. 5 goals 2nd R.S. 3 goals	
			The game was played in very bad weather. Great enthusiasm	
			displayed by spectators – General Sir Herbert P[illegible] commanding	

(A9175) Wt W2358/P360 600,000 12/17 D. D. & L. Sch. 52a. Forms/C2118/15

Instructions regarding War Diaries and Intelligence Summaries are contained in F. S. Regs., Part II. and the Staff Manual respectively. Title pages will be prepared in manuscript.

WAR DIARY
or
INTELLIGENCE SUMMARY.
(Erase heading not required.)

Army Form C. 2118.

Place	Date	Hour	Summary of Events and Information	Remarks and references to Appendices
[illegible]	[illegible]		[illegible]	

(A9175) Wt W2355/P360 600,000 12/17 D. D. & L. Sch. 52a. Forms/C2118/15.

Instructions regarding War Diaries and Intelligence Summaries are contained in F. S. Regs., Part II. and the Staff Manual respectively. Title pages will be prepared in manuscript.

WAR DIARY
or
~~INTELLIGENCE~~ SUMMARY.
(Erase heading not required.)

Army Form C. 2118.

Place	Date	Hour	Summary of Events and Information	Remarks and references to Appendices
	cont			
COLOGNE	10/3/19		51st N.F. – Battn visited Zoological Gardens. – Capt P.T. Pirie proceeded to III Div HQrs as A.D.C. to the Divisional Commander. Lieut R.C. Davidson MC took over the duties of A/Adjt.	
	11/3/19		2/Lt Ewing rejoined off [illegible] leave to U.K. – Draft of 75 O.Ranks proceeded to No 1 Con. Camp COLOGNE for dispersal to U.K.	
	12/3/19		A scratch team played a picked team of the 51st D.L.I. on the P&R.T. ground DEUTZ – result 1st G.H. 1 goal D.L.I. 0. – 2/Lts L.G. Farquhar and W.C. Ballas reported to the Battn for duty.	
	13/3/19		Capt. J.M. Keane MC 2/Lt T.H. EWING + 14 o.ranks proceeded to KERPEN to join 1/5th Bn Gordon Hrs	
	14/3/19		Pick up between 1st G.H. + 51st D.L.I. played on the Square: result 1st G.H. 3 goals 51st D.L.I. 1 goal. – 2/Lt W.H. Whyte + 6 o.ranks to 1/5th Bn Gordon Hrs at KERPEN	
	15/3/19		Inspections + walk in the morning – Brigade [illegible] attended by all Officers of the Bn.	
	16/3/19		50 o.ranks proceeded up the RHINE on a pleasure trip for the day	

(A9175) Wt W2350/P360 600,000 12/17 D. D. & L. Sch. 52a. Forms/C2118/15.

Instructions regarding War Diaries and Intelligence Summaries are contained in F. S. Regs., Part II. and the Staff Manual respectively. Title pages will be prepared in manuscript.

WAR DIARY
or
INTELLIGENCE SUMMARY.
(Erase heading not required.)

Army Form C. 2118.

Place	Date	Hour	Summary of Events and Information	Remarks and references to Appendices
COLOGNE	17/3/19		P.T. and Games [illegible]	
	18/3/19		10 ranks proceed to [illegible]	
			to No. 2 Con Camp DUREN for dispersal [illegible]	
	19/3/19		P.T. and Games + Walks [illegible]	
	22/3/19		Pte Means + Webster + [illegible]	
	23/3/19		12 Ranks went for a [illegible]	
	24/3/19		P.T. Games + Walks [illegible]	
			Con Camp for dispersal to [illegible]	
	27/3/19		Lt Col [illegible]	
			[illegible] to U.K. on [illegible]	
			took over command of the Con [illegible]	
	28/3/19		Lieut E. Mitchell to [illegible]	
	29/3/19		P.T. Games + Walk – 3 ranks [illegible]	
	30/3/19		Voluntary Church Parade	
	31/3/19		4 Ranks to KERPEN [illegible]	

[illegible signature]
Commanding
[illegible]

(A9475) Wt W2355/P360 600,000 12/17 D. D. & L. Sch. 52a. Forms/C2118/15.

1st Battalion The Gordon Highlanders

Nominal Roll of Officers on strength of Battalion 31-3-19

Major	V. G. Pearson MC	Commanding
Lieut	K. C Davidson MC	A/Adjutant
"	S. T. Jennings	Quartermaster
"	D. Hutton	Commanding B Coy
2/Lieut	R. Davidson	

ATTACHED

Captain Revd D Cameron C.F.

DETACHED.

Lieut Colonel	The Hon W Fraser DSO MC	Leave to UK
Captain	P. T. Pirie ADC	to G.O.C. Northern Division
Lieut	C.M. V. McConnachie	Leave to UK.
2/Lieut	W. G. Henderson MC	do
"	J. Grant	Conducting duty
"	A. Barnes	Hospital
Lieut	E. L. Mitchell	Mil Gov L of C.

Strength of Battalion

	O.	OR
Fighting Strength	12	153
Details	7	20

April 1919

1 Gordon Hrs

Army Form C. 2118.

Instructions regarding War Diaries and Intelligence Summaries are contained in F. S. Regs., Part II. and the Staff Manual respectively. Title pages will be prepared in manuscript.

WAR DIARY
or
~~INTELLIGENCE SUMMARY.~~
(Erase heading not required.)

Place	Date	Hour	Summary of Events and Information	Remarks and references to Appendices
COLOGNE	1.4.19		Usual morning parades (physical training [illegible])	
"	2.4.19		" "	
"	3.4.19		" "	
"	4.4.19		Notice received that the cadre battalion would proceed home on the 6th [illegible] [illegible].	
"	5.4.19		Battalion had baths and clean changes.	
"	6.4.19		Battalion proceeded home by train leaving Cologne Main station at 0700 hours. Major General Deverell + Brig Gen Metcalfe came to see the Batt^n off. Remainder of the Batt^n attached to 2nd Royal Scots. 6 OR. Transferred to 5th Gordon Highlanders. The journey was made in cattle trucks, about 12 men to each truck. Halts [illegible] were made at VERVIERS + HUY for meals.	COMDG. 1st BATT. THE GORDON HIGHLANDERS. [signature]
	7.4.19		Journey continued. The old lines were crossed at [illegible] and the battalion arrived at DUNKIRK at 23.45 hours but remained [illegible].	
	8.4.19		Marched to camp at DUNKIRK where men had baths [illegible] and were medically inspected.	
	9.4.19		Batt^n embarked from MONITOR QUAY DUNKIRK at 1100 hours on PRINCESS HENRIETTA. Boat sailed at 1200 hours + arrived DOVER at 1430 hours where train was taken for CROMARTY.	

Instructions regarding War Diaries and Intelligence Summaries are contained in F. S. Regs., Part II. and the Staff Manual respectively. Title pages will be prepared in manuscript.

WAR DIARY
or
INTELLIGENCE SUMMARY.
(Erase heading not required.)

Army Form C. 2118.

Place	Date	Hour	Summary of Events and Information	Remarks and references to Appendices
18.4.19			Arrived at Edinburgh at 0730 hours [illegible] breakfast there. Train left [illegible] [illegible] + changed trains for INVERNESS. Arrived INVERNESS about [illegible] hours. Arrived INVERGORDON at about 1900 hours. Met by Capt G.W.A. ALEXANDER [illegible] CROMARTY by ferry. Arrived in camp at CROMARTY at 2030 hours [illegible] was welcomed by the Brig. General + Major FOWKE, and then had a hot meal which had been prepared by the details.	

Cromarty
21. 4. 19.

G.H. Fowke Major
COMDG. 1ST BATT. THE GORDON HIGHLANDERS.

(A9175) Wt W2354/P360 600,000 12/17 D. D. & L. Sch. 52a. Forms/C2118/15.

www.ingramcontent.com/pod-product-compliance
Lightning Source LLC
Chambersburg PA
CBHW080807010526
44113CB00013B/2340

* 9 7 8 1 4 7 4 5 0 4 7 0 6 *